PROFESSIONAL TENNIS AND TRANSNATIONAL LAW

This book examines the intersection of professional tennis and legal regulation, unveiling a fascinating world where tennis meets domestic, international and transnational law, and showing the many ways these legal frameworks impact tennis. Filled with firsthand accounts of the legal landscape and its implication on tennis, the work provides an accessible, engaging portrait of the tennis ecosystem that is equally suited for academics, athletes, sports lawyers and journalists. It is an essential read for those working within sports law generally, and the tennis industry specifically. This title is also available as Open Access on Cambridge Core.

ILIAS BANTEKAS is Professor of Transnational Law at Hamad bin Khalifa University (a member of Qatar Foundation) and Adjunct Professor at Georgetown University. He has advised in the field of sports contracts, international law and human rights as part of his professional practice, and served as arbitrator chiefly in international commercial disputes. He has authored 22 books and close to 250 peer-reviewed articles.

MARKO BEGOVIĆ is Associate Professor of Sport History, and Sport Management at Molde University College in Norway. In 2022, he served as Director in charge of sport and youth affairs with the Government of Montenegro and is currently Program Director of the Sports Diplomacy Program at the Hungarian University and member of the UNESCO Chair on Governance and Social Responsibility.

PROFESSIONAL TENNIS AND TRANSNATIONAL LAW

Contractual and Regulatory

Edited by

ILIAS BANTEKAS
Hamad bin Khalifa University

MARKO BEGOVIĆ
Molde University College

Shaftesbury Road, Cambridge CB2 8EA, United Kingdom

One Liberty Plaza, 20th Floor, New York, NY 10006, USA

477 Williamstown Road, Port Melbourne, VIC 3207, Australia

314–321, 3rd Floor, Plot 3, Splendor Forum, Jasola District Centre, New Delhi – 110025, India

103 Penang Road, #05–06/07, Visioncrest Commercial, Singapore 238467

Cambridge University Press is part of Cambridge University Press & Assessment, a department of the University of Cambridge.

We share the University's mission to contribute to society through the pursuit of education, learning and research at the highest international levels of excellence.

www.cambridge.org
Information on this title: www.cambridge.org/9781009597654
DOI: 10.1017/9781009597616

© Cambridge University Press & Assessment 2025

This publication is in copyright. Subject to statutory exception and to the provisions of relevant collective licensing agreements, with the exception of the Creative Commons version the link for which is provided below, no reproduction of any part may take place without the written permission of Cambridge University Press & Assessment.

An online version of this work is published at doi.org/10.1017/9781009597616 under a Creative Commons Open Access license CC-BY-NC 4.0 which permits re-use, distribution and reproduction in any medium for non-commercial purposes providing appropriate credit to the original work is given and any changes made are indicated. To view a copy of this license visit https://creativecommons.org/licenses/by-nc/4.0

When citing this work, please include a reference to the DOI 10.1017/9781009597616

First published 2025

A catalogue record for this publication is available from the British Library

Library of Congress Cataloging-in-Publication Data
Names: Bantekas, Ilias, editor. | Begović, Marko, editor.
Title: Professional tennis and transnational law : contractual and regulatory / Ilias Bantekas, Marko Begović.
Description: 1. | New York : Cambridge University Press, 2025. | Includes index.
Identifiers: LCCN 2024059488 | ISBN 9781009597654 (hardback) | ISBN 9781009597609 (paperback) | ISBN 9781009597616 (ebook)
Subjects: LCSH: Sports – Law and legislation. | Tennis. | Tennis players – Legal status, laws, etc. | Intellectual property. | Tennis – Corrupt practices. | Doping in sports – Law and legislation.
Classification: LCC K3702 .P755 2025 | DDC 344/.099–dc23/eng/20250101
LC record available at https://lccn.loc.gov/2024059488

ISBN 978-1-009-59765-4 Hardback
ISBN 978-1-009-59760-9 Paperback

Cambridge University Press & Assessment has no responsibility for the persistence or accuracy of URLs for external or third-party internet websites referred to in this publication and does not guarantee that any content on such websites is, or will remain, accurate or appropriate.

CONTENTS

List of Abbreviations   page xiv
Table of Cases   xxi
Notes on Contributors   xxvii
Preface   xxxiii

1 The Intersection between Law and Tennis   1
ILIAS BANTEKAS AND MARKO BEGOVIĆ

  1 Introduction   1

  2 The Regulation of Professional Tennis by Transnational Law   2
    2.1 Professional Tennis as Part of the Transnational *Lex Sportiva*   4
    2.2 The Transnational Character of Dispute Resolution of Professional Tennis   5
    2.3 The Relationship between the ITF, the WTA and the ATP   7

  3 Professional Tennis and Domestic Law   9
    3.1 Tennis Governance   9
    3.2 The Relationship between National Tennis Federations and the ITF   11
    3.3 The Labor Status of Professional Tennis Players   12

  4 The Relevance of International Law   14
    4.1 Professional Tennis as Part of the Olympic Movement   15

  5 The Human Rights Standard-Setting Role of Transnational Tennis Entities   16

PART 1: **Contractual**   21

2 Legal and Contractual Aspects of Agency and Player–Agent Relations in Professional Tennis   23
WILLIAM BULL

  1 Introduction   23
  2 Agency in Tennis   24
    2.1 Background to Sports Agents in General and Tennis Agents in Particular   24
    2.2 Types and Roles of Agents in Professional Tennis   27
  3 The Regulation of Agents in Professional Tennis   29
    3.1 Domestic Rules   29
    3.2 Transnational Rules   35
  4 Contractual Agreements between Professional Tennis Players and Agents   36
    4.1 The Law on Player–Agent Contracts   36
    4.2 Legal Issues Arising from Player–Agent Relations in Professional Tennis   38

3 Protection, Commercialisation and Enforcement of Intellectual Property Rights in Professional Tennis   42
DÉSIRÉE FIELDS

  1 Introduction   42
  2 Overview of IP Rights   44
    2.1 Territoriality of IP Rights   44
      2.1.1 Ownership of IP Rights   44
  3 Trademarks   45
    3.1 What Is a Trademark?   46
      3.1.1 Types of Trademarks   47
        3.1.1.1 Traditional Trademarks   47
        3.1.1.2 Non-Traditional Trademarks   48
        3.1.1.3 Colour Marks   48
        3.1.1.4 Shape Marks   49
        3.1.1.5 Sound Marks   51
        3.1.1.6 Smell and Taste Marks   51
        3.1.1.7 Motion, Gesture Marks and Holograms   51

4 Scope of Trademark Protection 52
   4.1 Designs 53
   4.2 Copyright 54
   4.3 Image Rights/Rights of Publicity 55
   4.4 Patents 55
   4.5 Trade Secrets/Confidential Information 56

5 Commercialisation of IP Rights 56
   5.1 Sponsorship Agreements 56
      5.1.1 IP Provisions in Sponsorship Agreements 57
         5.1.1.1 Details of IP Rights Exploited during the Sponsorship 57
         5.1.1.2 Licensing Arrangements 58
         5.1.1.3 Ambush Marketing 59
   5.2 Endorsement Contracts 60
   5.3 Merchandising Agreements 60
   5.4 Broadcasting Rights Agreements 60

6 Enforcement of IP Rights 62
   6.1 Monitoring Infringements 62
   6.2 Enforcement Action 63
      6.2.1 Cease and Desist Letters 63
      6.2.2 Issuing Substantive Proceedings 63
         6.2.2.1 Trademark Oppositions 64
         6.2.2.2 Trade Validity and Revocation Actions 64
         6.2.2.3 Revocation 64
         6.2.2.4 Invalidity 65
         6.2.2.5 Trademark Infringement Proceedings 66
         6.2.2.6 Domain Name Complaints 66
         6.2.2.7 Company Name Complaints 67
   6.3 Remedies 67
      6.3.1 Injunctions 68
      6.3.2 Damages or Account of Profits 68
      6.3.3 Other Remedies 68

4 Morality Clauses in Tennis Agreements: Tennis, Social Media and the Digital World 69
MIGUEL CRESPO

1 Introduction 69

2 Players, Sponsors and Endorsement Agreements 72

    3 Reasons for Agreement Termination and Morality Clauses in Tennis   75

    4 The Application of Moral Clauses in Tennis: The Impact of Social Media and the Digital World   80

    5 Examples of Morality Clauses in Tennis Endorsement Agreements   83

    6 Conclusion   86

5 Restraint of Trade in Professional Tennis   88
   ILIAS BANTEKAS

    1 Introduction   88

    2 Restraint of Trade in the English Common Law   89

    3 Restraint of Trade in the Sports Context   92
       3.1 Restraints Arising from National Federations and State Regulation   92
       3.2 Restraints Arising from Players' Contracts with Agents   94

    4 Trade Restraints in Professional Tennis   96
       4.1 Restraints in Agency Agreements   96
       4.2 Disciplinary Bans as Restraint of Trade?   99
       4.3 Qualification for National Tennis Teams and Restraint of Trade   103

6 Professional Tennis Player Unions   105
   BRENDAN SCHWAB

    1 Introduction   105

    2 The Dual and Shifting Roles of Tennis Player Unions   105
       2.1 From Collective Action to Shared Governance   105
       2.2 What Is a Professional Tennis Players' Union?   106
       2.3 The Trade Union Rights of Professional Tennis Players   108

    3 Initial Attempts at Tennis Player Unionization   110
       3.1 The Pivotal Role of Player Unionization and the Development of Professional Tennis 1967–75   110

3.2 Pro Tennis's Labor Settlement – Business in Lieu of Bargaining   116

4 The "Seven Kingdoms": Player Voice, Rights, Pay and Conditions in Professional Tennis Today   124
    4.1 The Voice of the Players in the Governance of Professional Tennis   124
        4.1.1 The ITF   125
        4.1.2 The ATP   126
        4.1.3 The WTA   130
    4.2 Player Rights, Pay and Conditions in Professional Tennis   132

5 The PTPA   135
    5.1 Establishment of the PTPA in 2020 and the Reaction of the "Seven Kingdoms"   135
    5.2 The Developing Culture, Governance, Structure and Objectives of the PTPA   139

PART 2: **Regulatory**   145

7 Access to Justice in Tennis Disputes   147
    ILIAS BANTEKAS

    1 Introduction   147

    2 ADR in Tennis   148

    3 Internal ITF Mechanisms   149
        3.1 On-Site Quasi-Adjudicatory Mechanisms   149

    4 The Internal Adjudication Panel   151
        4.1 The Panel's Judicial Function, Jurisdiction and Powers   151
            4.1.1 The Panel's First-Instance Jurisdiction   154
            4.1.2 The Panel's Appellate Function   155
            4.1.3 The Panel's Supervisory Function   156

    5 The Independent Tribunal   157
        5.1 Procedures of the Independent Tribunal   159
        5.2 The Three Types of Jurisdiction Conferred on the Independent Tribunal   162
            5.2.1 The First-Instance Jurisdiction of the Independent Tribunal   162

    6 Appeals against the Independent Tribunal's Awards to CAS   164

    7 ATP Dispute Resolution   165

    8 WTA Dispute Resolution   166

    9 Contractual Disputes and the Role of National Courts   167

8 **The ITF, ATP and WTA and the Governance of Global Tennis**   170
MARKO BEGOVIĆ

    1 Introduction   170

    2 The Governance Structure of Tennis   174

    3 Players' Councils   176

    4 The Relationship between Players and the ATP/WTA   177

    5 The Relationship between National Tennis Federations and the ITF   179

    6 Contemporary Governance Setting and Challenges   180
        6.1 Commercialization, Corruption and Financial Governance Challenges   184

    7 Epilogue   189

9 **Safeguarding in Tennis: An Enforceable Duty of Care**   190
ILIAS BANTEKAS

    1 Introduction   190

    2 Safeguarding as a Duty of Care   192

    3 The Sporting Context of Abuse   194

    4 Safeguarding in Child–Adult Relationships in Tennis   195
        4.1 The WTA's Pioneering Safeguarding Role   195
        4.2 The ITF Safeguarding Policy for Children   196
        4.3 The ITF's Monitoring Process   198

    5 Safeguarding for Future Harm   202

    6 The Safeguarding of Adult Athletes   204

7 Health and Safety as a Safeguarding Duty   206

8 Consequences for Failure to Meet Safeguarding Obligations   207

9 The Boundaries of Safeguarding Duties   208

10 Integrity in Tennis: Doping, Match-Fixing and Other Corruption Offenses   210
ROSS BROWN, JAMIE SINGER AND LILY ELLIOTT

  1 Introduction   210

  2 Anti-Doping   211
    2.1 Legal Framework   211
      2.1.1 The Anti-Doping Offenses   212
        2.1.1.1 Presence   213
        2.1.1.2 Use   213
        2.1.1.3 Other ADRVs   214
    2.2 Proceedings   214
      2.2.1 Notice   215
      2.2.2 Charge Letter   215
      2.2.3 Hearing   216
    2.3 Sanctions   217
      2.3.1 Intention   218
      2.3.2 Identifying the Source   219
      2.3.3 Other Good Reason   221
      2.3.4 Fault   221
      2.3.5 No Fault or Negligence   222
      2.3.6 No Significant Fault or Negligence   225
    2.4 Appeals   228

  3 Anti-Corruption   229
    3.1 Legal Framework   230
      3.1.1 Jurisdiction   230
      3.1.2 Governing Law   231
      3.1.3 Burden/Standard of Proof   232
      3.1.4 Hearings   232
      3.1.5 Appeals   233
    3.2 Corruption Offenses   233
      3.2.1 Betting Offenses   235
      3.2.2 Fixing a Match   235
        3.2.2.1 Facilitating Others to Fix a Match   238
        3.2.2.2 Umpires Fixing a Match   238
      3.2.3 Failure to Report   239

3.2.4 Failure to Cooperate   239
3.2.5 Other Offenses   240
3.3 Sanction   240

11 Regulating On-Court Tennis Indiscipline   244
BEN LIVINGS

1 Introduction   244

2 The Code   246
2.1 Code Violations   248
2.1.1 Physical Violence   248
2.1.2 Audible Obscenity, Visible Obscenity and Verbal Abuse   251

3 Indiscipline and the Rising Popularity and Commercial Success of Tennis   252
3.1 The Influence of Sponsors   253

4 Adjudication and Enforcement   255

5 The Case of Grunting   256

6 Changes to the Rules   258
6.1 Coaching   258
6.2 Wimbledon   259
6.3 Changes in Adjudication and Enforcement Practices   260
6.3.1 Race   260
6.3.2 Mental Health   262

12 Compatibility of Selected ATP Rules with EU Economic Law   263
KATARINA PIJETLOVIC

1 Introduction   263

2 Good Governance Standards in Light of EU Law and Policy   264

3 Access to the Organisational Market for Rival Tennis Tours under Competition Law   266
3.1 Blocking Rivals from Accessing the Organisational Market   266
3.2 Applicable EU Legal Framework   268
3.3 Rules 1.07, 1.14 and 8.05A(2)(e) of the ATP Rulebook   272

3.4 Legality of the Rules 1.07, 1.14 and 8.05A(2)(e) and Reinforcing Practices under EU Competition Law   274
    3.4.1 Restrictions   274
    3.4.2 Legitimate Objectives and Proportionality   277

4 Wild Cards under the Lens of Article 56 of the TFEU on the Freedom to Provide Services   279
    4.1 Wild Cards in Tennis   279
    4.2 Legal Evaluation of Wild Cards under Article 56 of the TFEU   281

5 Recapitulation   283

13 The Regulation of Ethics in the ITF's Governance   285
ILIAS BANTEKAS

1 Introduction   285

2 What Are Ethics and Are They Different from Law?   286

3 The ITF's Substantive Ethical Rules   289
    3.1 Covered Persons   289
    3.2 Basic Obligations   290
    3.3 Other Substantive Duties and Obligations   291

4 The ITF Ethics Commission   294
    4.1 Investigations   296
    4.2 Decision Following the Investigator's Report: Aggravated and Non-Aggravated Breaches   298
    4.3 The Suspensive Effect of the Notice of Charge   299

5 Recourse to the Independent Tribunal and CAS   299
    5.1 Sanctions   300

6 The Elections and Eligibility Panel   302

Index   304

ABBREVIATIONS

AAA	American Arbitration Association
AAF	Adverse Analytical Finding
AC	*Appeals Cases* [Law Reports]
Admin LR	*Administrative Law Reports*
ADR	alternative dispute resolution
ADRV	anti-doping rule violation
AELTC	All England Lawn Tennis and Croquet Club
AER	Age Eligibility Rule
AG	Attorney-General
AGM	Annual General Meeting
AHO	Anti-Corruption Hearing Officer
AI	artificial intelligence
AICPA	American Institute of Certified Public Accountants
ALJR	*Australian Law Journal Reports*
All ER	*All England Reports*
Am U Bus L Rev	*American University Business Law Review*
APG	Professional Golfers America, Inc.
Ariz J Int & Comp L	*Arizona Journal of International & Comparative Law*
Ariz St U Sports & Ent LJ	*Arizona State University Sports & Entertainment Law Journal*
Ark L Rev	*Arkansas Law Review*
ATF	Asian Tennis Federation
ATP	Association of Tennis Professionals
Aus & NZ Sports LJ	*Australia & New Zealand Sports Law Journal*
BAT	Basketball Arbitral Tribunal
BBSA	British Bobsleigh and Skeleton Association
BCL Rev	*Boston College Law Review*
BIT	bilateral investment treaty
Bost U Int LJ	*Boston University International Law Journal*
Brigham Young U Pre L Rev	*Brigham Young University Pre-Law Review*
Brit J Sport Med	*British Journal of Sport Medicine*
BWF	Badminton World Federation
CADC	Czech Anti-Doping Committee

Camb J Int & Comp L	*Cambridge Journal of International & Comparative Law*
Canadian J App Sport Sci	*Canadian Journal of Applied Sport Science*
Cardozo Arts & Ent LJ	*Cardozo Arts & Entertainment Law Journal*
CAS	Court of Arbitration for Sport
CAT	Confederation of African Tennis
CBE	Commander, Order of the British Empire
CEO	Chief Executive Officer
Ch	Chancery [Reports]
Child Abuse Neg	*Child Abuse & Neglect*
CJEU	Court of Justice of the European Union
Colum JL & Arts	*Columbia Journal of Law & Arts*
Comm Law	*Communications Lawyer*
CONI	*Comitato Olimpico Nazionale Italiano*
COSAT	Confederación Sudamericana de Tenis
COTECC	Confederación de Tenis de Centroamérica y el Caribe
Cov LJ	*Coventry Law Journal*
CRC	Convention on the Rights of the Child
CRPD	Convention on the Rights of Persons with Disabilities
CtRC	Committee on the Rights of the Child
DePaul J Sport L & Cont Prob	*DePaul Journal of Sports Law & Contemporary Problems*
ECHR	European Convention on Human Rights
ECLI	European Case Law Identifier
ECR	*European Court Reports*
ECtHR	European Court of Human Rights
EEA	European Economic Area
EGM	Extraordinary General Meeting
EHRR	*European Human Rights Reports*
Ent & Sports Lawyer	*Entertainment & Sports Lawyer*
Ent & Sports LJ	*Entertainment & Sports Law Journal*
ESL	European Super League
Ethn Racial Stud	*Ethnic & Racial Studies*
EU	European Union
EUIPO	European Union Intellectual Property Office
Eur Comp L Rev	*European Competition Law Review*
Eur J Sport Sci	*European Journal of Sports Science*
Eur Sport Manag Q	*European Sport Management Quarterly*
EUTMR	European Union Trademark Regulation
EWCA Civ	England and Wales Court of Appeal, Civil Division
EWHC	England and Wales High Court

LIST OF ABBREVIATIONS

F.2d	*Federal Reporter, Second Series*
F.3d	*Federal Reporter, Third Series*
FA	Football Association
FC	Football Club
FedCFamC2G	Federal Circuit and Family Court [Australia]
FFT	Fédération française de tennis
FIBA	International Basketball Federation
FICA	Federation of International Cricketers' Associations
FIFA	Fédération International de Football Association
FIFPRO	Fédération Internationale des Associations de Footballeurs Professionnels
FIM	Fédération Internationale de Motocyclisme
FITP	Federazione Italiana Tennis e Padel
Fla St UL Rev	*Florida State University Law Review*
Fordham IP, Media & Ent LJ	*Fordham Intellectual Property, Media & Entertainment Law Journal*
Front Psychol	*Frontiers in Psychology*
F.Supp.	*Federal Supplement*
FU Phys Ed Sport	*Facta Universitatis, Series: Physical Education & Sport*
GB	Great Britain
Geo LJ	*Georgia Law Journal*
Geo Mas Int LJ	*George Mason International Law Journal*
German LJ	*German Law Journal*
Glob Sports Pol Rev	*Global Sports Policy Review*
GNOC	Georgian National Olympic Committee
GTF	Georgian Tennis Federation
HRIA	human rights impact assessment
IAP	Internal Adjudication Panel
IBA	International Bar Association
ICC	International Chamber of Commerce
ICCPR	International Covenant on Civil and Political Rights
ICESCR	International Covenant on Economic, Social and Cultural Rights
ICLQ	*International & Comparative Law Quarterly*
IDTM	International Doping Tests & Management
IFI	international financial institution
IHP	Independent Hearing Panel
ILO	International Labour Organization
ILTF	International Lawn Tennis Federation
IMG	International Management Group
IMTA	International Men's Tennis Association
Int J Hist Sport	*International Journal of the History of Sport*

Int JL Manag Human	*International Journal of Law, Management & the Humanities*
Int J Sport Exerc Psychol	*International Journal of Sport & Exercise Psychology*
Int J Sport Manag Mark	*International Journal of Sport Management & Marketing*
Int J Sport Pol & Politics	*International Journal of Sport Policy & Politics*
Int Rev Sociol Sport	*International Review for the Sociology of Sport*
Int Sports LJ	*International Sports Law Journal*
Int Sports L Rev	*International Sports Law Review*
IOC	International Olympic Committee
IP	intellectual property
IPIN	International Player Identification Number
ISF	International Sports Federation
ISU	International Skating Union
ITF	International Tennis Federation
ITIA	International Tennis Integrity Agency
ITPA	International Tennis Players Association
J Advert Res	*Journal of Advertising Research*
J Appl Bus Ec	*Journal of Applied Business & Economics*
J Child Sex Abus	*Journal of Child Sexual Abuse*
J Contemp Athl	*Journal of Contemporary Athletics*
J Gend Stud	*Journal of Gender Studies*
J Glob Mark	*Journal of Global Marketing*
J Int Arb	*Journal of International Arbitration*
J Leg Aspect Sport	*Journal of Legal Aspects of Sport*
J Spons	*Journal of Sponsorship*
J Sport Anal	*Journal of Sports Analytics*
J Sport Hist	*Journal of Sport History*
J Strat Mark	*Journal of Strategic Marketing*
J Strength & Cond Res	*Journal of Strength & Conditioning Research*
JIDS	*Journal of International Dispute Settlement*
KEA-CDES-EOSE	European Affairs-Centre de Droit et Economie du Sport-European Observatoire of Sport & Employment
Lewis & Clark L Rev	*Lewis & Clark Law Review*
LJ	Lord Justice
Lloyd's Rep	*Lloyd's Reports*
Loy LA Int & Comp L Rev	*Loyola Los Angeles International & Comparative Law Review*
LQR	*Law Quarterly Review*
LTA	Lawn Tennis Association

Manag Leis	*Managing Leisure*
Manag Mark-Craiova	*Management & Marketing-Craiova*
Manag Sci	*Management Science*
Manag Sport Leis	*Managing Sport & Leisure*
Mark Lett	*Marketing Letters*
Marq Sports L Rev	*Marquette Sports Law Review*
Md J Int L	*Maryland Journal of International Law*
Melb UL Rev	*Melbourne University Law Review*
MIPTC	Men's International Professional Tennis Council
MLB	Major League Baseball
MLBPA	Major League Baseball Players Association
MNC	multinational corporation
MTC	Men's Tennis Council
NBA	National Basketball Association
New Eng J Crim & Civ Confinement	*New England Journal on Criminal & Civil Confinement*
NFL	National Football League
NFLPA	NFL Players Association
NGO	non-governmental organization
NHL	National Hockey League
NOC	National Olympic Committee
NSF	National Sport Federation
NSPCC	National Society for the Prevention of Cruelty to Children
NTL	National Tennis League
NYU J Intell Prop & Ent L	*New York University Journal of Intellectual Property & Entertainment Law*
OHCHR	Office of High Commissioner for Human Rights
OHIM	Office for Harmonisation in the Internal Market
OJ	*Official Journal* [EU]
OTF	Oceania Tennis Federation
Oxford J Leg Stud	*Oxford Journal of Legal Studies*
PAC	Player Advisory Council
Pace IP Sports & Ent LF	*Pace Intellectual Property & Entertainment Law Forum*
PD	Practice Directive
PDP	Player Development Program
Pepp Disp Resol LJ	*Pepperdine Dispute Resolution Law Journal*
Pepp L Rev	*Pepperdine Law Review*
PFA	Professional Footballers' Association
PGA	Professional Golfers' Association
PILA	Private International Law Act (Swiss)

LIST OF ABBREVIATIONS

Psychol Sport Exerc	*Psychology of Sport & Exercise*
PTPA	Professional Tennis Players Association
QB	Queen's Bench
Qual Res Sport Exerc Health	*Qualitative Research in Sport, Exercise & Health*
Race Soc Probl	*Race & Social Problems*
RF	Roger Federer
San Diego Int LJ	*San Diego International Law Journal*
Santa Clara L Rev	*Santa Clara Law Review*
Scand J Med Sci Sports	*Scandinavian Journal of Medicine & Science in Sports*
SDNY	Southern District of New York
Seton Hall J Sport & Ent L	*Seton Hall Journal of Sport & Entertainment Law*
SGB	sport governing body
SMU L Rev	*Southern Methodist University Law Review*
South Carol J Int Law & Bus	*South Carolina Journal of International Law & Business*
Sport Bus Manag:	Int J *Sport, Business & Management: An International Journal*
Sport Educ Soc	*Sport, Education & Society*
Sport Ethics Philos	*Sport, Ethics & Philosophy*
Sport Hist	*Sport in History*
Sport Manag Rev	*Sport Management Review*
Sport Mark Q	*Sport Marketing Quarterly*
Sport Trad	*Sporting Traditions*
Sports Coach Rev	*Sports Coaching Review*
Sports LJ	*Sports Law Journal*
Stanford J Int L	*Stanford Journal of International Law*
Stanford L Rev	*Stanford Law Review*
TACP	Tennis Anti-Corruption Program
TADP	Tennis Anti-Doping Program
TE	Tennis Europe
Technol Forecast Soc Change	*Technological Forecasting & Social Change*
Tex Rev Ent & Sports L	*Texas Review of Entertainment & Sports Law*
TFEU	Treaty on the Functioning of the European Union
TIPP	Tennis Integrity Protection Programme
TISB	Tennis Integrity Supervisory Board
TIU	Tennis Integrity Unit
Tour Econ	*Tourism Economics*
TRIPS	Trade-Related Intellectual Property Rights
TUE	therapeutic use exemption
U Det L Rev	*University of Detroit Law Review*

U Miami Ent & Sports L Rev	*University of Miami Entertainment & Sports Law Review*
UAAA	Uniform Athlete Agents Act
UDPR	Universal Declaration of Player Rights
UDRP	Uniform Domain-Name Dispute-Resolution Policy
UK	United Kingdom
UKSC	United Kingdom Supreme Court [Reports]
ULEB	Union of European Leagues of Basketball
UN	United Nations
UNCITRAL	UN Commission of International Trade Law
UNDP	UN Development Programme
UNGPs	United Nations Guiding Principles
UNICEF	UN International Children's Emergency Fund
UNIDROIT	International Institute for the Unification of Private Law
US	United States
USC	*United States Supreme Court* [Reports]
USLTA	US Lawn Tennis Association
USTA	US Tennis Association
UTC	Ultimate Tennis Showdown
Va Sports & Ent LJ	*Virginia Sports & Entertainment Law Journal*
VSC	*Victoria Supreme Court* [Reports, Australia]
WADA	World Anti-Doping Agency
WADC	World Anti-Doping Code
Wake Forest J Bus & IP L	*Wake Forest Journal of Business & Intellectual Property Law*
WC	wild card
WCT	World Championship Tennis
WIPO	World Intellectual Property Organization
WIPTC	Women's International Professional Tennis Council
WITF	Women's International Tennis Federation
WLR	*Weekly Law Reports*
WLUK	*Westlaw United Kingdom*
WPA	World Players Association
WTA	Women's Tennis Association

TABLE OF CASES

SPORT TRIBUNALS and INTERNATIONAL COURTS

ATP Anti-Doping Tribunal
ATP v. Perry, Award (30 November 2005), 224 n.57

BWF Doping Hearing Panel
BWF v. Kate Jessica Foo Kune, Decision 2019/04, 295 n.42

CAS

Cilic v. ITF, CAS 2013/A/3335, 101 n.50
Coleman v. World Athletics, CAS 2020/A/7528, 158 n.39
Daniel Köellerer v. ATP and Others, CAS 2011/A/2490, 236 n.109
Dylan Scott v. ITF, CAS 2018/A/5768, 100 n.46, 161 n.54, 219 n.33
FINA v. Mellouli, CAS 2010/A/2268, 101 n.52
FINA & WADA v. Marco Tagliaferri, CAS 2008/A/1471 and 1486, 222 n.50
Halep v. ITIA, CAS Case 2023/A/10227, 134 n.148
Hans Knauss v. FIS, CAS 2005/A/847, 224 n.55
Hipperdinger v. ATP, CAS 2004/A/690, 227 n.71
I v. FIA, CAS 2010/A/2268, 222 n.50
Iannone v. FIM, CAS 2020/A/6978, 220 n.40
Ihab Abdelrahman v. Egyptian Anti-Doping Organization, WADA v. Ihab Abdelrahman & Egyptian Anti-Doping Organization, CAS 2017/A/5016 and 5036, 220 n.40
ITF v. Richard Gasquet, CAS 2009/A/1926, 224 n.58
ITIA v. Juan Carlos Saez (unreported), 240 n.129
Jose Paolo Guerrero v. FIFA and WADA v. FIFA and Guerrero, CAS 2018/A/5546 and 5571, 219 n.36
Kalashnikova and Gorgodze v. ITF, GNOC and GTF, CAS OG 20/05, 103
Klein v. ASDA, CAS A4/2016, 101 n.52
Luis Suarez v. FIFA, CAS Appeals Award (14 August 2014), 99 n.42
Maria Sharapova v. ITF, CAS 2016/A/4643, 226 n.65
Marin Cilic v. ITF, CAS 2013/A/3327, 226 n.67
Mauricio Fiol Villaneuva v. FINA, CAS 2016/A/4534, 221 n.43
Oleg Oriekhov v. UEFA, CAS 2010/A/2172, 236 n.107
Puerta v. ITF, CAS 2006/A/1025, 101 n.52, 224 n.59

Robert Kendrick v. *ITF*, CAS 2011/A/2518, 223 n.54
Roberto La Barbera v. *International Wheelchair & Amputee Sports Federation*, CAS 2010/A/2277, 220 n.38
Sara Errani v. *ITF*, CAS 2017/A/5301, 224 n.56
Squizzato v. *FINA*, CAS 2005/A/830, 101 n.52
Super Slam Ltd v. *ATP Tour Inc.*, Complaint filed in Delaware District Court dated 15 July 2021, 276 n.45
WADA v. *Abdelrahman*, CAS 2017/A/5036, 100, 100 n.44, 161
WADA v. *CADC & CSF & Kaskova*, CAS 2019/A/6213, 221 n.42
WADA v. *Darko Stanic & Swiss Olympic Association*, CAS 2006/A/1130, 222 n.51
WADA v. *FIM & Iannone*, CAS 2020/A/7068, 220 n.40
WADA v. *Hardy & USADA*, CAS 2009/A/1870, 226 n.68
WADA v. *International Weightlifting Federation & Yenny Fernanda Alvarez Caicedo*, CAS 2016/A/4377, 219 n.37
WADA v. *Swimming Australia, Sport Integrity Australia & Shayna Jack*, CAS 2021/A/7579 and 7580, 221 n.44
Walilko v. *FIA*, CAS 2010/A/2268, 101 n.52
X v. *ATP Tour*, 100 n.49, 157 n.37

CJEU

API – Anonima Petroli Italiana SpA and Others v. *Ministero delle Infrastrutture e dei Trasporti and Others*, Joined Cases C-184/13–C-187/13, C-194/13, C-195/13 and C-208/13, EU:C:2014:2147, 266 n.10
Audi AG v. *Office for Harmonisation in the Internal Market (Trade Marks and Designs) (OHIM)*, Case C-398/08 P, ECLI EU:C:2010:29, 48 n.11
Christelle Deliège v. *Ligue francophone de judo et disciplines associées ASBL, Ligue belge de judo ASBL, Union européenne de judo and François Pacquée*, Joined Cases C-51/96 and C-191/97 [2000] ECR I-2549, 281 n.60
David Meca-Medina and Igor Majcen v. *Commission*, Case C-519/04 P, EU:C:2006:492, 263 n.1
Dyson v. *Registrar of Trade Marks*, Case C-321/03, ECLI EU:C:2007:51, 50 n.16
European Super League v. *SL* v. *Fédération internationale de football association (FIFA) and Union of European Football Associations (UEFA)*, Case C-222/21, EU:C:2023:1011, 267 n.13
Gaetano Donà v. *Mario Mantero*, Case 13/76, EU:C:1976:115, 282 n.63
Heidelberger Bauchemie GmbH's Trade Mark Application, Case C-49/02, ECLI EU:C:2004:384, 49 n.12
Höfner and Elser v. *Macotron GmbH*, Case C-41/90, EU:C:1991:161, 268 n.16
International Skating Union v. *European Commission*, Case C-124/21 P, EU:C:2023:1012, 94 n.31, 267 n.14
International Skating Union v. *European Commission (ISU)*, Case T-93/18, EU:T:2020:610, 94 n.30, 271 n.27

International Skating Union's Eligibility Rules (ISU), Case AT.40208, C(2017) 8240 final, 94 n.29, 269 n.19, 270 n.26
Jaguar Land Rover Ltd v. *Office for Harmonisation in the Internal Market (Trade Marks and Designs)*, Case T-629/14, ECLI:EU:T:2015:878, 50 n.19
Lego Juris A/S v. *OHIM*, Case C-48/09, ECLI EU:C:2010:516, 50 n.15
Motosykletistiki Omospondia Ellados NPID (MOTOE) v. *Elliniko Dimosio*, Case C-49/07, EU:C:2008:376, 269 n.22
Noah Clothing v. *EUIPO*, Case T-562/22, EU:T:2024:23 (24 January 2024), 65 n.46
Ordem dos Técnicos Oficiais de Contas, Case C-1/12, EU:C:2013:127, 271 n.31
Reinhard Gebhard v. *Consiglio dell'Ordine degli Avvocati e Procuratori di Milano*, Case C-55/94, EU:C:1995:411, 263 n.2
Schecke and Eifert v. *Land Hessen*, Joined Cases C-92/09 and C-93/09 [2010] ECR-I-11063, 3 n.11
Smart Technologies ULC v. *Office for Harmonisation in the Internal Market (Trade Marks and Designs) (OHIM)*, Case T-523/09, ECLI EU:T:2011:175, 48 n.48
Union Royale Belge des Sociétés de Football Association ASBL v. *Jean-Marc Bosman, Royal club liégeois SA* v. *Jean-Marc Bosman and Others and Union des Associations Européennes de Football (UEFA)* v. *Jean-Marc Bosman*, Case C-415/93, ECLI:EU:C:1995/463, 184 n.30
Walrave and Koch v. *Union Cycliste Internationale and Others*, Case 36/74, ECLI:EU:C:1974:140, 282 n.63
Wouters and Others v. *Algemene Raad van de Nederlandse Orde van Advocaten*, ECLI:EU:C:2001:390, 268 n.17

Committee on the Rights of Children
Y. B. and N. S. v. *Belgium*, CtRC Views, UN Doc. CRC/C/79/D/12/2017, 197 n.29

ECtHR

Mutu and Pechstein v. *Switzerland*, App. Nos. 40575/10 and 67474/10, 17 n.49
Neulinger and Shuruk v. *Switzerland* (2012) 54 EHRR 31, 197 n.30
Riva, Akal and Others v. *Turkey*, App. Nos. 30226/10, 17880/11, 17887/11, 17891/11 and 5506/16, 17 n.50
Semenya v. *Switzerland*, App. No. 10934/21, (2023) ECHR 219, 17 n.49

ITF Independent Anti-Doping Tribunal
ITF v. *Jamie Burdekin*, 222 n.50
ITF v. *Mariano Puerta*, 222 n.50
ITF v. *Stefan Koubek*, 223 n.53

ITF Independent Tribunal
Evgeniy Zukin v. *ITF*, SR/076/2024, 290 n.20
Federación de Tenis de Chile & Rios v. *ITF*, Independent Tribunal Appeal, SR/48/2018, 102 n.57

Ilie Nastase v ITF, Independent Tribunal Decision, SR/913/2017, 6 n.18, 101 n.51, 102 n.57, 159 n.40, 247 n.17
ITF and Anti-Doping Organization v. Kratzer, SR/085/2020, 163 n.61
ITF and Anti-Doping Organization v. Lepchenko, SR/254/2021, 100 n.48, 161 n.56
ITF and Anti-Doping Organization v. Shoshkyna, SR/262/2020, 100 n.45, 161 n.53
ITF and Anti-Doping Organization v. Stephane Houdet, SR/005/2022, 101 n.53, 158 n.39

ITF Ethics Commission
ITF Ethics Commission v. Guidicelli, Decision (16 November 2020), 298 n.63
ITF Ethics Commission v. Majoli, Decision (3 August 2022), 291 n.26, 301 n.87
ITF Ethics Commission Re. Art. 12 Candidate Rules, Decision (15 July 2019), 293 n.37
ITF Ethics Commission Re. Art. 14 Candidate Rules, Decision (15 July 2019), 293 n.36
ITF Ethics Commission v. Zukin, Decision (25 February 2022), 19 n.57, 290 n.20

ITIA Sanctions
ITIA v. Karen Khachatryan, 241 n.132

TACP AHO

ITIA v. Baptiste Crepatte, 232 n.92
ITIA v. Edvinas Grigaitis, 238 n.122
ITIA v. Franco Feitt, 238 n.120
ITIA v. Jules Okala, 236 n.109, 237 n.116
ITIA v. Majd Affi, Abderahim Gharsallah and Mohamed Ghassen Snene, 239 n.123
ITIA v. Mick Lescure, 236 n.110, 236 n.112
ITIA v. Sanjar Fayziev, 236 n.111, 237 n.115, 237 n.117
ITIA v. Simohamed Hirs, 237 n.114
ITIA v. Timur Khabibulin, 236 n.111, 236 n.112, 237 n.119

UK Anti-Doping Tribunal
UKAD v. Buttifant, SR/NADP/508/2016, 220 n.41
UKAD v. Catana (unreported), 223 n.52

WIPO Arbitration Panel
Grand Slam Tennis Properties Ltd v. Contact Privacy Inc. Customer 0152960105 / Darryl Cazares, Grand Slam Nutrition Corp., Case D2020-1034, 67 n.50

NATIONAL COURTS

Australia
Djokovic v. Minister for Immigration, Citizenship, Migrant Services & Multicultural Affairs [2022] FedCFamC2G 7, 9 n.25

England and Wales
AAA v. Unilever Plc [2018] EWCA Civ 1532 (QB), 3 n.9
A-G of Commonwealth of Australia v. Adelaide Steamship Co. [1913] AC 781, 91 n.18

TABLE OF CASES

Age Old Builders Pty Ltd v. *Swintons Pty Ltd* [2003] VSC 307, 152 n.19
Alec Lobb (Garages) Ltd v. *Total Oil (Great Britain) Ltd* [1985] 1 WLR 173, 91 n.19
AT&T Corp. v. *Saudi Cable Co.* [2000] 2 Lloyd's Rep 127, 288 n.12
Buckley v. *Tutty* (1971) 45 ALJR 23, 93 n.25
Cavendish Square Holding BV v. *Makdessi* [2016] AC 1172, 92 n.22
Clarke v. *Newland* [1991] 1 All ER 397, 91 n.14
Dickson v. *Pharmaceutical Society of Great Britain* [1970] AC 403, 91 n.19
Donoghue v. *Stevenson* [1932] AC 562, 193, 193 n.15
Douglas Harper v. *Interchange Group Ltd* [2007] EWHC 1834 (Comm), 152 n.18
Eastham v. *Newcastle United Football Club Ltd* [1964] Ch 413, 93, 93 n.25, 119 n.70
Enderby Town FC Ltd v. *Football Association Ltd* [1971] Ch 591, 89 n.5
Esso Petroleum Ltd v. *Harper's Garage (Stoutport) Ltd* [1968] AC 269, 98 n.39
Faccenda Chicken Ltd v. *Fowler* [1987] Ch 117, 91 n.16
Greig v. *Insole* [1978] 1 WLR 302, 93, 93 n.26
Herbert Morris Ltd v. *Saxelby* [1916] 1 AC 688, 91 n.15
Imageview Management Ltd v. *Jack* [2009] EWCA Civ 63, 38, 38 n.93
Instone v. *Schroeder Music Publishing Co. Ltd* [1974] 1 WLR 1308, 90 n.12, 97 n.36
JW Spear & Son Ltd v. *Zynga Inc.* [2014] 1 All ER 1093, 50 n.16
Kalma v. *African Minerals Ltd* [2020] EWCA Civ 144 (QB), 3 n.9
Mason v. *Provident Clothing & Supply Co Ltd* [1913] AC 724, 91 n.13
Nagle v. *Feilden* [1966] 2 QB 633, 94 n.27
Nordenfelt v. *Maxim Nordenfelt Guns and Ammunition Co. Ltd* [1894] AC 535, 91 n.13
Patel v. *Mirza* [2016] UKSC 42, 92 n.21
Peninsula Securities Ltd v. *Dunnes Stores (Bangor) Ltd* [2020] 3 WLR 521, 91 n.15, 98
Petrofina (Great Britain) Ltd v. *Martin* [1966] Ch 146, 90 n.8
Proactive Sports Management Ltd v. *Rooney* [2011] EWCA Civ 1444, 90 n.9, 95 n.33, 168 n.81
Schroeder Music Publishing Co. Ltd v. *Macaulay* [1974] 1 WLR 1308, 90 n.11
Shone v. *British Bobsleigh Ltd* [2018] 5 WLUK 226, 193 n.16
Stevenage Borough Football Club v. *Football League Ltd* (1996) 9 Admin LR 109, 93 n.24
Texaco Ltd v. *Mulberry Filling Station Ltd* [1972] 1 WLR 814, 90 n.10, 91 n.20
Union Discount v. *Zoller* [2002] 1 WLR 1517, 152 n.18
Vedanta Resources Plc and Another v. *Lungowe and Others* (2019) UKSC 20, 3 n.8
Walker v. *Crystal Palace Football Club Ltd* (1910) 1 KB 87, 119 n.69
Watson v. *Praeger* [1991] 1 WLR 726, 95, 96 n.34
Wilander v. *Tobin* [1997] 2 Ll Rep 293, 162, 162 n.57
Zverev v. *Ace Group International Ltd* [2020] EWHC 3513 (Ch), 6 n.19, 40, 96 n.35, 168 n.80

Switzerland
A v. *International Biathlon Union*, Case 4A_232/2022 (22 December 2022), 153 n.20

United States of America
Brandeis Instel Ltd v. *Calabrian Chemicals Corp.*, 656 F.Supp. 160 (SDNY 1987), 288 n.13
Burleson v. *Earnest*, 153 S.W.2d 869 (Court of Civil Appeals of Texas 1941), 38 n.95

Deutscher Tennis Bund v. *ATP Tour Inc.*, 610 F.3d 820 (3d Cir. 2010), 2 n.2, 168, 168 n.82, 187, 187 n.40

Lendl v. *ProServ Inc.*, No. B-88–254 (District of Connecticut 1988), 39

Merit Insurance Co. v. *Leatherby Insurance Co.*, 714 F.2d 673 (7th Cir. 1983), 288 n.13

Reeves Brothers, Inc. v. *Capital-Mercury Shirt Corp.*, 962 F.Supp. 408 (SDNY 1997), 288 n.13

Volvo North America Corp. v. *Men's International Professional Tennis Council*, 857 F.2d 55 (2d Cir. 1988), 2 n.3, 169 n.84

Washington v. *USTA*, No. 99-CV-5148IJG, 2002 WL 1732801 (EDNY, 22 July 2002), 13 n.38

NOTES ON CONTRIBUTORS

ILIAS BANTEKAS is Professor of Transnational Law at Hamad bin Khalifa University (a member of Qatar Foundation) and Adjunct Professor at Georgetown University. He has advised in the fields of sports law, international law and human rights as part of his professional practice and served as arbitrator in commercial disputes, as well as before the Court of Arbitration for Sport (CAS). He has held full- and part-time academic positions at Brunel, Westminster, Harvard, Miami, Lausanne, London and elsewhere. He was the founder and CEO of Doha High Performance Tennis Academy, the only academy in the Gulf catering for professionally oriented tennis players. He was the joint winner in 2024 of the UNDP/ROLACC excellence award on safeguarding sport from corruption. He has written over 250 peer-reviewed articles and twenty-two books, fourteen of which with Oxford and Cambridge University Press, including: *Introduction to International Arbitration* (Cambridge University Press, 2015); *Cambridge Companion to Business and Human Rights* (Cambridge University Press, 2021 with M. A. Stein); *International Human Rights Law and Practice*, 4th edn (Cambridge University Press, 2023, with L. Oette); *International Law*, 5th edn (Oxford University Press, 2022, with E. Papastavridis); *Commentary on the UNCITRAL Model Law on International Commercial Arbitration* (Cambridge University Press, 2020, with P. Ortolani et al.); and *Commentary on the Court of Arbitration for Sport Arbitration Code* (under review with Cambridge University Press, 2026, with M. Diaconu and Z. Calo).

MARKO BEGOVIĆ is Associate Professor of Sport History and Sport Management at Molde University College in Norway. He is Senior Lecturer of Sport Law, Policy and Politics at the Faculty of Sport in Belgrade, Guest Lecturer of the Centre for Interdisciplinary and Multidisciplinary Studies at the University of Montenegro, Program Director of the Sports Diplomacy Program at the Hungarian

University of Sports Sciences and member of the UNESCO Chair on Governance and Social Responsibility in Sport. In parallel, Begović is acting as an associated academic at the Institute of European Sport Development and Leisure Studies at the German Sport University, and a member of the UNESCO Task Force on Anti-Doping. Between 2021 and 2022, he served as Director in charge of sport and youth affairs with the Government of Montenegro and was appointed as Program Director for the Master of Sport Management at the American University in the Emirates. He has written extensively on sports law, history, sport policy and politics. He was a member of the Governing Bureau for Sport and task force on good governance and Gender Equality Rapporteur at the Council of Europe. His extensive experience in sport politics and research impacted work on Council of Europe conventions and resolutions and the development of sports policies across Europe. Currently, combining academic, policy, legal and political knowledge and experience, he serves as Senior Policy Advisor for a number of sports organizations across the globe. He is a former professional tennis player and member of the national teams of Yugoslavia, and the Davis Cup team of Montenegro.

ROSS BROWN is a partner in the London office of the leading boutique sports law firm, Onside Law. He is particularly known for his regulatory dispute experience through acting for governing bodies, sports teams and individuals across various areas, including anti-corruption, anti-doping, contractual, disciplinary, safeguarding and selection disputes. He also regularly acts as lead advocate for his clients in their disputes. Among others, Ross has acted for (1) World Rugby on its anti-doping caseload, including at CAS, (2) the International Tennis Integrity Agency (ITIA) in over sixty proceedings under the Tennis Anti-Corruption Program, including before the CAS on several occasions, as well as the Tennis Anti-Doping Program (TADP), and (3) the England and Wales Cricket Board in relation to its regulatory investigations involving racism in cricket, its anti-doping caseload before the National Anti-Doping Panel and various disciplinary and safeguarding proceedings. Ross is also a qualified solicitor advocate and sits on the Sport Resolutions National Panel, the Sport Resolutions pro bono panel and the England Boxing National Disciplinary Panel.

WILLIAM BULL is Assistant Professor of Private Law at Maastricht University (UM) and a member of the Maastricht European Private Law Institute. Prior to obtaining his doctorate degree, he also worked as a researcher for the European Institute of Public Administration in Luxembourg. Since defending his PhD, he has conducted research into private and public-private aspects of sports law. His most recent articles have focused on sports agents and especially the regulation of access to and conduct of the profession of football intermediary, both from a comparative perspective and in the light of law and economics theory – the latter having been published in the *International Sports Law Journal*. In addition, he has completed a joint research project on the application of anti-money laundering legislation to the professional football sector (including football agents) in Belgium in the context of the UEFA Research Grant Programme, and subsequently co-authored a book on the subject, entitled *Professional Football and Anti-Money Laundering* (Intersentia, 2022). He is also a member of the International Advisory Board of the *Rivista di Diritto ed Economia dello Sport* and has taught for a number of years on UM's elective course on Introduction to Sport and Law, in collaboration with the Asser Institute's International Sports Law Centre.

MIGUEL CRESPO is the Head of Participation and Education of the Development Department at the International Tennis Federation. In this capacity, he oversees education and participation programs, organizes courses and conferences, and drives and conducts research on a variety of topics in close cooperation with organizations such as the National and Regional Tennis Federations, Olympic Solidarity from the International Olympic Committee, or Higher Education institutions. Prior to this, Miguel was the Coach Education Director for the Royal Spanish Federation (RFET), and he was also captain of Spain's junior national teams. He is a former professor in various universities such as Universidad Politécnica de València, Universidad Miguel Hernández de Elche and Universitat de València. He holds three PhDs, in Law (morality clauses in endorsement contracts), Psychology (leadership in tennis) and Business and Administration (innovation strategies of sports organizations), and is certified as a National Professor in Tennis by the RFET. He has written extensively on tennis-related law and sport science topics, including more than 100 articles, thirty book chapters and twenty books. He is the co-editor of the journal *ITF Coaching &*

Sport Science Review, a journal published for over thirty years which covers many topics related to sport science applied to tennis, and he is also on the editorial board of the *International Journal of Sports Sciences & Coaching*. He is also the Treasurer of the International Council for Coach Excellence.

LILY ELLIOTT is Senior Associate at Onside Law in the litigation and regulatory department. She advises governing bodies, clubs, teams and commercial organizations both nationally and internationally on contentious matters. Her practice primarily involves advising clients on sports regulatory proceedings and investigations, in particular in relation to disciplinary proceedings with cases focusing on misconduct, anti-doping and anti-corruption. She also has extensive experience advising governing bodies on the drafting and implementation of regulations, including spending a year with the England and Wales Cricket Board in their Regulatory Team. Alongside her regulatory practice, Lily also advises clients on High Court litigation, primarily on commercial matters. Prior to Onside Law, Lily trained and qualified at Freshfields Bruckhaus Deringer LLP, where she worked on High Court litigation and in particular mass litigation, consumer actions and product liability disputes. Lily studied classics at Cambridge University for her undergraduate degree before converting to law.

DÉSIRÉE FIELDS is a Legal Director in the London office of international law firm Pinsent Masons, specializing in intellectual property. Her practice focuses on worldwide trademark and design portfolio management, international prosecution and clearance, enforcement, exploitation and commercialization of trademarks and designs. She has been involved in complex multi-jurisdictional trademark oppositions and litigation and has experience with coordinating trademark projects on a global basis. Dual-qualified as a solicitor in England & Wales and as an attorney-at-law in New York, she has a deep understanding of multi-jurisdictional matters. Désirée has worked with clients across a diverse range of sectors, including luxury and consumer brands, food and beverages, media, technology and communications, sports, entertainment, hospitality and leisure. Her particular focus on the tennis industry is a result of her lifelong interest in the sport in which she has become widely regarded for her extensive knowledge and insight. She is also a leader in Pinsent Masons' sports practice and heads up the tennis sub-sector initiative and manages the firm's relationship with the Tennis Industry Association UK. Désirée is a Trustee of Middlesex Tennis having joined the board in October 2023 and has been a participant in the Lawn Tennis Association's Inspire Leadership Programme for Women Volunteers in Tennis in 2024/25. Désirée has authored numerous articles for various intellectual property and other legal publications (including in respect of brand protection in the tennis industry) and has been consistently recognized by leading legal directories and publications. She has been named as a top trademark professional for trademark prosecution and strategy by World Trademark Review's WTR 1000 (2017–25) and recommended for trademark and brand protection work in the Legal 500 (2018–25). Désirée's outstanding contributions to The Trademark Reporter Committee of the International Trade Mark Association since 2018 have resulted in her elevation to Senior Editor for 2023. She is the Co-Subcommittee Chair of the Content Solicitation and Development Subcommittee. Désirée is also an editor of the *UK Trade Mark Handbook*.

BEN LIVINGS has held academic positions at universities in the United Kingdom, France and Australia. He is currently Associate Professor of Criminal Law and Evidence in Justice and Society at the University of South Australia. Ben received his doctorate from the University of Warwick. His thesis examined the way in which participant violence in sport is regulated and permitted according to a mixture of sports regulation and the law. He continues to be interested in the intersection between law and regulation in sports governance and administration. Ben realized early in life that he would never be a proficient tennis player, but he likes to watch it anyway.

KATARINA PIJETLOVIC, LLM, LLLic, LLD, is Professor of EU Competition and Sports Law at Católica University of Portugal, Global School of Law in Lisbon. Previously, she served as Associate Professor at Manchester Law School, a sports law module leader at Liverpool University Football Industries MBA Programme and a visiting scholar at ISDE Global Sports Law Master Programme in New York, among others. She is the sole author of *EU Sports Law and Breakaway Leagues in Football* (Springer, 2015). In 2021, during its incorporation process, she was a member of the advisory board of the Professional Tennis Players Association set up by Novak Djokovic and Vasek Pospisil. She is the co-founder and former General

Secretary of the Union of European Clubs in football. One of her professional passions is protecting the fundamental rights of athletes, non-elite clubs and national teams in the sports ecosystem.

BRENDAN SCHWAB, LLB, MBA, is an Australian lawyer and architect of the global and Australian player association movements, having co-founded and led the World Players Association, FIFPRO Asia/Oceania, the Australian Athletes' Alliance and Professional Footballers Australia. Over a thirty-year career, he has represented and worked with the strongest player associations in the world, as well as multiple teams and athletes, including Australia's Socceroos and Matildas. Brendan has written extensively on global sport's responsibility to protect, respect and fulfill human rights. He was the principal author of the landmark *Universal Declaration of Player Rights* and has had articles published in the *Maryland Journal of International Law*, the *International Sports Law Journal*, the *Journal on the Legal Aspects of Sport*, Sweet & Maxwell's *International Sports Law Review* and various other publications and media outlets, including *Law in Sport*.

JAMIE SINGER is an English Qualified solicitor and a founding partner of Onside Law. He qualified as a solicitor into the Commercial department at Clifford Chance in 1998 before joining International Management Group in 2001 as principal legal advisor to IMG's tennis and sponsorship divisions. With two colleagues, he launched Onside Law in 2005. Jamie has been advising on high-profile commercial, intellectual property, governance and regulatory matters across the sports and entertainment industries for twenty-five years. His commercial practice includes sponsorship, media rights, licensing, hosting, image rights and talent management. His regulatory practice focuses, in particular, on integrity and match-fixing cases. He regularly speaks at conferences, writes articles and appears on television as a sports law expert and is recommended as a leading sports law practitioner in all the independent legal directories. He co-authored the 'Sponsorship and Commercial Rights' chapter of the textbook *Football and the Law* edited by Nick de Marco KC, and is a Guest Lecturer on the Sports Law Masters at ISDE in Barcelona and on De Montfort University's Sports Law Diploma. He is also the global editor of *Chambers Sports Law Review*.

PREFACE

A book on tennis and the law faces many challenges from the very outset. Despite the fact that it is one of the most popular sports, attracting large crowds throughout the world, there is an absence of scholarship in the legal literature. One may perhaps think that there is not all that much to write about. However, the governance of global tennis constitutes one of the most complex in the world of sports since it is subject to no less than three governing bodies, all with autonomy, but also in relative synergy. This fact alone should have been enough for an expansive literature, but it has hardly attracted any attention in the intersection between law and tennis. While putting this book together, the editors were faced with several dilemmas. Was this a book about professional tennis or tennis in general? From a practical perspective, as opposed to the definition of the ATP and WTA, it is difficult to discern who is or who claims to be a professional tennis player. In equal measure, a junior player going into debt in order to cover his or her expenses with a view to climbing the rankings and ultimately making money from the sport may have as much claim to a professional status as any seasoned player earning guaranteed profits from participation in various circuits. As a result, our definition of professional tennis should be perceived in a broad sense, which necessarily involves thousands of persons around the world who view their efforts as professional or from a professional angle. Just like other individual sports, tennis is hardly about the two opponents on the court; rather, there is an entire mechanism off the court without which a high-level game could never be played. This includes a dedicated entourage (mostly parents) that travel around the circuits, book the courts (and sweep them almost every time!), pay coaches and act as psychologists and counselors to their children. One of the editors of this book was a tennis dad and is perfectly aware of all the highs and lows this full-time endeavor offers. In addition to parents, the off-court entourage includes coaches and other tennis professionals, tennis clubs and academies, national tennis associations, event organizers, sponsors, equipment producers, media, advertisers and others. When one watches the finals of ATP or WTA tournaments, this is simply the pinnacle of the game of tennis, and it is easy to ignore the labor of millions of stakeholders throughout the world.

A major challenge in writing a book on law and tennis is the absence of material and as a result a lack of wholesome expertise. By way of distinction, it may be surmised that contract law in the United Kingdom is comprised of the common law and a handful of statutes. A specific law of tennis contracts, on the other hand, cannot rely on an identifiable body of law because relevant contracts are confidential, and the availability of tennis-specific cases is miniscule. Legal counsel in the three tennis governing bodies have access to a relatively small body of law and regulation, which in turn creates ultra-specialization. Lawyers representing tennis players and tennis stakeholders are the guardians of contracts and it is natural that they shape much of the game of tennis off the court. It was clear to the editors that all of these varied types of expertise were required if they were to produce a comprehensive book on the intersection between tennis and the law. It is for this purpose that contributors are derived from all walks of the tennis legal spectrum, including from academia, legal practice and in-house counsel in one or more of the three tennis governing entities. All of the contributors thus have a strong interest in tennis, besides their legal expertise. In addition, one of the editors was an ATP-ranked player and senior advisor to several national tennis associations, while the other editor was the founder and CEO of the first high-performance tennis academy in the Middle East.

It is also apt to declare our dilemma about what could have been an appropriate title for this book, besides the use of the word "professional." Is tennis regulated by domestic law, international law or that part of transnational sports law (*lex sportiva*) as applied to the specific governance requirements of tennis? Readers will come to realize that all three components are relevant to this discussion. While it was felt that both transnational (and also global) and international law were appropriate, ultimately only one of the two had to remain. The choice was certainly not an easy one.

The editors would like to pay their gratitude to all the contributors to this book for their professionalism and their efforts to uncover material that was largely inaccessible. Without them, this book would not have been possible. In addition, the editors would like to extend their appreciation to Marianne Nield, senior commissioning editor at Cambridge University Press, for believing in this project despite the absence of a dedicated sports law concentration at the Press. The editors certainly hope that this is a first attempt to map the intersection of law and tennis and that the younger generation of sports lawyers expands and improves on this work. The editors are happy to receive comments and suggestions for possible improvement in a second edition. The production of the book was delayed on account of unforeseen circumstances. Despite several rounds of updating, by the time of the last round until the book had gone to production, all three tennis entities had amended pertinent institutional rules at least once. Readers may well need to consult the newest versions of rules. Alas, the law stated herein is accurate as of May 1, 2024.

1

The Intersection between Law and Tennis

ILIAS BANTEKAS AND MARKO BEGOVIĆ

1 Introduction

This chapter endeavors to identify the place of professional tennis in the realms of domestic, transnational and international law. It serves as a background platform to all subsequent chapters. As the reader will come to appreciate in this and subsequent chapters, the key protagonists in professional tennis, namely, the International Tennis Federation (ITF), the Women's Tennis Association (WTA) and the Association of Tennis Professionals (ATP), rely on contracts in order to interact and communicate with third parties within their sphere of activities. Given the transnational nature of tennis, with tournaments and outreach throughout the globe, it is only natural that these contracts are equally transnational in nature, whatever this might mean. This also explains the legal personality of these entities. Even so, because all of these entities must by necessity be headquartered or incorporated in at least one jurisdiction, they are subject to the domestic laws of the forum. In this sense, the regulatory dimension of tennis becomes entangled with the transnational character of the ITF, the WTA and the ATP and their capacity to enter into transnational contracts and dispute resolution mechanisms. It is no wonder, therefore, that all of these entities are headquartered in liberal jurisdictions that are both arbitration-friendly and amenable to transnational legal processes. At the same time, it should be emphasized that professional tennis is also an integral part of public international law. The three aforementioned entities, as well as the association of the ITF with the International Olympic Committee (IOC), renders them akin to global non-governmental organizations (NGOs) or multinational corporations (MNCs) and by extension the expanding body of soft law applicable thereto.[1] This is particularly true

---

[1] See Ilias Bantekas, "Corporate Social Responsibility in International Law" (2004) 22 Bost U Int LJ 309; Ilias Bantekas, "The Emerging UN Business and Human Rights Treaty and Its Codification of International Norms" (2021) 12 Geo Mas Int LJ 1.

of the ITF which is incorporated as a commercial company with activities throughout the globe. In equal measure, it is now clear that international human rights law governs the operation of non-state actors, even if ultimately the obligation burdens the state and its institutions. Moreover, there is little doubt that the ITF, at least, satisfies the criterion of foreign investment in several bilateral investment treaties (BITs), although it has not officially claimed such a status. Overall, the purpose of this chapter and the book as a whole is to bring to light the patchy set of rules (institutional or otherwise) and norms that govern professional tennis and highlight their relevance.

2 The Regulation of Professional Tennis by Transnational Law

Strictly speaking, professional tennis is not "regulated" by transnational legal processes. Rather, the structures under which it is organized benefit from such transnational processes. A key illustration is the organization of the ITF as a corporate entity under the laws of the Bahamas, yet headquartered in London. This allows it to contract in its own name and not on behalf of a state entity or on the behest of one or more governments. Its Board of Directors dictates its corporate agenda, while at the same time it benefits from membership in the IOC and likewise its own members/shareholders consist of national tennis federations, the majority of which retain some kind of public dimension, whether through funding, legal personality or other association.

One of the key profit-making activities of the ITF, the ATP and the WTA is the organization of tennis tournaments in professional and amateur circuits, as well as attendant media and image rights. Although any entity is free to organize tournaments, these three entities have placed themselves in a position to dominate prizes, media coverage, branding and the trust of the top players.[2] Generally speaking, the organization and allocation of tennis tournaments is not excluded from domestic and transnational anti-trust laws[3] and all three entities must tread carefully to avoid accountability.

---

[2] See *Deutscher Tennis Bund* v. *ATP Tour Inc.*, 610 F.3d 820 (3d Cir. 2010), *cert. denied*, 562 US 1064, 131, which confirmed that the ATP can re-organize professional tournaments and relegate one or another to a lower tier without breaching anti-trust rules (in this case the Hamburg and Qatar tournaments).

[3] See George A. Metanias, Thomas J. Cryan and David W. Johnson, "A Critical Look at Professional Tennis under Anti-Trust Law" (1987) 4 U Miami Ent & Sports L Rev 57; equally, *Volvo North America Corp.* v. *Men's International Professional Tennis Council*, 857 F.2d 55 (2d Cir. 1988), one of the earlier cases concerning whether an international tennis federation is susceptible to the Sherman Act, 15 USC § 1 (1982).

1 THE INTERSECTION BETWEEN LAW AND TENNIS

All three entities and their attendant members, as transnational corporate actors, are subject to an increasing body of regulation. As a matter of unilateral state practice, extra-territorial laws regulating particular aspects of corporate conduct are on the rise, chief among these being the United Kingdom's Modern Slavery Act of 2015[4] and the Australian Modern Slavery Act of 2018.[5] Section 54 of the United Kingdom's Act requires commercial entities with a turnover of £36 million, irrespective of their place of incorporation, but which undertake even a part of their business in the United Kingdom, to prepare annual slavery and trafficking audits.[6] The ITF has issued a policy statement in implementation of the Act.[7] Significantly, such liability is not limited to tort, particularly given the public nature and importance of the violated rights involved, the gravity of their breach, the impact on the domestic and global rights objectives, and the need to deter subsequent breaches.[8] English courts have held that the extra-territorial reach of such laws concern specific conduct and do not encompass the impact of MNCs on human rights.[9] These extra-territorial laws were preceded by the introduction of human rights impact assessments (HRIAs) and due diligence requirements by international financial institutions (IFIs), UN bodies[10] and the European Union,[11] among others.

---

[4] Modern Slavery Act 2015 (c. 30) (UK).
[5] Modern Slavery Act 2018 (No. 153/2018) (Austl.).
[6] Modern Slavery Act 2015 (c. 30) (UK).
[7] ITF, Modern Slavery and Human Trafficking Statement, available at: www.itftennis.com/en/about-us/modern-slavery/, which is consistent with the United Kingdom's Modern Slavery Act 2015, to which it is bound given its seat in London.
[8] Ibid. See equally *Vedanta Resources Plc and Another v. Lungowe and Others* (2019) UKSC 20, at 45–6, 92, which unlike other cases did find a duty of care arising from a company's overseas business operations.
[9] See e.g. *AAA v. Unilever Plc* [2018] EWCA Civ 1532 (QB) (holding no duty of care by a UK parent company in respect of third parties harmed by the business conduct of a foreign subsidiary); equally, *Kalma v. African Minerals Ltd* [2020] EWCA Civ 144 (QB) (deciding that there was no liability for a UK company's operations in Sierra Leone mired by police abuse).
[10] See Guiding Principles on Human Rights Impact Assessment for Trade and Investment Agreements, UN Doc. A/HRC/19/59/Add.5 (December 19, 2011); Guiding Principles on extreme poverty and human rights, UN Doc. A/HRC/21/39 (July 18, 2012); Committee on Economic, Social and Cultural Rights, General Comment No. 24 (August 10, 2017), paras 17, 21–2; Committee on the Rights of the Child, General Comment 19, UN Doc. CRC/CG/19 (July 10, 2016), para. 47.
[11] EU Commission Working Paper Operational Guidance on taking account of fundamental rights in Commission impact assessments, SEC(2011) 567 Final (May 6, 2011). The Court of Justice of the European Union has, in fact, emphasized the importance of such HRIAs in the adoption of primary and secondary EU legislation. See *Schecke and Eifert v. Land Hessen*, Joined Cases C-92/09 and C-93/09 [2010] ECR-I-11063. HRIAs are also required through two EU instruments, namely: the Directive on Public Procurement and

Crucially, the ITF, the WTA and the ATP interact with third parties through the medium of contract. Although contract law is quintessentially national in character, there is an ever-growing consensus and state practice whereby certain principles, practices and wholesale legal systems are given prominence and authority as a matter of transnational governing laws. This is true, for example, as regards the UNIDROIT Principles of Transnational Commercial Contracts as well as English contract law, the latter serving as governing law for several specialized transnational commercial contracts.[12] Hence, none of the three tennis entities is bound to operate within the narrow confines of the contract laws of their headquarters or place of incorporation and given that contracts are the only form of interaction with third entities throughout the globe, the existence and recognition of uniform and harmonized contractual practices significantly minimizes all transaction costs.

2.1 Professional Tennis as Part of the Transnational Lex Sportiva

The game of tennis is situated within a complex and interrelated set of regimes that consists of both legislative and institutional (internal) elements, all of which are governed by the ITF. The universality of contemporary tennis has been achieved primarily through formalization of the rules of the game that includes matters such as the size of tennis courts and types of balls, as well as specific match or competition formats. Cumulatively, this rather rigid structure of rules serves to maintain legislative and organizational transnationality, along with the dominant role of the ITF and the two professional tennis associations, namely, the WTA and the ATP. The ITF develops the rules that effectively define the game of tennis at both the amateur and professional levels, while together with the WTA and ATP, they serve to regulate the organization of competitions under their aegis. The allocation of tournaments as major competition formats is subjected to a number of requirements to which host federations or organizers are bound to adhere. As a result, all of these stakeholders adopt and implement these rules and standards as part of the broader *lex*

---

the Directive on Non-Financial Information Disclosure. Under the latter, companies with over 500 employees are required to disclose information on policies, risks and results as regards their respect for human rights.

[12] See, in particular, Stefan Vogenauer (ed.), *Commentary on the UNIDROIT Principles of International Commercial Contracts* (Oxford University Press, 2015); Michael J. Bonell (ed.), *The UNIDROIT Principles in Practice* (Brill, 2006).

sportiva. These rules, policies and standards trickle down to national tennis federations who go on to adopt and enforce them within their domestic sphere of authority, whether as a matter of law (infrequent) or institutional prowess, in their capacity as primary units of the ITF.

At the same time, the institutional law of the Olympic Movement, including the Olympic Charter, is binding on the ITF because of its institutional relationship with the IOC. As part of the Olympic structure, the IOC exercises authority over members of the Olympic Movement (including all international sports federations). This in turn entails that all IOC-related commitments, such as those arising from the World Anti-Doping Agency's (WADA) anti-doping regulations, are binding on the ITF and its direct stakeholders. With the establishment of the WADA, the adoption of the World Anti-Doping Code (WADC)[13] has become an inextricable part of the professional tennis ecosystem, especially since the enforcement of the WADC falls under the jurisdiction of the Court of Arbitration for Sport (CAS).

2.2 The Transnational Character of Dispute Resolution of Professional Tennis

The ITF – and to a lesser degree the WTA and ATP – has followed the example of other international sports federations[14] by setting up internal dispute resolution and disciplinary mechanisms, rather than opting for general commercial arbitration or litigation. All of these specialized sports arbitral mechanisms are related by reason of agreement (which is reflected in their constitutions or other internal instruments) to the CAS, which broadly speaking serves either as an appellate forum for disputes already adjudicated by these specialist institutions or as first instance arbitral recourse.[15] The type of arbitral and quasi-judicial mechanisms envisaged in ITF-related instruments constitute an exception to the general rule that all private disputes are subject to the jurisdiction of

---

[13] Available at: www.wada-ama.org/sites/default/files/resources/files/2021_wada_code.pdf.
[14] A good example is offered by FIBA's Basketball Arbitral Tribunal (BAT). See Dirk R. Martens, "Basketball Arbitral Tribunal: An Innovative System for Resolving Disputes in Sport (Only in Sport?)" (2011) 1 Int Sports LJ 54.
[15] According to Art. 57 of the FIFA Statutes, FIFA recognizes the independent CAS with headquarters in Lausanne (Switzerland) to resolve disputes between FIFA, member associations, confederations, leagues, clubs, players, officials, intermediaries and licensed match agents. Strictly speaking, CAS comprises an ordinary arbitration division, an anti-doping division and an appellate arbitration division. See CAS Code of Sports-Related Arbitration (2022), S3.

the courts. No doubt, preference for such internal mechanisms is dictated by several factors, including: speed, confidentiality (although awards and decisions are made public), cost and ultimately authority over the process. Moreover, given that sporting disputes generally engage issues that are the same or similar across all sports,[16] the case law of the CAS has assumed a universal value that is consistently applied as precedent before domestic courts as well as sports arbitral institutions.[17] The only notable exception that has been identified as such by the ITF Independent Tribunal concerns the application of sanctions.[18] Hence, an underlying consensus in favor of solidifying and expanding the so-called *lex sportiva* is essential in understanding both the adoption and complexity of internal dispute mechanisms by the ITF, WTA and ATP and other international sporting federations.

Within this context, the ITF has set up its own distinct organs for the resolution of disputes arising from tennis. The ambit of these organs excludes contractual disputes, such as those between players and agents,[19] or between the ITF and tournament organizers. All three sporting entities have promulgated discreet tournament rules, as have also national tennis federations, which further provide for penalties and sanctions.[20] Finally, the ITF has instituted an Ethics Commission that has

---

[16] By way of illustration, the ITF is a signatory to the WADA Anti-Doping Code and as part of its commitment thereof it has issued the Tennis Anti-Doping Program (TADP), which establishes the WADA Code-compliant Anti-Doping Rules for professional tennis. In particular, the ITF contracts International Doping Tests & Management (IDTM) to collect samples from players under the TADP so that they can be tested for the presence of prohibited substances under the WADA Code.

[17] See Johan Lindholm, "A Legit Supreme Court of World Sports? The CAS(e) for Reform?" (2021) 21 Int Sports LJ 1 (who argues that the concept of judicialization and the related models of arbitration can help us understand the Court of Arbitration for Sport and its role in the development of a transnational legal order in sports).

[18] In *Ilie Nastase* v. *ITF*, Independent Tribunal Decision, SR/913/2017, at para. 101, the Independent Tribunal held that the applicable principle concerning sanctions is that of "correctness trumps consistency," as referred to in previous sports decisions. Hence, "if a sanction granted in another similar matter – although, as was just said, there is no such case that the Tribunal is aware of – is greater or smaller than the one imposed by the [Panel or Tribunal], this should not bind the Tribunal and prevent it from electing the sanction which it determines to be the fairest in light of all the circumstances of the case."

[19] *Zverev* v. *Ace Group International Ltd* [2020] EWHC 3513 (Ch) (which effectively concerned a restraint of trade claim before English courts, but which was ultimately settled to the benefit of the tennis player).

[20] For fines imposed by tournament organizers, see Jimmy Hascup, "Australian Tennis Player Gets Fined $56,100 for Failing to Meet 'Professional Standard' in Wimbledon Loss," *USA Today* (July 5, 2019), available at: www.usatoday.com/story/sports/tennis/wimb/2019/07/05/wimbledon-2019-bernard-tomic-fined-prize-money-lackluster-effort/

authority to investigate ethical infractions attributed to ITF officials, as well as monitor the electoral process for the ITF Board of Directors.[21] This is more fully explored in Chapter 13 of this volume.

2.3 The Relationship between the ITF, the WTA and the ATP

The organizational structure of the world of tennis is an expression of the evolution of the game towards commercialization and professionalization. The ITF was created more than a century ago as a major governing body for the world of tennis. The changes that led to its current status were shaped with the abolition of the long-standing rule that only amateur athletes can compete in the Olympics and the introduction of tennis as part of the Olympic program, which culminated in the elimination of the distinction between professional and amateur tennis. Further transformation took place through the struggle for gender equality, whereby Billie Jean King founded the WTA as a global stakeholder for women's tennis. Both associations, the WTA and the ATP, were created to quintessentially safeguard players' rights. These new institutional regimes led to the creation of a new ranking system and fairer allocation of funds. Further development unfolded on the basis of the institutional cooperation between players' associations and tournament organizers. However, the major shift occurred in the 1990s, whereby the ATP announced the development of a new format that would revolutionize the game, focusing on the business ecosystem structured around sponsors, media and other related organizations and institutions. The ITF remains the coordinating authority of the Grand Slam tournaments (Australian Open, Roland Garros, Wimbledon Championships and US Open), future tournaments and ITF junior circuit tournaments, while, as already explained, the ATP is in charge of two categories of tournaments: (1) ATP Tour tournaments (ATP Tour Finals singles/doubles, United Cup, ATP Tour Masters

---

1655166001/. In practice, national tennis federations promulgate their own rules, which include conduct obligations and the imposition of fines. See US Tennis Association (USTA), Handbook of Rules and Regulations (2022), available at: www.usta.com/content/dam/usta/2022-pdfs/2022%20Friend%20at%20Court.pdf, Chapter IV.C(1), which stipulates that: "The Chair of any tournament may withhold all or part of any prize money or expenses payable to any player charged by the Chair or by the Referee of the tournament with conduct inconsistent with the principles in USTA Regulation IV.C., provided a written grievance is filed in accordance with USTA Regulation V.B. and Bylaw 43. Any prize money or expenses so withheld shall be withheld until a final determination of the charges in the grievance has been made. Immediately after the final determination, the funds withheld, less the amount of any fine, shall be promptly paid to the player."

[21] ITF Code of Ethics, available at: www.itftennis.com/media/7246/2023-itf-code-of-ethics-english.pdf.

1000, ATP Tour 500, ATP Tour 250); and (2) ATP Challenger Tour tournaments. The WTA, in turn, under the terms of the WTA Tour, enjoys authority for the organization of two categories of events: (1) WTA Tour tournaments (WTA 250, WTA 500, WTA 1000 and Finals); and (2) WTA Challenger Tour tournaments.

Therefore, the current organizational structure is complex as two professional entities and the main governing body are in charge of organizing a series of professional, and at times competing or overlapping, tennis events. Some of these events are organized jointly between the ATP and the WTA in order to maximize media attractiveness, visibility, sponsorship and the sport's fan base. That said, the relationship between these stakeholders is complex as all of them are entitled to organize events and deal with athletes in respect of tournaments and events under their respective authority. This complexity requires the adoption of separate rules by each entity that entails a significant degree of coordination and delineation of competencies and responsibilities. The Grand Slam Rules adopted by the Grand Slam Board include the Grand Slam Tournament Regulations and the Grand Slam Code of Conduct.[22] The aim of these rules is to structure the organization of the four Grand Slam Tournaments, to maintain organizational standards, and to ensure that the conduct of both players and organizers contributes to safeguarding the integrity of the world of tennis. The Grand Slam Board is responsible for coordinating and governing activities associated with the Grand Slam Tournaments. Besides adopting rules, the Grand Slam Board is engaged in officiating, drafting tournament calendars and maintaining contractual relationships with other stakeholders from the world of tennis or third parties. As global governing bodies for men's and women's professional tennis, the ATP and the WTA adopt rulebooks, a specific set of rules for each competitive year aimed at regulating the organization of tournaments, their financial, branding, personnel, facilities-related aspects, as well as set out a code of conduct, dispute resolution and anti-corruption mechanisms.[23] Both professional tennis bodies have gone on to establish a governing authority – the Board of Directors – in charge of implementing policies and maintaining a contractual relationship between players and tournament organizers.[24]

---

[22] 2023 Official Grand Slam Rulebook, available at: www.itftennis.com/media/5986/grand-slam-rulebook-2023-f.pdf.
[23] 2023 ATP Official Rulebook, available at: www.atptour.com/en/corporate/rulebook.
[24] 2023 WTA Official Rulebook, available at: https://photoresources.wtatennis.com/wta/document/2023/05/04/181c679e-d187-4e7a-a7b2-25677d3eeec4/2023-WTA-Rulebook-5-4-2023-.pdf.

The current strategy for planning and coordinating activities aims to eliminate potential overlaps with a view to maximizing the income generated from the organization of these events.

3 Professional Tennis and Domestic Law

While a large part of professional tennis is regulated under transnational law, domestic laws are hugely relevant to a variety of stakeholders. The following sections will only touch on governance and labor laws. Domestic laws dictate all aspects of national tennis federations and their members, as well as the distinct relationships between players, academies, coaches and agents. Domestic laws and institutions are responsible for professional tennis policies, such as the state's relationship with the ITF and the IOC. Finally, all issues related to tournaments, whether criminal or administrative, are subject to the laws of the host state and the jurisdiction of its courts.[25]

3.1 Tennis Governance

Although the governance of transnational tennis entities may be perceived as a matter suitable to transnational regulation, every corporate or other entity must be set up and registered under the laws of a single state. If such corporate entity desires to establish "subsidiaries" in other states, it can only do so through new and distinct legal persons under the laws of that third state. The only link between the mother entity and its foreign "subsidiaries" is that of intra-shareholding. It is difficult to fully understand the complexity of governance among the various international tennis entities without a solid foundation of the modern history of the game. The majority of fans do not fully comprehend the existence of several entities, nor the nuanced rivalry between players, organizers and to some degree also the ITF. While such rivalries are not uncommon in team sports, such as football and basketball,[26] the creation of bifurcated –

---

[25] As was the case with the immigration/visa status of Novak Djokovic and his deportation for his refusal to be vaccinated ahead of the Australian Open. *Djokovic v. Minister for Immigration, Citizenship, Migrant Services & Multicultural Affairs* [2022] FedCFamC2G 7. See Vasilije Markovic, "The Djoković Case: The Limits of God-Like Power of Australia's Immigration Minister," available at: www.cirsd.org/en/expert-analysis/the-djokovic-case–the-limits-of-god-like-power-of-australias-immigration-minister.

[26] E.g. the dispute between FIBA and ULEB (Union of European Leagues of Basketball) which ultimately culminated in an agreement in 2004, but was reignited again in 2015, concerning the hosting of Europe's most significant tournament, the Euroleague.

yet to some degree synergetic – structures is highly unusual. Professional tennis is organized under a complex contractual and intra-regulatory web. To understand the role of the ITF in this complex web, one must first appreciate the interests of the various stakeholders that make up the world of professional tennis.

A brief look at the most recent history is pertinent. The ATP[27] was set up in 1972 and the Men's International Professional Tennis Council (MIPTC), also known as the Men's Tennis Council (MTC), was set up in 1974 as the governing body of men's professional tennis. Its composition consisted of ITF and ATP representatives. By 1988, the ATP had become frustrated with the way the sport was managed and its lack of influence and so it withdrew from the MIPTC, setting up a distinct ATP tour in 1990. The MIPTC now had no reason for existence and was disbanded in 1989.[28] Professional tennis is a confusing array of several transnational entities, each controlling certain fragments of the game. By way of illustration, the ATP, which is organized as a non-profit entity, is the governing body of only some men's professional circuits, namely, the ATP Tour, the ATP Challenger Tour and the ATP Champions Tour. The ATP is governed by a Board of Directors, consisting of tournament members, player members and a Chairman/President.[29] The relationship between the ATP and the ITF can be characterized as both synergetic and contentious. The ITF organizes the four Grand Slams,[30] and on behalf of the IOC it also administers the Davis Cup and the Olympic tennis tournament.[31] The ITF's role in professional tennis is paramount. It functions as organizer of three major events (Grand Slam, Davis Cup and Olympic tennis tournament) and several less publicized ones. This allows it to generate significant income as well as yield authority. Its authority stems from the fact that as the mother of all national tennis federations,[32] these are dependent

---

[27] Available at: www.atptour.com.
[28] See Robert Lake (ed.), *Routledge Handbook of Tennis: History, Culture and Politics* (Routledge, 2019).
[29] ITF Constitution (2022), Art. 19, available at: www.itftennis.com/media/2431/the-constitution-of-the-itf-2024-web.pdf.
[30] The four Grand Slams (Australian Open, French Open, Wimbledon and US Open) as well as the Davis Cup are regulated by the ITF. There is agreement between the Grand Slams and ATP as to the use of ATP entry and ranking systems for qualification and ultimate ranking, save for Wimbledon. which in addition to the ATP formula applies its own rules.
[31] ITF Bylaws, Art. 2.2(2)(a).
[32] National tennis federations are tiered members and shareholders of the ITF corporate vehicle. See ITF Constitution, Art. 2 (2025).

on the ITF for admission into its tournament calendars and organization of national team events.

While national and sub-national federations may organize their own tournaments, if these are not part of the ITF tours and hence do not generate ATP/WTA ranking points, it is unlikely that any top names will ever agree to take part, particularly since the ITF/ATP/WTA calendar is already loaded with tournaments. It is worth noting that the ITF is organized and registered as a limited liability company under the laws of the Commonwealth of the Bahamas,[33] albeit its headquarters are in London. A key reason for incorporating in the Bahamas is the country's preferential tax regime.[34] The United Kingdom, in turn, finds the ITF an attractive commercial enterprise because it generates employment opportunities and uses other UK companies to sub-contract with. It is no surprise, therefore, that during the Covid-19 crisis, the UK tax authorities offered a tax credit of £455,000 to the ITF for income generated in the United Kingdom.[35]

One of the oddities of professional tennis is that the organization of the women's game is the domain of an entity that is distinct from that of the men's game. The WTA,[36] founded in 1973, governs the WTA Tour, but not the Grand Slam, the Davis Cup or the Olympic tennis tournament, all of which are organized in the same manner as the men's game by the ITF. In all other respects, the WTA and ATP are similar in nature, function and organization.

3.2 The Relationship between National Tennis Federations and the ITF

The historical dominance of particular national tennis federations remains vibrant to the present day, subject to minor variations. The world of tennis as governed by the ITF encompasses 213 national tennis

---

[33] ITF Constitution, Art. 1.
[34] Until 2018, companies registered in the Bahamas but operating exclusively outside of the country, as was the case with the ITF (which is headquartered in London and without any events in the Bahamas), were entitled to preferential exemptions from taxes in accordance with the International Business Companies Act (Ch. 309); the Exempted Limited Partnership Act (Ch. 312); the Investment Condominium Act, 2014 (No. 38 of 2014); and the Executive Entities Act, 2011 (the "Preferential Exemption Acts"). Under pressure from the Organisation for Economic Co-operation and Development, such laws had to be scrapped and in 2018 they were replaced by the Removal of Preferential Exemptions Act.
[35] Available at: www.insidethegames.biz/articles/1110765/strict-financial-discipline-to-be-main.
[36] Available at: www.wtatennis.com.

federations as members, from which 160 enjoy voting rights. According to the ITF Constitution, voting rights are divided into two classes, namely, Class B and Class C. The ITF Constitution recognizes "exclusive voting rights" for Class B members.[37] The leading five national federations (Australia, Great Britain, France, Germany and the United States) possess twelve votes. Another set of fourteen countries enjoy nine votes. Within the Class B category there are groups of members with seven, five, three and one votes. There are fifty-three members within Class C without voting rights. There are six continental federations operating with the framework of the ITF:

- Asian Tennis Federation;
- Central American and Caribbean Tennis Confederation;
- Confederation of African Tennis;
- Oceania Tennis Federation;
- South America Tennis Confederation; and
- Tennis Europe.

Application for membership to the ITF by a national tennis federation presupposes a capacity to effectively operate in the territory where it is established. Both elements must conform to the laws in place in the country in question. According to the ITF's criteria, the national federation will be granted membership status within two existing classes by the Council's resolution at the Annual General Meeting (AGM). The ITF's Council may take action against a member federation (suspension or expulsion) in accordance with Article 4.g of the ITF Constitution, where in its opinion the actions of a national federation damage the reputation of tennis or fail to comply with the rules stipulated by the ITF. The participation of national federations in the decision-making work of the ITF through its AGM, however, is rather limited since only a few members possess voting rights.

3.3 The Labor Status of Professional Tennis Players

In the context of individual sports, such as tennis, there exists a certain level of specificity, and contrary to professional team sports, tennis players are generally viewed as independent contractors. While in some professional sports athletes are capable of arranging collective bargaining agreements between themselves and competition organizers, chiefly through appropriate representation in the form of unions or players' associations, this is not the

---

[37] See ITF Constitution, Art. 11.

case in the world of tennis. Functionally, professional tennis players remain under the control of the ATP/WTA in the form of independent contractors lacking collective bargaining agreements or other institutional rules for articulating or safeguarding labor rights. As a result, professional tennis players are exempted from a number of benefits, such as health insurance or pension plans, as well as the possibility of setting up professional unions.

The complexity of the governing structure between the ITF and the ATP and WTA, especially with the latter two serving as intermediaries between players and tournament organizers, reflects players' labor status. In practice, professional tennis players are self-employed, while ATP/WTA are currently organized as bodies reflecting the interests of different stakeholders, where players have more consultative rather than executive roles. Both the WTA and the ATP are governed by an executive body, namely, a Board of Directors that is comprised of three player representatives, tournament representatives and the President of the ATP; or, in the case of the WTA, the WTA CEO. Their interests are often opposing or conflicting and generally fail to adequately articulate or protect players' rights. This is particularly evident with regard to profit-sharing because players do not possess sufficient institutional power to influence player-based allocation of proceeds. Such labor ambiguity is exacerbated by the decisions of national tennis federations in their selection of players for Davis/Fed Cup/Olympics tournaments or any other selection procedure as none of these may be challenged before national courts.[38] As a result, professional tennis players are exempt from any institutional or legal protection in respect of their labor rights. As will be explained Chapter 6, there is a growing unionization between professional players, chiefly through the Professional Tennis Players Association (PTPA).[39] Another way that

---

[38] *Washington v. USTA*, No. 99-CV-5148IJG, 2002 WL 1732801 (EDNY, July 22, 2002) (the court used the "agency test" to decide whether Washington was an employee of the USTA. Because, however, the USTA had no control over the "manner and means" of how Washington did his job (of playing tennis), he could not be considered an employee of USTA); see Elizabeth Priest, "Working toward Breaking Point: Professional Tennis and the Growing Problem with Employee and Independent Contractor Misclassifications" (2022) 75 SMU L Rev 343 (who argues in favor of a single ABC test for the employment purposes of professional tennis players, rather than their incorrect classification as independent contractors); equally Collin R. Flake, "Note, Getting to Deuce: Professional Tennis and the Need for Expanding Coverage of Federal Antidiscrimination Laws" (2014) 16 Tex Rev Ent & Sports L 51, 62.

[39] See Simon Cambers, "Vasek Pospisil Exclusive: Why Time Was Right to Form the PTPA (Professional Tennis Players' Association)," ATP (September 20, 2020), available at: www.tennismajors.com/atp/vasek-pospisil-exclusive-ptpa-interview-289067.html/amp?__twitter_impression=true.

athletes may claim a higher percentage and better working conditions (including access to health care) and cover their cost of training and travel, as well as make a decent living, is by collective bargaining agreements.[40] In the field of tennis, the ATP, through some of its most famous members such as Novak Djokovic, have made significant strides in their collective bargaining agreements.[41] Even so, such agreements are limited in scope and number, covering only a fraction of athletes, and do not encompass mid- and lower-tier athletes.

4 The Relevance of International Law

International law regulates the relationship between states and their subdivisions, and it is only since the end of World War II that it has taken a keen interest in the treatment of people within the borders of a state as a matter of international obligation. From the perspective of professional tennis, the chapter confines itself to the pursuit of human rights objectives by the ITF, as well as the investment capacity of the three transnational tennis entities. Whether and to what degree they may be considered as foreign investors[42] in countries other than their headquarters or place of incorporation and whether their activities constitute investments under applicable BITs and host state laws is a matter of investigation.[43] The general nature of this chapter does not allow us to elaborate on the foreign investment dimension of professional tennis. The ITF has shown significant reluctance to engage with human rights issues, unlike other international sports federations, albeit it is clear that all three entities can play a significant role in the promotion of human rights throughout the world. In Section 2.2, we discussed developments

---

[40] Ibid.; see also "Collective Labor Agreements in the Sports Sector," available at: www.fnv.nl/getmedia/144f6021-8e2d-41f9-8cee-d3a92c140403/341-sport-cao-english-2016-2018.pdf.
[41] See Priest, "Working toward Break Point."
[42] For instance, Art. 3 of the 2008 Germany Model BIT defines an "investor" as any legal entity and any commercial organization or association with or without legal personality as the owner, possessor or shareholder of an investment within the jurisdiction of another contracting state; equally, Art. 13(a)(iii) of the Multilateral Investment Guarantee Agency Convention. For a fuller exposition, see Ilias Bantekas and Hakan Sahin, "Non-Profit Entities as Foreign Investors: The Case of International Sport Governing Bodies" (2023) 60 Stanford J Int L 70.
[43] See generally Ilias Bantekas, *Introduction to International Arbitration* (Cambridge University Press, 2015), 285–92.

pertaining to human rights commitments of corporate entities, chiefly in the European Union. These apply to the ITF and readers should consult that section for a fuller analysis. The following section examines the role of professional tennis in the IOC.

4.1 Professional Tennis as Part of the Olympic Movement

Tennis and the Olympic Movement have a long and complex history as tennis was on the program of the First Olympic Games in 1896. During these Games, only men were allowed to compete, while four years later this was extended to women tennis players. Due to the frictions between the IOC and the ITF (at that time, the International Lawn Tennis Federation, ILTF) that was associated with the monopolistic position of the IOC and exclusion of the tennis governing body, tennis was removed from the Olympics in 1924. These frictions reflected not only a conservative orientation of the IOC in respect of the status of professional athletes, but also an inadequate organization of the particular Olympic event during the Games in Antwerp in 1920. In an attempt to resolve this situation, the IOC proposed that during the Olympic year, all major events in tennis should be cancelled, including the Davis Cup.[44] The leading national tennis federations, in particular the Lawn Tennis Association (LTA), refused this proposal and demanded more active representation for the tennis governing body in decision-making processes. The IOC Executive Board's decision to remove tennis was approved by the twenty-seventh IOC Session in 1928.[45] In 1956, the formal request for tennis to be reinstated by the ILTF was not welcomed, primarily due to integrity issues associated with tennis and the fear that professionalism would effectively eliminate amateurism. It was reinstated in 1968 under the guise of a demonstration sport and as part of the gradual changes to the notion of amateurism. In 1973, the rigid interpretation of amateurism under a variety of influences within the IOC and the world of tennis was toned down, chiefly because the IOC was under financial pressure as a result of geopolitical dynamics. In 1981, during the eighty-fourth IOC Session, the decision for major changes included the status of tennis as an Olympic event, as demonstration sports ceased to exist. Under the Samaranch

---

[44] See Matthew P. Llewellyn and Robert J. Lake, "'The Old Days of Amateurism Are Over': The Samaranch Revolution and the Return of Olympic Tennis" (2017) 37 Sport Hist 4.
[45] See History of Tennis at the Olympic Games, available at: https://stillmed.olympic.org/media/Document%20Library/OlympicOrg/Factsheets-Reference-Documents/Games/OG/History-of-sports/Reference-document-Tennis-History-at-the-OG.pdf.

doctrine and broader commercialization of professional sport, tennis became once again part of the Olympic program in 1988. The Games in Los Angeles played a crucial role, since that event represented a blueprint for the commercialization of sports.

Currently, there are two men's and two women's events – in addition, one mixed (doubles) event – at the Olympic Games. The tennis tournament in the Olympic Games is managed by the ITF. The ITF adopts Regulations on Eligibility for the Olympic Tennis event in accordance with the Olympic Charter (Rule 41) related to nationality. Further, the age limit is set at 14 years and above, with a mandatory provision that a player "must be in good standing with his/her" national federation and the ITF, in addition to satisfying the eligibility criteria of the ITF Davis Cup Regulations and the ITF Billie Jean King Cup Regulations. This provision on eligibility represents an agreement between the IOC and the ITF, pushed by the latter to maintain its monopoly in the world of tennis. Besides this, the ITF's Independent Panel may, under the following circumstances, exercise discretionary powers concerning the composition of the Olympic event: injury, newcomer, strength of nation and player's prior results.[46] The significance of professional tennis for further development of the Olympic Movement was notable, particularly because of its exposure to commercialization, broadening of the sport's fan base and media attractiveness. Following the example of tennis, the door for other professional sports in the Olympic Games became a reality, and four years later the US basketball Dream Team came to the forefront. Consequently, the rule on amateurism in the Olympic Charter was abolished.

5   The Human Rights Standard-Setting Role of Transnational Tennis Entities

There is no tennis-specific human rights regime. Professional tennis is subject to the same set of human rights rules, principles and fundamental guarantees as all other sporting activities and phenomena. In the realm of professional tennis, there exist interactions and relationships between private actors alone (e.g. WTA and female athletes), as well as relationships between public and private actors (e.g. criminal sanctions against an athlete by a state organ, stripping an athlete from state

---

[46] See Regulation on Eligibility for the Olympic Tennis Event, available at: www.itftennis.com/media/7241/olympic-tennis-event-eligibility-rule-paris-2024.pdf.

funding as a result of a doping violation or awarding a tournament to a state). In the first scenario, the parties' relationship is contractual, and the obligations owed by the WTA and its female athlete members is of a contractual nature. Any violation of their mutual obligations amounts to a breach thereof, which if found to be sufficiently gross entitles the aggrieved party to terminate the contract. In the event of loss, the breaching party is also liable to the payment of damages. In the exercise of its activities, the ITF interacts with third parties (e.g. contractors, tournament organizers) and hence must necessarily adopt human rights policies to deal with such third parties, as part of its supply chain due diligence obligations.[47] Moreover, in the event that the ITF's dispute resolution processes[48] fail to satisfy all pertinent fair trial requirements, the state is obliged to offer access to the courts or force the ITF mechanism in question to apply particular guarantees, lest the outcome be annulled.[49] The European Court of Human Rights (ECtHR) has made it clear that private dispute resolution mechanisms must satisfy fundamental fair trial guarantees.[50]

Sports diplomacy is a significant driving force for human rights standard-setting and promotion of human rights more generally. The vast majority of labor reforms in Qatar in the last decade can and have been directly attributed to its hosting of the 2022 FIFA World Cup.[51] The ITF, WTA and ATP

---

[47] See e.g. the ITF's Modern Slavery and Human Trafficking Statement, available at: www.itftennis.com/en/about-us/modern-slavery/, which is consistent with the United Kingdom's Modern Slavery Act 2015, to which it is bound given its seat in London.

[48] See Chapter 4 of this volume.

[49] On the right to fair trial before specialized sporting judicial and quasi-judicial entities, see *Mutu and Pechstein* v. *Switzerland*, App. Nos. 40575/10 and 67474/10, Judgment of 2 October 2018, where the ECtHR held that CAS proceedings amounted to compulsory arbitration, which in turn was obliged to provide all the procedural safeguards enunciated in Art. 6 of the European Convention on Human Rights (ECHR), including the right to a public hearing. See more recently the ongoing case of *Semenya* v. *Switzerland*, App. No. 10934/21, (2023) ECHR 219, which challenged a CAS award on procedural and substantive grounds. The ECtHR found that the applicant had not been afforded sufficient institutional and procedural safeguards in Switzerland to allow her to have her complaints examined effectively, especially since her complaints concerned substantiated and credible claims of discrimination. It was immaterial for the Court that the Regulations in question were agreed to by all national track-and-field federations.

[50] Ibid. See also *Riva, Akal and Others* v. *Turkey*, App. Nos. 30226/10, 17880/11, 17887/11, 17891/11 and 5506/16, where the ECtHR found a violation of Art. 6(1) ECHR on the ground that the Arbitration Committee of the Turkish Football Federation suffered from structural deficiencies, such that allowed external influence and lack of full independence in its decision-making capacity.

[51] Andrew Spalding, *A New Mega-Sport Legacy: Host Country Human Rights and Anti-Corruption* (Oxford University Press, 2021).

can play a positive role in advancing particular human rights in countries that violate these, as well as sensitize people about those rights. This is possible because these entities control the allocation of tennis tournaments. Non-state actors have been criticized not only for failing to exert their influence over governments with which they are in close collaboration, but also for undermining the realization of rights and the environment by "exerting undue influence over domestic and international decision-makers and public institutions." This phenomenon is known as corporate capture. The exertion of influence and defiance of arbitrary laws and practices by powerful non-state actors has been found to give them a reputational advantage in the global consumer market. Consumer pressure is a significant aspect in the voluntary human rights policies and public pledges of MNCs and to a large degree has helped shape these policies.[52] It is no wonder that several models of corporate responsibility have been suggested by reference to corporate involvement in structural injustice. Iris Young's social connection model of responsibility, for example, posits that all agents who contribute by their actions to the structural processes that produce injustice have responsibilities to work to remedy these injustices.[53] The ITF in particular has been severely criticized for its handling of the deprivation of liberty of the Chinese female tennis professional Peng Shuai. When Shuai spoke publicly about a high-ranking official of the Chinese Communist Party who she alleged was sexually abusing her, she disappeared from the professional circuit. Yet, the ITF failed to exert pressure on the Chinese government, nor did it suspend tournaments and activities taking place in China.[54] On the contrary, the WTA has called for an independent investigation and threatened to pull out of all tournaments in China.[55]

---

[52] A study conducted in 2002 by Cone revealed that of US consumers aware of a corporation's negative corporate social responsibility practice, 91 percent would most probably prefer another firm, 85 percent would disseminate this information to family or friends, 83 percent would refuse to invest in that company, 80 percent would refuse to work at that company and 76 percent would boycott its products. Opinion Research Corporation International, *2002 Cone Corporate Citizenship Study*.

[53] See Iris M. Young, "Responsibility and Global Justice: A Social Connection Model" (2006) 23 Social Philosophy & Policy 102.

[54] See Helen Davidson, "Peng Shuai: International Tennis Federation Does Not Want to Punish 1.4bn People with a China Boycott," *The Guardian* (December 6, 2021), available at: www.theguardian.com/sport/2021/dec/06/peng-shuai-international-tennis-federation-does-not-want-to-punish-14bn-people-with-a-china-boycott.

[55] See "WTA's Stance on Peng Has Made It Human Rights Champion, Says Former U.S. Official," CNN (November 24, 2021), available at: https://edition.cnn.com/2021/11/24/tennis/peng-shuai-wta-spt-intl/index.html.

1 THE INTERSECTION BETWEEN LAW AND TENNIS 19

A survey of ITF rules and instruments exhibits two policy commitments to human rights. The first is Article 1 of its Constitution, whereby it pledges to abide with the fundamental principles of the Olympic Charter,[56] but without directly setting out a firm commitment to human rights. It is no surprise, therefore, that there is nothing in the membership requirements of the ITF Constitution requiring adherence to human rights by any of its existing or aspiring members. The second and most concrete manifestation of human rights commitment can be found in Article 2.1 of the 2023 ITF Code of Ethics. It states that all ITF officials must:

2.1.1. act in accordance with the highest standards of honesty and integrity in all of their activities as Officials;
2.1.2. respect human rights that may be impacted in their actions as Officials, including:
    2.1.2.1. respect human dignity;
    2.1.2.2. not discriminate improperly against or denigrating anyone on grounds of race, colour, sex, gender, sexual orientation, language, religion, political or other opinion, national or social origin, disability, or any other unlawful ground.

Although this is a powerful statement, it simply dictates what is required of ITF employees and does not seek to spell out a human rights policy for the ITF as an organization.[57]

The ITF is engaged in numerous initiatives to influence national human rights policies at the domestic level, albeit it is not clear that these constitute definitive conditions for the granting of tournament rights or for retaining tournaments. One such initiative is the WeThe15, the aim of which is to sensitize people and governments about disability rights and make diversity work in practice[58] by

---

[56] Art. 2 of the Olympic Charter, which sets out the mission and role of the IOC, does not specifically mention human rights as a goal or policy objective. The IOC website suggests that principles 1, 2, 4 and 6 of its Fundamental Principles and Art. 2 of the IOC Charter enshrine human rights; these authors suggest that this is hardly the case.

[57] This is evident, for example, in the ITF Ethics Commission's Decision in the case of Evgeniy Zukin (February 25, 2022) (*ITF Ethics Commission v. Zukin*), available at: www.itftennis.com/media/8735/itf-ethics-commission-decision-zukin-25-july-2022-publication.pdf, which relied on Art. 2.1 of the Code of Ethics in respect of a personal act of assault and battery by an ITF official.

[58] See ITF, "WETHE15: ITF Marks Launch of Movement for Persons with Disabilities," available at: www.itftennis.com/en/news-and-media/articles/wethe15-itf-marks-launch-of-human-rights-movement-for-persons-with-disabilities/.

effectively implementing the key standards set out in the UN Convention on the Rights of Persons with Disabilities (CRPD). In the same manner, the ITF has been content to take a soft approach to the participation of Russian athletes in the aftermath of the Russian invasion of Ukraine, allowing them to participate under condition that they do not represent their country and make no political statements.[59]

A more preferable strategy would have been for the ITF to adopt a concrete human rights policy through the adoption of a policy statement, such that would allow its stakeholders to fully understand its stance against entities that violate human rights. Its modern slavery statement is merely a reflection of its otherwise statutory obligations under the laws of England. Such a policy would allow all future contracting to undergo a human rights impact assessment, with specific human rights requirements demanded of tournament organizers and other entities with which it has a commercial or other relationship. In fact, the ITF should emulate the IOC and adopt similar policy documents in respect of its suppliers[60] and its corporate stance in the field of human rights, as well as its human rights position regarding tournaments under its aegis.[61]

---

[59] See ITF Statement, "Russian and Belarusian Athletes Entry in UK Events" (March 31, 2023), available at: www.itftennis.com/en/news-and-media/articles/itf-statement-russian-and-belarusian-athletes-entry-into-uk-events/; equally, "ITF Suspends Russia and Belarus from Its ITF Membership and Team Competitions," available at: www.itftennis.com/en/news-and-media/articles/itf-statement-itf-suspends-russia-and-belarus-from-itf-membership-and-international-team-competition/.

[60] IOC Supplier Code, available at: https://stillmed.olympics.com/media/Document%20Library/OlympicOrg/IOC/What-We-Do/celebrate-olympic-games/Sustainability/Spheres/IOC-Supplier-Code-Final.pdf?_ga=2.113239940.1862512609.1685599548-642320309.1674043337.

[61] IOC Olympic Agenda 2020+5, available at: https://stillmedab.olympic.org/media/Document%20Library/OlympicOrg/IOC/What-We-Do/Olympic-agenda/Olympic-Agenda-2020-5-15-recommendations.pdf, which suggests adopting an overarching IOC human rights strategic framework with specific action plans for each of the IOC's three different spheres of responsibility; linking the overarching IOC human rights strategic framework to various existing or forthcoming IOC strategies; amending the Olympic Charter and the "Basic Universal Principles of Good Governance" of the Olympic and Sports Movement to better articulate human rights responsibilities; and enabling the newly created IOC Human Rights unit to develop the IOC's internal capacity with regard to human rights.

PART 1

Contractual

2

Legal and Contractual Aspects of Agency and Player–Agent Relations in Professional Tennis

WILLIAM BULL

1 Introduction

Just as in the context of other professional sports, agency plays an important behind-the-scenes role in professional tennis. Whether it is in the representation of players, the management of their sporting careers and schedules, or even the promotion of tournaments, the work of agents in the shadows of the sport of tennis is of increasing significance. At the same time – or rather, in conjunction with this – the profession and activities of tennis agents give rise to an ever-expanding array of legal questions and issues of both a regulatory and a contractual nature, which have yet to be elucidated, let alone investigated. Accordingly, this exploratory chapter seeks to offer an inceptive account of the central legal and contractual aspects of agency and player–agent relations in professional tennis, as well as an initial foray into the key legal issues arising from, and possible regulatory approaches to, the work of tennis agents. The chapter will begin with an overview of agency in tennis – including the history (and indeed heritage) of tennis agents in the wider context of sports agency, the different types of tennis agents active on the market and the roles that agents perform in the world of professional tennis – before proceeding to set out the multifaceted legal landscape in which these agents operate and the diverse regulatory frameworks governing the exercise of their professional activities. In the latter part of the chapter, the focus will then shift to contractual agreements between professional tennis players and player agents, by sketching the legal rules that are (potentially) applicable thereto and particularly the contractual duties to which tennis agents may be subject, and ultimately examining a number of specific legal issues relating to player–agent contracts and relations in professional tennis. In so doing, this chapter will shed light on the implications both of and for the law in respect of tennis agency.

2 Agency in Tennis

The following sub-section will outline the essential nature and broader context of tennis agency, starting with a brief excursus into the historical development of agency in tennis, against the more general backdrop of agency in professional sport. It will then centre on the present-day phenomenon of agency in tennis, identifying the different kinds of agents that provide services on the professional tennis market, the main characteristics of this market and the principal roles that these agents fulfil. This summary will enable readers to gain an understanding of the tennis agents' industry and an appreciation of the relevance of their profession to the sport itself, which will serve as a useful background to the subsequent depiction and discussion of the rules and regulations applicable to their activities.

2.1 Background to Sports Agents in General and Tennis Agents in Particular

While little has been written to date on the law pertaining to professional tennis agency, there are relatively comprehensive works to be found in the literature on the sport of tennis per se, including its societal context and historical evolution[1] – and in some of these publications one does encounter references to tennis agents in particular, with at least one such work dedicating an entire chapter to the subject.[2] As Ruth eloquently expounds, player agents and sports managers have a long history in the realm of tennis, to the extent that the origins of tennis agency can be traced back to, and are actually intertwined with, those of professional sports agency itself. Indeed, whereas much of the attention in the literature (and certainly in legal scholarship) on sports agency has (perhaps understandably) been devoted to popular team sports (and most

---

[1] By way of illustration, see Robert J. Lake (ed.), *Routledge Handbook of Tennis: History, Culture and Politics* (Routledge, 2019); John Grasso, *Historical Dictionary of Tennis* (Scarecrow Press, 2011); Peter Doherty, *Empire, War, Tennis and Me* (Melbourne University Press, 2022); or Warren F. Kimball, *The United States Tennis Association: Raising the Game* (University of Nebraska Press, 2017).

[2] See Greg Ruth, *Tennis: A History from American Amateurs to Global Professionals* (University of Illinois Press, 2021), and specifically ch. 11 thereof, entitled 'The Impact of Sports Agents and Agencies on Professional Tennis'.

frequently to football,[3] as well as the traditional major league sports in North America[4]), it is worth recalling that the very first agencies to provide professional athlete representation services originally concentrated their activities on individual sports, and most notably on tennis, alongside golf.[5] This was true of 'the earliest, most successful, and most historically significant agency',[6] namely, the US-based International Management Group (IMG), which at its outset in the 1960s preferred to enrol tennis players and golfers as clients over players of team sports.[7] This was in large part due to financial considerations, as it was cheaper to ferry individual athletes to sporting exhibitions than entire teams, thereby making them more versatile in terms of their earning potential, for they could then also generate income from such events at the same time as bringing revenues from product endorsements (i.e. particularly clothing and equipment).[8] And while IMG's very first clients were golfers,[9] the company's expansion coincided with the International Tennis Federation's (ITF) opening of hitherto exclusively amateur tennis tournaments (including the Grand Slam competitions) to professional tennis players[10] and the signing of its first tennis client in 1968 in the form of the world number 1 at the time, the legendary Australian player Rod Laver. In fact, tennis also lay at the root of the well-documented tussle between IMG and its historically closest and similarly renowned competitor, ProServ, whose first clients were Arthur Ashe and Stan

---

[3] For a brief account of the prominence of football agents in the wider context of sports agency, see William Bull and Michael Faure, 'Agents in the Sporting Field: A Law and Economics Perspective' (2022) 22 Int Sports LJ 17, at 19.

[4] Take, for example, Charles W. Ehrhardt and J. Mark Rodgers, 'Tightening the Defense against Offensive Sports Agents' (1988) 16 Fla St UL Rev 633; Alec Powers, 'The Need to Regulate Sports Agents' (1994) 4 Seton Hall J Sport & Ent L 253; and, more recently, Justin Park, 'The Role of Athlete-Agents and the Law: A Conflict of Interest? (2015) 29 Brigham Young U Pre L Rev 107; Jodi S. Balsam, '"Free My Agent": Legal Implications of Professional Athletes' Self-Representation' (2016) 16 Wake Forest J Bus & IP L 510.

[5] Ruth, *Tennis*, 200 ff.

[6] Ibid., 199.

[7] It should also be noted that the very first individual sports agents actually date back to the 1920s, although these industry pioneers also collaborated with tennis players, among others; see Kenneth L. Shropshire and Timothy Davis, *The Business of Sports Agents* (University of Pennsylvania Press, 2008), 11.

[8] Ruth, *Tennis*, 200. Another factor Ruth identifies is rather contractual in nature, insofar as, unlike players of team sports, tennis players enjoyed greater contractual freedom, since they were not bound to any franchise (at 211).

[9] IMG's founder, Mark McCormack, famously signed professional golfers Arnold Palmer, Gary Player and Jack Nicklaus – often referred to as 'the Big Three' – as his first clients.

[10] Cf. Men's International Professional Tennis Council (MIPTC) Official Yearbook (1987), 7.

Smith, the top two American players at the time. ProServ was founded in 1970 by Donald Dell, the former US Davis Cup captain (and teammate of Ashe and Smith). Dell had received overtures of allegiance two years earlier from IMG's founder and fellow lawyer Mark McCormack, who was afraid of the potential competition Dell could bring to bear should he decide to venture into the sports agency business on his own account, given Dell's more sizeable network in the tennis world.[11] But when contract talks between IMG and Ashe – arranged by Dell – came to nothing, Dell ultimately did just that, agreeing to represent Ashe himself through his own sports management firm, which would specialise in the representation of tennis players.[12] In this way, Dell became what one might term the first tennis agent proper, and the arena of professional sports management firms emerged.

IMG and ProServ would go on to dominate this arena for the rest of the century, amassing between them a broad and star-studded array of clients along the way. Among these were the biggest names in tennis of the era (from Bjorn Borg to Martina Navratilova), as well as superstars of other sports (like Muhammad Ali and Michael Jordan).[13] Furthermore, these agencies extended their representation services to other bodies in tennis (such as the Russian Tennis Federation[14]), and even to tennis events themselves, including Wimbledon, or more precisely the All England Lawn Tennis and Croquet Club (AELTC).[15] And, in turn, this also precipitated an expansion of their areas of representation, beyond merchandising and licensing deals and into sponsorship agreements and broadcasting contracts.[16] By the turn of the millennium, IMG (which remained the largest sports management agency, dwarfing even ProServ) had represented hundreds of sportspeople and sporting entities and was grossing over a billion dollars a year, with operations in multiple countries across the globe.[17] At the same time, a number of other prominent sports agents and management firms had also entered the scene.[18]

---

[11] Ruth, *Tennis*, 207.
[12] Ibid., 209.
[13] See further Shropshire and Davis, *The Business of Sports Agents*, 16 ff.
[14] Ruth, *Tennis*, 210.
[15] Ibid., 212.
[16] On this expansion, see also George A. Metanias, Thomas J. Cryan and David W. Johnson, 'A Critical Look at Professional Tennis under Antitrust Law' (1987) 4 Ent & Sports LJ 57, at 58.
[17] Daniel S. Mason and Gregory H. Duquette, 'Globalisation and the Evolving Player–Agent Relationship in Professional Sport' (2005) 1 Int J Sport Management & Marketing 93, at 99.
[18] Shropshire and Davis, *The Business of Sports Agents*, 17.

2.2 Types and Roles of Agents in Professional Tennis

Since the dawn of corporate sports agency in the 1960s, the sector has come to be populated by agents with differing backgrounds; commonly legal, but also financial and commercial.[19] Many of these work for large-scale transnational agencies such as IMG or Octagon (a successor to ProServ), which provide a range of services to players, entities and event organisers in a variety of sports, including tennis. However, more recent years have also seen the emergence, alongside these 'all-inclusive' agencies, of smaller 'bespoke' firms, which are focused specifically on tennis representation and talent management, and 'built around a stable of select player clients'.[20] These are often established by players themselves, such as Roger Federer, who left IMG together with his long-lived agent to found the Team 8 Global management firm in 2012.[21] In addition, agency and representations services may also be provided, to one extent or another, by specialised law practices, accountants, financial advisers, investment companies and sports marketing firms, or some combination of them.[22] Indeed, agents may perform a variety of different roles in professional tennis. When it comes to player agency, as was already alluded to, contract representation constitutes the tennis agent's core activity, including contracts of endorsement and sponsorship[23] and licensing (e.g. for exhibitions or of image rights), as well as negotiations with coaches and (significantly, in terms of both the potential sporting and legal implications) for entries and appearances at tournaments.[24] At the same time, player agents may also (or possibly instead) provide tennis players with a range of managerial and administrative services, such as career counselling and advice, handling sporting schedules, travel and accommodation arrangements, or press and social media relations.[25] Furthermore, tennis agents may

---

[19] Balsam, 'Free My Agent', 515.
[20] See Michael Long, 'Switching Pitch: The Rise of the Boutique Tennis Agency', Sports Pro (16 November 2017), available at: www.sportspromedia.com/analysis/switching-pitch-the-rise-of-the-boutique-tennis-agency/?zephr_sso_ott=Iufxvf.
[21] Ibid.
[22] See Balsam, 'Free My Agent', 529–32. This is also not to mention the fact that many professional athletes opt to represent themselves or rely on family members in contract negotiations, and increasingly so; on this, see further ibid., 513 ff.
[23] On such deals, see further Tim Newcomb, 'The Anatomy of a Tennis Player's Sponsorship Deals', Forbes (4 May 2020), available at: www.forbes.com/sites/timnewcomb/2020/05/04/the-anatomy-of-a-tennis-players-sponsorship-deals/?sh=6612e912789c; see also Mason and Duquette, 'Globalisation and the Evolving Player', 98 ff.
[24] See Metanias et al., 'A Critical Look', 59; and also Ruth, *Tennis*, 211.
[25] See Marc Hervez, 'What's the Role of a Good Tennis Agent?', We Are Tennis (5 March 2013), available at: https://wearetennis.bnpparibas/en/news-tennis/news-results/2065-whats-the-role-of-a-good-tennis-agent; and also John P. Sahl, 'The Changing Landscape

also, or alternatively, represent other bodies in the sport, or even play a role in the promotion and management of tournaments, including the solicitation of sales and sponsorship therefor, as well as television rights.[26] In so doing, the agent's primary function is to maximise revenues for the client (or 'principal'), through the deployment of specialist knowledge and expertise, which the principal does not necessarily possess.[27]

As far as the market on which tennis agents operate is concerned, while the sport itself continues to generate ever-larger profits, earning multiple millions from broadcasting rights and ticket sales to one Grand Slam event alone,[28] the size of the tennis agency sector would appear to remain relatively limited. Admittedly, statistics on sports agency are hard to come by, but, according to one rare study on sports agency that was produced for the European Commission in 2009,[29] there were an estimated twenty-two official tennis agents active in the European Union across eleven Member States at that time.[30] This is likely due in part to the tendency for individual players to engage one of the larger management firms,[31] combined with the fact that the higher earning potential is concentrated in the top-ranked tennis players, with a wide financial gap existing between these more dominant players and those ranked outside the top 100.[32]

---

of Intercollegiate Athletics – the Need to Revisit the NCAA's "No Agent Rule"' (2020) 61 Santa Clara L Rev 1, at 20–4.

[26] Metanias et al., 'A Critical Look', 61–2.

[27] See further Mason and Duquette, 'Globalisation and the Evolving Player', 94 ff.; Mark Smienk, 'Regulation in the Market of Sports Agents: Or No Regulation at All?' (2009) 3–4 Int Sports LJ 70, 75 ff.; Bull and Faure, 'Agents in the Sporting Field', 22.

[28] Eric Barget, 'The Economics of Tennis' in Wladimir Andreff and Stefan Syzmanski (eds), Handbook on the Economics of Sport (Edward Elgar, 2006), 423.

[29] KEA-CDES-EOSE, 'Study on Sports Agents in the European Union' (2009), available at: https://ec.europa.eu/assets/eac/sport/library/studies/study-sports-agents-in-eu.pdf.

[30] Ibid., 35–40. Although, as this study also cautions, it is difficult to ascertain the size of the sports agent population with any degree of accuracy (at 30). Still, the numbers would appear to be of a similar magnitude in the United States, with roughly ten professional tennis agencies active on the US market as of 2014; see Scott Kestenbaum, 'Uniform Alternative Dispute Resolution: The Answer to Preventing Unscrupulous Agent Activity' (2014) 14 Pepp Disp Resol LJ 55, at 67.

[31] Ibid., 52.

[32] See D'Arcy Maine, '"Why Am I Here, Playing for Literally $6?": The Stunning Financial Reality of Pro Tennis', ESPN (17 January 2023), available at: www.espn.com/tennis/story/_/id/35414286/the-stunning-financial-reality-high-cost-pro-tennis.

3 The Regulation of Agents in Professional Tennis

The rules that are (or may be) applicable to tennis agents and their activities are varied, both in terms of their content and their sources. The focus in this chapter will be on two central aspects of the law of professional tennis agency: first, the regulation of the profession itself; and second, the rules governing contractual relations between agents and players. We will begin in this sub-section by laying out the regulatory framework surrounding the exercise of (if not even the access to) the tennis agent's profession per se, and in the next sub-section we will move to consider the regulations and legal standards applicable to player–agent contracts, with a view to identifying certain concrete legal issues arising from such agreements. In each of these respects, it will be seen that the activities of tennis agents can be subject not only to domestic rules of both public and private origin, but also to transnational sporting regulations.

3.1 Domestic Rules

Depending on the given jurisdiction, there may exist an assortment of domestic rules of specific application to the work of tennis agents. More precisely, there may be special rules relating to sports in general or tennis in particular that are material to the tennis agent's vocation, which might derive from contract-based regulations and in some cases could even be laid down in statutory law. Alternatively, in other countries there may be no *lex specialis* on the matter at all. Furthermore, of those jurisdictions where pertinent sports-related rules do exist, the scope of such rules may be limited to certain aspects of the conduct of agents and provision of agency services in the tennis sector, or could even extend to tennis agency as a lawful occupation.

To depart from the non-specialised end of the regulatory spectrum, there are many countries in which no specific provision has been made for professional tennis agency, either in national law or by means of private regulations of national tennis governing bodies. Take the United Kingdom, for example: not only is there an absence of statutory legislation on the subject there,[33] but the regulations of the national governing body in Britain (the Lawn Tennis Association, LTA) are also silent on the matter.[34] Obviously, this is not to say that the activities of tennis agents

---

[33] See KEA-CDES-EOSE, 'Study on Sports Agents', 30.
[34] Cf. LTA Rules (2023).

on British soil are entirely unregulated. On the contrary, being registered as self-employed workers or as businesses, tennis agents in the United Kingdom are officially recognised in one way or another by government authorities and, as such, must adhere to all attendant laws and statutes.[35] These will comprise not only applicable labour and/or company laws, but also statutes like the Fraud Act 2006 or the Bribery Act 2010, to name but just two. In addition, as will be further elaborated in the next sub-section, the common law of agency has developed an intricate body of legal authority covering the activities of intermediaries, including those active in the sport of tennis. However, beyond such regulations, legal rules specially applicable to tennis agency – whether of state origin or of a private nature – are essentially non-existent in Britain.[36] And the same can be said about various other countries one might care to mention, including civil law jurisdictions such as Germany and the Netherlands.[37] In many of these jurisdictions, one finds statutory regulations on private employment agencies and job placement services that may be of application to the business of sports agents as they are to other forms of agency;[38] but apart from these laws the activity has not been the object of any particular regulatory attention.

At the other end of the spectrum, there are other (if apparently fewer) countries in which one encounters both national legislation specific to sports agents (i.e. including tennis agents) and relevant regulations adopted by national tennis associations or federations. The prime example in this respect is France, where the sports agent's profession is primarily regulated in the *Code du sport*. This special codified statute, created in the 2000s, contains various provisions applicable to sports agents, which lay down strict requirements and standards on sports agency.[39] Most notable among these is the requirement for individuals to hold an official licence in order to legally carry

---

[35] KEA-CDES-EOSE, 'Study on Sports Agents', 30.
[36] To be precise, this is the case as far as regards purely domestic regulations. As will be seen in what follows, however, there also exist specific rules laid down by international governing bodies, which are applicable by extension in the countries of member associations, including Great Britain.
[37] KEA-CDES-EOSE, 'Study on Sports Agents', 65, 68–9. See also more recently, and for further detail, Richard Parrish, Andrea Cattaneo, Johan Lindholm et al., 'National Association Intermediary Regulations' (2018), available at: www.edgehill.ac.uk/wp-content/uploads/documents/National-Associations-Report.pdf.
[38] Ibid., 70.
[39] On the *Code du sport* in a comparative perspective, see further William Bull and Michael Faure, 'Regulation of Football Agents in Europe: A Comparative Law and Economics Analysis' (2023) 12 Am U Bus L Rev 1, at 23 ff.

out sports agency activities in the French jurisdiction.[40] Unlicensed individuals who undertake sports agency activities in France face a possible criminal penalty of two years' imprisonment along with a fine of at least €30,000,[41] and this may also be accompanied by a temporary or even permanent ban on obtaining the licence and carrying on the occupation.[42] At the same time, the issuance of said licence and the precise conditions attached thereto are assigned by the *Code du sport* to competent national sports federations[43] – which in the case of tennis corresponds to the *Fédération française de tennis* (FFT). For this purpose, the FFT constitutes a Sports Agents Commission within the meaning of the *Code du sport*[44] and maintains a list of sports agents authorised to exercise the profession in the realm of tennis.[45] In order to obtain the requisite licence from the FFT, the applicant must, among other things, pass an entry examination.[46] This exam consists of two parts, the first of which is designed to assess the candidate's aptitude to exercise the sports agent's profession (particularly in terms of their cognisance of relevant social, legal and sporting matters), while the second tests their knowledge of regulations enacted by the FFT, by international federations of which the FFT is a member, by the Association of Tennis Professionals (ATP) and by the Women's Tennis Association (WTA).[47] Applicants must also meet strict conditions of integrity, which prohibit access to the profession inter alia to persons 'convicted of acts contrary to honour, probity or rules of morality'[48] or 'affected by personal bankruptcy or a ban on management'.[49] Additionally, once licensed, FFT agents must comply with several good practice rules, including reporting obligations (such as the duty to regularly communicate activity reports, accounting documentation and contractual agreements to the FFT),[50] as well as conflict-of-interest-related requirements

---

[40] *Code du sport*, Art. L.222-7. As far as citizens of other EU or EEA States are concerned, these persons may perform sports agency activities on the French territory without obtaining a licence if they are already qualified as a sports agent in their country of origin (i.e. where the profession is regulated in the country in question), or if they have already been carrying on such activities for a period in their 'home' state (i.e. in the case that it does not regulate the profession); Art. L.222-15.
[41] *Code du sport*, Art. L.222-20.
[42] Ibid., Art. L.222-21.
[43] Ibid., Art. L.222-7.
[44] Ibid., Art. R.222-1.
[45] *Statuts et règlements FFT* 2023, Art. 134.I.4.
[46] Ibid., Art. 149.1(a).
[47] Ibid., Art. 144.2.
[48] Ibid., Art. 134.II.1(f).
[49] Ibid., Art. 134.II.1(g).
[50] Ibid., Art. 154.

(and particularly the duty to refrain from the so-called *double mandat*, or dual representation).[51] Failure to do so can result in disciplinary sanctions being imposed by the FFT on the licensed agent, including pecuniary fines as well as temporary suspension, if not permanent revocation of their licence.[52] Thus, the applicable sports law in France, as enshrined in the *Code du sport* and transposed in the FFT's *Règlement des agents sportifs*, not only prescribes rigorous requirements for access to the tennis agent's profession, but also couples these with stringent professional conduct regulations.

France is certainly not alone in having regulations governing the occupation and activities of tennis agents – although other states that have also introduced statutory legislation specifically on sports agency while delegating its promulgation in specie to regulatory authorities for the sport concerned, such as Hungary and Italy,[53] have adopted a registration-based model.[54] In Italy, for instance, a budgetary law of 2017[55] established the requirement for all sports intermediaries to be registered with the National Olympic Committee (the *Comitato Olimpico Nazionale Italiano*, CONI) and, in turn, with the relevant national sporting federation, which for tennis is the *Federazione Italiana Tennis e Padel* (FITP). Contracts entered into by professional sportspeople with unregistered agents would thereafter be deemed null and void.[56] An individual's registration is subject to successful completion of a habilitation exam intended to determine the candidate's suitability, especially with regard to knowledge of the sport and attendant law (in the same vein as the French licence exam).[57] To be eligible to take this qualifying test, applicants must be in possession of a secondary school diploma and free from certain criminal convictions (again, along similar lines to the French conditions of integrity).[58] Accordingly, only agents entered in the FITP's register are permitted to operate as 'agents of FITP athletes'[59] and those associated tennis players are only allowed to enlist the services of FITP-registered agents.[60] For their part, the FITP regulations stipulate a series of obligations and rules of conduct to which registered

---

[51] Ibid., Art. 156.1.
[52] Ibid., Art. 152.
[53] KEA-CDES-EOSE, 'Study on Sports Agents', 68–72.
[54] For an economic analysis of registration- and licence-based agency regulation, see Bull and Faure, 'Agents in the Sporting Field'.
[55] *Legge 27 dicembre 2017 n. 205*.
[56] Ibid., Art. 1.373.
[57] Ibid., Art. 1.373 and *Regolamento CONI degli Agenti Sportivi*, Art. 11.
[58] *Legge 27 dicembre 2017 n. 205*, Art. 1.373 and *Regolamento CONI degli Agenti Sportivi*, Art. 13.
[59] *FITP Regolamento Organico* 2019, Art. 4.2.1.
[60] Ibid., Art. 4.1.1.

tennis agents must adhere, from general principles of honesty, good faith and professional diligence[61] to accounting and fiscal duties,[62] as well as the duty to avoid conflicts of interest with their clients and FITP members in general.[63] Furthermore, upon registering, the agent is bound to respect CONI's 'Code of sporting conduct'.[64] The infringement of any of these requirements may give rise to disciplinary and pecuniary punishments administered by the FITP's federal tribunal,[65] which can include suspension of the agent from the register.[66] Furthermore, players themselves can be sanctioned for making use of unregistered or suspended agents.[67]

As far as the United States is concerned, arguably the situation lies somewhere in the middle of the two extremes just described. In addition to general rules of the law of obligations that are applicable to fiduciary relationships (comparable to those applicable in the United Kingdom under the English common law of agency), there do exist statutory regulations on sports agents' activities (including in the field of tennis) at state level, which are modelled on the National Conference of Commissioners on Uniform State Laws' Uniform Athlete Agents Act (UAAA), adopted in 2000 and last amended in 2019.[68] Yet, while these model rules have been enacted in most States of the Union, they have not been introduced in all fifty and, moreover, they are specifically targeted at sports agents representing student (i.e. amateur) athletes.[69] It is true that the involvement of agents in the collegiate context stretches up to the intersection of amateur with professional sports (i.e. when college athletes complete their university studies and look to turn professional),[70] but the point remains that the UAAA only covers agents who recruit, advise or manage student athletes[71] – and this would appear to

---

[61] Ibid., Art. 4.6.1.
[62] Ibid., Art. 4.8.3(d).
[63] Ibid., Art. 4.8.2(g).
[64] Ibid., Art. 4.5.2.
[65] Ibid., Art. 4.10.1.
[66] Ibid., Art. 4.5.5.
[67] Ibid., Art. 4.10.2(b).
[68] For a detailed introduction to and overview of the UAAA, see Shropshire and Davis, *The Business of Sports Agents*, 157–64.
[69] KEA-CDES-EOSE, 'Study on Sports Agents', 79–80. This is also the case with the one federal intervention in the domain of sports agents, namely, the Sports Agent Responsibility and Trust Act of 2004; see further Kestenbaum, 'Uniform ADR', 64 ff.
[70] Ibid. On the transition from collegiate to professional sport examined specifically through the lens of tennis, see further Christopher M. Hartley, 'Double Fault: How the NCAA's No-Agent Rule Serves Legal and Policy Errors into the Courts of Tennis' (2019) 72 Ark L Rev 553, at 555 ff.
[71] Revised Uniform Athlete Agents Act (2015) (last amended 2019), § 2.2.

be reflected in most of the individual state enactments.[72] However, individual states are of course at liberty to adapt the UAAA when implementing it into their own laws, and some have done so. The California athlete agents regulation (now known as the Miller-Ayala Act), for example, is not limited to amateur athletes, but rather applies to sports agents in their dealings with both student athletes and professional athletes.[73] In addition, the Miller-Ayala Act provides greater substantive requirements and stricter sanctions for infringements as compared to those envisaged in the UAAA, with agents found to have violated the Act being subject to a mandatory revocation of their entitlement to operate in the state for at least one year, not to mention punishment by a fine of up to $50,000 and/or imprisonment of up to one year.[74] Similarly, while the vast majority of states that have implemented the UAAA have adopted the registration system and accompanying integrity standards and duties that are foreseen by the UAAA,[75] not all have opted to impose registration requirements on sports agents[76] and even those that have may have chosen differing modalities (such as the need to register with a Secretary of State, or a department of professional registration, or a labour commission).[77] Still, these registration systems do converge around the position of the UAAA that, unlike in Italy, the passing of an examination does not form part of the requirements for registration. Instead, certification is based on an individual's prior training and experience, along with an absence of convictions for crimes involving moral turpitude and the like.[78]

In short, then, there exist sharply contrasting regulatory approaches of relevance to the profession and activities of tennis agents, not only

---

[72] Cf., for instance, the Mississippi Uniform Athlete Agent Act, § 73.42.3(b), or the Texas Occupations Code § 2051.001.2 juncto 3.
[73] California Business and Professions Code, § 18895.2(b)(1).
[74] Ibid., § 18897.93(a) and (b). See also Paul C. Weiler, Stephen F. Ross, Michael C. Harper et al., *Sports and the Law: Text, Cases, and Problems* (West Academic Publishing, 2023), 750.
[75] Revised Uniform Athlete Agents Act (2015) (last amended 2019), § 4 ff.
[76] Weiler et al., *Sports and the Law*, 751. See also Noah Henderson, 'Student-Athletes Need an Updated Uniform Athlete Agents Act', Sports Illustrated, NIL Daily (19 November 2023), available at: www.si.com/fannation/name-image-likeness/news/student-athletes-need-a-nil-updated-uniform-athlete-agents-act-noah9.
[77] Philip N. Fluhr Jr, 'The Regulation of Sports Agents and the Quest for Uniformity' (1999) 6 Sports LJ 1, at 6–7.
[78] Revised Uniform Athlete Agents Act (2015) (last amended 2019), § 5. Cf. Mississippi Uniform Athlete Agent Act, § 73.42.9; Texas Occupations Code § 2051.102; California Business and Professions Code, § 18896.

between but even within individual countries. For reasons of scope, we have limited ourselves to looking at a few prominent examples, but these alone serve to demonstrate some of the salient differences in this respect. In particular, it has become apparent that jurisdictions diverge in terms of whether to specifically regulate the sports agency business at all; whether to regulate only the conduct of the profession or also access to it; whether to make such access subject to a system of licensing or registration, based on an entry examination or some other criteria; and which sanctions to impose in the event of non-compliance. These kinds of disagreements are certainly not confined to the sport of tennis, but clearly they do impinge upon it as in other sports.[79]

3.2 Transnational Rules

Before turning our attention to the contracts that agents enter into with professional tennis players, the place of the regulations of international governing bodies in the regulatory panorama of tennis agency should also be acknowledged. Indeed, there are some rules of significance to tennis agents contained in the ITF Code of Conduct, the ATP Rulebook and the WTA Rulebook. Admittedly, these are not so extensive[80] and for the most part are applicable to agents insofar as they fall under the broader category of 'related persons' to players (i.e. along with coaches, physicians, family members, etc.), rather than dealing distinctly with their particular activities.[81] Nevertheless, these regulations do provide some standards of behaviour with which player agents (among others) are bound to agree and

---

[79] The sport that has attracted most attention in the debate surrounding the optimal approach to the regulation of sports agents is, again, football, where the international governing body, the *Fédération internationale de football association* (FIFA), introduced a licensing system for players' agents in 1991, which was made subject to a qualifying exam in 1994. FIFA later replaced this licence with a registration system in 2015 and eliminated the habilitation exam in the process, before coming full circle with the enactment of the current FIFA Football Agent Regulations in 2023: for a discussion of this regulatory controversy in the context of football, see Bull and Faure, 'Agents in the Sporting Field'.

[80] To the extent that sports agents' activities are regulated in their own right by rules of sporting bodies – save in exceptional cases such as those of France and Italy that were already explained – this tends to be in team sports, where agents are involved in player transfers between clubs; KEA-CDES-EOSE, 'Study on Sports Agents', 77.

[81] ITF World Tennis Tour Code of Conduct 2023, Art. I; ATP Rulebook 2024, § VIII 8.05 (A)(1)(a); WTA Rulebook 2023, § XVII(B)(1)(f) (which instead employs the term 'player support team member'). In the case of the WTA Rulebook, agents of elite young players (i.e. up to 18 years of age) are also specifically required to sign a Code of Ethics; § X(B)(5)(c)(ii)(b).

to comply in providing their services during the tournaments concerned. In particular, as persons assisting players in their participation in tennis tournaments, agents are under an obligation to refrain from engaging in aggravated or abusive behaviour or other conduct that is contrary to the integrity of the game of tennis.[82] Infractions of these rules can lead to an agent being stripped of their tournament accreditation and denied access to any tournament governed by the given association, potentially even permanently.[83] Being established by private regulatory authorities, these rules are grounded not in state laws but in contracts, meaning their enforcement is also necessarily contractual. On the other hand, because the rules laid down by the ITF, ATP and WTA – to which players and national tennis federations also agree to adhere – are inherently transnational, unlike domestic legislation they are not territorially limited (or at least not in and of themselves), and are therefore applicable to the actions of tennis agents across different jurisdictions.[84]

4 Contractual Agreements between Professional Tennis Players and Agents

Having surveyed the statutory and contract-based regulations applicable to the profession of tennis agency itself, in this final sub-section we will zoom in on contractual agreements between professional tennis players and agents and the rules that govern these contracts, as well as the distinct legal issues to which such agreements can give rise. Of course, the primary source of obligations in player–agent relations is the contract between the parties, but this is subject to the relevant law on player–agent contracts.

4.1 The Law on Player–Agent Contracts

In general terms, unlike the law on tennis agency as a profession, there are greater similarities in the regulatory approaches taken to tennis agency contracts across distinct jurisdictions. While the specific rules applicable to player–agent contracts and sources thereof may well differ, a broad

---

[82] ITF World Tennis Tour Code of Conduct 2023, Art. VI(A) and (B); ATP Rulebook 2024, § VIII 8.05(A)(1) and (2); WTA Rulebook 2023, § XVII(H)(1). See further Ben Livings and Karolina Wlodarczak, 'Procedural Fairness in the International Tennis Federation's Disciplinary Regime' (2020) 18 Ent & Sports LJ 1, at 2 ff.

[83] ITF World Tennis Tour Code of Conduct 2023, Art. VI(A) and (B); ATP Rulebook 2024, § VIII 8.05(A)(1)(b) and (2)(e); WTA Rulebook 2023, § XVII(H)(3)(c).

[84] On the transnational nature of these rules, see Chapter 1 of this volume.

concordance can be identified in the substance of the laws governing such contracts, and particularly in terms of the standards to which agents are under a duty to adhere in their contractual dealings with players. In fact, it was already seen that where there exist sports laws governing the activities of tennis agents, such laws impose duties of good faith and conflict-of-interest-related obligations on them, including in their contractual relations with players. And the same is true of the general rules of private law that are applied to player–agent contracts in different countries.

In the case of civil law jurisdictions, the overarching, mandatory principle of good faith under general contract law (which is often enshrined in the national civil code[85]) governs the negotiation, formation, construction, interpretation and execution of contracts, including contracts of agency, and being a 'super-provision' this obviously has wide-ranging applications and far-reaching implications in and of itself. There may also be special rules of civilian contract law applicable to agency contracts, however. In Germany, for example, the civil code also contains a number of provisions covering brokerage contracts, such as rules on brokerage fees.[86] Similarly, the French civil code comprises a separate title on 'mandates' whereby a party confers upon an authorised representative the power to act in their name.[87] This prescribes certain obligations for the representative (not to mention the mandator), like the obligation for the agent to report to the mandator on their management of the mandate.[88] As for common law countries, there exist comparable obligations – which include an expansive utmost good faith obligation – under predominantly precedential rules of agency and fiduciary relationships.[89] Indeed, while the requirement to act in good faith is not a typical feature of the common law of contract in general, it famously is of the law on fiduciary relations in particular. Thus, as already alluded to, both the English and American legal systems recognise a common law doctrine of agency controlling the principal–agent relationship, by virtue of its fiduciary

---

[85] Cf. *Bürgerliches Gesetzbuch*, § 242; *Burgerlijk Wetboek*, Art. 6:248; *Code civil*, Art. 1104; *Codice civile*, Art. 1175.
[86] *Bürgerliches Gesetzbuch*, § 652 ff.
[87] *Code civil*, Art. 1984 ff.
[88] Ibid., Art. 1993.
[89] Among the obligations prescribed by the common law of agency, another conduct standard that is worth noting in this context is the duty of competence that the agent owes to the principal, insofar as it relates to the suitability of the agent's performance (and, in this sense, reflects similar concerns to those underpinning the access requirements in other jurisdictions discussed previously). On common law agency principles as applied specifically to the agent–athlete relationship, see further Shropshire and Davis, *The Business of Sports Agents*, 88 ff., and also Weiler et al., *Sports and the Law*, 686 ff.

nature as one where an agent is given authority to act on behalf of a principal in their dealings with third parties.[90] The fiduciary duty of good faith requires the agent to act in accordance with general private law obligations of loyalty, honesty and openness, which fundamentally entail that fiduciaries must pursue their beneficiary's interest and place it above their own.[91] In the words of Lord Justice Jacob in the English case of *Imageview Management Ltd* v. *Jack* (which involved a football intermediary):

> The law imposes on agents high standards. Footballers' agents are not exempt from these. An agent's own personal interests come entirely second to the interest of his client. If you undertake to act for a man you must act 100%, body and soul, for him. You must act as if you were him. You must not allow your own interest to get in the way without telling him.[92]

More particularly, it follows from these long-standing and well-established standards of fidelity that the sports agent is duty-bound to disclose to their athlete-client any real possibility of a conflict of interest that may arise in the agent's performance of his representative role, and to obtain the client's consent to said conflict before proceeding.[93] While this does not go as far as the outright ban on dual representation provided under the French sports law code,[94] it does mean that as a matter of principle the common law 'denies the right of an agent to assume any relationship that is antagonistic to his duty to his principal'.[95]

4.2 Legal Issues Arising from Player–Agent Relations in Professional Tennis

Following directly on from the previous point, one of the most notable legal issues that can arise from player–agent relations is that of conflicts

---

[90] Shropshire and Davis, *The Business of Sports Agents*, 19. Of course this is not to mention other common law jurisdictions. For an account of the application of the common law of fiduciary duties to player agency also in Australia, for example, see Simon Johnson, 'Show Me the Money!!! Player Agents and Conflicts of Interest' (2006) 1 Aus & NZ Sports LJ 103.
[91] Ibid., 20. See also Sukhninder Panesar, 'The Nature of Fiduciary Liability in English Law' (2007) 12 Cov LJ 1.
[92] [2009] EWCA Civ 63, at para. 6.
[93] Weiler et al., *Sports and the Law*, 687; *Imageview Management Ltd* v. *Jack* [2009] EWCA Civ 63, at paras 6–8. Furthermore, the measure of disclosure that is required is stringent, such that there is little prospect of consent being granted by the client; see further Johnson, 'Show Me the Money!!!', 111.
[94] *Code du sport*, Art. L.222–17.
[95] *Burleson* v. *Earnest*, 153 S.W.2d 869 (Court of Civil Appeals of Texas 1941), at 874.

of interest on the part of agents; a potential issue that is all but inherent in the multitude of services that player agents provide[96] and one that has only grown in magnitude since the advent of large-scale sports agencies.[97] As regards specifically professional tennis, such conflicts can arise not only due to the fact that (especially larger) agencies usually represent a plurality of players, whereby serving the interests of one player may come at the expense of another,[98] but also because (as already mentioned) tennis agents have also expanded their operations into the management of tournaments, which can give rise to legal questions if they wish for players they represent to appear in the tournaments they promote.[99] Both of these scenarios arose in the case of *Lendl v. ProServ Inc.*,[100] for instance, which concerned an action brought by Ivan Lendl against ProServ, his erstwhile representative agency, on the ground of breach of fiduciary duty. Lendl argued that ProServ had engaged in practices amounting to a conflict of interest in two respects: first, by signing him up to merchandising agreements and sporting events together with other tennis player clients as a way of securing more income for those clients, but on less advantageous conditions for himself; and second, by having him participate in events managed by ProServ for fees that were lower than the market rate he could command, in order to acquire greater profits for themselves.[101] While the case was ultimately settled out of court, it provided an early example of the contractual disputes between players and agents that can ensue under the common law of agency. Furthermore, the added role of player agents in the promotion of tennis tournaments might also give rise to issues under competition law. Since tennis agents (and again particularly all-inclusive agencies) can effectively attain monopoly power in their representation of top players, this may result in a spill-over monopolisation of their management of tournaments, to the illegal exclusion of actual and potential competing tournaments.[102] As Hainline puts it, '[w]ith this power,

---

[96] Park, 'The Role of Athlete-Agents', 110.
[97] Mason and Duquette, 'Globalisation and the Evolving Player', 102.
[98] Ibid.
[99] Metanias et al., 'A Critical Look', 62.
[100] No. B-88-254 (District of Connecticut 1988).
[101] Johnson, 'Show Me the Money!!!', 111.
[102] Jon S. Hainline, 'Matchpoint: Agents, Antitrust, and Tennis' (1987) 64 U Det L Rev 481, at 497–8. On competition law aspects of tennis more generally, see further Katarina Pijetlovic's contribution in Chapter 12 of this volume, and also Ryan M. Rodenberg and Daniel Hauptman, '*American Needle's* Progeny? Tennis and Antitrust' (2012) 2 Pace IP Sports & Ent LF 10.

the player agents can determine the success of any tournament by deciding what top ten players will participate in a given event. If the players follow their agent's advice, the agent's event is likely to succeed at the expense of his competitors.'[103] It was in light of these concerns that the now-disbanded Men's International Professional Tennis Council (MIPTC) actually adopted a 'conflicts of interest rule' prohibiting player representatives from simultaneously promoting and managing professional tournaments.[104] This itself led to an asserted violation of competition law in the United States, however, in the case of *Volvo* v. *MIPTC*.[105] In that case (which was also ultimately settled), IMG and ProServ (both of which were frequently involved in the management of tournaments) joined Volvo, a sponsor-client of ProServ, in challenging the MIPTC's rule on the basis that it infringed the Sherman Antitrust Act[106] – while the MIPTC counterclaim alleged anti-trust violations based on the agents' dual roles.[107]

Another important (and related) legal issue that was raised in that case – and that also concerns agents in their dealings with players – is that of restraint of trade. This common law doctrine rather concerns contractual restrictions on freedom to conduct business, and assesses the extent to which such restrictions are enforceable according to a reasonableness standard and with regard to public policy and the interests of the parties.[108] The most well-known tennis-specific case illustrating the issue of restraints in agency agreements is that of *Zverev* v. *Ace Group International Ltd*,[109] which involved a dispute between Alexander Zverev and his former sports agency Ace. In that case, Ace claimed a breach of

---

[103] Hainline, 'Matchpoint', 499.
[104] MIPTC Official Yearbook, Supp. 1 (1987).
[105] *Volvo North American Corp.* v. *Men's International Professional Tennis Council*, 857 F.2d 55 (2d Cir. 1988).
[106] See further Ryan M. Rodenberg, 'Age Eligibility Rules in Women's Professional Tennis: Necessary for the Integrity, Viability and Administration of the Game or an Unreasonable Restraint of Trade in Violation of Antitrust Law?' (2000) 7 Sports LJ 183, at 196 ff.
[107] See also Metanias et al., 'A Critical Look', 62–3.
[108] On the application of the restraint of trade doctrine specifically in the context of professional tennis, see Ilias Bantekas, 'Professional Tennis and Restraint of Trade in the English Common Law' (2023) 22 Va Sports & Ent LJ 1. See also more generally David Capper, 'When Is the Restraint of Trade Doctrine Engaged?' (2023) 1 Contract and Comm L Rev 196; and Stephen F. Ross, 'Labor Restraints under Antitrust Law' in James A. R. Nafziger, Thomas B. Stoel and Ryan Gauthier (eds), *Handbook on International Sports Law* (Edward Elgar, 2022), 423.
[109] [2020] EWHC 3513 (Ch).

contract on the part of Zverev (as well as his parent guarantors), since he had purported to end his relation with Ace notwithstanding the fact that the term of the representation agreement he had entered into with the agency at the age of 15 was not due to expire for another nine years. Zverev then sought a declaration before the UK High Court that the contract was unfair and oppressive. More precisely, Zverev contended that the lengthy duration of the contract, given its exclusive character, amounted to an unlawful restraint of trade that was not justified as reasonable, and was therefore unenforceable. And while the parties again eventually settled, the nature of the settlement firmly in Zverez's favour suggests that the High Court would have agreed with Zverez's contentions.[110] What is particularly remarkable about this outcome is that Zverev did not even claim to have sustained any financial disadvantage by reason of his protracted contract with Ace, which is the traditional line of argumentation in actions founded on the restraint of trade doctrine. Instead, it was the interest in having an agency relationship based on continued trust and confidence that motivated Zverev's claim, bearing in mind the particular importance of tournament prizes and image rights in professional tennis.[111] This case could therefore have significant ramifications for player–agent agreements and the ability of players to make alternative representational choices. Conversely, for agents this could entail a further limitation on the degree of contractual autonomy that they enjoy and the freedom to shape their relations with players as they desire.

---

[110] Bantekas, 'Professional Tennis', 11 ff.
[111] Ibid., 13.

3

Protection, Commercialisation and Enforcement of Intellectual Property Rights in Professional Tennis

DÉSIRÉE FIELDS

1 Introduction

Intellectual property (IP) rights have always played an important role in the development of sports generally, as well as tennis specifically, and have assisted in developing the global sports industry into the US$350 billion business that we know today.[1] As the fourth most popular sport in the world, the value of the global tennis market achieved US$914.53 million in 2021 and is anticipated to grow by 3.01 per cent year upon year, reaching a projected value of US$1,092.47 million in 2028.[2]

One of the reasons why IP rights play such an important role in the development of sports is because it is highly innovative and constantly evolving, for example, with the rise of eSports, which now reaches a global audience of 500 million.[3] Particular examples of where IP rights play a role in tennis can be seen with inventions such as Hawk-Eye Live, which will imminently completely replace (human) lines-people. Tennis apps are hugely popular among tennis players and fans alike and perform a variety of functions, from monitoring live scores and finding tennis partners to tracking and improving performance and finding sponsorship opportunities. Virtual reality trainers are also revolutionising the

---

[1] Business Research Company, 'Sports Global Market Report 2022: By Type, Revenue Source, Ownership' (February 2022), cited in Jacques de Werra, 'Reference Guide to Sustaining Sport and Its Development through Intellectual Property Rights', 4, available at: www.wipo.int/documents/d/sports/guide-sustaining-sport-ipr-2022.
[2] 'Global Tennis Industry Research Report 2023, Competitive Landscape, Market Size, Regional Status and Prospect' (18 January 2023), available at: www.researchreportsworld.com/enquiry/request-sample/22376172?trk=article-ssr-frontend-pulse_little-text-block.
[3] De Werra, 'Reference Guide', 4.

tennis world. Many tennis players now complement their on-court training with technology such as virtual reality trainers which scan and process a player's biomechanical data and calculate the optimal pattern of movements.

In June 2022, the Association of Tennis Professionals (ATP) Tour released its 'One Vision' plan, a long-term transformational strategic plan designed to take tennis to new heights from 2023. The plan recognises that nowadays tennis is much more than a sport – it is an entertainment business and 'superstar players' are one of the factors setting up the sport for success in the digital age.[4] The plan acknowledges that times have moved on, and live tennis matches are not enough; they cannot be the only product that the industry offers. A fan experience must be heightened because tennis is competing with other entertainment platforms such as Netflix, social media platforms and music streams, as well as other sports. And tennis players can no longer be seen as just playing the sport, they must also be building rapport with and entertain a global audience. Building this rapport can be achieved by tennis players significantly investing in their personal branding strategies and by recognising that their audience is not merely interested in live coverage from the tennis court, but the real-life dramas of the individual sports stars, their background stories and sneak peaks into their private lives. This is why documentaries such as Netflix's Break Point (which has been showing the behind-the-scenes moments of numerous successful tennis players both on and off the court) are becoming increasingly popular.

Given the ever-growing attention around the private lives of tennis stars, brands will inevitably want to increase their investment into them through sponsorship deals and this is where IP comes in – it is increasingly more important for tennis stars to have a strong brand protection strategy (trademark applications for their names or nicknames is a good starting point) so that they have more control over how their names/brand is being used and how stars can leverage income from that personal brand. The efficient protection and enforcement of IP rights is of significance for the commercial success of the tennis industry and allows all participants therein to prosper: individual players, tennis clubs, tournament organisers and sponsors. This chapter explores the importance of protection, commercialisation and IP rights in the context of professional tennis. While the chapter provides a brief overview of relevant IP rights, the particular emphasis is on trademarks and brand

[4] Available at: https://onevision.atptour.com/onevision/.

protection, given that brands are at the heart of commercialisation. The chapter will then highlight legal and contractual issues pertaining to commercialisation, as well as other matters pertinent in the context of enforcement. The reader is advised that the chapter is aimed at providing a basic introduction to this highly complex area. It is therefore highly advisable to seek specialist advice when considering IP protection and strategy.

2 Overview of IP Rights

The following sub-section will explore in brief the different IP rights relevant to the tennis industry. While trademarks and copyright are traditionally considered the most important categories of IP rights for the tennis industry, there are a broad range of other relevant intangible rights.

2.1 *Territoriality of IP Rights*

As a preliminary matter, it should be noted that all IP rights are territorial in nature. As far as registered trademark rights are concerned, it is therefore necessary to obtain protection in all countries in which the rights are commercialised or intended to be commercialised in the future. While the basic concept of IP rights is similar worldwide, there are significant differences between the various legal systems. The registration and protection of IP rights are governed by local law in each country. Unless otherwise indicated, the following sections will refer to the position under EU and/or UK IP law.

2.1.1 Ownership of IP Rights

Ownership of IP rights in the tennis industry, as in other sports industries, is complex due to the many stakeholders involved and the variety of contexts in which IP rights can be monetised. Individual tennis players are arguably the most important category of stakeholder in the tennis industry as they constitute the backbone of the industry. Individual tennis players are increasingly aware of the importance of building a personal brand, own registered or unregistered IP rights, and can often be involved in IP issues.

National, regional and international tennis federations as well as other sports governance bodies may also own and control certain IP rights, in particular relating to events, and play a huge role in promoting and implementing sport development activities. Furthermore, a broad range of players in the private sector may own IP rights due to the activities they are involved in and the goods and services they provide. Such activities include the organisation of tennis tournaments, the broadcasting of tennis events, the management of rights related to individual tennis players and sports events, the manufacture and commercialisation of sporting goods, the operation of tennis clubs and other tennis venues, and the sponsoring of individual tennis players, tennis organisations, tennis tournaments and venues.

When considering an IP protection strategy, it is important to carefully consider who should own the relevant IP rights and, where multiple stakeholders are involved, to ensure that relevant agreements are put in place to govern the relationship between the parties. By way of example, many tennis players, either alone or through their sponsors or management companies, have registered trademarks for their names, nicknames, initials, portraits, signatures or other distinctive features. It is crucial to consider in advance what will happen to any trademarks in the event that a relationship, such as a sponsorship agreement, is terminated. One of the most famous cases in tennis related to the famous RF logo, which was undoubtedly always associated with Roger Federer. The rights in the logo initially belonged to Federer's long-term former sponsor, Nike. When the relationship terminated in 2018, Federer was unable to commercialise the logo for two years even though these were his own initials. It was only in or around February 2020 that Federer managed to acquire those rights. His initials are found on many clothing items and have a high brand value.[5]

3 Trademarks

Trademark protection is crucial for all stakeholders in the tennis industry, including athletes, national and international tennis federations and, in particular, sporting goods manufacturers.[6]

---

[5] See e.g. Dan Parkes, 'Important Lessons for Athletes from the Nike/Federer "RF" Logo Dispute', Law in Sport (8 August 2018), available at: www.lawinsport.com/topics/item/important-lessons-for-athletes-from-the-nike-federer-rf-logo-dispute; LGV Avvocati, 'Roger Federer Takes "His" RF Logo Back', Lexology (17 March 2020), available at: www.lexology.com/library/detail.aspx?g=e472a59f-bee0-4eda-b071-a5a4d1b30eea.

[6] Désirée Fields, 'Protecting Tennis and Sports Brands Holistically, beyond Words and Logos', Pinsent Masons (25 August 2022), available at: www.pinsentmasons.com/out-law/analysis/protecting-tennis-sports-brands; Désirée Fields, 'Maximising Your Brand

3.1 What Is a Trademark?

A trademark is any sign, or any combination of signs, capable of distinguishing the goods or services of one undertaking from those of other undertakings.[7] As such, the primary purpose of a trademark is to indicate the origin of the good and services concerned. The registration of a trademark conveys exclusive rights on the trademark owner to use and enforce the trademark. There are certain signs that cannot be registered as trademarks, as defined under national legislation or case law. If a sign applied for which an application is made falls within one of those defined categories, it is likely to be refused by the relevant trademark office. Most commonly, trademark applications will be refused if their subject matter cannot be clearly identified, or they lack distinctive character, are descriptive of the goods and services applied for, or have become customary in trade.[8] Particular challenges can arise in the context of event-related trademarks, which may often be considered non-distinctive – for example, because they refer to a particular sport, location and/or the year in which the event takes place (e.g. the US

Value as a Tennis Player', Pinsent Masons (27 June 2022), available at: www.pinsentmasons.com/out-law/analysis/maximising-brand-value-tennis-player.

[7] Trade-Related Intellectual Property Rights (TRIPS) Agreement, Art. 1(1); Council Regulation No. 2017/1001/EC (EUTMR), Art. 4, clearly provides that a trademark must function as a source identifier: 'An EU trade mark may consist of any signs, in particular words, including personal names, or designs, letters, numerals, colours, the shape of goods or of the packaging of goods, or sounds, provided that such signs are capable of: (a) distinguishing the goods or services of one undertaking from those of other undertakings; and (b) being represented on the Register of European Union trademarks ("the Register"), in a manner which enables the competent authorities and the public to determine the clear and precise subject matter of the protection afforded to its proprietor.' Similar provisions are found in the national legislation of individual EU Member States, as well as UK Trademarks Act 1994, s. 1.

[8] TRIPS Agreement, Art. 1(1); EUTMR, Art. 7(1), provides: 'The following shall not be registered: (a) signs which do not conform to the requirements of Article 4; (b) trademarks which are devoid of any distinctive character; (c) trademarks which consist exclusively of signs or indications which may serve, in trade, to designate the kind, quality, quantity, intended purpose, value, geographical origin or the time of production of the goods or of rendering of the service, or other characteristics of the goods or service; (d) trademarks which consist exclusively of signs or indications which have become customary in the current language or in the bona fide and established practices of the trade.' However, it is possible to overcome a refusal under Art. 7(1)(b), (c) or (d) if 'the trademark has become distinctive in relation to the goods or services for which registration is requested as a consequence of the use which has been made of it'; similarly, UK Trademarks Act 1994, s. 3.

Open). There are also other grounds for refusal which are outside the scope of this chapter.[9]

Trademarks are widely regarded as the strongest form of IP protection as they are capable of being protected indefinitely, provided that the trademark owner keeps using it and pays the renewal fees when they are due, whereas all other IP rights have limited life spans. Registered trademarks provide the strongest form of protection against third-party infringements. Some countries, such as the United Kingdom, equally recognise unregistered trademarks which may become enforceable by means of an action of passing off. In addition to requiring proof of reputation and goodwill in a trademark, it is also necessary to show that there has been a misrepresentation that could mislead the public, as well as proof of damage, such as financial loss or damage to goodwill. An action for passing off can therefore be both difficult to prove and expensive.

3.1.1 Types of Trademarks

Trademarks may be categorised into so-called 'traditional' and 'non-traditional' trademarks. Both are explored in the following sub-sections.

3.1.1.1 Traditional Trademarks Traditional trademarks are those that all businesses have or should have, and which are encountered on a daily basis, namely, word marks (e.g. Lacoste, Roger Federer, Wimbledon), logos or figurative marks (e.g. the Lacoste crocodile) or a combination of words and images (e.g. the Wimbledon logo which contains the words 'The Championships Wimbledon' or Fred Perry's signature).

Slogans (such as the famous phrase 'You cannot be serious', coined by John McEnroe) may also be viewed as a type of word mark.[10] However, slogans are generally very difficult to register because trademark offices and courts tend to find they lack distinctiveness if they are no more than a mere advertising message extolling the qualities of the goods or services in question, unless it can be shown that they have acquired distinctiveness through use in the sense that consumers would immediately recognise the

---

[9] EUTMR, Art. 7.
[10] John McEnroe's famous catch phrase 'YOU CANNOT BE SERIOUS' was registered with the US Trademark Office until September 2014 in relation to T-shirts under US Trademark Registration No. 3379565.

slogan as referring to particular goods or services provided by one undertaking, or alternatively if they possess some unique qualities.[11]

3.1.1.2 Non-Traditional Trademarks As their name suggests, non-traditional trademarks are quite unusual. However, they are increasingly being considered by all types of businesses as part of a comprehensive brand protection strategy. Non-traditional trademarks encompass other aspects of a brand, such as colours, shapes, sounds, smell, tastes, movements/gestures and holograms. The increase in applications for non-traditional trademarks in the European Union is in part attributable to the fact that until recently it was only possible to register a trademark if it was capable of being represented graphically. For example, a sound mark would have to be represented by notes, clefs and ledger lines, which meant that it was often difficult to capture the essence of a sound. However, amendments to the relevant trademark legislation recognised technical advancements. Hence, it is now possible to submit sound or video files for a trademark application.

Nonetheless, it is often an uphill struggle to obtain protection for non-traditional trademarks because trademark offices usually find that such marks are not capable of indicating origin unless there is something unique about them.

3.1.1.3 Colour Marks Colour marks constitute one of the most common applications for non-traditional trademarks. According to EU case law, single colours can be registered if they have acquired distinctiveness. Colour combinations can also be protected, provided that the application for registration includes a systematic arrangement associating the colours

---

[11] The Court of Justice of the European Union (CJEU) has provided a helpful list of criteria that should be used when assessing the distinctive character of a slogan. See *Audi AG v. Office for Harmonisation in the Internal Market (Trade Marks and Designs) (OHIM)*, Case C-398/08 P, ECLI EU:C:2010:29, at para. 47; *Smart Technologies ULC v. Office for Harmonisation in the Internal Market (Trade Marks and Designs) (OHIM)*, Case T-523/09, ECLI EU:T:2011:175, at para. 37. An advertising slogan is likely to be distinctive whenever it is seen as more than a mere advertising message extolling the qualities of the goods or services in question because it: (i) constitutes a play on words; (ii) introduces elements of conceptual intrigue or surprise; (iii) has some particular originality or resonance; (iv) triggers in the minds of the relevant public a cognitive process; (v) contains unusual syntactic structures; and/or (vi) uses linguistic and stylistic devices, such as alliteration, metaphors, rhyme, paradox, etc.

in a predetermined and uniform way.[12] When assessing whether the mark has a distinctive character, trademark offices will consider whether, in the perception of the relevant public, the colour is capable of identifying the source of the goods or services and distinguishing them from competing products. This is balanced against a general interest not to unduly restrict the availability of colours for other traders who offer goods or services of the same type. Applications covering a large number of goods or services are less likely to be granted protection as opposed to those that are more specific. In addition, there are only a limited number of colours in internationally accepted codes, meaning that strong evidence would be required to show that the public expects goods sold under a particular colour to represent the goods of a discreet trader.

In tennis, undoubtedly, the most historic and iconic colour scheme is the dark green and purple which has been associated with the Wimbledon Championships for more than 100 years. For many years, the All England Lawn Tennis and Croquet Club (AELTC) has faced numerous issues in relation to preventing unauthorised third-party use of their signature colours. In 2016, the AELTC was successful in registering two colour trademarks for both vertical and horizontal green and purple stripes in the United Kingdom.[13] Prior to this registration, the club had to rely on the law of 'passing off' to prevent third parties from piggybacking on the goodwill of the Championships by using those colours to imply an association with Wimbledon, when no such association existed.

3.1.1.4 **Shape Marks** Trademark offices are generally reluctant to grant registrations for shape marks as these are often perceived as falling more within the scope of design rights or patents. It is often only possible to get a shape mark over the line if it also includes distinctive verbal elements. In particular, signs cannot be registered if they consist exclusively of:

> (i) signs or indications which may serve, in trade, to designate the kind, quality, quantity, intended purpose, value, geographical origin, or the time of production of the goods or of rendering the service, or other characteristics of the goods; and

---

[12] *Heidelberger Bauchemie GmbH's Trade Mark Application*, Case C-49/02, ECLI EU: C:2004:384.
[13] UK Intellectual Property Office, Trademark No. UK000003095408, available at: https://trademarks.ipo.gov.uk/ipo-tmcase/page/Results/1/UK00003095405; https://trademarks.ipo.gov.uk/ipo-tmcase/page/Results/1/UK00003097108.

(ii) the shape which results from the nature of the goods themselves, or the shape of goods which is necessary to obtain a technical result, or the shape which gives substantial value to the goods.[14]

While adding further elements to a mark may mean that it does not consist 'exclusively' of one of the features set out in (ii) above, such shape marks may still be ineligible for registration if the shape of the goods merely denotes those goods to the relevant customer; because, for example, the shape is seen to be descriptive or non-distinctive.[15] Additionally, applications to register shape marks based on their verbal descriptions may be rejected if they lack clarity, precision and objectivity.[16] Examples of successful sports-related shape mark applications include the World Cup Trophy owned by FIFA.[17] The AELTC recently sought protection for its trophies, albeit it elected to file these applications in the form of logo marks as opposed to shape marks, presumably because registration is usually easier to obtain for logo than shape marks.[18]

As with most non-traditional trademarks, the important point to remember is that the sign for which protection is sought must deviate significantly from the norms and customs in the sector.[19] It is possible to imagine that there could be other tennis-related shapes, such as the umpire's chair and related accessories, that could potentially qualify for registered trademark protection if they depart from the norms and customs of the sector. It is more likely, though, that elements like this

---

[14] EUTMR, Art. 7(1)(c) and (e).
[15] See *Lego Juris A/S* v. *OHIM*, Case C-48/09, ECLI EU:C:2010:516.
[16] In *Dyson* v. *Registrar of Trade Marks*, Case C-321/03, ECLI EU:C:2007:51, the CJEU held that Dyson could not register the concept of 'a transparent bin or collection chamber forming part of the external surface of a vacuum cleaner', as this could take on any number of different appearances. Similarly, in *JW Spear & Son Ltd* v. *Zynga Inc.* [2014] 1 All ER 1093, the manufacturers of Scrabble were prevented from registering the shape of a Scrabble playing tile, described as 'a three dimensional ivory-coloured tile on the top surface of which is shown a letter of the Roman alphabet and a number in the range of 1 to 10'. This mark was held not to be a 'sign' as it potentially covered many different signs achievable through the permutations, presentations and combinations of the numbers and letters on each tile.
[17] EUIPO, 'Trademark without Text', No. 009096736, available at: https://euipo.europa.eu/eSearch/#details/trademarks/009096736.
[18] The registration of EUIPO is available at: https://euipo.europa.eu/eSearch/#details/trademarks/018975150 and equally at: https://euipo.europa.eu/eSearch/#details/trademarks/018974902.
[19] *Jaguar Land Rover Ltd* v. *Office for Harmonisation in the Internal Market (Trade Marks and Designs)*, Case T-629/14, ECLI:EU:T:2015:878.

would be protected by registered designs and/or copyright, and not by reference to trademark law.

3.1.1.5 Sound Marks An example of a sports-related sound mark that has been registered successfully by FC Barcelona is for the spoken word BARCA.[20] Looking at the field of tennis, there may be certain unique sounds that could be registrable as trademarks. For example, a number of tennis players are known for their very distinctive grunts and would be instantly recognisable – for example, Andrey Rublev's 'Bwehhhh'. The question is whether there is any commercial value in protecting such a mark. It is possible that such a mark could increase the value of a fashion-related trademark. For example, if a tennis enthusiast were to visit a clothing store and heard the distinctive grunt of their favourite player in the background, this may well awake positive emotions or memories and entice the tennis enthusiast to purchase something from that particular player's clothing range.

3.1.1.6 Smell and Taste Marks Smell and taste marks are quite rare. Even so, in 1996, the EU Intellectual Property Office (EUIPO) accepted: 'The smell of fresh cut grass' in respect of 'tennis balls'.[21] This registration has since expired.[22]

3.1.1.7 Motion, Gesture Marks and Holograms An increasingly popular category of non-traditional trademarks in the sports sector is the motion or gesture mark. In particular, there is a sub-category of motion marks, known as gestures, which are unique identifiers of certain athletes. To be registrable, such motions would normally need to be relatively short and repetitive and not purely functional. A recently high-profile case arose when Usain Bolt applied to register his famous 'lightning bolt' gesture in the United States for which he already had long-standing trademark protection in relation to clothing, sports equipment and other merchandising classes in the United Kingdom and European Union.[23]

---

[20] EUIPO, 'Trademark without Text', No. 01770361, available at: https://euipo.europa.eu/eSearch/#details/trademarks/017700361.
[21] WIPO, 'Smell, Sound and Taste: Getting a Sense of Non-Traditional Trademarks', *WIPO Magazine* (25 February 2009), available at: www.wipo.int/wipo_magazine/en/2009/01/article_0003.html.
[22] EUIPO, 'The Smell of Fresh Cut Grass', registration available at: https://euipo.europa.eu/eSearch/#basic/1+1+1+1/100+100+100+100/000428870.
[23] Désirée Fields, 'Bolt Trademark Could Inspire Tennis Stars to Follow', Pinsent Masons (23 August 2022), available at: www.pinsentmasons.com/out-law/news/bolt-trade-mark-

In tennis, Niclas Kroon was known for the 'Vicht' salute as a form of celebration and went on to register rights to an associated trademark in 1988. Kroon held rights in the mark together with Mats Wilander. However, when they forgot to renew the registration, Lleyton Hewitt, who had adopted this symbol himself, took advantage and registered the mark for clothing and accessories.

4 Scope of Trademark Protection

Trademarks are not protected in relation to everything but in respect of particular goods and services that fall into different Classes of the Nice Classification system.[24] There are forty-five Classes in total: thirty-four Classes of goods and eleven Classes of services. Each Class has a general Class heading which relates to a longer alphabetical list of goods and services. The Nice Classification is updated annually, albeit it is not always adept at keeping up with the pace of new technological developments.

The Classes of goods and services relevant to the tennis sector will very much depend on the individual or business concerned. For example, a tennis player might wish to protect its name and, if applicable, logo very broadly in relation to a range of goods and services in order to keep the door open for future merchandising opportunities. While the scope of trademark protection may differ in each case, the following Classes tend to be the most popular in the tennis/sports industry, depending on the nature of the trademark owner's business/activities:

- **Class 3**: Cosmetics, toiletry preparations; perfumery, essential oils;
- **Class 9**: Computer software; mobile applications; eyeglasses;
- **Class 12**: Vehicles;
- **Class 14**: Jewellery, precious and semi-precious stones; horological and chronometric instruments;
- **Class 16**: Paper and cardboard; printed matter; photographs; stationery;

---

tennis; equally, EUIPO, 'Trademark without Text', No. 008669236, available at: https://euipo.europa.eu/eSearch/#details/trademarks/008669236; and EUIPO, 'Trademark without Text', No. 009787573, available at: https://euipo.europa.eu/eSearch/#details/trademarks/009787573.

[24] The current version of the Nice Classification system is available at: www.wipo.int/classifications/nice/nclpub/en/fr/.

- **Class 18:** Leather goods; luggage and carrying bags; umbrellas and parasols;
- **Class 21**: Household or kitchen utensils and containers; cookware and tableware; glassware, porcelain and earthenware;
- **Class 24**: Textiles and substitutes for textiles; household linen; curtains of textile or plastic;
- **Class 25**: Clothing, footwear, headwear;
- **Class 28**: Games, toys and playthings; video game apparatus; gymnastic and sporting articles;
- **Class 35**: Advertising; business management, organisation and administration; office functions; organisation of promotional events;
- **Class 38**: Telecommunications; broadcasting;
- **Class 41**: Education; provision of training; entertainment; sporting and cultural activities;
- **Class 43**: Services for providing food and drink; temporary accommodation.

The foregoing are mere examples of what may be included within these Classes. In practice, they include many more items. Again, it is highly advisable to seek the advice of a trademark lawyer to ensure that a comprehensive specification of goods and services is included with any application.

4.1 Designs

Design rights are intended to protect the appearance of a product in whole or part. In the European Union and United Kingdom, designs can be either registered or unregistered. Design rights are of particular importance in the sports industry to protect innovative shapes and designs of products in 2D or 3D, such as the design of shoes, trophies and mascots. Unregistered design protection protects against unauthorised copying of the design and the mechanism in place arises automatically. Unregistered UK design rights provide protection for the lesser of (1) fifteen years from the end of the calendar year when the design was first recorded in a design document or (if earlier) from when an article was first made to the design; or (2) ten years from the end of the calendar year when articles made to the design were first made available for sale or hire.[25] EU unregistered design rights last for three years.[26]

---

[25] Copyright, Designs and Patents Act 1988, Pt III, s. 216(1).
[26] Council Regulation No. 6/2002 of 12 December 2001 on Community Designs, OJ L 3, 5.1.2002, Art. 11.

In the European Union and United Kingdom, it is possible to apply for registered designs as long as they are (1) novel; (2) of individual character; and (3) not excluded by statute.[27] Unlike trademarks, registered design protection lasts for a maximum of twenty-five years, provided renewal fees are paid every five years. The protection of designs at the international level can benefit from the World Intellectual Property Organization's (WIPO) international protection Hague System.[28]

4.2 Copyright

Copyright is intended to protect original artistic, musical, dramatic and literary works, including computer programs, certain databases, sound recordings, films, broadcasts and typographical arrangements of published works. It arises automatically upon creation of the work. Copyright in relation to artistic, musical, dramatic and literary works lasts for seventy years from the death of the author. Sound recordings are protected for seventy years from the date of publication, whereas broadcasts are protected for a period of fifty years from the date of making.[29]

It is important to note that copyright does not protect the idea itself, but only the expression of an idea. Therefore, it only protects against the copying of a work and not the independent development of the same idea. The copyright owner is entitled to prevent the unauthorised use of the work, for example, making copies.

The sports industry is an image industry which is built on images of athletes and teams. Accordingly, copyright is an important means of protecting the visual content associated with sports events. However, there is a lack of harmonisation of copyright protection internationally, which gives rise to challenges. The main areas in which copyright is relevant in the tennis industry include: (1) protection of sports performances and of the recording of sports performances; (2) protection of broadcasters; (3) protection of organisers of sports events; and (4) protection of databases relating to sports events.[30]

---

[27] Ibid., Art. 4(1); UK Registered Designs Act 1949, s. 1B ff.
[28] De Werra, 'Reference Guide', 21; WIPO, 'Hague System – The International Design System', available at: www.wipo.int/hague/en/; WIPO, 'Sport and Design', available at: www.wipo.int/web/sports/design.
[29] UK Copyright, Designs and Patents Act 1988, ss. 12–15.
[30] De Werra, 'Reference Guide', 20–30.

4.3 Image Rights/Rights of Publicity

The image of tennis players can be protected by so-called 'image rights' or 'rights of publicity' which play a very important role in the sports industry. Image rights are not recognised everywhere in the world and the scope of protection can differ significantly depending on the legal system in question. Broadly speaking, the term 'image rights' covers all the identifying features of an individual (such as names, initials, signatures, voice, body features and achievements). Some of these elements can also be protected by other IP rights, in particular trademarks or copyright. The commercialisation of image rights can yield significant revenues for prominent tennis players. Image rights can also provide tennis players with a means of preventing the unauthorised commercial use of their image or other personal features.

4.4 Patents

Given that the sports industry is very much driven by innovation, patents are also of prime importance in the tennis industry. While individual athletes might not own patent rights, they rely extensively on technology to improve their performance. By way of example, many tennis players, such as the top German player Alexander Zverev, use virtual reality trainers alongside their normal on-court training.[31] The sports goods industry also invests heavily in technological developments. Perhaps the most famous example is electronic line calling, such as Hawkeye, that is phasing out the need for human lines-people.

Patent protection provides inventors with a twenty-year monopoly[32] over inventions and protects new and inventive technical features of products and processes. In order to attract patent protection, an invention must be new, involve an inventive step, be capable of industrial application and not be specifically excluded from protection.[33] Examples of matters that are excluded from protection are computer programs, business methods and methods of medical treatment.[34] Patents are difficult and expensive to maintain.

---

[31] Improvr, available at: https://goimprovr.com/.
[32] UK Patents Act 1997, s. 25.
[33] Ibid., s. 1.
[34] Ibid., ss. 1(2) and 4(A).

4.5 Trade Secrets/Confidential Information

Trade secrets or confidential information are not strictly speaking IP rights, but serve to protect sensitive information, which can be commercial, technical or both in nature. They play a very important role in the tennis industry, giving a competitive advantage to athletes and the highly innovative sporting goods industry which relies on trade secrets and confidential information to commercialise its products. Accordingly, robust protection of trade secrets is very important in this sector. Protection of confidential information is implemented by local IP laws.[35] Generally speaking, in order to be considered enforceable, the information concerned must (1) be confidential in nature; and (2) have been imparted in circumstances in which an obligation of confidence arises. Furthermore (3), its unauthorised use must be to the detriment of the person imparting it.

5 Commercialisation of IP Rights

Just like other sports industries, the reason why the tennis industry is so dependent on the efficient protection of IP rights is because it derives a significant part of its revenues from control over IP rights relating to events and institutions which allow commercialisation of said rights internationally. In addition to IP laws, contract law plays an important role in the commercialisation of tennis-related IP rights because this area is heavily underpinned by contracts in a wide variety of contexts, including sponsorship, endorsement and broadcasting agreements.

5.1 Sponsorship Agreements

Sponsorship is a prime source of revenue for a number of stakeholders in the tennis industry and refers to a form of marketing whereby a sponsor (usually a business organisation) pays for marketing rights to associate itself with the particular event, activity, venue, content, organisation, individual athlete or sporting team being sponsored. Sponsorship can offer businesses exposure for a brand, the chance to reach new audiences and reinforce, or change, existing consumer perceptions while providing those sponsored with much-needed revenue. However, there are risks and pitfalls inherent in any sponsorship arrangement to navigate. For

---

[35] TRIPS Agreement, Art. 39.

example, the actions taken by those sponsored as well as event organisers will be linked to the sponsor and the sponsor has no control over the same. Thus, negative behaviour by a sponsored party could significantly impact the brand value of the sponsor.[36]

Stakeholders first need to have a clear understanding of what they want to achieve from the sponsorship relationship. There are many commercial factors to be considered, such as whether the relationship provides the right exposure, reaches the right audience, and fits with the brand values of the sponsors and those being sponsored. Planning the communication and implementing a clear branding strategy, as well as a carefully drafted sponsorship agreement, can make all the difference. A formal, written sponsorship agreement is a major tool in safeguarding any brand. A contract that gives sponsors robust protection will include morality clauses, which will specify prohibited behaviours that trigger other rights under the contract – such as the right to suspend payments or terminate the agreement. Robust termination provisions within the contract are important, as are *force majeure* clauses that account for unforeseeable events that prevent performance of the contract.

Other important aspects of a title sponsorship agreement will include payment provisions that facilitate staggered payments, which are weighted against large upfront payments. Exclusivity clauses will help protect the investment made by the sponsor in the event and can be supported by further contractual safeguards against 'ambush marketing' activities – where other brands look to unfairly piggyback on an event to leverage marketing of their own brand. IP and associated rights will shape the strategy around any potential co-branding activities. Each stakeholder will aim to ensure that they have as much control as possible over how their brand is used and monitor that any brand guidelines are strictly adhered to.

5.1.1 IP Provisions in Sponsorship Agreements

There are certain key considerations in respect of IP rights that need to be taken into account when considering sponsorship agreements.

5.1.1.1 Details of IP Rights Exploited during the Sponsorship The sponsorship agreement should clearly set out the details and ownership of all IP rights to be exploited during the sponsorship, as well as the

---

[36] Désirée Fields and George Campbell, 'How to Maximise Your Title Sponsorship of Tennis Events', Pinsent Masons (13 June 2022), available at: www.pinsentmasons.com/out-law/analysis/title-sponsorship-of-tennis-events.

owner of the relevant IP rights. This can be particularly difficult where IP rights are created jointly, such as a new logo, or where IP rights incorporate features of a tennis player. By way of example, Lacoste owns trademark registrations for logos associated with Daniil Medvedev and Novak Djokovic, both of which incorporate their personal name.[37] A prudently drafted sponsorship agreement would need to deal with not only the current trademark ownership arrangements, but also include provisions about rights ownership following the termination of any sponsorship agreement.

When reviewing a sponsorship agreement, the parties need to consider whether the name and logo that constitute the IP subject matter of the sponsorship are registered or whether it is desirable to do so. While it is advisable to obtain registrations for all IP rights, there may be some situations where a combined mark simply consists of a side-by-side placement of the parties' existing trademarks. In a scenario like this, options include registering ownership of the combined logo in both parties' names or dealing with ownership and use as part of ordinary licensing arrangements. Where a logo has been created by a third party, it is also necessary to ensure that any rights in the logo have been assigned to the entity or person intending to use and register the mark.

5.1.1.2 Licensing Arrangements The sponsorship agreement needs to clearly set out the licences that each party grants to the other to use its intellectual property rights. By way of example, the sponsor may require a licence from the athlete to use their trademarks, names and likeness, as well as any specific marketing assets created for a sponsorship campaign for the purposes of certain marketing activities. In turn, the sponsored party will expect a licence from the sponsor to use its trademarks in a number of ways, for example, on clothing or otherwise publicising the sponsorship. The licence terms pertaining to IP would include terms such as: (1) the types of usage which are permitted; (2) whether the licence is exclusive or non-exclusive; (3) whether either party has the right to grant sub-licences; (4) who is entitled or required to take action against third-party infringement of IP rights; and (5) any approval

---

[37] See e.g. EUIPO, 'International Trade Mark Registration No. 1720387 for a logo incorporating Daniil M', available at: https://euipo.europa.eu/eSearch/#details/trademarks/W01720387; and EUIPO, 'International Trade Mark Registration No. 1360540 (based on EUTM Registration No 016792591) for the silhouette of Novak Djokovic incorporating his full name', available at: https://euipo.europa.eu/eSearch/#details/trademarks/016792591.

requirements for use of IP rights. It is important to bear in mind that there may be jurisdictional differences in legal protection and formalities, especially in relation to personality rights. It is also important to include details regarding the duration of the licensing arrangement, the territories covered and robust termination provisions. Licence agreements further include financial terms, which could include lump-sum payments, royalty percentages and others.

5.1.1.3 Ambush Marketing Ambush marketing is a marketing strategy in which a non-official advertiser 'ambushes' an event to compete for exposure against official sponsors. Ambush marketing campaigns are usually clever, carefully thought out and entertaining, and are therefore often more memorable than 'regular' advertising. Some forms of ambush marketing are legal, some are illegal and some tread a fine line between the two. The concept itself refers to a situation where a non-sponsoring company attempts to deflect attention to itself and away from the sponsoring company, which undermines the effectiveness of the sponsorship communication and also the value of the sponsorship.[38]

By way of example, in 2011, Heineken was the official beer sponsor of the US Open. Stella Artois chose to advertise their brand on the rail station platform closest to the Bille Jean King National Tennis Centre, with large posters featuring tennis themes, such as: 'Your trophy awaits'; 'A Perfect Match'; and 'The top-seeded Belgian'. This led to confusion as to who was the official sponsor.[39]

The legal, statutory and regulatory framework in relation to ambush marketing differs from country to country and is outside the scope of this book. There is no single law protecting against ambush marketing. However, IP rights such as trademarks, copyright and designs may be of assistance. Additionally, there are certain contractual provisions that may be included in sponsorship agreements and practical steps that can be taken. Indeed, sponsorship agreements should set out who is expected to act against ambushers, who should pay for related fees and expenses, and whether a sponsor is due any compensation if ambushing occurs. There are a number of steps that can be taken to mitigate the effects of ambush marketing, such as renaming a tournament with the main

---

[38] Phillip Johnson, *Ambush Marketing and Brand Protection: Law and Practice*, 3rd edn (Oxford University Press, 2021), 656.
[39] Jess Blissett, 'The Impact of Ambush Marketing on Official Partnerships', Sporting Her (2 January 2022), available at: https://sportingher.com/the-impact-of-ambush-marketing-on-official-partnerships/.

sponsor's brand, operating a 'clean venue' policy or restricting external non-sponsored goods to be brought into the venue.

5.2 Endorsement Contracts

The terms 'sponsorship agreement' and 'endorsement contract' are often used interchangeably and as a result their contractual mechanisms and content tend to be similar. However, while a sponsorship deal is primarily focused on a financial transaction, an endorsement deal usually involves a contract between an individual athlete and a company, whereby the athlete actively endorses a particular product, for example, by appearing in marketing campaigns and being a brand ambassador. The provisions relating to the licensing of IP rights would closely mirror those in sponsorship agreements, as explained above.

5.3 Merchandising Agreements

A merchandising agreement grants a licence to a third party to use IP rights for the creation of consumer products in respect of distribution, sale and marketing. By way of example, all tournaments offer a wide range of branded products to tennis enthusiasts during the event and, in the case of prestigious Grand Slams, all year long. A merchandising agreement includes the same terms as other licensing agreements in the sports industry. Additionally, a robust merchandising agreement will also include quality control provisions allowing a licensor to examine the quality of the licensed merchandise and related advertising before the parties' mutual release and during the term of the merchandising agreement. This is crucial for the licensor in order to be able to control its reputation and brand image, as inferior merchandise could devalue a brand. This is particularly vexing in situations where products might not be fit for purpose and give rise to product liability claims.

5.4 Broadcasting Rights Agreements

Broadcasting rights, also known as media rights, generate the highest revenue for sports organisations and are highly sought after by broadcasters who make lucrative offers for the exclusive right to broadcast sporting events live. By way of example, Sky Sports entered a blockbuster deal with the ATP and WTA at the end of 2023 to broadcast live tennis tournaments in the United Kingdom and Ireland for forty-eight weeks of the year. The deal covers eighty tournaments a year, with the broadcaster reportedly paying £10 million per year for the rights.[40]

The grant of broadcasting rights is complex and can involve granting rights in all media for one or more territories or a split according to the types of rights and media involved. There are different legal and regulatory frameworks for broadcasting in television and television available over the Internet. This complexity is further exacerbated by the range of IP laws governing broadcasting, which vary significantly from country to country. Copyright and related rights govern the relationship between sports organisations and broadcasters.[41]

Piracy in live sport broadcasting is a growing issue, which disincentivises investment. It is estimated to cost event organisers up to €28 billion in lost revenue each year. Illegal streams of live sports events can also harm end users by exposing them to identity theft, malware or theft of credit card details and other personal data. Existing legislation is not necessarily robust enough to protect event organisers, broadcasters and their significant investment.[42] It is therefore crucial that sports bodies and owners of broadcasting rights for sports events invest in monitoring for illegal streaming and consider the options they have for enforcing their rights against infringers in the context of their commercial objectives.[43]

---

[40] 'Tennis Gets Major Boost in UK with Blockbuster New Sky Sports Deal', tennishead (27 November 2023), available at: https://tennishead.net/tennis-gets-major-boost-in-uk-with-blockbuster-new-sky-sports-deal/.

[41] The Rome Convention for the Protection of Performers, Producers of Phonograms and Broadcasting Organisations of 1961 establishes minimum standards of international protection for broadcasting organisations. Under the Convention, broadcasting organisations have the right to authorise or prohibit certain acts, namely: (i) the re-broadcasting of their broadcasts; (ii) the fixation of their broadcasts; (iii) the reproduction of fixations of such broadcasts; and (iv) the communication to the public of television broadcasts if such communication is made in places accessible to the public against payment of an entrance fee. The Rome Convention provides that the term of protection provided by signatories must last at least twenty years computed from the end of the year in which (i) the fixation was made – for phonograms and for performances incorporated therein; (ii) the performance took place – for performances not incorporated in phonograms; or (c) the broadcast took place – for broadcasts. However, many national laws provide for a longer term protection.

[42] Gill Dennis and Tom Nener, 'Action Needed to Protect Value of Sports Broadcasting Rights amidst Piracy Risk', Pinsent Masons (23 March 2023), available at: www.pinsentmasons.com/out-law/analysis/protect-value-sports-broadcasting-rights-amidst-piracy-risk;
Tom Nener, 'Delay in EU-Wide Legislation to Tackle Live Sports Piracy "Harmful to Rights Holders"', Pinsent Masons (24 May 2023), available at: www.pinsentmasons.com/out-law/news/delay-in-eu-wide-legislation-to-tackle-live-sports-piracy-harmful-to-rights-holders.

[43] Julian Diaz-Rainey and Tom Nener, 'Sports Bodies Have Options for Tackling Illegal Streaming, Say Experts', Pinsent Masons (2 June 2023), available at: www.pinsentmasons.com/en-gb/out-law/news/sports-bodies-have-options-tackling-illegal-streaming?utm_

6 Enforcement of IP Rights

Obtaining relevant IP protection and putting contractual arrangements in place is only part of a balanced brand protection strategy. IP rights do not enforce themselves and it is up to IP rights owners to take appropriate steps against third-party infringements and misuse of such rights. Failing to properly police IP rights and take appropriate enforcement action can significantly reduce the value of a brand.

6.1 Monitoring Infringements

To identify infringements, brand owners must monitor third-party uses and infringements and take appropriate enforcement action where such infringements are identified. There are a variety of different services available to monitor third-party infringements, including trademark watches, domain name watches and company name watches. Subscribing to such services will allow brand owners to identify any trademarks, domain names or company names applied for or registered by third parties that are in contravention of identical or similar trademarks and which are lawfully registered.

Infringement often takes place online – for example, on social media platforms. Combatting infringement of IP rights online can be challenging and requires a clear enforcement strategy. IP rights holders can undertake manual searches online on an ad hoc or regular basis, although this is unlikely to eradicate the problem. Online platforms are typically fitted with reporting tools and take-down procedures so that IP rights holders can complain of IP infringements. However, the manual approach and reporting has the downside of potentially missing infringements.

There are comprehensive brand protection solutions which allow rights holders to monitor and enforce the use of their IP rights online through a single platform that can be used to identify potential infringements. These platforms can be utilised to issue take-down notices. These services also have the added benefit of maintaining a record of infringing activity which can be used to provide proof of infringements on a platform existing in real time. Many of the brand protection solutions are equally able to provide more sophisticated brand protection

source=vuture&utm_medium=email&utm_campaign=newsletter%20-%20english&utm_content=your%20weekly%20round-up%20-%20rest%20of%20the%20world%20(109).

solutions, such as monitoring of online abuse of athletes on social media (which is becoming an increasingly serious issue).[44]

6.2 Enforcement Action

The appropriate cause of action depends in large part on the type of IP right involved, the nature of the infringement and jurisdictional variations. Examples include litigation against trademark, design and copyright infringement (using the same or similar logo) and counterfeiting (imitating of genuine goods), as well as piracy (i.e. unauthorised copying, use, reproduction or distribution of materials protected by copyright). In respect of registered IP rights, in particular trademarks and designs, it is also possible to take action before the relevant IP registries in extrajudicial proceedings. Registered IP rights, in particular trademarks and design rights, are likely to be the most frequently invoked and strongest enforcement tools in combatting IP infringements. Other proceedings can include domain name complaints and company name complaints. The available enforcement actions and associated procedures will differ depending on the country in question.

6.2.1 Cease and Desist Letters

Regardless of the cause of action involved, it is usually recommended to send a 'cease and desist' letter to the infringing party to put them on notice that they are using certain IP rights without consent and request that they cease using these immediately and refrain from using them in the future. Indeed, in some cases, especially in court proceedings, it is mandatory to send a letter before issuing proceedings to avoid adverse consequences. The content of 'cease and desist' letters may indeed be prescribed by regulations – for example, the Civil Procedure Rules in the United Kingdom.[45] Making a mistake may severely impact the ability to take legal action and/or succeed with any legal claim.

6.2.2 Issuing Substantive Proceedings

Where a 'cease and desist' letter is ignored, taking enforcement action is usually the only means of challenging a potential infringer. The precise

---

[44] Associated Press, 'Tennis Players to Get Protection from Online Abuse through New Monitoring Service' (20 December 2023), available at: www.tennis.com/baseline/articles/tennis-players-social-media-online-abuse-protection-threat-matrix-service-ai-signify-group. See Chapter 8 of this volume on safeguarding.
[45] Civil Procedure Rules, available at: www.justice.gov.uk/courts/procedure-rules/civil.

enforcement action to be taken will depend on the circumstances of the case and the IP rights involved. It is outside the scope of this chapter to discuss all potential actions in detail. A brief summary of potential available enforcement mechanisms relating to trademarks is set out below.

6.2.2.1 Trademark Oppositions All trademark applications are examined by local trademark registries. In some countries, such as Australia and the United States, the examiner may raise earlier third-party rights as a bar to registration. In other jurisdictions, like the European Union and the United Kingdom, it is entirely up to the earlier rights holder to take action. Trademark applications are published for opposition purposes following a successful examination process. Trademark oppositions can be filed both on the basis of absolute grounds, such as where the trademark concerned is descriptive and non-distinctive and should be free for all traders to use; or on the basis of relative grounds, such as where the trademark is identical or confusingly similar to an existing registered mark or conflicts with existing prior common law rights established under the tort of passing-off. The length of an opposition period differs from country to country. The process of any opposition proceedings will also differ depending on the country in question, but it involves (1) filing an opposition notice and grounds of opposition; (2) filing a defence; (3) evidence rounds; (4) final submissions and/or hearing; and (5) issuance of a decision.

6.2.2.2 Trade Validity and Revocation Actions A registered trademark does not guarantee indefinite rights. A trademark registration can be challenged on various grounds, including invalidity of the mark (where a third party seeks a declaration that the registration is invalid) or revocation (where a third party seeks the revocation of the trademark on the ground that it has not been used, has become generic or is likely to mislead the public). Such challenges are often brought against registered trademarks as part of a wider infringement dispute. It is therefore crucial for IP rights owners in tennis to take the necessary steps to ensure their IP rights remain valid and enforceable by regularly reviewing their trademark portfolios.

6.2.2.3 Revocation A revocation action can be brought in respect of an entire registration or for specific goods and services. Revocation actions may be brought where a trademark has not been used, has become generic or may mislead the public. Where a party has not put a mark to genuine use within a five-year period, it will need valid reasons for that non-use. A trademark must be used in relation to each of the goods and services for which it is registered. By way of example, the EU General Court has upheld an EUIPO Board of Appeal decision confirming that an EU trademark registration for the figurative sign NOAH owned by former Grand Slam Champion and tennis legend Yannick Noah remained registered in respect of 'polo shirts' and 'sweaters'. In reviewing the Board's decision, the General Court conducted an extensive analysis of the law surrounding genuine use. Notably, the General Court found that use in a slightly different form from its registered form, insofar as the mark included the first initial of Yannick Noah's name followed by a full stop, did not alter its distinctive character. The General Court also confirmed that the mark was used in relation to the marketing of sweater vests, which was sufficient to maintain the registration for the broader category of 'sweaters'. Further, given the consistent marketing strategy of limited-edition clothing, the General Court found that the mark had been put to genuine use for 'polo shirts' and 'sweaters'.[46] However, Yannick Noah did have his rights cut down considerably in scope.[47]

Prominent sportspeople are increasingly cultivating a brand during their active years that they can continue to commercially exploit into retirement. This case highlights the risk athletes face by losing trademark rights if they do not put those marks to 'genuine use' in respect of the goods or services for which they were registered. Accordingly, athletes should think carefully about the scope of trademark rights they will need during and after their careers and ensure that their trademark protection extends to all relevant goods and services. Careful consideration should also be given to whether the mark used is sufficiently similar to the one registered in order to be able to fend off any potential non-use cancellation actions. Athletes are therefore advised to develop a strategy to ensure 'genuine use' is made of their trademark rights.[48]

6.2.2.4 Invalidity Invalidity actions can be broadly brought on two grounds. First, bad faith is an absolute ground of refusal and so if it can be

---

[46] *Noah Clothing* v. *EUIPO*, Case T-562/22, EU:T:2024:23 (24 January 2024).
[47] Désirée Fields, 'Yannick Noah Case Highlights Athlete Brand Longevity Challenge' (2024) 35 Ent L Rev 1.
[48] Désirée Fields, 'Yannick Noah Case Highlights Athlete Brand Longevity Challenge', Pinsent Masons (16 January 2024), available at: www.pinsentmasons.com/out-law/news/yannick-noah-case-highlights-athlete-brand-longevity-challenge.

shown on the balance of probabilities that a party has not registered a trademark in good faith, it will be invalidated. It is on the party alleging bad faith to prove it. Persuasive evidence will be required. The owner of an earlier trademark can also challenge a later trademark registration if this is identical or similar to its own trademark and registered in relation to identical or similar goods and services (and there exists a likelihood of confusion where these are similar). Where a third party registers an identical or similar trademark in respect of dissimilar goods and services, it will be crucial for IP rights owners to demonstrate a reputation in a mark and that the later registration takes advantage of the earlier mark or is detrimental to its distinctive character or repute. This is likely to be easier for sizeable brands, but will be more difficult for smaller, newer brands.

6.2.2.5 Trademark Infringement Proceedings Unlike trademark opposition proceedings, which are concerned with preventing the registration of a trademark, trademark infringement proceedings are concerned with the use of an identical or similar trademark in relation to identical or similar goods or services in the course of trade without the proprietor's consent. Trademark infringement proceedings can be brought by the trademark owner. A licensee can also bring infringement proceedings in its own name in certain circumstances, which is often detailed in applicable licence agreements. It depends on the individual IP rights owner and the licensing relationship as to whether the licensor prefers to remain in control of all enforcement actions or put the burden on a licensee.

6.2.2.6 Domain Name Complaints All domain name registrars must follow the Uniform Domain-Name Dispute-Resolution Policy (often referred to as the UDRP). Disputes alleged to arise from abusive registrations of domain names (e.g. cybersquatting) may be addressed by expedited administrative proceedings initiated by a trademark rights holder through the filing of a complaint with an approved dispute resolution service provider. Generally speaking, a trademark owner can either file a complaint against a domain name registrant in a court that has jurisdiction or submit a complaint to an approved dispute resolution provider. The appropriate provider will depend on the domain name involved.[49] In order to succeed in a domain name complaint, it is

---

[49] ICANN, 'Uniform-Domain Name Dispute Resolution Policy', available at: www.icann.org/resources/pages/help/dndr/udrp-en.

necessary for the complainant to establish that: (1) the disputed domain name is identical with, or confusingly similar to, the complainant's trademark rights; (2) the respondent has no rights or legitimate interests in the disputed domain name; and (3) the disputed domain name has been both registered and used in bad faith by the respondent.[50] For example, Grand Slam Tennis Properties Ltd[51] successfully obtained transfer of the domain name *tennisgrandslam.net* on the basis that it established that the term 'Grand Slam' had been used by the operators of the four prestigious Grand Slam tournaments since the 1930s, and that the public referred to the events as such and that in addition the respondent had taken advantage of the complainant's trademark without the licence of the complainant or other justification in bad faith.

6.2.2.7 Company Name Complaints One possible and effective way to stop a company that has registered the same or a very similar company name in the United Kingdom with UK Companies House is to submit a complaint to the Company Names Tribunal.[52] Like domain name complaints, it is crucial to establish rights in the name and substantiate the claim that the company name has been registered in bad faith. Similar types of procedures may also be available in other countries.

6.3 Remedies

It is important to note that in proceedings before IP registries, there are no remedies as such. The result of such proceedings is that the registry will determine whether the relevant IP right has been infringed and the third-party application will be refused, allowed to proceed or declared invalid. There may also a be a small costs award. However, a successful claim before IP registries will not automatically lead to an alleged infringer stop using the particular mark in question. Therefore, if an infringer decides to continue using a mark without registration, the only redress is often to bring legal action in the courts, which tends to be a time-consuming and expensive process.

---

[50] *Grand Slam Tennis Properties Ltd v. Contact Privacy Inc. Customer 0152960105 / Darryl Cazares, Grand Slam Nutrition Corp.*, Case D2020-1034.

[51] Grand Slam Tennis Properties Ltd was established in 2009 to administer the intellectual property associated with the four prestigious tennis tournaments known as the Grand Slams.

[52] A list of decisions issued by the Company Names Tribunal is available at: www.gov.uk/government/publications/company-names-tribunal-undefended-decisions-and-orders.

If an IP owner is successful, the courts may award a variety of remedies. The available remedies depend on the type of IP rights that was infringed and the specifics of the situation. Ultimately, the IP rights owner will be keen to maintain brand value for commercialisation purposes and be compensated for any losses incurred as a result of an infringement.

6.3.1 Injunctions

The most common remedy for all IP infringements is an injunction. This is a court order requiring the named persons to refrain from using the IP rights in question. There are different types of injunctions. An interim injunction can be granted as an emergency measure prior to the commencement of or during proceedings while the case is being decided. However, the courts will carefully weigh up the facts and only grant an injunction where there is a serious issue to be tried and where damages may be an adequate remedy. The courts will also consider the respective inconvenience or loss to each party depending on whether or not the interim injunction is granted.

Perpetual injunctions are typically granted as a final relief by the court, prohibiting the unauthorised use of the IP rights concerned. Failure to adhere to an injunction can result in fines and even imprisonment.

6.3.2 Damages or Account of Profits

Where an IP infringement has occurred, an IP rights owner will be entitled to compensation. Typically, the IP rights owner will be able to elect either damages or an account of profits, but not both. The preferable remedy will depend on the facts of a particular case. Damages are intended to cover the value of the damage caused to the IP rights owner, while an account of profits covers the profits that the infringing party has made as a result of their infringement.

6.3.3 Other Remedies

Other remedies include (1) an award of costs (intended to compensate the successful party for all or part of their costs incurred in the proceedings); (2) delivery up and/or destruction of infringing items; and (3) tracing orders.

4

Morality Clauses in Tennis Agreements
Tennis, Social Media and the Digital World

MIGUEL CRESPO

1 Introduction

Tennis is a global sport, and the top professional players are its great ambassadors. Companies associate their brands with the images of these players as fans consider some of them celebrities. This is achieved through traditional sponsorship contracts. If a scandal occurs due to the misbehavior that affects the underlying agreement, typically coming to the public domain through its circulation on social media, the parties endeavor to protect themselves from any adverse impact by including in these contracts a specific provision known as a "morality clause." This chapter will provide an overview of the tennis ecosystem, its business and industry, and explain the origin, history, relevance, types and characteristics of this clause, with special attention to its place in the ever-expanding digital world.

Played in more than 215 countries around the world by more than 100 million people, tennis is one of the most popular sports and probably the most practiced racket sport in the world. During recent decades, it has become considerably popular, and in addition to approximately 100,000 clubs around the world, it is also played in parks and public facilities on more than half a million tennis courts. As per the gender distribution of players, data from the latest research concludes that tennis is played by 41 percent of women and approximately 59 percent of men, thus demonstrating that it is the most gender-balanced sport in the world. The game is taught by more than 150,000 coaches around the world, all of whom are responsible for introducing anyone to the advantages of this excellent sport.[1] Nonetheless, tennis as a spectacle also attracts more than

---

[1] See on this International Tennis Federation, "ITF Global Tennis Report" (2024).

a billion fans around the world who follow the achievements of the great players on the professional circuits. Certainly, tennis can be considered a global show due to the large crowds of fans it attracts. The business is supported by a global tennis industry made up of a variety of actors with varying roles in the different areas of its existence.[2]

From a historical perspective of tennis as a business, the tennis industry has grown from a sport reserved for the highest social classes to an activity that has managed to be present at all levels of society.[3] In this context, the latest data indicates that between 2023 and 2030 the size of the global tennis market will reach US$4.59 billion.[4]

As per the global sports governance, tennis is composed of a classic structure that includes the International Tennis Federation (ITF) as the body that governs the destinies of the sport in the international context, to which six regional associations (Tennis Europe – TE, Asian Tennis Federation – ATF, Oceania Tennis Federation – OTF, Confederation of African Tennis – CAT, Confederación Sudamericana de Tenis – COSAT, and Confederación de Tenis de Centroamérica y el Caribe – COTECC) belonging approximately to the different continents and around 200 member nations are affiliated. In turn, as is the case in most sport disciplines, the national federations consider their respective provincial associations, players, coaches, officials and clubs as their affiliated members.[5]

The fundamental task of all of these federative organizations is to govern tennis in their respective areas of influence, whether international, national or local.[6] Thus, they are responsible for carrying out different tasks, which may include but are not limited to the following: the promulgation of rules and regulations for resolving disputes in competitions organized under their aegis; the representation of teams from their organization in competitions in which they participate; the organization of tournaments and championships of different categories, which also includes the publication and management of player and team

---

[2] Infosys Tennis Radar, "The Next Big Era" (2020).
[3] See for an overview Eric Barget, "The Economics of Tennis" in Wladimir Andreff and Stefan Szymanski (eds), *Handbook on the Economics of Sport* (Edward Elgar, 2006), 418.
[4] Grand View Research, "Tennis Equipment Market Size Worth $4.59 Billion by 2030" (2022), available at: www.grandviewresearch.com/press-release/global-tennis-equipment-market.
[5] ITF Constitution (2023).
[6] For a historical overview of tennis governance, see Robert J. Lake, "Tennis Governance: A History of Political Power Struggles" in Robert L. Lake (ed.), *Routledge Handbook of Tennis* (Routledge, 2019), 341.

rankings; the provision and organization of training for players of different levels, which may include the management of one or several training centers and talent selection programs for those players; representation and participation before the corresponding sports entities; the organization of development programs, promotion and participation of tennis in order to achieve a greater number of players and fans; the education of coaches, officials, players and other stakeholders, among others.[7]

As per the sports governance at the international and professional competitive level, tennis has a characteristic that distinguishes it from other sports, chiefly the existence of two organizations that represent the interests of professional players and their circuits: the Association of Tennis Professionals (ATP)[8] for male players and the Women's Tennis Association (WTA) for their female counterparts, which organize their own professional tours that are held in forty countries around the world.

Furthermore, due to its great relevance and historical tradition, it is important to point out the existence of another organization, the Grand Slams, which encompasses the four most important individual professional tournaments on the international calendar, namely, the Australian Open, Roland Garros, Wimbledon and the US Open.[9]

Manufacturers, tournament and event organisers, player agents, court builders, media and other relevant stakeholders play a crucial role in the global tennis industry that shapes the current complex, dynamic and evolving tennis ecosystem. In this scenario, tennis looks into the future, trying to position the game as equal, inclusive, sustainable and innovative.

Among all the various tennis constituents, players are at the center of the game, and among them, the professional players, and the great champions who are truly considered as legends of the sport in a way

---

[7] See Miguel Crespo, Dolores Botella-Carrubi and Jose Jabaloyes, "Innovation Programs of the Royal Spanish Tennis Federation" (2022) 175 Technol Forecast Soc Change 1.

[8] For the ATP Tour, see Amy D. Gibson, "The Association of Tennis Professionals: From Player Association to Governing Body" (2010) 10 J Appl Bus Econ 5, at 23, as well as Alessandra Sorrentini and Tommasina Pianese, "The Relationships among Stakeholders in the Organization of Men's Professional Tennis Events" (2011) 3 Glob Bus Manag Res: Int J 141.

[9] A comprehensive view is provided in Robert J. Lake, "Grand Slams: Tennis at the Forefront of Women's Professionalised Sport" in Ali Bowes and Alex Culvin (eds), *The Professionalisation of Women's Sport: Issues and Debates* (Emerald, 2021), 19. See also a comparison among these events as per prize money in Martin Svoboda and Zuzana Rakovská, "How Big Is the Prize Money Gap? Analysis of Prize Money in 2016 Grand Slam Tournaments" (2017) 8 Financial Assets & Investing 1, at 40.

that culminates in the pinnacle of tennis heroes.[10] They are usually the ones who gather the attention in a sport that has generated iconic champions since its very beginnings by combining style, etiquette, tradition and an appeal that identifies with cultures, nations and individuals.[11]

2 Players, Sponsors and Endorsement Agreements

The popularity of tennis on a global scale puts the great champions at the center of attention around the world as this focus is enhanced by the prominent role of media proper and social media in the current digital environment. In most cases, great tennis players are rightly considered role models by people in general and fans in particular who follow with interest not only their performance on the court, but also everything that occurs off it.[12] In this context, it is not surprising that sponsoring companies vigorously seek player endorsements and wish to associate their brand with the image of both the sporting and the social success of top tennis players, particularly those considered idols or celebrities.[13] Through this association, the sponsoring companies ensure that fans and potential clients understand that the sponsored tennis player supports

---

[10] There is an abundance of studies on the consideration of tennis players as heroes and celebrities. The case of Tim Henman is discussed in Gill Lines, "Villains, Fools or Heroes? Sports Stars as Role Models for Young People" (2011) 20 Leis Stud 285. The scenario in Germany with Steffi Graf and Boris Becker is analyzed in Anne Feddersen and Wolfgang Maennig, "Sports Heroes and Mass Sports Participation – the (Double) Paradox of the 'German Tennis Boom'" (2009) 29 Hamburg Contemporary Economic Discussions 1, at 29. The image of former world number one Simona Halep in Romania is explored in Diana-Luiza Dumitriu, "Media Construction of Sport Celebrities as National Heroes" (2018) 20 Revista Română de Comunicare și Relații Publice 2, at 21. In the US context, see Jacqueline D. Lee and Andrea N. Eagleman, "From Tennis Skirt to Catsuit: A Qualitative Analysis of Serena Williams' Impact on Women's Tennis Fashion" (2013) 7 J Contemp Athl 1, at 27.

[11] The concept of cultural economy of tennis is explored in Barry Smart, "The World's Game? Globalisation and the Cultural Economy of Tennis" in Lake, *Routledge Handbook of Tennis*, 96. From a national endorsement perspective, the case of the famous Thai tennis player Paradorn Shrishapan is discussed in Fabrice Desmarais, "Global Issues in Selecting Athlete Endorsers for National Markets: A Macroinvestigation" (2014) 27 J Glob Mark 308.

[12] An overview is provided by Mara Konjer, Michael Mutz and Henk Erik Meier, "Talent Alone Does Not Suffice: Erotic Capital, Media Visibility and Global Popularity among Professional Male and Female Tennis Players" (2019) 28 J Gend Stud 1, at 3.

[13] For an interesting example on the branding of women tennis players, see Norman O'Reilly and Anne L. Braedley, "Celebrity Athletes and Athletic Clothing Design: Branding Female Tennis Players" (2008) 3 Int J Sport Manag Mark 119.

the brand and, therefore, a relationship is established that both parties believe will be favorable for their respective interests.[14]

This mutual endorsement implies a benefit that usually occurs if the relationship develops within the general channels of the legal business and as long as both parties respect what was agreed.[15] The positive economic value of tennis celebrity endorsements and the considerable financial and social impact of player-related sponsorship on specific aspects such as return on investment, purchase habits, brand identification, marketing recognition and other indicators has been extensively studied in the literature.[16]

Tennis players are usually at the top of the lists of endorsed athletes.[17] Historically, they have been considered among the most marketable athletes as their image has usually transcended the tennis court and impacted on brand preference, user satisfaction, customer appreciation and, most importantly, purchase intention.[18]

In this scenario of an endorsement cooperation, the benefits are high when the underlying relationship is well managed by both parties and the desired alignment is achieved. However, the attendant risks and potential negative outcomes can also be high, as it is well known that on some occasions, both in sport in general and tennis in particular, sponsored athletes or endorsement organizations may be involved in situations labeled as scandalous and which are obviously not desired by any of the parties.[19] Scandals in sports settings have been defined in a variety of

---

[14] The difference between technical sponsorship and endorsement specifically applied to tennis is explained in Vlad Roșca, "Celebrity Endorsement in Advertising" (2010) 2 Manag Mark-Craiova 365.

[15] See Juan Luis Nicolau and María Jesús Santa-María, "Celebrity Endorsers' Performance on the 'Ground' and on the 'Floor'" (2013) 24 Mark Lett 143 (for a discussion of Rafa Nadal).

[16] See Anita Elberse and Jeroen Verleun, "The Economic Value of Celebrity Endorsements" (2012) 52 J Advert Res 149. Also Dirk F. Gerritsen and Saskia van Rheenen, "The Value of Winning: Endorsement Returns in Individual Sports" (2017) 28 Mark Lett 371. For the impact of Rafa Nadal on Spanish tourism, see Juan Luis Nicolau and María Jesús Santa-María, "Sports Results Creating Tourism Value: Rafael Nadal's Tennis Match Points Worth €12,000,000" (2017) 23 Tour Econ 697.

[17] An interesting comparison is provided by Gashaw Abeza, Norm O'Reilly, Benoit Séguin et al., "The World's Highest-Paid Athletes, Product Endorsement, and Twitter" (2017) 7 Sport Bus Manag: Int J 332.

[18] The case of the success of tennis in Serbia and its impact on customer purchase intention is explored in Sretenka Dugalić and Snežana Lazarević, "The Impact of Celebrity Athlete Endorsement on Purchasing Habits" (2017) 14 FU Phys Ed Sport 435.

[19] For the specific case of a given endorsement agreement rejected by the WTA, see John L. Crompton, "Potential Negative Outcomes from Sponsorship for a Sport Property" (2014) 19 Manag Leis 420.

ways as they have attracted considerable attention from the academic literature. Due to the difficulty of adhering to a single definition, it is perhaps more appropriate to mention some of the key aspects identified as the main characteristics of a scandal.[20] These include an action that: (1) is either unethical or illegal; (2) involves multiple parts; (3) occurs or it is believed to have occurred; (4) affects the reputation and integrity of the sport and its stakeholders; (5) is of public notice; (6) can happen either on- or off-field; (7) implies a transgression of social norms or values; (8) causes public indignation.

Sports scandals have also been typified according to their most salient features. Authors have distinguished among: (1) competition scandals (i.e. doping, unsportsmanlike conduct); (2) governance scandals (i.e. corruption, manipulation); and (3) off-field scandals (i.e. from minor incidences such as social media posts to violence or murder).[21] These scandals are often triggered because of unwanted conduct by one of the parties. The most usual concerns inappropriate ethical (i.e. cheating, opinions or views), illegal or criminal behavior (i.e. doping, betting or drug abuse) by the endorsed athletes. Other cases have witnessed more serious criminal conduct (i.e. assault, sexual abuse, homicide, etc.). In this scenario, some names of athletes who have seen their sponsoring companies cancel their sponsorship contracts after having been involved in scandals that became public include great champions such as Mike Tyson, Tiger Woods, Oscar Pistorius, Michael Phelps, Marion Jones, Manny Pacquiao, Ray Rice, Gilbert Arenas, Barry Bonds, Jason Giambi, Adrian Peterson, Michael Vick, Wayne Rooney, Ben Johnson, Rashard Mendenhall and Ronaldinho, among others.[22] In tennis, probably the best-known case in recent years was the one involving Maria Sharapova.[23]

---

[20] Some of the most relevant studies on the definition of scandals in sport may be found in Stephanie Hughes and Matt Shank, "Defining Scandal in Sports: Media and Corporate Sponsor Perspectives" (2005) 14 Sport Mark Q 214; and Sarah J. Kelly, Clinton S. Weeks and P. Monica Chien, "There Goes My Hero Again: Sport Scandal Frequency and Social Identity Driven Response" (2018) 26 J Strat Mark 56.

[21] For an in-depth study, see Mark Ludwig and Inga Oelrichs, "More than a Marginal Phenomenon: Relevance and Content-Related Aspects of Mediated Sport Scandals" (2020) 17 Sport & Gesellschaft 185.

[22] A comprehensive list including descriptions and examples of many cases is provided in Miguel Crespo, *Las Cláusulas de Moralidad en los Contratos de Patrocinio Deportivo* (Reus, 2019). The ethics perspective of athlete scandals is explored in Felicia M. Miller and Gene R. Laczniak, "The Ethics of Celebrity-Athlete Endorsement: What Happens When a Star Steps Out of Bounds?" (2011) 51 J Advert Res 499.

[23] In the case of Maria Sharapova and the way in which sponsorship crises can affect brands, see Jakob Ivarsson, Carolin Bruder and Helena Lübeck, "Should We Stay or Should We

There are also scenarios in which someone in the player's entourage (i.e. a coach, captain, agent, family member, etc.) is the one directly involved in controversial behavior.[24] Another situation arises where the endorsement company engages in conduct that the sponsored player or organization considers as likely to cause a loss of reputation and is therefore contrary to their interest. In many cases, these situations involving players, teams or federations have considerable consequences which both parties should effectively prevent and address.

3 Reasons for Agreement Termination and Morality Clauses in Tennis

Sport endorsement agreements as all contracts are based on trust and goodwill. They usually include a series of so-called boilerplate clauses, as well as succinct termination terms.[25] Sponsorship agreements in sport can be terminated by either party due to a variety of reasons, such as financial or economic causes, a *force majeure* event, impossibility to deliver or perform, applicable legal changes or negative impact due to particular misbehavior.[26]

Sponsors typically include penalty clauses in sport sponsorship contracts. A novel option in tennis was provided by Yonex, which introduced a controversial contractual clause entitling the manufacturer to financially penalize its sponsored players for each racket they intentionally break.[27] This provision refers to the duty-of-care obligation for the

---

Go? Key Brand Elements that Can Be Affected by Sponsorship Issues and How to Communicate the 'Go-Decision,'" LBMG Strategic Brand Management – Masters Paper Series, 4th edn (2018), available at: https://lup.lub.lu.se/luur/download?func=downloadFile&recordOId=8963959&fileOId=8963960.

[24] In the specific case of tennis, see Akriti Singh, "A Light on the Jurisprudential Remedies to Controversies in Tennis" (2021) 2 Glob Sports Pol Rev 64, for an analysis of the situation generated by the behavior of Illie Nastase during a Fed Cup tie.

[25] For a comprehensive overview of the most relevant clauses in sport endorsement agreements, see Ian S. Blackshaw, *Sports Marketing Agreements: Legal, Fiscal and Practical Aspects* (Asser, 2012), 121. The most relevant clauses are covered in Adam Epstein, "An Exploration of Interesting Clauses in Sports" (2011) 5 J Legal Aspects Sport 5.

[26] The termination provisions in these specific agreements are explored in Mary Hutchings Reed, Monique N. Bhargava and Jason Myja Kjaer, "Terminating a Sponsorship Relationship: Conditions and Clauses" (2010) 4 J Spons 79.

[27] Obviously, this is an unprecedented decision in the world of tennis that has met with some resistance from its sponsored players. See Michael Chammas, "Nick Kyrgios' Racquet Manufacturer Yonex Starts Fining Its Players for Smashes," *Brisbane Times* (January 20, 2017), 1, for more details on Yonex's most prominent sponsored athletes and the brand's decision.

equipment that the sponsor makes available to the sponsored party in the sports advertising sponsorship contract.

It has been noted that in the current global digital world the behavior of top players is under constant public scrutiny. In light of behavior considered unacceptable by the parties, the fans or the public, which in turn may affect the reputation of the endorsement companies or players, it seems appropriate that the parties seek legal tools and alternatives to defend their interests under these circumstances.[28] So, how do parties prevent the occurrence of these situations and the negative consequences of the impugned conduct?

A clause that has received considerable attention in contract law due to its general use in sport endorsement agreements is that which is commonly known as the "moral clause."[29] A moral clause in sport sponsorship contracts has been defined as a contractual provision "which identifies one or several conducts carried out by one of the parties that the other party considers unacceptable and which, consequently, allows it to adopt a series of measures linked to the contractual development, among which may be contractual termination."[30] These have been labeled using different terms such as moral, morality, disrepute, good conduct or behavior, ethical, etc. This provision is widely used in almost all sports endorsement agreements due to the obvious increase in sports sponsorship, and because of the usual occurrence of scandals involving sport celebrities.[31] Its broad use is justified by its growing relevance, as evidence has shown that the impact of players' behavior, whether off- or on-court, on the endorsement cooperation can have unprecedented financial, ethical and social consequences for both parties. Furthermore, such clauses have been viewed as tools for setting out adequate moral

---

[28] See Qi Ge and Brad R. Humphreys, "Athlete Off-Field Misconduct, Sponsor Reputation Risk, and Stock Returns" (2021) 21 Eur Sport Manag Q 153, for the conclusions on the negative effect on endorsers of inappropriate behavior from sport celebrities.

[29] The seminal paper is Daniel Auerbach, "Morals Clauses as Corporate Protection in Athlete Endorsement Contracts" (2005) 3 DePaul J Sport L & Cont Prob 1, at 1. Other interesting views can be seen in Fermando M. Pinguelo and Timothy D. Cedrone, "Morals – Who Cares about Morals – Examination of Morals Clauses in Talent Contracts and What Talent Needs to Know" (2009) 19 Seton Hall J Sport & Ent L 347; and Caroline Epstein "Morals Clauses: Past, Present and Future" (2015) 5 NYU J Intell Prop & Ent L 72.

[30] See Miguel Crespo Celda, *Las Cláusulas de Moralidad en los Contratos de Patrocinio Deportivo* (Reus, 2019), 34.

[31] Anne Philipps, "When Crime Pays, Does Anyone Lose?" (2019) 35 Ent & Sports Lawyer 29.

standards and fulfillment of social responsibility obligations, and to lead by example by controlling unwanted behavior. Moreover, the importance of these clauses has been further acknowledged by the immediacy with which scandals involving sport celebrities are spread through the media and brought to the attention of sponsors, organizations, fans and the public.[32]

Historically, these clauses were first utilized by the film industry in Hollywood during the 1920s as an attempt to control the misbehavior of some of its best-known celebrities.[33] These clauses were then emulated by teams of US professional leagues such as baseball and football, later adapted to contracts with script writers and ultimately ended up as a common practice for all endorsement agreements in the sport and entertainment industry.[34] In terms of frequency, the inclusion of morality clauses in the sports industry is very common – not only in sponsorship contracts between endorsement companies and players or other organizations, but also in employment contracts of athletes with teams or organizations that do not include a sponsorship dimension. The clauses are incorporated in endorsement agreements for both professional and college athletes.[35] It has been stated that in light of the impact of sport scandals, "moral clauses are more important than ever."[36] From a geographical point of view, it has been noted that morality clauses are used more frequently in Anglo-Saxon countries such as the United States, Great Britain, Canada and Australia. This is because the sports industry is considerably broad and powerful within these countries. Furthermore, these clauses originally came into use in the United States. However,

---

[32] William H. Baaki, "'Morals Clauses' in Sports Contracts – More Important Now than Ever Before?" Sports and Entertainment Law Insider (September 16, 2014). In terms of the intentions and reasons for the use of these clauses, from an ethical perspective, these provisions have also been considered as a way of linking moral or ethical behavior with endorsement opportunities. They are seen as tools that assist in promoting a sports ethical atmosphere, maintaining the image of the industry and controlling player behavior.

[33] See Noah B. Kressler, "Using the Morals Clause in Talent Agreements: A Historical, Legal and Practical Guide" (2005) 29 Colum JL & Arts 235; and J. Haskell Murray, "Morality Clauses and Escrow Accounts in Sports Contracts" (2017) 17 Va Sports & Ent LJ 119.

[34] The evolution of the use of these provisions in different industries and contexts is covered in Kira N. Buono, "Athletes Sacked by Moral Turpitude Clauses: Presumed Guilty Unless Proven Innocent" (2015) 41 New Eng J Crim & Civ Confinement 367.

[35] For an example of the application of morality clauses in college sport, see Adam Epstein, "Moral Clauses and UofL Head Basketball Coach Rick Pitino: Extension and Extortion" (2019) 30 Marq Sport L Rev 1, at 130.

[36] Char Pagar, "Athletes, Scandals and Sponsorships: Why Morals Clauses Are More Important than Ever," VLP Law Group (2016), 6, available at: www.vlplawgroup.com/blog/athletes-scandals-sponsorships-morals-clauses-important-ever/.

their use is also common in Continental Europe and gradually they have spread to the entire world.[37]

In terms of drafting, they are usually the product of negotiation as parties may adopt different positions depending on their power. Obviously, the negotiating power of a great champion or a well-known company is considerably greater than that of a young talent or a start-up. In these unequal bargaining scenarios, it is crucial that morality clauses should be drafted with a view to ensuring that both parties are protected, lest they may be deemed unenforceable on a variety of grounds. There is a crucial controversy on this issue as some authors recommend that these provisions should be very precise in the description of what the athlete must not do.[38] However, in terms of the wording of the terms of morality clauses, endorsers propagate a broad view to cover as many types of behavior and circumstances as possible. This is obviously not always fair to the athlete, who may be unaware that private behavior in his or her personal life could lead to the termination of a sponsorship agreement. Therefore, the scope of the clause may vary depending on the interests of each party. Companies usually tend to prefer broad clauses that include as many situations or types of behavior as possible, whereas players are more inclined to advocate for narrower clauses or those that include a precise description of each behavior sought.

In terms of the negotiation process, a fair recommendation would be for athletes and endorsement companies to agree on concrete and clear terms as related to the application of this clause. It is crucial that the wording is precise for the athlete to understand the conduct expected, the violation of which will result in termination of the contract. If this is not the case, everyone will be unsatisfied: the athlete, the endorser and the fans.[39] From a practical perspective, and as this is related to the social media context, before any public statement, whether a tweet, post or message, the parties should carefully consider its possible implications

---

[37] These provisions are common practice not only due to the relevance of professional sport in these countries, but also because of the importance of college sport. Nowadays, they are used in countries such as the United Kingdom, Italy, Spain, China, India, Taiwan and even Kenya, to name a few.

[38] See Caysee Kamenetsky, "The Need for Strict Morality Clauses in Endorsement Contracts" (2017) 7 Pace IP Sports & Ent LF 289, for one approach; and Stephen M. Gallagher, "Who's Really 'Winning'? The Tension of Morals Clauses in Film and Television" (2016) 16 Va Sports & Ent LJ 88, for the other.

[39] For a list of possible behaviors that could be included in an exhaustive clause, see Tushar Katheria, "Importance of Moral Clause in Sports Contracts" (2020) 3 Int JL Manag Human 2025.

considering the mutual contractual obligations and the morality clauses included in their endorsement agreements.

Should morality clauses encompass private behavior of the endorsed player or only that related to the sport? This is an often-debated issue. Sponsors will tend to include all behavior no matter where it occurs. Sponsored players will look to avoid intrusion into their private lives and limit the agreed behavior to that taking place on or off the field, but directly related to their sport.[40] It is suggested that in drafting morality clauses the parties should consider the athlete's personality as well as the company's culture and brand image, among other relevant factors.

One of the most relevant controversies related to the use of morality clauses is the definition of morality itself. It is widely accepted that the evolution over time of moral standards is an obvious fact as those behaviors that were considered unacceptable a few decades ago are viewed as perfectly acceptable today. Some of these behaviors include conduct viewed as reprehensible in the past, such as sexual orientation, political beliefs and others.[41]

Another interesting facet concerning the application of morality provisions arises where it is the sponsoring company, and not the player, that engages in conduct that, in the views of the sponsored player, is unacceptable to its interest. In this case, the nature of the organization's behavior can negatively affect the image of the player, such that it can lead to a considerable loss of reputation. Such clauses, where they exist, are known as "reverse" moral clauses.[42]

A crucial question is when and how to use morality provisions. It has been suggested that they be used with caution and following a careful, balanced and thorough assessment of whether the nature of the behavior is so damaging to the reputation of the harmed party that maintaining the agreement would be more disadvantageous than termination. In this case, to avoid ambiguity, it has also been indicated that these provisions should not only include the typology of the prohibited behavior that

---

[40] Steve Nwabwueze, "Morals Clauses in Professional Player Contracts: Their Uses and Limitations," Sportsbarng (2024).

[41] See Eleni Polymenopoulou, *Artistic Freedom in International Law* (Cambridge University Press, 2023), 161.

[42] One of the most interesting articles is that of Taylor Porcher, Fernando M. Pinguelo and Timothy D. Cedrone, "The Reverse-Morals Clause: The Unique Way to Save Talent's Reputation and Money in a New Era of Corporate Crimes and Scandals" (2010) 28 Cardozo Arts & Ent LJ 65.

would trigger the clause, but also the circumstances in which the resolution can be legitimately used.[43]

The possibility of using other alternatives to morality clauses has also created a considerable debate as there may be preferable options to the unilateral termination of the agreement.[44] As mentioned above, provisions related to fines, sanctions, activities or community service, as well as options offering financial incentives for good behavior, are common in some contracts, so that appropriate conduct is duly rewarded.

4 The Application of Moral Clauses in Tennis: The Impact of Social Media and the Digital World

These challenging circumstances are not new in tennis. In the early periods of the game, great champions were involved in situations considered ethically inappropriate by society at that time.[45] Research has also explored the period of the so-called "bad boys" of tennis, an era in which unsportsmanlike behavior on court attracted the attention of fans and tabloids.[46] The endorsement agreements of some famous tennis players were also affected by their activism, as was the case with Arthur Ashe, who advocated for civil rights during the 1960s and 1970s. Billie Jean King also threatened to boycott the US Open if equal pay was not offered to all players.[47] Other personal orientations equally affected the

---

[43] For a consideration related to the use of these provisions in the social media context, see Rick G. Morris, "Media Moguls Risking It All: Contract Clauses in the Entertainment Business in the Age of #MeToo" (2019) 9 Ariz St U Sports & Ent LJ 1.

[44] For a social media perspective, see Annamarie White Carty, "Cancelled: Morality Clauses in an Influencer Era" (2022) 26 Lewis & Clark L Rev 565.

[45] See on this John Carvalho and Mike Milford, "'One Knows that This Condition Exists': An Analysis of Tennis Champion Bill Tilden's Apology for His Homosexuality" (2013) 33 Sport Hist 554. Also "Bill Tilden: A U.S. Tennis Hero, But with a Morals Clause," Tennis.com (April 28, 2016), available at: www.tennis.com/news/articles/bill-tilden-a-u-s-tennis-hero-but-with-a-morals-clause. See also Nathan Titman, "Making Work Out of Play: The Troubling Gender Performances of Bill Tilden" in Lake, *Routledge Handbook of Tennis*, 96.

[46] Robert J. Lake, "The 'Bad Boys' of Tennis: Shifting Gender and Social Class Relations in the Era of Nastase, Connors, and McEnroe" (2015) 42 J Sport Hist 179.

[47] See on this Sarah Brown and Natasha Brison, "More than an Athlete Constitutional and Contractual Analysis of Activism in Professional Sports" (2017) 7 Ariz St U Sports & Ent LJ 249. Also, a broad perspective is provided in Sungho Cho, "Termination of Athlete Endorsement Contract under Morals Clause: Event Study Analysis of Social Activism and Incidents of Moral Turpitude," Sports Litigation Alert (April 8, 2022), available at: https://sportslitigationalert.com/termination-of-athlete-endorsement-contract-under-morals-clause-event-study-analysis-of-social-activism-and-incidents-of-moral-turpitude/.

sponsorship contracts of tennis players, particularly in the 1980s and 1990s, whereby sponsors of certain female tennis champions terminated their agreements because of their sexual orientation. These sponsors added a clause that specifically referred to any behavior that could bring the company or the game into disrepute or otherwise stir or cause a negative public image.[48]

In 1981, some sponsors of the great champion Billie Jean King terminated their endorsement agreements, approximately up to $2 million, when the alimony suit filed by the player's partner became public.[49] Similarly, in 1981, Martina Navratilova's sponsorship deals were unilaterally terminated when she openly declared being gay, following which she was unable to sign any new sponsorship agreement. She felt that one of the main reasons that endorsement companies refused to sign sponsorship agreements with her was on account of her sexual orientation.[50] The case of Nick Kyrgios was one where morality clauses could have been used. According to one of his sponsors, namely, the underwear brand Bonds, which also sponsored former Australian World No. 1 Pat Rafter, Kyrgios's borderline permissible behavior was the main cause for its unilateral termination.[51]

One example among the various criteria used in the application of morality clauses in endorsement agreements of top tennis players is that of Maria Sharapova. At a press conference held on March 7, 2016, the player revealed that following a doping test conducted after losing at the Australian Open in January, she had tested positive for the substance meldonium. In 2016, the World Anti-Doping Agency (WADA) placed this substance on its banned list because it was considered as a performance-enhancing drug. She claimed full responsibility for her actions, but indicated that she had not realized the substance was illegal

---

[48] Mariah Burton Nelson's *Are We Winning Yet? How Women Are Changing Sports and Sports Are Changing Women* (Random House, 1991) states that athletes who had those sexual preferences were forced to hide them to protect their earnings.

[49] On this, see Stan Grossfeld, "No Royalty Like King: NU Honor Is Just Latest for True Tennis Pioneer," *Boston Globe* (December 3, 2006), 1.

[50] Adidas announced the inclusion of a clause in its sponsorship contract with athletes stating that publicly declaring themselves to be gay or lesbian would not constitute grounds for termination of the contract. See Bruce Browning, "Adidas Encourages Star Athletes to Come Out," *Advocate* (February 15, 2021), 1.

[51] Lorenzo Ciotti, "Nick Kyrgios Dumped by Brand Sponsor," Tennis World USA (August 15, 2015), 1, reports that the company's head of sponsorship said that "immediately after Wimbledon 2014, we signed the contract, but the agreement was for three months, so it is no longer in effect since last October."

and she had taken it throughout her career.[52] The ITF informed Sharapova of the positive test on March 2 and provisionally suspended her from March 12. Porsche, Nike and Tag Heuer terminated their endorsement agreements with the player as soon as she announced she had tested positive. Despite the player's admission of the positive test, the manufacturer of her racquet, Head, however, communicated it was looking to extend their agreement with the Russian Federation.[53] Later on, Nike's head of marketing left the door open for Sharapova.[54] Sharapova was also suspended from her position as a goodwill ambassador for the UN Development Programme (UNDP), which she had assumed since 2007. This foundation works to promote education in areas affected by the 1986 Chernobyl disaster. In November 2016, the UNDP overturned the player's suspension five months before the end of her doping ban.

The Australian player Bernard Tomic was involved in two situations related to morality clauses arising from his endorsement contracts. In 2014, it was reported that IMG, the international talent management company, which was in charge of ensuring sponsorship agreements since he was 12, terminated its contract with him before it was due to expire, mostly on the ground of allegations concerning inappropriate on-court behavior.[55] Years later, his racquet sponsor Head decided to unilaterally terminate his contract following the player's statement after losing at the 2017 Wimbledon event, where he said: "It's a rollercoaster and I can't find the commitment to work hard, enjoy myself and win trophies. It's definitely a mental problem, I wasn't mentally and physically on the court to perform. I don't know why, but I felt a bit bored on the court to be

---

[52] On Sharapova's earnings during 2015 and her sponsorship contracts, see "Sponsors Act after Maria Sharapova's Failed Drug Test," Sky Sports (March 8, 2016), 1.

[53] For statements by Nike, which had been Sharapova's sponsor since she was 11 years old, see Michael Shields, "Swiss Watch Brand TAG Heuer Won't Renew Contract with Sharapova," Reuters (March 15, 2016), 2.

[54] Emma Thomasson, "Nike Brand Chief Leaves Door Open to Sharapova after Doping Scandal," Reuters (March 17, 2016), 1, in an interview with Trevor Edwards, Nike's head of marketing: "Whenever these situations happen, we are saddened and disappointed. At the same time, there are many athletes who inspire us. At the end of the day, athletes are human beings just like the rest of us, and they have the same weaknesses that the rest of us have, and sometimes those situations become teaching opportunities."

[55] See Associated Press, "Cut Loose: Talent Agency Severs Ties with Tennis Bad Boy Bernard Tomic Due to His Off Court Behaviour ... before His Contract Had Even Expired," Daily Mail Online (July 15, 2014), available at: www.dailymail.co.uk/news/article-2692453/Talent-agency-severs-ties-tennis-player-Bernard-Tomic.html.

completely honest."[56] Other recent cases include that of Illie Nastase, which has already been mentioned (see note 24), and those of Justin Gimelstob, Dan Evans and Simona Halep, which are related to doping offenses.

The relationship between morality clauses, social media and the digital world is explained by the globalization of the game and its sponsorship, and the fact that tennis as a mass phenomenon transcends borders and cultures.[57] Social networks are an invaluable tool to foster endorsement alliances and impact consumer trends. The fact that the new social media platforms allow the sharing of content immediately and globally has tremendous advantages to facilitate this process. The dangers are also obvious, as the use by endorsed players of platforms such as Instagram, Facebook, Tik Tok or Snapchat may not always be appropriate.[58] In this sense, social media platforms are a double-edged sword as any statement made in social media may bring about both expressions of support or dismay in equal force. Regarding the application of morality clauses in situations where endorsed athletes post or tweet on social media, it has been suggested that, before impulsively invoking a morality clause, endorsement companies should analyze the situation carefully and critically assess whether such action or conduct is actually covered by the clause.[59] A hasty termination of the sponsorship contract may be problematic for the sponsor in case the other party seeks judicial determination, in addition to attracting media attention that may be unwanted.

5 Examples of Morality Clauses in Tennis Endorsement Agreements

This section will present several examples of morality clauses included in tennis sponsorship contracts. It is important to emphasize that as the nature of these agreements is confidential, it is considerably difficult to

---

[56] For more details on the sponsor's comments, see Simon Evans, "Sponsor Head Drops Tomic after 'Bored' Comments," Reuters (July 6, 2017), 1.
[57] See James J. Zhang and Brenda G. Pitts (eds), *Globalized Sport Management in Diverse Cultural Contexts* (Routledge, 2019).
[58] For a specific reference to social networks, see Miguel Crespo and Andrés Crespo Dualde, "Las Cláusulas de Moralidad en Contratos de Patrocinio Deportivo y Las Redes Sociales" in *Cuestiones de Derecho del Deporte: Libro Homenaje al Profesor Gabriel Real Ferrer* (Reus, 2023), 161.
[59] See Sungho Cho, "Termination of Athlete Endorsement Contract under Morals Clause: Event Study Analysis of Social Activism and Incidents of Moral Turpitude" (2022) 23 Legal Issues in Collegiate Athletics 1.

access these or obtain credible direct information concerning the specific content of these clauses. Therefore, the examples provided hereinafter should be considered as draft templates. In the following contract between a sponsoring company and a professional tennis player, explicit reference is made to the statements that the sponsored player may not make:

> 8. Public Exposure. Image Consultant.
>> 8.1. The player shall at all times, both in his public activities and in his private life, maintain decorum in accordance with his activity, avoiding at all times any act or omission that could directly or indirectly cause damage to his public image. To this end, the player shall lead a lifestyle consistent with the professional practice of tennis, and shall refrain from attending inappropriate places, frequenting unsuitable persons, or maintaining any kind of relationship with those who could hinder his or her professional career.
>> 8.2. The player shall refrain from making public statements or representations that reflect a religious, racial, sexual, or political preference unless authorised in writing by . . .

The following example includes a morality clause in the termination section of the sponsorship contract between a professional tennis player and a sports equipment sponsoring company, with special mention of actions that the player cannot take, as this would be detrimental to the sponsor.

> N. Termination
>
> The Company shall have the right to terminate this contract immediately upon written notice to the Athlete and without prejudice to any other rights the Company may have at law or in equity, if: (i) the Athlete fails to comply with its obligations specifically but not only, in conjunction with Sections E – "Company Products", 2 / – and J – "Use of Products"; (ii) the Athlete commits any act which is known to the media and which adversely affects the Company's brand (including being charged with any criminal offence, testing positive in an ITF doping control test or failing to be admitted to a substance abuse treatment programme); (iii) the Athlete carries out any act which is known to the media and which adversely affects the Company's brand (including being charged with any criminal offence, testing positive in an ITF doping control test or failing to be admitted to a substance abuse treatment programme); (iii) the Athlete takes any action that is inconsistent with his or her recommendation and advertising of the Company's products and/or disparages the Company's brands, or does not advise the use of the Company's products; (iv) the Athlete obscures, removes or covers any

4 MORALITY CLAUSES IN TENNIS AGREEMENTS 85

Company product logos in any manner; (v) the Athlete ceases, for any reason, to be a professional tennis player for a period of ninety (90) consecutive days or more during the contract period; or (vi) the Athlete is unable, for any reason, to use the Company's products in accordance with this contract and in particular fails to use the Company's products during the entire course of matches and at other competitions and/or exhibitions as required under this contract. The parties agree that in the event that the Company terminates this contract pursuant to this paragraph, the Athlete shall not be entitled to receive any pro-rata compensation for services rendered and rights granted prior to the effective date of termination without prejudice to the possibility of the Company suing the Athlete for compensation.[60]

The following is an example of a morality clause in a sponsorship contract between a sports federation and a professional athlete where the provision appears in the declarations and commitments section, which is of rather new import. It reads as follows:

5. Representations and Undertakings

   5.1 [The sponsored athlete] represents and undertakes that it:

   (a) will comply throughout the Term with all reasonable instructions of the [Federation] in relation to its obligations under clause 3 above; ...
   (c) is and will remain throughout the Term in good standing with his National Federation (except to the extent approved in writing by the [Federation]);
   (d) shall not, during or after the term [of the contract], do or say anything which is, in the reasonable opinion of ... or could be seen to be negative, disparaging, or derogatory about the [Federation] or unbecoming of a professional tennis player.[61]

Advertising sponsorship of sporting events is also a modality in which morality clauses can be included. The following is an example of a morality clause between a sponsor and a tennis tournament whereby the tournament is prevented from contracting with other sponsors

---

[60] This example is characterized by the great precision in the enumeration of the conduct that is considered a cause for termination of the contract under this clause. In fact, the conduct of concealing, removing or covering any logos on the company's products in any way, a practice that sometimes occurs in professional tennis, is striking.

[61] In this example, the ambiguity of the last section of the clause should be noted, as it does not define what is meant by appropriate representations to the professional tennis player. Furthermore, it prohibits representations after the end of the contractual relationship.

who have not only a similar activity to that of the sponsor in question, but also activities related to aspects that the sponsor might consider immoral:

> (4) the organiser shall inform the sponsor of the identity of all potential secondary sponsors / suppliers of the tournament at least ten (10) working days before it enters into agreements with such third parties and confirm that it will not appoint as tournament sponsors organizations whose main activity is:
>
>> (i) tobacco, gambling (lotteries, betting, or similar activities) or pornography; and / or
>> (ii) any other activities, products, or services which, in the reasonable opinion of the sponsor, are not in keeping with the tournament or a healthy lifestyle.[62]

6 Conclusion

From its origins and first application in the Hollywood film industry of the 1920s to its adoption in the sports industry today, morality clauses in sponsorship agreements have been utilized as an instrument to help the parties in the event of an undesired circumstance. The increasing presence of social networks in today's world and the fact that the lives of tennis players are under constant scrutiny by the public and fans provide greater relevance to the inclusion of morality clauses in sports sponsorship contracts.

These provisions have not been free from criticism as their use has been considered objectionable, unenforceable and ambiguous. The fact that the term "morality" is dynamic and changes according to the evolution of society means that the application of these provisions is clearly complex. This is in contrast to many cases where the courts have repeatedly held that contract termination based on morality clauses is enforceable and valid.[63] Recent calls have been made for an increase in the

---

[62] In this example, it is worth noting the reference to the concept of "healthy lifestyle," an expression that lends itself to countless interpretations.
[63] For the United States, see David E. Fink and Sarah E. Diamond, "Morality Clauses in the Age of #MeToo and Time's Up" (2018) 34 Comm Law 2, at 4. In the case of Spain, see Miguel Crespo, "Las Cláusulas de Moralidad en Contratos de Patrocinio Deportivo: A Propósito de la Sentencia de la Audiencia Provincial de Alicante 901/2008, de 30 de Diciembre" in *Estudios sobre el Deporte Federado en la Comunitat Valenciana: (Regulación y Resolución de Conflictos)* (Reus, 2020).

precision of the drafting of these provisions to clarify the scope of their application for the benefit of both parties.[64]

In this connected world in which news travels from one part of the world to another immediately and instantaneously, the role of these clauses in regulating how endorsement companies and players balance their interests may be crucial. In a changing context, characterized by uncertainty and immediacy, the only way in which morality clauses can remain useful to the parties is by adapting to the era of the Internet and social networks.

---

[64] See Rohit Krishna, "The Need to Reset Morality Clauses in Athlete Contracts" (2021) 2 Glob Sports Pol Rev 70.

5

Restraint of Trade in Professional Tennis

ILIAS BANTEKAS

1 Introduction

As will be shown, restraint of trade effectively prohibits a person from exercising their chosen profession or trade and hence of making a livelihood. Such restraint is achieved by means of a contract entered into by the restricted person and which while freely entered into achieves this undesirable outcome. In the field of sport, young athletes often enter into contracts that bind them to work for a particular team, agent or other entity in a manner that is unconscionable and where the athlete is unable to break free, lest he or she is in breach of its contractual obligations. This chapter will focus more on agency contracts and at the end it will consider whether bans or penalties imposed by the International Tennis Federation (ITF), Association of Tennis Professionals (ATP) and Women's Tennis Association (WTA) equally constitute unconscionable restraints of trade.

There is good reason why this chapter sets out to examine restraint of trade for professional tennis players from the lens of English common law. Article 33(d) of the ITF Constitution stipulates that where the ITF is a party to a dispute it is agreed in advance that the governing law of the pertinent agreement is English law and unless otherwise agreed by the ITF the dispute will be entertained in London. This is consistent with transnational practice which suggests that parties typically subject transnational commercial disputes to English law.[1] Moreover, the ATP headquarters are in London and by extension all pertinent contracts are chiefly governed by English law. In addition, a good number of tennis representation agencies are premised in England, and it is only natural that their agency agreements be governed by English law. English law is equally central to the ITF's Independent

---

[1] See Ilias Bantekas, 'The Globalization of English Contract Law: Three Salient Illustrations' (2021) 137 LQR 130 (exemplifying the dominance of English contract law in sovereign finance agreements, Islamic finance contracts, as the substantive law of special economic zones, among others).

Tribunal. Under the ITF's Internal Adjudication Panel Rules, the Independent Tribunal is an arbitral tribunal, whose proceedings are governed by English law and subject to the English Arbitration Act.[2] This is equally reiterated by Article 1.3 of the Tribunal's own Procedural Rules. Finally, unless stated otherwise in the ITF's procedural rules or its Constitution, English courts possess exclusive jurisdiction over disputes arising out of proceedings before the ITF Independent Tribunal.[3] For all these reasons, English contract law, which is quintessentially the product of the common law (with little codification), is central to restraint of trade claims by professional tennis players.

2 Restraint of Trade in the English Common Law

The concept of restraint of trade originally developed in the English common law.[4] It is quintessentially a contractual remedy, which naturally requires the existence of a contractual relationship. Even so, the effects of the underlying restraint suggest that there is no reason why the remedy may not be invoked in circumstances lacking a clear contractual relationship. In such cases, it must be clearly shown that the restraint is effectively imposed, as is the case with the decisions of sports governing bodies, such as the ITF, on the capacity of athletes to pursue a professional career. The remedy emerged in relation to professions predicated on contract and was subsequently applied to the field of sport. To a large decree, this and associated remedies have been justified on the basis of public policy.[5] In the common law scholarship and English case law, restraint of trade has been classified within the remit of illegality.[6]

Its underlying rationale is that any action, whether contractual or not, that restricts a person's trade is unenforceable and hence void, unless

---

[2] ITF Constitution 2022, Arts 7.3 and 7.4; this is also reiterated in Art. I.E.5 of the Men's World Tour Regulations, which emphasises that any dispute arising 'out of or in connection' with the Regulations, including also non-contractual claims, shall be governed and construed in accordance with English law, to the exclusion of English private international law.

[3] Procedural Rules Governing Proceedings before an Independent Tribunal Convened under ITF Rules (2019), Arts 1.3 and 7.5; International Tennis Integrity Agency (ITIA), Procedural Rules Governing TADP Proceedings Before an Independent Tribunal (2022), Art. 1.3.

[4] See Stephen A. Smith, 'Reconstructing Restraint of Trade' (1995) 15 Oxford J Leg Stud 566; equally, the classic treatise by Michal Jefferson, *Restraint of Trade* (John Wiley & Sons, 1996).

[5] *Enderby Town FC Ltd* v. *Football Association Ltd* [1971] Ch 591, at 606.

[6] See Jack Beatson, Andrew Burrows and John Cartwright, *Anson's Law of Contract*, 30th edn (Oxford University Press, 2016), ch. 11.

such restriction may otherwise be justified.⁷ The concept of 'trade' is broad, encompassing any activity or opportunity to earn a living. It has been defined as an agreement 'in which a party agrees with any other party to restrict his liberty in the future to carry on trade with other persons not parties to the contract in such manner as he chooses'.⁸ No doubt, not all agreements that exhibit some restraint fall under the remit of this remedy. Two types of agreements have been recognised as giving rise to restraint of trade, namely: those between employer and employee; and seller (of a business) and buyer, whereby the employee and buyer are prevented from any action that competes with that of the employer or seller. The question, however, remains that since some restraint is permissible, how does one definitively conclude which restrains are unenforceable? English courts have made it clear that the boundaries are fluid,⁹ and that in any event the restraint cannot violate competition rules in force,¹⁰ and in principle courts will seek to protect the weaker party against oppression and abusive terms.¹¹

In general, a restraint is deemed enforceable unless: (1) it is unreasonable in the interests of the parties; (2) it is unreasonable in the interests of the public. As regards (1), several factors are relevant in assessing reasonableness. Contracts that restrict one's economic freedom over a long period of time, especially where the employee's professional career is relatively short, have been held to be unnecessary and oppressive.¹² Even so, a contract that otherwise restricts a party's economic freedom, but which is counterbalanced by other benefits that would adequately address the shortfall from the restriction, is enforceable because of the special

---

⁷ See Prince Saprai, *Contract Law without Foundations: Toward a Republican Theory of Contract Law* (Oxford University Press, 2019), 214, arguing that in the republican worldview of contract law, freedom resides not in the absence of interference per se, but in the absence of arbitrary interference or dominium by others. This situates restraint of trade in the republican camp.
⁸ *Petrofina (Great Britain) Ltd* v. *Martin* [1966] Ch 146, at 180 as per Diplock LJ.
⁹ *Proactive Sports Management Ltd* v. *Rooney* [2011] EWCA Civ 1444.
¹⁰ *Texaco Ltd* v. *Mulberry Filling Station Ltd* [1972] 1 WLR 814, at 827. In the sports law context, anti-competitive practices, particularly monopolies by domestic and international sports federations, are not necessarily addressed as restraint of trade, although there is no good reason why they cannot. See Katarina Pijetlovic, 'EU Competition Law and Organisational Rules in Sports' in Antoine Duval and Ben Van Rompuy (eds), *The Legacy of Bosman: Re-visiting the Relationship between EU Law and Sport* (Asser Press, 2016), 117.
¹¹ *Schroeder Music Publishing Co. Ltd* v. *Macaulay* [1974] 1 WLR 1308, at 1315 as per Diplock LJ.
¹² *Instone* v. *Schroeder Music Publishing Co. Ltd* [1974] 1 WLR 1308, per Reid LJ, holding that a ten-year exclusive recording contract was an unreasonable restraint of trade.

justifying circumstances.[13] Hence, the context, including the factual circumstances, the aim sought to be achieved, as well as any counterbalances to the restraint are crucial to judicial determination of the enforceability of the contract or the particular provision thereto.[14] In employer–employee relationships, apart from oppressive long-duration contracts lacking counterbalances, the legitimate interests of the parties are fewer as compared to contractual restraints among businesses.[15] As a result, save for restraints concerned with imparting trade secrets and influence over existing customers and clients,[16] it is generally unreasonable for the parties to be restrained from using skills acquired in their previous employment, or from competing in any way with their previous employer.

The second criterion that justifies the non-enforcement of a contract is its lack of reasonableness 'in the interests of the public'. In *Proactive Sports Management* v. *Rooney*, Arden LJ explained the public's interest as follows: 'Public policy is concerned with the manner in which a person may properly realize his potential, not only for the good of that individual but for the economic benefit of society generally.'[17] Although in the early part of the twentieth century, the likelihood of restraints deemed unreasonable in the public interest were viewed as extremely rare occurrences,[18] this view is no longer accepted. The case law has paid particular attention to agreements between experienced commercial actors who, while capable of deciding what restraints are reasonable in their own interests, pay scant attention to the detrimental effect of the restraint on the public interest as such.[19] This is not to say that the courts have not taken a cautious approach to the public interest test when assessing restraints between parties with similar bargaining power.[20] In a recent UK Supreme Court case, a nine-judge panel majority ruled that 'the public interest is best served by a principled and transparent assessment of the considerations identified, rather [than by] the

---

[13] *Nordenfelt* v. *Maxim Nordenfelt Guns and Ammunition Co. Ltd* [1894] AC 535; for 'special justifying circumstances', see also *Mason* v. *Provident Clothing & Supply Co. Ltd* [1913] AC 724.
[14] *Clarke* v. *Newland* [1991] 1 All ER 397.
[15] *Herbert Morris Ltd* v. *Saxelby* [1916] 1 AC 688, at 713. See also the UK Supreme Court in *Peninsula Securities Ltd* v. *Dunnes Stores (Bangor) Ltd* [2020] 3 WLR 521, discussed in more detail below.
[16] *Faccenda Chicken Ltd* v. *Fowler* [1987] Ch 117, at 137.
[17] At para. 93.
[18] *A-G of Commonwealth of Australia* v. *Adelaide Steamship Co.* [1913] AC 781, at 795.
[19] *Dickson* v. *Pharmaceutical Society of Great Britain* [1970] AC 403; *Alec Lobb (Garages) Ltd* v. *Total Oil (Great Britain) Ltd* [1985] 1 WLR 173, at 191.
[20] Especially, *Texaco Ltd* v. *Mulberry Filling Station Ltd* [1972] 1 WLR 814, at 826–9, per Ungoed-Thomas J.

application of a formal approach capable of producing results which may appear arbitrary, unjust or disproportionate'.[21] This test has been applied in other contractual situations and represents good law.[22]

3   Restraint of Trade in the Sports Context

The following sub-sections endeavour to contextualise the application of the common law doctrine of restraint of trade to sporting activities more generally.[23] This analysis will set the stage for the final section, where the application of the doctrine to professional tennis will become more apparent, despite the existence of a small amount of past precedent.

3.1   Restraints Arising from National Federations and State Regulation

Sports governing bodies (SGBs) have developed internal rules that govern their relationship with their corporate members, namely, clubs that are parties to a national league/federation, as well as with tournament organisers. In some instances, as is the case with professional tennis, these internal rules govern the relationship between the federation and players. It is not rare for such internal rules to impose restraints on what their members/signatories can and cannot do. Many of these restraints, although otherwise incompatible with competition law, are justified under national and regional anti-competition rules for a number of public interest objectives, namely: in order to maintain the integrity and stability of national and international sporting competitions; to reinforce the sport's commercial and cultural viability; to encourage youth development and promote the sport's competitive balance; and to protect national teams. Even so, drawing a sensible balance is not always easy and restraint of trade claims have been raised by players in an

---

[21] *Patel* v. *Mirza* [2016] UKSC 42, per Lord Toulson, at para. 120.
[22] See *Cavendish Square Holding BV* v. *Makdessi* [2016] AC 1172, especially para. 7 as per Lords Neuberger, Sumption and Carnwath, concerning an equitable approach to contractual penalties.
[23] There is little doubt that the bargaining disparity in sports contracts between athletes and federations/clubs/managers is also a human rights issue and claims of this nature have reached the European Court of Human Rights. This dimension is beyond the narrow purview of this chapter. See Katarina Pijetlovic, 'Fundamental Rights of Athletes in the EU Post-Lisbon' in Tanel Kerikmäe (ed.), *Protecting Human Rights in the EU: Controversies and Challenges of the Charter of Fundamental Rights* (Springer, 2013).

individual capacity and by clubs.[24] Often, the internal rule posited by a federation against its members is the result of domestic law. This notwithstanding, the interplay of interests involved in such rules, irrespective of their origin, may well motivate the club, the national team or other entity to impose an unnecessary, unfair and undue restraint of trade on athletes.

The leading case in English sports law is *Eastham v. Newcastle United Football Club Ltd.* During the 1960s, according to the rules of the Football Association (FA) which were framed in a contract with FA-registered clubs, a player could be 'retained' by his club at the end of the season, even without a new contract. During such retention the player was not allowed to sign for any other club willing to offer him a contract. Clearly, this rule was in the interest of clubs and could be applied in a manner that effectively prevented a player from earning a living from the sport. The player moved for a declaration against the club and the Association that the system of retention was invalid because it restrained players' freedom of employment. The Chancery Division of the High Court and Wilberforce J in particular accepted that while some restriction was essential for the proper administration of professional football in England, the restriction imposed by the rules was far too disproportionate on liberty of employment.[25] In *Greig v. Insole*, the International Cricket Conference and the English Test and Country Cricket Board had issued resolutions disqualifying players from test and country matches if they had competed in games or tournaments organised by a private promoter. Greig was banned after signing a contract to play in the World Cricket series, which was at the time a lucrative event for cricket players who earn their living during the English summertime. The Chancery Division of the High Court and Slade J, in particular, held that such a restriction constituted an unreasonable restraint of trade.[26] English courts have generally taken the position that restraints unjustified by any professional or public interest

---

[24] In *Stevenage Borough Football Club v. Football League Ltd* (1996) 9 Admin LR 109, a club that had won its respective league and was thus entitled to promotion to a higher league was refused because among others its ground did not satisfy the requirements for that higher league (6,000-seat stadium). The club argued that the timeframe to augment size capacity was far too short. The Court held that although the timeframe was indeed short, all clubs had knowledge of the criteria from the beginning of the season and had time to make the necessary adjustments.

[25] *Eastham v. Newcastle United Football Club Ltd* [1964] Ch 413, at 432; equally *Buckley v. Tutty* (1971) 45 ALJR 23.

[26] *Greig v. Insole* [1978] 1 WLR 302.

imposed by sporting entities are unenforceable, as was the case with the Jockey Club's prohibition of trainer licences to women.[27]

In a similar manner, the International Skating Union (ISU) foresaw the danger to its own financial interests from rival skating organisers trying to 'poach' its athletes by offering them more lucrative participation deals. It subsequently proceeded to issue Communication No. 1974, titled 'Open International Competitions',[28] which demanded advance authorisation for the organisation of a competing event, as well as participation therein (so-called 'prior authorisation rules'). The EU Commission had no problem seeing the obvious incompatibility of the ISU Communication with fundamental tenets of EU competition law, chiefly Article 101 of the Treaty on the Functioning of the European Union (TFEU).[29] This was followed suit by the General Court, which came to the same conclusion regarding the ISU's eligibility rules.[30] Although the General Court did not rely on restraint of trade, it emphasised that SGBs are free to safeguard their legitimate interests, but any rule they promulgate must not deprive members or non-members from access to the same market, especially where the market in question generates profit.[31]

3.2 Restraints Arising from Players' Contracts with Agents

Restraints arising from agreements between agents and players are not uncommon.[32] Depending on the subject matter of the agreement, they concern two issues. The first relates to royalties from direct sports earnings, while the second revolves around royalties from image rights.

---

[27] *Nagle v. Feilden* [1966] 2 QB 633.

[28] Communication No. 1974 is available at: https://insightplus.bakermckenzie.com/bm/attachment_dw.action?attkey=FRbANEucS95NMLRN47z%2BeeOgEFCt8EGQJsWJiCH2WAWuU9AaVDeFgq9gxTxSJepG&nav=FRbANEucS95NMLRN47z%2BeeOgEFCt8EGQbuwypnpZjc4%3D&attdocparam=pB7HEsg%2FZ312Bk8OIuOIH1c%2BY4beLEAeOus5uxTYXe0%3D&fromContentView=1.

[29] EU Commission, *International Skating Union's Eligibility Rules*, Case AT-40208, available at: https://ec.europa.eu/competition/antitrust/cases/dec_docs/40208/40208_1579_5.pdf.

[30] *International Skating Union v. European Commission (ISU)*, Case T-93/18, ECLI:EU:T:2020:610, Judgment of 16 December 2020.

[31] Ibid., at para. 67. Iterated again in *International Skating Union v. European Commission*, Case C-124/21 P, EU:C:2023:1012, Judgment of 21 December 2023, available at: https://curia.europa.eu/juris/document/document.jsf?text=&docid=280763&pageIndex=0&doclang=en&mode=lst&dir=&occ=first&part=1&cid=8144980.

[32] See Robert Siekmann, Janwillem Soek, Richard Parrish et al., *Players' Agents Worldwide: Legal Aspects* (Asser Press, 2007).

English courts have drawn a further distinction between restraints imposed during the ordinary life cycle of the contract, which are subject to the criteria identified above, and those imposed post-termination of the contracts, which have been found to be unlawful.

In *Proactive Sports Management Ltd* v. *Rooney*, the 17-year-old football star had entered into an image rights representation agency agreement with a company called Stoneygate. The latter agreed to pay a 20 per cent commission to Proactive for the duration of its agreement with Rooney. When a few years later Rooney terminated its contract, the agent sued for breach of contract. The Court of Appeal found the particular terms of the agency agreement unenforceable on two grounds, namely: (1) Rooney at the time was a minor without the benefit of legal advice; (2) the duration of the contract was unduly long and certainly far beyond what was customary at the time. What is more interesting is the fact that the restraint was held to be questionable even though Rooney's image rights were not his primary trade; at the time he was a highly paid footballer and top of his game. Moreover, the Court of Appeal, while invalidating the image rights clause in Rooney's contract with Proactive, had no issue retaining the contract as a whole. It was never in doubt that Proactive provided significant services to Rooney, all of which led to lucrative deals.[33]

The most serious manifestation of restraint of trade concerns restrictions to the competitive life of professional athletes in a manner that not only prevents them from making a living from their 'trade', but most importantly because such restrictions negatively impact athletes' competitive edge and drive away their self-confidence. Athletes lacking these two qualities find it hard to get back to top form and ultimately this produces negative consequences on their game and their earnings. In this light, any agreement with an agent that effectively causes an athlete to forego significant part of his or her income without reasonable effort on behalf of an agent, or any action by which the agent can sideline an athlete because the latter refuses to honour an unreasonable commission, may constitute unnecessary and abusive restraints. In *Watson* v. *Praeger*, a professional boxer and his manager had entered a contract whose form was prescribed by the British Boxing Board of Control. The agency contract was subject to a term of three years, but was extendable for a further three-year term at the option of the agent, without the consent of the athlete. When the agent/manager exercised this option, the boxer

---

[33] *Proactive Sports Management Ltd* v. *Rooney* [2011] EWCA Civ 1444.

refused to concede that it was enforceable. Scott J agreed on the grounds that the contract was not the result of free negotiation by the parties, but had been proscribed by the governing body. He further considered that this restraint of trade could not be justified on the basis of the interests of the parties and the public.[34]

In the next section, we will examine the outcome in the *Zverev* case as a particular manifestation of contractual player–agent restraints in the field of professional tennis.

4   Trade Restraints in Professional Tennis

The types of trade restraints examined in the previous sections set out the groundwork for assessing whether they apply in the same or similar ways in the field of professional tennis. The application of the general principle is beyond doubt and common law courts would have little problem applying it. No doubt, the particularities of professional tennis and in fact the entire rationale of the concept of 'professional' play a significant role in ascertaining whether a restraint is justified and reasonable. Moreover, while the game is individual in nature, getting on the court in the first place is based on a complex contractual interplay between the ITF, players' associations, national tennis federations and tournament organisers. Even within this framework, the role of agents/managers is critical, because the vast majority of players will have progressed through the ranks of the game with the assistance of an agent or agent/manager. The following sub-sections explore the variety of contractual and regulatory contexts whereby restraints of trade can and usually do arise.

4.1   Restraints in Agency Agreements

The tennis-specific case that stands out is *Zverev v. Ace International Group Ltd*, despite the fact that the parties ultimately settled.[35] At the age of 15, Alexander Zverev entered into a representation agreement with the sports agency Ace. The term of the agreed representation was for a period of eleven years, albeit commission was payable for sixteen years, which meant that Zverev would effectively be shackled to his contract from the very beginning of his playing career until close to its end. It is crucial to note that Zverev's parents were fully engaged in the negotiations and

---

[34] *Watson v. Praeger* [1991] 1 WLR 726.
[35] *Zverev v. Ace Group International Ltd* [2020] EWHC 3513 (Ch).

agreed to act as guarantors thereof. Seven years into his contract, Zverev decided to leave Ace, which sued for breach of contract and made a claim against the player's parents. Zverev's legal team argued that the duration of the contract, coupled with its exclusive nature, was unreasonable and constituted a restraint of trade.[36] It is interesting to highlight here that like other sports-related trade restraint cases, Zverev did not argue that he suffered financial harm or that he could make more money through another agency; quite the contrary, Ace had worked hard to bring lucrative endorsements for Zverev. This is important to note because it provides a non-financial dimension to the restraint of trade doctrine, which in theory, at least, should invalidate any pertinent claim. If this non-financial dimension is viewed by the common law courts as an integral part of the doctrine, then the very concept of 'trade' is not only about making a living from one's sporting endeavours, but also about the right to choose those partners that instil confidence and trust in an athlete.

It is no wonder, therefore, that Ace centred its arguments not only on *pacta sunt servanta* (i.e. that contracts are enforceable), but that the agency had amassed a fortune for Zverev. In fact, Ace called in an expert who produced a comparative report of players' earnings and contract durations in order to demonstrate that Zverev's contract duration was hardly unusual in professional tennis and his earnings comparatively higher as compared to other players. The expert report was crucial in the progression of the trial, but parts of it were redacted, namely, players' names. The report was confidential and obviously unavailable, and when Zverev's legal team sought to lift the redacted parts,[37] Ace decided to drop its entire case and settle. The settlement suggests that Zverev's

---

[36] In *Instone v. Schroeder Music Publishing Co. Ltd* [1974] 1 WLR 1308, which involved a recording contract, the House of Lords made it clear that an exclusive contract over a long period of time is not in and by itself a restraint of trade. Lord Reid emphasised, however, that a ten-year exclusive contract was an unreasonable restraint of trade. He went on to note that: 'If contractual restrictions appear to be unnecessary or to be reasonably capable of enforcement in an oppressive manner, then they must be justified before they can be enforced.'

[37] For a large part of the professional legal community, the case stands out because of the order made by the Court to reveal the names of the players in the expert report. The application relied on Rules and Practice Direction, which are tantamount to the English Civil Procedure Rules, and particularly Practice Directive 51U.21.1(5), which allows a party at any time to request a copy of a document that was not disclosed in a party's original bundle, but which is nonetheless mentioned in an expert's report. Ace's legal team argued that the Court lacked authority under PD 51U.21.1(5) to force its expert to provide evidence in breach of confidentiality given to the players whose contracts were mentioned in the report.

contractual duration, as well as perhaps the age at which he entered into the contract, made it crystal clear to all the parties witnessing the expert report that the High Court could only come to the conclusion that the particular terms constituted a restraint of trade. This in turn demonstrates that there is a consensus in the sporting legal community that a contract of this duration, especially when entered into by a 15-year-old player, fails to provide the right to seek alternative choices. Moreover, it confirms what was suggested elsewhere in this section, that for athletes earning significant sums of money from tournament prizes and image rights, restraint of trade gives rise to altogether different issues as compared to professional athletes simply making a living from their sport. For top-earning tennis players such as Zverev, the prospect of a non-acrimonious relationship with an agent, the proximity of the agent to tennis rather than all sports and the availability of more choices (e.g. in branding) are perhaps more important than earning additional income.

While the Zverev proceedings were progressing, the UK Supreme Court had the opportunity to reshape the restraint of trade doctrine in *Peninsula Securities Ltd* v. *Dunnes Stores (Bangor) Ltd*.[38] A developer of a shopping centre granted a long (exclusive) lease encompassing part of the property to an anchor tenant. Under the terms of the lease, the tenant undertook not to set up a retail unit of a particular size that was commercially active in the trade of textiles or groceries. Several decades after the adoption of the lease, the tenant sought a declaration that the exclusion was unenforceable on the ground that it was an unjustified restraint of trade. In parting with the House of Lords' judgment in *Esso Petroleum Co. Ltd*,[39] the Supreme Court adopted the so-called 'trading society' test. According to this test, a term in an exclusive agreement will not engage the restraint of trade doctrine if the term in question 'passed into the accepted and normal currency of commercial or contractual or conveyancing relations' and which may therefore be taken to have 'assumed a form which satisfies the test of public policy'.[40] Although the judgment in *Peninsula Securities* is seemingly unrelated to professional sport, this is not the case. It will be recalled that the turning point in Zverev's claim was the comparator in the expert's report. If it were determined that it was 'normal currency' in tennis representation agreements for young athletes to sign long-term contracts in return for lucrative agreements, it is doubtful that the parties or the courts could reach an

---

[38] (2020) UKSC 36.
[39] *Esso Petroleum Co. Ltd* v. *Harper's Garage (Stoutport) Ltd* [1968] AC 269.
[40] *Peninsula Securities*, at paras 45–8.

outcome that the contract in question restrained Zverev's ability to apply his trade. It remains to be seen how in practice English courts will come to reconcile the trading society test with the non-financial interests inherent in restraint of trade claims brought by tennis players against their agents. The balance is a delicate one, but the *Zverev* outcome clearly demonstrates that it is 'normal currency of commercial or contractual' tennis relations for parties to value the player–agent relationship on grounds that are not exclusively financial.

4.2 Disciplinary Bans as Restraint of Trade?

English courts have not yet encountered claims whereby disciplinary bans imposed by clubs or sporting federations may amount to a restraint of trade. Indeed, the likelihood of such claims being upheld are slim, particularly since the grounds for disciplinary bans are limited and the steep sentences involved are justified in the public interest, as is the case with doping and illegal gambling.[41] Even so, the Appellate Chamber of the Court of Arbitration for Sport (CAS) in *Luis Suarez and Others* v. *FIFA* considered that the four-month ban from all football activities imposed on the FC Barcelona (at the time) star, although correct on merit, was disproportionate as to its outcome on the athlete. It held that 'the stadium ban and the prohibition to engage in "any football-related activity" was excessive in this case given the fact that such measures are not appropriate to sanction the fault committed by the player and that they would still have an impact on his activity beyond the end of the suspension'.[42] The rationale here is that a four-month ban from all football activities (including training with his team, playing in friendly games, etc.) imposed against a player at the top of his form meant that he could not be conditioned into his club once the ban expired and there was the danger that the player's overall form would deteriorate beyond repair.

In the tennis context, disciplinary bans are related to discreet offences set out in the ITF's Rules. The most common among these are corruption and doping offences. Article 6.1 of the Independent Tribunal's Procedural

---

[41] Several bans are for life, as in the case of Franco Feitt; see LTIA, 'Franco Feitt Banned from Tennis for Life' (13 April 2021), available at: https://itia.tennis/news/sanctions/franco-feitt-banned-from-tennis-for-life/; see equally lifetime bans for two Russian female players found guilty of match fixing; see LTIA, 'Two Russian Tennis Players Given Lifetime Bans' (27 January 2021), available at: www.itia.tennis/news/sanctions/two-russian-tennis-players-given-lifetime-bans/.

[42] *Luis Suarez* v. *FIFA*, CAS Appeals Award (14 August 2014), available at: www.tas-cas.org/fileadmin/user_upload/communique20medias2036652020_FR_1420082014.pdf.

Rules stipulates that 'facts may be established by any reliable means'.[43] The consistent practice of the CAS and other specialised sports tribunals, especially as regards doping and corruption, has created an elaborate body of evidentiary rules that have attained precedential value and which the ITF Independent Tribunal cannot depart from. By way of illustration, the ITF Tribunal has accepted the CAS approach in *WADA v. Abdelrahman*,[44] whereby it was held that the standard of evidence tendered has to be persuasive, specific, objective and concrete.[45] As to the burden of proof in doping cases, in following CAS jurisprudence, the ITF Tribunal has held that the literal reading of Article 10.2.3 of the Tennis Anti-Doping Program (TADP) 2020 requires the player to disprove engaging in conduct that he or she 'knew constituted an Anti-Doping Rule Violation' or 'knew that there was a significant risk that the conduct might constitute or result in an Anti-Doping Rule Violation and manifestly disregarded that risk'. This means that the player must not only be unaware that the action constituted an anti-doping rule violation (ADRV), she or he must also have not known that there was a significant risk.[46] Moreover, other instruments already set out evidentiary rules[47] to which the ITF Tribunal must turn to when deciding pertinent cases.[48]

The CAS Appeals Chamber has not reversed on merit any bans imposed by the ITF Independent Tribunal,[49] although in practice the CAS will assess

---

[43] This is very close to the language in ICC Arbitration Rules, Art. 25(1), which refers to 'all appropriate means'.

[44] *WADA v. Abdelrahman*, CAS 2017/A/5036.

[45] *ITF and Anti-Doping Organization v. Shoshkyna*, SR/262/2020, at para. 78.

[46] Ibid., at para. 124; equally, in agreeing with *Dylan Scott v. ITF*, CAS 2018/A/5768, the ITF Tribunal held that should there be a gap in scientific knowledge and that it is not known whether or not a particular proposition is true, and therefore the hypothesis as to source remains unverified, the benefit of the doubt goes against the player, because it is the player who bears the burden of proof on this point.

[47] Pursuant to TADP, Art. 3.1.1, the burden is on the ITF to establish each of the elements of the ADRVs charged 'to the comfortable satisfaction of the hearing panel, bearing in mind the seriousness of the allegation that is made. This standard of proof in all cases is greater than a mere balance of probability but less than proof beyond a reasonable doubt.'

[48] See *ITF and Anti-Doping Organization v. Lepchenko*, SR/254/2021, at para. 38, where the ITF Tribunal accepted that where an athlete is unable to identify how a prohibited substance entered his or her body, it is very difficult for the athlete to discharge the burden of proof that his or her conduct that led to the positive test was not intentional.

[49] In *X v. ATP Tour*, decided by the CAS Appellate Chamber, the duration of the suspension was reduced. More significantly, the tennis player had signed waiver of the right to bring setting-aside proceedings against future arbitral awards against the ITF. The CAS was unambiguous in its decision that such waiver agreements are not valid, even if express among the parties, in accordance with Art. 192 of the Swiss (Federal) Private International Law Act (PILA).

whether the ban is proportionate by reference to whether a clear departure from the text of a rule would violate public policy.[50] The same approach has been adopted also by the ITF's Independent Tribunal.[51] Fairness is paramount in the ITF Independent Tribunal's practice, as well as sports tribunals more generally[52] concerning fines and penalties imposed on athletes.[53] Given that the offences and their attendant sanctions are known in advance and the ITF Independent Tribunal, as well as the CAS, apply these sanctions proportionally and fairly, it is natural that no claims of restraint of trade have been raised in respect of disciplinary sanctions in tennis, and sports more generally. Even the *Suarez* appeal did not specifically refer to this doctrine or other equivalents. There are several reasons for this. First, the doctrine has been developed and enforced by common law courts. All disciplinary bans have been imposed by specialised tribunals, which need not rely on English law, since their own internal rules suffice for the imposition of sanctions. Second, a restraint of trade claim, even if applicable, would be pointless, particularly since bans for serious offences such as doping and cheating/illegal gambling are part and parcel of the commercial and contractual currency of tennis and all athletes are aware of the severe consequences.

The same cannot be said, however, for infractions of rules of conduct other than doping and illegal activities. Penalties for rage,[54] walking off the court without being injured, and insulting umpires and the audience are subject to misconduct fines under the ITF's Welfare Rules, as well as tournament organisers and national tennis federations.[55] No doubt, if

---

[50] *Cilic* v. *ITF*, CAS 2013/A/3335, Award (11 April 2014).
[51] In *Ilie Nastase* v. *ITF*, Independent Tribunal Decision, SR/913/2017, at para. 101, the Independent Tribunal held that the applicable principle concerning sanctions is that of 'correctness trumps consistency', as referred to in previous sports decisions. Hence, 'if a sanction granted in another similar matter – although, as was just said, there is no such case that the Tribunal is aware of – is greater or smaller than the one imposed by the [Panel or Tribunal], this should not bind the Tribunal and prevent it from electing the sanction which it determines to be the fairest in light of all the circumstances of the case'.
[52] *Squizzato* v. *FINA*, CAS 2005/A/830; *FINA* v. *Mellouli*, CAS 2010/A/2268; *Klein* v. *ASDA*, CAS A4/2016; *Walilko* v. *FIA*, CAS 2010/A/2268; and *Puerta* v. *ITF*, CAS 2006/A/1025.
[53] See *ITF and Anti-Doping Organization* v. *Stephane Houdet*, SR/005/2022, at para. 132, where the ITF Tribunal stated that 'it enjoys a broad discretion in how it defines "fairness" in the particular case'.
[54] ITF Pro-Circuit Code of Conduct, available at: www.itftennis.com/media/7285/09-2022-wtt-code-of-conduct-v2.pdf.
[55] For fines imposed by tournament organisers, see Jimmy Hascup, 'Australian Tennis Player Gets Fined $56,100 for Failing to Meet "Professional Standard" in Wimbledon Loss', *USA Today* (5 July 2019), available at: www.usatoday.com/story/sports/tennis/wimb/2019/07/05/wimbledon-2019-bernard-tomic-fined-prize-money-lackluster-effort/1655166001/. In practice, national tennis federations promulgate their own rules,

a minor disciplinary offence were to receive a ban that was so disproportionate that it prevented an athlete from retaining his or her form, it would rightly be subjected to a reversal on grounds similar to or with the same effect as restraint of trade.[56] Some commentators have argued that even if the sanction imposed by the ITF is not oppressive, the lack of procedural fairness is nonetheless disturbing[57] and may (in the opinion of this author) justify claims concerning restraint of trade if the appropriate threshold is met.[58]

In some instances, a disciplinary sanction may not culminate in significant financial loss for a tennis athlete, yet it may cause high levels of distress and exacerbate an existing condition. When US star Naomi Osaka felt compelled to withdraw from the French Open, subsequently facing fines because she did not want to make media appearances, she was poorly portrayed in the press and no accommodation was made available even though she was undergoing mental health issues.[59] Although the fine was insignificant for the athlete, it exacerbated her mental health issues and the distress caused prevented her from competing for some time.

which include conduct obligations and the imposition of fines. See US Tennis Association (USTA) Handbook of Rules and Regulations (2022), available at: www.usta.com/content/dam/usta/2022-pdfs/2022%20Friend%20at%20Court.pdf, Chapter IV.C(1), which stipulates that: 'The Chair of any tournament may withhold all or part of any prize money or expenses payable to any player charged by the Chair or by the Referee of the tournament with conduct inconsistent with the principles in USTA Regulation IV.C., provided a written grievance is filed in accordance with USTA Regulation V.B. and Bylaw 43. Any prize money or expenses so withheld shall be withheld until a final determination of the charges in the grievance has been made. Immediately after the final determination, the funds withheld, less the amount of any fine, shall be promptly paid to the player.'

[56] See Rosmarjin Van Kleef, 'Reviewing Disciplinary Sanctions in Sports' (2015) 4 Camb J Int & Comp L 3.

[57] See Ben Livings and Karolina Wlodarczak, 'Procedural Fairness in the International Tennis Federation's Disciplinary Regime' (2020) 18 Ent & Sports LJ 1. The authors discuss two particular tennis awards, namely: *Ilie Nastase* v. *ITF*, Independent Tribunal Decision, SR/913/2017, Award of 6 February 2018; *Federación de Tenis de Chile & Rios* v. *ITF*, Independent Tribunal Appeal, SR/48/2018, Award of 28 March 2018.

[58] See Martin Kosla, 'Disciplined for "Bringing a Sport into Disrepute" – a Framework for Judicial Review' (2001) 25 Melb UL Rev 654.

[59] Matthew Futterman, 'Naomi Osaka Quits the French Open after News Conference Dispute', *New York Times* (31 May 2021), available at: www.nytimes.com/2021/05/31/sports/tennis/naomi-osaka-quits-french-open-depression.html.

5 RESTRAINT OF TRADE IN PROFESSIONAL TENNIS

4.3 Qualification for National Tennis Teams and Restraint of Trade

Although the battleground for professional tennis is predicated around ITF/ATP and WTA tournaments and the ranking therefrom, selection and participation in national teams is highly sought after by players at all ranks. It is not only that national teams pay salaries to players,[60] but more importantly, national team selection brings several privileges to players who do not as a rule make a viable living from tournament prizes. A player selected in a national team may play in the Olympics, become employed in his or her country's civil service, be granted a pension or simply accumulate sufficient recognition to be given a wild card in a tournament for which he or she would not have otherwise qualified. For all of these reasons, at the very least, wrongful exclusion from a national team may give rise to a justifiable claim for restraint of trade.

In principle, each national federation recommends athletes for the Olympics, irrespective of merit, and this decision is transmitted to the federation's National Olympic Committee (NOC), which then transmits the names of those selected to the International Olympic Committee (IOC).[61] The same is true in the case of tennis. In *Oksana Kalashnikova and Ekaterine Gorgodze v. ITF, Georgian National Olympic Committee (GNOC) and Georgian Tennis Federation (GTF)*,[62] the applicants were the top-ranked female doubles team in Georgia. Prior to the 2020 Tokyo Olympics, they had received verbal assurances that they would be placed on Georgia's entry list. It turned out that the GNOC failed to enter them in the original and revised entry lists. The two players requested that it was unfair that they were excluded, and that the ITF intervene through a revised list. They further argued that the verbal assurances received from the GNOC and GTF estopped the latter from reneging on their promise. The CAS was forced to reject the players' application on the grounds explained above, albeit a different outcome might have transpired if the same dispute was submitted to an English court (assuming

---

[60] See 'Davis Cup Prize Money 2021', Perfect Tennis, available at: www.perfect-tennis.com/prize-money/davis-cup/.
[61] Appendix E to the ITF Constitution includes several rules extracted verbatim from the Olympic Charter. The By-Law to Rule 40(1) of the Charter stipulates that each international federation establishes its own rules for participation in the Olympics, albeit such criteria must be approved by the IOC Executive Board. Paragraph 2 further clarifies authority for selection by suggesting that this is done by international federations, in conjunction with their affiliated national federations and national organizing committees.
[62] CAS OG 20/05, Award (22 July 2021).

it possessed jurisdiction) pursuant to a restraint of trade claim. The application of this doctrine is not necessarily reliant on the legality of a particular rule, but whether its otherwise oppressive nature is justified and reasonable in the public interest and whether in the process it deprives an athlete of his or her livelihood. In the case at hand, the two female athletes ranked 73 and 108 in the WTA singles rankings and were in their early 30s. If one assumes that at that point in their career their best chance to make a living from the sport was through their participation in the Georgian national team (assuming that they could not expect to seriously contend for prize money), then being deprived of this opportunity on unfair and discriminatory grounds constitutes a restraint of trade. While national tennis federations possess sole authority to determine access to national teams, it is advisable and in the best interests of the ITF to amend its rules and demand that membership in national teams be achieved on a competitive basis. This could be based on ATP/WTA rankings or by competing in national rounds. This author sees no legal impediment for the ITF to suggest that any other outcome would violate an athlete's right to make a living and would be discriminatory.

6

Professional Tennis Player Unions

BRENDAN SCHWAB

1 Introduction

At critical junctures in the history of the game, the world's best tennis players have attempted to unionize. When they have, the impacts have been profound, even revolutionary. Professional tennis player unions are therefore a critical element of the global governance and law of the game and are the focus of this chapter. The discussion starts with an overview of the dual and shifting roles that tennis player unions have played: first, as a demonstration of collective action and trade union rights; and second, as central actors in the governance of the game. The initial attempts of the players to unionize are then examined, especially the pivotal years between 1967 and 1975, which resulted in professional tennis's first "labor settlement," the legacy of which continues to this day. Next, the position, rights, pay and conditions of today's players are explored. The players' current unionization effort – the Professional Tennis Players Association (PTPA) – is also considered, which is developing at a time when sport globally is experiencing a new wave of athlete organizing and the industry of professional tennis is once again contemplating seismic change.

2 The Dual and Shifting Roles of Tennis Player Unions

2.1 From Collective Action to Shared Governance

Some fifty years ago, the world's greatest professional tennis players – both women and men – successfully unionized when the game was tumultuously shifting from a sport to a business. They acted militantly, collectively, innovatively, with principle, and, in so doing, led and accelerated the game's economic and cultural transformation. The players – unlike their counterparts in major professional team sports – didn't convert their activism into collective bargaining. Instead, they chose to be business partners in the tours. The legacy of that monumental decision is still being felt and understood today.

For the greatest part of the professional era of "Open Tennis" since 1968, the players have sought to influence the governance and business of the game through the transformation of their two main player associations – the Association of Tennis Professionals (ATP) and the Women's Tennis Association (WTA) – into the governing bodies of the respective professional tours and significant transnational businesses in their own right.[1] The reasons driving these transformations and whether they have been in the best interests of the generations of players who have followed raise necessary questions that are likely to inform the future development of both the governance of the professional game and the collective representation of the players, including the potential role and impact of the PTPA.

2.2 What Is a Professional Tennis Players' Union?

A fundamental question in this discussion is what is a professional tennis players' union? Given that tennis players – like all professional athletes – are workers, the most appropriate way to approach this question is through the principles and standards of the International Labour Organization (ILO), including its fundamental conventions: Freedom of Association and Protection of the Right to Organise Convention, 1948 (No. 87);[2] and Right to Organise and Collective Bargaining Convention, 1949 (No. 98).[3] In essence, a tennis players' union is one in which: players "have the right to establish and ... join ... of their own choosing without previous authorisation"; exists for the purposes of "furthering and defending the interests" of the players;[4] and, inter alia, "is protected against acts of interference," including acts designed to support the organization "by financial or other means, with the object of placing [it]

---

[1] Elizabeth Priest, "Working toward Break Point: Professional Tennis and the Growing Problem with Employee and Independent Contractor Misclassifications" (2022) 75 SMU L Rev 943, at 947–9.
[2] ILO, Freedom of Association and Protection of the Right to Organise Convention, 1948 (No. 87), available at: www.ilo.org/dyn/normlex/en/f?p=NORMLEXPUB:12100:0::NO:: P12100_INSTRUMENT_ID:312232.
[3] ILO, Right to Organise and Collective Bargaining Convention, 1949 (No. 98), available at: www.ilo.org/dyn/normlex/en/f?p=NORMLEXPUB:12100:0::NO::P12100_Ilo_Code: C098.
[4] ILO, Convention No. 87, Arts 2 and 10.

under the control of employers or employers' organisations."[5] The ILO sees "recognition of the principle of freedom of association" as "a means of improving conditions of labour" and "essential to sustained progress," so much so that the enunciated "principles should form the basis for international regulation."[6]

The ATP and the WTA can only be considered as having been professional tennis player unions when they were functioning as player associations and prior to their transformations into governing bodies, a fact unaltered by both having player representatives within their governance structures. Under international human rights principles and standards, the ATP and the WTA shifted from being *holders* of the human rights of players (including their trade union rights) to having the *responsibility to respect* those rights. The recent evolution of global sports law to encompass internationally recognized human rights is therefore highly relevant.[7] That legal evolution has occurred due to the myriad of egregious and adverse human rights impacts with which global sport has been associated and the recognition by international sports governing bodies – especially the International Olympic Committee (IOC) and the Fédération Internationale de Football Association (FIFA) – that the business of global sport and global sports law must be conducted in accordance with the United Nations Guiding Principles (UNGPs) on Business and Human Rights.[8] Meeting the corporate responsibility to respect human rights is therefore a minimum standard

---

[5] ILO, Convention No. 98, Art. 2.
[6] ILO, Convention No. 87, Preamble.
[7] For a working definition of "global sports law," see Brendan Schwab, "'Celebrating Humanity': Reconciling Sport and Human Rights through Athlete Activism" (2018) J Leg Aspect Sport 170, at 172–4.
[8] See UN Office of High Commissioner for Human Rights (OHCHR), UN Guiding Principles on Business and Human Rights (2011), available at: www.ohchr.org/sites/default/files/documents/publications/guidingprinciplesbusinesshr_en.pdf; IOC, Olympic Charter (October 15, 2023), Fundamental Principles of Olympism (FPO) 1 and 4, available at: https://olympics.com/ioc/olympic-charter; IOC, "Respecting Human Rights," available at: https://olympics.com/ioc/human-rights; IOC, IOC Strategic Framework on Human Rights (2022), available at: https://stillmed.olympics.com/media/Documents/Beyond-the-Games/Human-Rights/IOC-Strategic-Framework-on-Human-Rights.pdf; IOC, "Recommendations for an IOC Human Rights Strategy" (2020), available at: https://stillmed.olympics.com/media/Document%20Library/OlympicOrg/News/2020/12/Independent_Expert_Report_IOC_HumanRights.pdf; FIFA, FIFA Statutes (2022), Art. 3, available at: https://digitalhub.fifa.com/m/3815fa68bd9f4ad8/original/FIFA_Statutes_2022-EN.pdf; FIFA, "FIFA's Human Rights Policy" (May 2017), available at: https://digitalhub.fifa.com/m/1a876c66a3f0498d/original/kr05dqyhwr1uhqy2lh6r-pdf.pdf.

of expected conduct of the ATP and the WTA, as it is of the International Tennis Federation (ITF), tennis's world governing body.[9]

2.3 The Trade Union Rights of Professional Tennis Players

Trade union rights comprise the rights to freedom of association (including to form or join trade unions), to organize and to effective recognition of collective bargaining. Being one of five fundamental principles of work declared by the ILO in the ILO Declaration on Fundamental Principles and Rights at Work (1998), as amended in 2022 (ILO Declaration),[10] they are among the internationally recognized human rights expressly referred to in the UNGPs.[11] Trade union rights are also expressed in the International Bill of Human Rights.[12] The Universal Declaration of Human Rights provides that "[e]veryone has the right to form and join trade unions for the protection of his [sic] interests,"[13] as does the International Covenant on Civil and Political Rights (ICCPR) in the context of the broader enabling right of freedom of association.[14] The International Covenant on Economic, Social and Cultural Rights (ICESCR) expands on the rights by making it clear that they encompass the right to join a union of one's "choice," the right of unions themselves to form "national federations or confederations" as well as "international trade-union organizations," the right of those unions to "function freely" and "the right to strike."[15]

In practical terms, the ATP, ITF, WTA and other enterprises involved in the governance and business of professional tennis are expected by the UNGPs to "undertake human rights due diligence in order to assess and address adverse human rights impacts across their value chains, including impacts on [the] trade union rights [of professional tennis players]." The tennis bodies, for example, should not interfere with any decision of the players to associate, appreciate that the players are free to

---

[9] Brendan Schwab, "Protect, Respect and Remedy: Global Sport and Human Rights" (2019) 3 Int Sport L Rev 52–3.
[10] ILO, ILO Declaration on Fundamental Principles and Rights at Work (1998), as amended in 2022, para. 2(a), available at: www.ilo.org/dyn/normlex/en/f?p=1000:62:0::NO:62:P62_LIST_ENTRIE_ID:2453911:NO.
[11] OHCHR, UN Guiding Principles on Business and Human Rights, 13–14.
[12] OHCHR, International Bill of Human Rights, available at: www.ohchr.org/en/what-are-human-rights/international-bill-human-rights.
[13] OHCHR, Universal Declaration of Human Rights (1948), Art. 23(4), available at: www.ohchr.org/en/human-rights/universal-declaration/translations/english.
[14] ICCPR (1966), Art. 22.
[15] ICESCR (1966), Art. 6(1).

unionize and recognize representative organizations for the purpose of collective bargaining.[16] Moreover, according to Shift:

> In addition to being important rights in and of themselves, trade union rights are enabling rights, meaning that respecting these rights can, in many cases, lead to the fulfillment of a number of other rights (e.g. adequate wages, reasonable working hours, and a healthy and safe workplace that is free from discrimination and harassment). Addressing risks to trade union rights is therefore important on its own, but is also critical in addressing the root causes of many other workplace-related human rights impacts.[17]

The ILO Declaration states that "the guarantee of fundamental principles and rights at work ... enables the persons concerned to claim freely and on the basis of equality of opportunity their *fair share of the wealth* which they have helped to generate, and to *achieve fully their human potential*."[18]

In 2017, the World Players Association (WPA) launched the Universal Declaration of Player Rights (UDPR), which – "anchored in international human rights law and core [ILO] standards" – includes "labor rights" (including the trade union rights of players) as one of four pillars of player rights, alongside "access to sport," "personal rights" and "legal rights."[19] WPA research reveals that in the world of sport, professional players and athletes face many threats against and risks to the realization of their trade union rights, including the denial of the status of athletes as workers, widespread cultures of anti-union behavior, anti-union conduct including direct discrimination and harassment of union members, and union avoidance strategies, where management-controlled forms of athlete representation are imposed.[20]

In 2020, the ILO began to comprehensively address the labor rights of professional athletes by convening for the first time in its 100-year history representatives of employers, athletes, player associations, sports bodies and governments to discuss the challenges facing working athletes and

---

[16] Shift Project, "Respecting Trade Union Rights in Global Value Chains: Practical Approaches for Business" (2019), 15, available at: https://shiftproject.org/resource/respecting-trade-union-rights-in-global-value-chains-practical-approaches-for-business/.

[17] Ibid., 14.

[18] ILO Declaration on Fundamental Principles and Rights at Work, Preamble (emphasis added).

[19] WPA, Universal Declaration of Player Rights (2017), available at: https://uniglobalunion.dev-zone.ch/sites/default/files/files/news/official_udpr.pdf and https://uniglobalunion.dev-zone.ch/sites/default/files/files/news/wpa_udpr_portico_v3.pdf.

[20] UNI Global Union, "Landmark New Report Finds Trade Union Rights a Top Concern for Players Worldwide" (June 22, 2023), available at: https://uniglobalunion.org/news/right-to-organize-in-sport/.

the application of international labor standards.[21] The consensus points reached include that "[a]ll workers, including athletes, regardless of the type of employment relationship, require, as a minimum, to be protected by the fundamental principles and rights at work."[22] This consensus accords with the well-established jurisprudence of the ILO's Committee on Freedom of Association that the right to organize exists "without distinction whatsoever," including "of any kind based on occupation."[23] The "criterion for determining the persons covered by the right to organize is not based on the existence of an employment relationship. Workers who do not have employment contracts should have the right to form the organizations of their choosing if they so wish."[24] Consequently, the trade union rights of professional tennis players are unaffected by their individualistic pursuit of sport as a career and their legal status as independent contractors.[25] Measures should also be taken to ensure that the presence of elected worker representatives, such as player representatives within the governance of the ATP and the WTA, "is not used to undermine the position of the trade unions concerned." In particular, the enterprise should "encourage co-operation on all relevant matters between the elected representatives and the trade unions concerned."[26]

3   Initial Attempts at Tennis Player Unionization

3.1   The Pivotal Role of Player Unionization and the Development of Professional Tennis 1967–75

Despite the emergence of professional tennis as early as the 1920s,[27] it was not until the late 1960s that the world's best tennis players effectively

---

[21] ILO, "Global Dialogue Forum on Decent Work in the World of Sport" (January 20–22, 2020), available at: www.ilo.org/meetings-and-events/global-dialogue-forum-decent-work-world-sport.

[22] ILO, "Global Dialogue Forum on Decent Work in the World of Sport – Points of Consensus," 1, available at: www.ilo.org/sites/default/files/wcmsp5/groups/public/%40ed_dialogue/%40sector/documents/meetingdocument/wcms_735388.pdf.

[23] ILO, "Compilation of Decisions of the Committee on Freedom of Association Sixth Edition" (2018), 59, para. 315, available at: www.ilo.org/sites/default/files/wcmsp5/groups/public/%40ed_norm/%40normes/documents/publication/wcms_632659.pdf.

[24] Ibid., 62, para. 330.

[25] Priest, "Working toward Break Point," 961–71, argues that professional tennis players are misclassified as independent contractors.

[26] ILO, Workers' Representatives Convention, 1971 (No. 135), Art. 5, available at: www.ilo.org/dyn/normlex/en/f?p=NORMLEXPUB:12100:0::NO::P12100_INSTRUMENT_ID:312280.

[27] John Arlott (ed.), *The Oxford Companion to Sports & Games* (Oxford University Press, 1975), 608.

exercised the right to organize and form player unions as a solution to the many challenges confronting them, their careers and the industry of professional tennis. The matters requiring resolution were fundamental and wide-ranging in nature. Professionalism itself was being resisted by the game's governors, principally the "old guard" at the world governing body,[28] the International Lawn Tennis Federation (ILTF).[29]

The players had a bold vision of "Open Tennis," where the elite could all play as professionals in the world's most prestigious tournaments and venues, including Wimbledon, Roland Garros and Forest Hills. Only Open Tennis could maximize fan interest in the sport and provide a legitimate livelihood for players who were taking to "small-venue barnstorming" and "shamateurism" to survive.[30] Contracts, playing fees, prize money, expenses and tournament conditions, as well as the schedule and eligibility, all needed to be negotiated.[31] Tennis, the players asserted, also had to boldly lead society on acute issues of the day, including matters of human rights, especially the battle for gender equality. Addressing these matters required the players – as a collective – to overcome many internal and naturally occurring divisions. But it was, in the end, one issue that prompted unprecedented and historic displays of player solidarity and militancy – the obsession of the old guard to remain in control and put commercialism and upstart players well and truly back in their place.[32] The players resisted, and the resulting labor unrest would finally propel tennis into the modern era.

In less than a decade – eight years in fact from 1967 to 1975 – the players would collectively drive a professional, business, and player and human rights revolution of the sport. The pace and extent of player-driven change was – and remains even with the benefit of hindsight – simply breathtaking.

1967

The establishment of World Championship Tennis (WCT) offering "an unprecedented level of prize money" had "a major influence on the evolution of Open Tennis." Initially signing a cluster of players who

---

[28] Raymond Arsenault, *Arthur Ashe: A Life* (Simon & Schuster, 2018), 96.
[29] The ILTF became the ITF in 1977. See ITF, "Frequently Asked Questions: Governance," available at: www.itftennis.com/en/about-us/organisation/faqs/?type=governance.
[30] Arsenault, *Arthur Ashe*, 97; Billie Jean King with Johnette Howard and Maryanne Vollers, *All in: An Autobiography* (Viking, 2021), 135.
[31] Arsenault, *Arthur Ashe*, 96–7.
[32] Matthew Futterman, *Players: The Story of Sports and Money, and the Visionaries Who Fought to Create a Revolution* (Simon & Schuster, 2016), 86.

became known as the "Handsome Eight," including 1967 Wimbledon men's singles champion John Newcombe and his fellow semi-finalists, WCT conducted a raft of major tournaments from 1968.[33]

1968

Wimbledon, under the influence of younger and reform-minded administrators and supported by the players, was declared "open" to professionals by Britain's Lawn Tennis Association (LTA), with the distinction between professionals and amateurs dropped and competitors simply designated as "players." The "open era" had started.[34]

1969

The International Tennis Players Association (ITPA) was established in London before Wimbledon "despite signs that several parts of the tennis establishment felt threatened by the players' assertive stance." Under Newcombe's interim chairmanship, the ITPA aimed to "force the issue of player rights" and address the "world tennis situation [which was] in turmoil."[35]

1970

The "Original Nine" – under the astute and courageous leadership of Billie Jean King – signed $1 contracts with *World Tennis* magazine to trigger the creation of the professional women's tour, address gross disparity in prize money between men and women professionals, and defy threats of suspension from the tennis authorities, including the US Lawn Tennis Association (USLTA).[36]

1970

Arthur Ashe, the treasurer of the ITPA, led the creation of the "Association of *Independent* Tennis Professionals" because of rising tension and conflict between the so-called "independent" and "contract" professionals, which was causing the ITPA to falter. The future of Open Tennis was already looking uncertain after the WCT announced plans to hold fourteen invitational tournaments with no scope to include independent professionals like Ashe who depended on prize money from the

---

[33] Arsenault, *Arthur Ashe*, 205.
[34] Arlott, *The Oxford Companion to Sports and Games*, 609.
[35] Arsenault, *Arthur Ashe*, 248–9.
[36] King, *All in: An Autobiography*, 174. All references to dollars or $ in this chapter are to US dollars.

Davis Cup and the major tournaments to eke a living and, failing that, turned to the increasingly lucrative world of celebrity product endorsements. The ILTF had also taken a stand against the "contract pros," with a ban slated to take effect on January 1, 1972.[37]

1972

The ATP was established at the US Open with Jack Kramer, a former Wimbledon and US Open champion who had promoted professional tennis for men since the late 1940s,[38] installed as its inaugural Executive Director.[39] The new players' union replaced the ITPA and brought together fifty male players from sixteen different nations all willing to pay $400 a year in dues for the services of Kramer and lawyer and player manager Donald Dell, whose clientele included Ashe, the ATP's first vice-president. Kramer and Dell had, only months earlier, negotiated a peace deal on behalf of the USLTA which saw all WCT tournaments become ILTF-sanctioned events, the coordination of non-WCT events to avoid conflict or competition, the elimination of the distinction between contract and independent pros, with all pros (after the expiry of all extant WCT contracts) to compete for prize money on the same terms, and all players (including WCT players) strongly encouraged to participate in the four Grand Slam tournaments. The ATP was necessary, Ashe said, because he and his peers were "tired of being stepped upon by two elephants," the WCT and ILTF, and would "unite, promote and protect" the common interests of the players.[40] The ATP – like the ITPA before it – rejected requests from King that women also be members.[41] The ATP also made a constitutional commitment that players would compete solely for prize money and not individual salaries.[42]

1973

King led the establishment of the WTA in player meetings before Wimbledon. Determined not to be dictated to by either the tennis authorities or the ATP, the players committed 10 percent of their prize

---

[37] Arsenault, *Arthur Ashe*, 257, 269 and 296 (emphasis added to the name of the association).
[38] Arlott, *The Oxford Companion to Sports and Games*, 609.
[39] Richard Evans, *Open Tennis: The First Twenty Years* (Bloomsbury, 1988), 6.
[40] Arsenault, *Arthur Ashe*, 297 and 300.
[41] King, *All in: An Autobiography*, 164.
[42] Arsenault, *Arthur Ashe*, 314.

money to funding the new organization. King had long felt that "officials were behaving like feudal overlords." Among the issues to be addressed were unequal prize money. In 1970, Kramer's Pepsi Pacific Southwest Championship offered $65,000 to the men and $7,500 to the women, a ratio of 8:1, evidence of a cultural approach that under Kramer's leadership had infected the entire ATP. But the problem extended beyond the ATP. The 1973 Wimbledon men's champion was slated to receive £5,000 to the women's £3,000.[43]

1973

The ATP led a historic and unprecedented boycott of Wimbledon in response to the All England Club's ruling to uphold a decision of Yugoslavia's tennis federation and the ILTF to deem that Nikola Pilic was no longer of "good standing" and suspend him for nine months. History now suggests that Pilic "may be the most important tennis player almost no one outside of tennis has heard of."[44] The arbitrary and capricious use of disciplinary powers by tennis authorities lay at the heart of the power imbalance between the players and the game's rulers, with the ITPA's initial objectives having been stated to include, "[i]f necessary ... act[ing] as one to discipline players who misbehave[d], and ... fight[ing] to protect players who [were] unjustly treated."[45] Pilic, a twelve-year Yugoslav Davis Cup veteran, had missed a Davis Cup tie against New Zealand due to a competing professional commitment with the WCT. If Pilic couldn't play due to a ban incurred simply because he was trying to make a living, then neither would the world's best, and more than seventy professionals boycotted the world championship of tennis, an unprecedented act.[46] Moreover, "[t]he players had brought tennis's powers to their knees and they would do it again if they needed to. They didn't need Grand Slams or the Davis Cup as much as those events needed them."[47] Fourteen years later, ILTF President Philippe Chatrier admitted the players' action inflicted "a blow from which the ILTF never fully recovered."[48]

---

[43] King, *All in: An Autobiography*, 136, 166, 227 and 228.
[44] Futterman, *Players*, 83 and 84.
[45] Arsenault, *Arthur Ashe*, 248.
[46] Futterman, *Players*, 103; Arlott, *The Oxford Companion to Sports and Games*, 610.
[47] Futterman, *Players*, 104.
[48] Evans, *Open Tennis*, 94.

1973

Only a year after King as US Open champion took home 40 percent of Ille Nastase's US$25,000 winner's cheque, the US Open became the first major tournament to award equal prize money to its men's and women's champions. King had informed tournament organizers that she would "show up in 1972, but [she] wouldn't play in the 1973 U.S. Open if they didn't level the prize money, and most of the top women would walk out with [her]." King backed her militancy with intelligence and entrepreneurial flare. She commissioned market research which attested to the power of the top women players as drawcards, players such as Chrissie Evert, Rosie Casals, Evonne Goolagong and Margaret Court, and secured a sponsor to fund the prize money differential of $55,000.[49]

1973

The new women's tour, by then incorporated into the Women's International Tennis Federation (WITF), settled a law suit it had launched against the ongoing threats from the USLTA to ban players from the majors. The settlement resulted in the WITF being disbanded and the new tour – then sponsored by Phillip Morris's *Virginia Slims* brand – operating with the sanctioning of the USLTA.[50]

1974

The fight to control men's professional tennis between the ATP and the ILTF was settled with the establishment of the Men's International Professional Tennis Council (MIPTC), which gave the players "a say in everything from scheduling to work conditions."[51] With the ATP and ILTF having worked through necessary rule changes in response to the Wimbledon boycott of 1973 (including lifting Pilic's suspension in time for the US Open), the new MIPTC consisted of four nominees of the ILTF and three from the ATP. The ATP were reluctant signatories, concerned about always finding themselves in the minority, especially given the demonstrated determination of the ILTF to retain control. The players were, according to Dell, "willing to place [themselves] under the total control of the council," and proposed that it be made up of three representatives of the ILTF, three of the ATP and three tournament directors. If the players were to find themselves in a minority, Dell

---

[49] King, *All in: An Autobiography*, 208.
[50] Ibid., 222.
[51] Futterman, *Players*, 104.

asserted, they wanted "the swing votes to be in the hands of knowledgeable people who have a real stake in the game."[52] The MIPTC was soon to be reconstituted to accord with the ATP's proposal.[53]

1975

The ILTF and the WTA similarly settled their governance dispute, with the establishment of the Women's International Professional Tennis Council (WIPTC), a joint venture of sorts between the ILTF and the WTA and including representatives from the tournaments and sponsors. The "purpose of the Council was to promote, control and govern the organisation and development of the women's professional circuit throughout the world."[54]

3.2 Pro Tennis's Labor Settlement – Business in Lieu of Bargaining

And so, by 1975, the framework for labor relations in professional tennis had largely been set. The settlements achieved by both the ATP and the WTA were historic and were to deliver real outcomes that would place the world's very best tennis players at the top of global athlete earnings and prestige.[55] The players had unquestionably won the rights to compete as professionals and to have a meaningful say in all decisions that affected them (especially on the questions of prize money, scheduling, governance and discipline). They had a seat at the table determined to drive the expansion of the professional men's and women's tennis and, in turn, the players' prize money pools.[56]

It is noteworthy that both labor settlements took the form of the two player associations – the ATP and the WTA – taking seats in the global governance of the professional tours, and not the form of collective bargaining. In the same period, professional team athletes especially in the United States and European football were unionizing, legally challenging the long-standing restraints imposed by leagues and owners on their freedoms and earning capacities, and securing collective bargaining agreements which addressed essential player needs such as a minimum wage, guaranteed contracts, pensions and, through free agency, the right

---

[52] Evans, *Open Tennis*, 95–6.
[53] ITF, "Frequently Asked Questions: Governance."
[54] Ibid.
[55] See Sportico, "100 Highest-Paid Athletes in the World" (7 February 2024), available at: www.sportico.com/feature/highest-paid-athletes-in-the-world-1234765608/.
[56] Futterman, *Players*, 80–1.

to offer one's services to an employer of choice in a competitive labor market.[57] The latter proved to be critical in ensuring that players would be paid, individually, their market rate and, collectively, a fair share of the game's overall revenues.[58] Upon the establishment of the WTA, Marvin Miller, the Executive Director of the Major League Baseball Players Association (MLBPA), had sent King and the players his congratulations in an interview with United Press International.[59] Between 1968 and 1975, Miller had secured US pro-sports' first ever collective bargaining agreement, led a successful strike over pension fund payments and secured free agency for his members.[60] King regarded the "groundbreaking" Miller as "one of [her] heroes," and said that his endorsement "meant the world" to her.[61]

Yet, the world's best tennis players took a very different path from that of their Major League Baseball (MLB) counterparts, which would fundamentally shift the purpose, structure and culture of both the ATP and the WTA away from trade unionism.

The world's leading professional golfers had won a similar battle in 1968 against their governing body, the Professional Golfers' Association of America (PGA), which had formed in 1916 as an organization of golf pros – the people who ran pro shops and gave golf lessons. Occasional events initially organized by the PGA to promote "golf tourism" had developed by the 1950s into an expanded schedule of events capable of supporting tour pros on a full-time basis. Add stars Arnold Palmer, Jack Nicklaus, Gary Player and television to the mix, and by 1968 tour prize money sat at $5.6 million, but was under the control of the PGA, with the old golf pros holding sway over the world-class professional golfers who played the tour. The tour's best players – some 205 of them – established Professional Golfers America, Inc. (APG), and following a dispute fought over two years that threatened the PGA championships of 1967 and 1968, a settlement was finally reached. The settlement saw the PGA form a separate Tournament Players' Division, a standalone entity governed by a ten-member policy board consisting of four APG-nominated players, three PGA executives

---

[57] See Brendan Schwab, "'When We Know Better, We Do Better.' Embedding the Human Rights of Players as a Prerequisite to the Legitimacy of Lex Sportiva and Sport's Justice System" (2017) 32 Md J Int L 4, at 18–25.
[58] Schwab, "Celebrating Humanity," 192–3.
[59] King, *All in: An Autobiography*, 229.
[60] MLB, "History," available at: www.mlbplayers.com/history.
[61] King, *All in: An Autobiography*, 229.

and three consulting businessmen. A commissioner would run the tour, answerable only to the board.[62]

It is perhaps not surprising that the tennis players – like their golfing counterparts – would choose a model based on governance, entrepreneurialism and business, instead of the trade union rights and commitment to collective bargaining that were then transforming professional team sports and continue to this day to do so.[63] Unlike the well-established professional team sports such as baseball and football, the business of tennis was rapidly evolving and constantly changing, with new organizers and tour concepts quickly emerging. There possibly was not yet a stable managerial counterpart with whom the players could reliably bargain. That had to be found and, if it couldn't be, it would have to be created. But, more than that, tennis was a "rich man's sport":[64] the men's revolution had been shaped by Kramer – himself arguably the most established tennis promoter in the world – together with the game's *very best* players who *all* could be sure to win a lion's share of the increasing prize money that was bound to follow. King's immense struggle for the women's game is as remarkable for her success as a player and businessperson as it is her courage and principle. Working initially in partnership with Gladys Heldman,[65] she relentlessly promoted and developed the tour and readily accepted the sponsorship of Phillip Morris as a business necessity despite her moral and health concerns with the tobacco company.[66]

In contrast, the unionization of professional footballers began at the turn of the twentieth century in industrial Manchester. It was, from the earliest of days, an industrial dispute between "Masters and Servants,"[67] with professionalism "legalized" by the game's authorities as early as 1885 (albeit reluctantly). The Players' Union – now the Professional Footballers' Association (PFA) – was established in 1907 after a struggle that started in the 1890s.[68] A footballer's status as a worker was legally recognized in

---

[62] Jim Gorant, "War for the Tour: The Day the PGA Championship Nearly Died," Golf (August 8, 2018), available at: https://golf.com/news/tournaments/pga-championship-nearly-died/.
[63] Schwab, "Celebrating Humanity," 186–8.
[64] Harry Gordon, "Arthur Ashe Has to Be Aware That He Is a Pioneer in Short White Pants," *New York Times* (January 2, 1966).
[65] Evans, *Open Tennis*, 97–106.
[66] King, *All in: An Autobiography*, 179.
[67] John Harding, *For the Good of the Game: The Official History of the Professional Footballers' Association* (Robson Books, 1991), 84.
[68] Ibid., 1, 25, 40.

1910,[69] and the early 1960s finally saw England's best soccer players start to enjoy their rights and greater income-earning opportunities through a combination of a successful threatened strike which resulted in the abolition of the long-standing maximum weekly wage and litigation which ended the retain and transfer system.[70] Similarly, a key part of Miller's success at the MLBPA was instilling a "union consciousness" among the players.[71]

Just as freedom of contract and free agency had transformed the earnings of English football and MLB players (and would, over time, transform the earnings of almost all professional team athletes), the competition between the main factions in the tennis wars had driven up player payments enormously, such as that between the WCT and the ILTF's Grand Prix Masters tournament in the early 1970s. Even Ashe – dedicated to his status as an independent professional – found the opportunities irrefusable, signing a five-year WCT contract in 1971 worth $750,000, putting him on a par with the best-paid stars in the MLB, PGA and other major leagues.[72] Yet – as we have seen – the players became a driving force in the settlement of the tennis wars on terms which even saw the end of such rewarding and secure contracts and the embedding of an individualistic albeit potentially lucrative performance-based pay structure exclusively dependent on prize money. The players were – perhaps inadvertently – agreeing to stifle the very competition that had helped put them in such a strong position, a position powerfully reinforced by the solidarity demonstrated at Wimbledon in 1973. According to Evans, "[a]lthough the ATP was to squander the position it had earned for itself in later years," the creation of the MIPTC meant that "the battle was not in vain."[73] This raises a question of cause and effect. The players had agreed to a seat at the industry's top table while allowing the same industry to evolve into a monopsony, a buyers' cartel for player services.

Ashe would reflect on the impact of the reforms years later: "For many of us, the deluge of money led to confusion and an unholy scrambling after dollars. Certain values and standards that had bonded players in my

---

[69] Walker v. Crystal Palace Football Club Ltd (1910) 1 KB 87, at 93.
[70] See Harding, For the Good of the Game, 276–88; Eastham v. Newcastle United Football Club [1964] Ch 413.
[71] Marvin Miller, A Whole Different Ballgame: The Sport and Business of Baseball (Birch Lane Press Books, 1991), 75.
[72] Arsenault, Arthur Ashe, 271–2.
[73] Evans, Open Tennis, 95.

earlier years – certain codes of honor and a spirit of cooperation and camaraderie – disappeared." He wondered, "how much we, the leaders of the players during the transition, contributed to the fall."[74] Perhaps one factor was the ATP's inability to ensure that the game's wealth was shared more equitably among all players on the tour. As early as 1972, Ashe had said that "the present prize-money breakdown gives too much money to a man at the top."[75]

Within a decade, King was also questioning the state of things. "The trouble is, as ever, the players fight too much against each other and not enough against the real enemy."[76] She even grew concerned about the long-term impact of her early victory for equal prize money:

> Part of the problem is that, a decade ago, I was too successful in helping obtain parity in prize money for the women. This was important at the time but, looking back, I can see that it was a Pyrrhic victory. It helped the federation to turn the men more against us – divide and conquer – and made it easier for the major tournaments and the tennis-federation establishment to keep us down. What difference does it really make if the women can earn as much as the men, if both sexes are underpaid? The major tournaments, like the US Open, like Wimbledon, rip the players off terribly.[77]

The ATP was to grow frustrated with the constraints of the MIPTC. In 1988, players including Mats Wilander and Stefan Edberg led the decision of the ATP to leave the MIPTC, by then renamed the Men's Tennis Council.[78] "We should be in control of our own destiny," Edberg said, recalling that the "ATP was founded for the players by the players, but it [now] has no control. We've been continually told where to go ... now we want our say." Hamilton Jordan, the ATP's CEO, announced in a carpark outside the US Open that the ATP would run its own tour.[79] In 1995, the WTA merged with the WIPTC (by then the Women's Tennis Council) to establish the WTA Tour.[80] In so doing, both the ATP and the

---

[74] Arsenault, *Arthur Ashe*, 313.
[75] Ibid., 302–3.
[76] Billie Jean King and Frank Deford, *Billie Jean King: The Autobiography* (Granada, 1982), 169.
[77] Ibid.
[78] Lisa Dillman, "Tennis Federation Rejects Players' Demands: Wilander, Edberg Outspoken in Requesting Shift of Power in Men's Council," *LA Times* (August 30, 1988).
[79] ATP, "The Tour Born in a Parking Lot" (August 30, 2013), available at: www.atptour.com/en/news/heritage-1988-parking-lot-press-conference-part-i.
[80] WTA, "About the WTA," available at: www.wtatennis.com/about.

WTA effectively completed their transformations from player unions to tennis governing bodies and businesses.

Business autonomy did not resolve the tension and division among the players. In 2003, the players again tried to unionize, with the establishment of the International Men's Tennis Association (IMTA) with leading players such as Roger Federer, Marit Safin and Lleyton Hewitt signing up. The players' concerns included the declining financial position of the ATP, the diminishing popularity of men's tennis, and the inherent conflict of interest that existed in a body such as the ATP being responsible for advancing player rights while administering player discipline.[81] Federer, however, "consistently preferred to work within the system, lobbying and cajoling behind the scenes." The IMTA would not succeed, and Federer would later serve as President of the ATP Player Advisory Council (PAC) – an advisory body within the ATP's structure – from 2008 to 2014.[82] In the midst of his presidency and despite a substantial increase in ATP prize money between 2006 and 2011, players met to consider a boycott of the first tournament of 2012 – the Australian Open – over the prize money allocation of around $26 million from tournament revenues of $250 million, demonstrating that player complaints were focused on the Grand Slam tournaments as well as the ATP. Players indicated that prize money should at least be 30 percent of tournament revenues, arguably a "paltry" share in comparison with the major professional team sports in the United States.[83]

Ashe and King may have reflected harshly on themselves and their legacy, but they also did so presciently. Forty years after equal prize money was achieved at the US Open, the four highest paid women athletes in the world were all tennis players: Maria Sharapova, Li Na, Serena Williams and Caroline Wozniacki, each of whom made between $13 million and $27 million.[84] When Ashe won the US Open in 1968, his prize money was $14,000, a reward he could not accept because of his army service.[85] In 2021, both men and women US Open champions received $4 million.[86]

---

[81] Tom Fordyce, "Tennis: Where the Power Lies," BBC Sport (January 14, 2004).
[82] Christopher Clarey, *The Master: The Brilliant Career of Roger Federer* (John Murray Press, 2021), 351–2.
[83] Bradley Raboin, "Accepting a Double-Fault: How ADR Might Save Men's Professional Tennis" (2014) 3 Mississippi Sports L Rev 211, at 224–5.
[84] Futterman, *Players*, 107.
[85] Michael Steinberger, "A Few Tennis Pros Make a Fortune. Most Barely Scrape by," *New York Times Magazine* (June 29, 2021), available at: www.nytimes.com/2021/06/29/magazine/tennis-players-association.html.
[86] Ibid.

These amounts are relative and do not give the complete picture, however. Whether the world's best tennis players are receiving a fair share of the revenue and wealth they create as well as keeping pace with the world's best athletes in the 2020s are more salient questions, as is the position and well-being of *all* members of the profession. In 2023, only two tennis players were in the top 100 earning athletes – Novak Djokovic (46) and Carlos Alcaraz (56) – with prize money earnings of $15.9 million and $15.2 million and sponsorships of $29 million and $27 million, respectively. No woman was in the top 100, although women tennis players remained the world's highest paid female athletes, with Coco Gauff being the top-earning female athlete, receiving $22.7 million in total combined earnings for her work and business activities on and off the court.[87] Yet, tennis no longer monopolized the top 10 female income-earners, as it last did in 2019. Seven of the top 10 earners in 2022 and 2023 were tennis players, but only three were in 2021, highlighting the precarity of the tennis pay system in the context of the Covid-19 pandemic.[88] In addition to the dramatic reductions in available prize money in 2020 and 2021,[89] the players' off-court earnings were also hit. According to Sportico, "almost every tennis sneaker and apparel contract is designed with minimum play requirements."[90]

Unionized athletes in the intensely competitive sports of football, American football, baseball and basketball occupied eighty places in the top 100 in 2023.[91] The National Basketball Association (NBA) will pay its 450 players an average wage of $10.8 million in 2023/24,[92] an amount exceeded in 2023 prize money earnings by only three tennis players (all men) – Djokovic ($15.9 million), Alcaraz ($15.2 million) and Daniil Medvedev ($11.5 million). The 450th-ranked male tennis player in

---

[87] Sportico, "100 Highest-Paid Athletes"; and Lev Akabas, "Djokovic Tops 2023 Tennis Earnings with $16m. His ATP Bonus? $0," Sportico (December 18, 2023), available at: www.sportico.com/personalities/athletes/2023/tennis-prize-money-2023-djokovic-1234758778/.

[88] Kurt Badenhausen, "Highest Paid Female Athletes 2023: Coco Scores Top Slot at $23m," Sportico (December 6, 2023), available at: www.sportico.com/personalities/athletes/2023/highest-paid-female-athletes-2023-coco-gauff-1234751998/.

[89] For WTA end of year prize money lists, see WTA, "Match Notes & Historical Records," available at: www.wtatennis.com/match-notes.

[90] Badenhausen, "Highest Paid Female Athletes 2023."

[91] Sportico, "100 Highest-Paid Athletes"; and Akabas, "Djokovic Tops 2023 Tennis Earnings."

[92] Eric Fisher, "NBA Sees $100M Annual Player Salaries in Its Future," Front Office Sports (October 23, 2023), available at: https://frontofficesports.com/nba-sees-100m-annual-player-salaries-in-its-future/.

terms of annual prize money – Czechia's Petr Nouza – earned a mere $48,428,[93] while a rookie NBA player will be paid a guaranteed minimum wage of $1.1 million.[94] And unlike NBA players, players like Nouza are "independent," which means they are self-employed and responsible for overheads such as travel, coaching and other expenses, resulting in players commonly losing money on the tour.[95] Many players don't see this or the tour's gross income inequality as unjust. When Covid-19 shut down the world of professional tennis in 2020 – even resulting in the cancellation of Wimbledon – the players were unable to reach a consensus on how to help the players most in need. Austria's Dominic Thiem was one who refused to contribute to a relief fund: "There are many, many players who don't put the sport above everything else and don't live in a professional manner ... I don't really see why I should give such players money. None of us top players got anything handed to us, we all had to fight our way up."[96] The four majors, the ITF, the ATP and the WTA combined to fill a fraction of the need by establishing a $6 million Covid-19 relief package.[97]

In 2020, when Canadian Vasek Pospisil joined forces with Djokovic to establish the PTPA, he had already formed the view that "[t]here's no way that tennis shouldn't have 300 players making decent livings," yet Chris O'Connell, the 139th best men's tennis player, was "barely solvent." As a Canadian, Pospisil had looked into the National Hockey League (NHL). There, the guaranteed minimum was $700,000 a season, and more than half were earning more than a million dollars. The answer, Pospisil was convinced, wasn't because the NHL owners were benevolent. The players had a union.[98] Djokovic had worked within the ATP PAC for years, alongside Federer and Rafael Nadal, then the undisputed "Big Three" of men's tennis. Federer's biographer Christopher Clarey writes, Djokovic was to "ultimately become the most radical of the Big Three" and led the launch of the PTPA that

---

[93] ATP, "ATP Prize Money Leaders (US$)" (December 25, 2023).
[94] Kevin McCormick, "NBA Minimum Salary: How Much Is an NBA Player Paid?" Sportskeeda (August 2, 2023), available at: www.sportskeeda.com/basketball/news-nba-minimum-salary-how-much-nba-player-paid.
[95] Steinberger, "A Few Tennis Pros Make a Fortune."
[96] Cody Atkinson, "Dominic Thiem May Not Care, But Most Tennis Professionals Lose Money Playing the Game," ABC (April 29, 2020), available at: www.abc.net.au/news/2020-04-30/coronavirus-tennis-most-players-lose-money-playing-the-game/12198950.
[97] Steinberger, "A Few Tennis Pros Make a Fortune."
[98] Ibid.

"sought to be an independent voice from the *traditional* men's tour."⁹⁹ Some fifty years on, the players had come full circle.

4 The "Seven Kingdoms": Player Voice, Rights, Pay and Conditions in Professional Tennis Today

4.1 The Voice of the Players in the Governance of Professional Tennis

According to Rothenberg, professional tennis is governed by "Seven Kingdoms": the ITF, the ATP, the WTA and the four Grand Slam tournaments: the Australian Open, the French Open, the US Open and Wimbledon.¹⁰⁰ Furthermore, given that tennis is an Olympic sport, the IOC – as the "supreme authority" of the Olympic Movement – exercises significant regulatory authority and control through international federations such as the ITF.¹⁰¹ The IOC, for example, requires the "statutes, practice and activities" of the ITF to "be in conformity with the Olympic Charter," including through "the adoption and implementation of the World Anti-Doping Code" (WADC). Moreover, the Court of Arbitration for Sport (CAS) has jurisdiction over all disputes involving a participant in the Olympic Games, challengeable decisions of the IOC, any dispute "arising on the occasion of, or in connection with, the Olympic Games"¹⁰² and any appeal under the WADC.¹⁰³ The ITF also recognizes the jurisdiction of the CAS in addition to its own adjudicating bodies.¹⁰⁴ In 2021, the "Seven Kingdoms" established the International Tennis Integrity Agency (ITIA) "to promote, encourage, enhance and safeguard the integrity of their tennis events worldwide,"¹⁰⁵ including by having carriage of the Tennis Anti-Doping Program (TADP) (which must accord with the WADC) and the Tennis Anti-Corruption Program (TACP), the focus of which includes the fight against match-fixing.¹⁰⁶ This brings the total number of international bodies exercising legal and regulatory control

---

⁹⁹ Clarey, *The Master*, 352 (emphasis added).
¹⁰⁰ Ben Rothenberg, *Naomi Osaka: Her Journey to Finding Her Power and Her Voice* (Text Publishing, 2024), 388.
¹⁰¹ IOC, Olympic Charter, FPO 3.
¹⁰² Ibid., FPO 3, Rules 25, 44, 44.6, 61.1 and 61.2.
¹⁰³ WADA, World Anti-Doping Code (January 1, 2021), Art. 13, available at: www.wada-ama.org/sites/default/files/resources/files/2021_wada_code.pdf.
¹⁰⁴ Despina Mavromati, "The Justice System of the International Tennis Federation" in Massimo Coccia and Michele Colucci (eds), *International Sports Justice* (Sports Law and Policy Centre, 2024), 736.
¹⁰⁵ ITIA, "About," available at: www.itia.tennis/about/.
¹⁰⁶ Mavromati, "The Justice System of the ITF," 746 and 748.

over the rights, pay and conditions (including discipline) of professional tennis players to at least eleven. All eleven adopt modes of player and athlete engagement, representation and input into their decision-making bodies and processes, which: "regulate and control who can represent athletes"; are internal, subordinate and avoid player unions; and, in the case of the CAS, even involve – according to investigative journalist Grit Hartmann and sports governance think-tank, "Play the Game" – "[f]aking athletes' representatives."[107]

Moreover, the structures established to give players a voice exist within the tennis bodies and stand apart from one another. They are not designed and do not incorporate a player voice to *holistically advance the rights and interests of the players* in a way which is capable of addressing all eleven bodies at the same time in a united manner. In particular – absent the PTPA – there isn't a directly organized player counterpart to the "Seven Kingdoms." This also means – again absent the PTPA – that there isn't a player body designed and structured to *holistically support the players (both as athletes and people)* as they navigate the various tours and confront the many professional and personal challenges involved in individually pursuing an elite playing career which, by its very nature, is transnational, short term and precarious, and will, for too many on the tour, define their sense of identity and self-worth.[108]

4.1.1 The ITF

The ITF is, pursuant to The Constitution of ITF Limited (trading as International Tennis Federation), governed by a Board of Directors (ITF Board) consisting of an elected President, fourteen other elected Directors and two "Athlete Representative Board members," one female

---

[107] See WADA, "Athlete Engagement," available at: www.wada-ama.org/en/athletes-support-personnel/athlete-engagement; WADA, "Athlete Council: A WADA Permanent Special Committee," available at: www.wada-ama.org/en/athletes-support-personnel/athlete-engagement/athlete-council; IOC, "Athletes' Commission," available at: https://olympics.com/ioc/athletes-commission; WPA, "#Right2Organise Survey & Report: Effective Athlete Representation in Global Sport" (2023), 32, available at: https://uniglobalunion.org/wp-content/uploads/WPA-R2O-Report_Digital-2.pdf; WPA, "WADA Governance Review: A Missed Opportunity for Urgently Needed Reform" (November 24, 2021), available at: https://uniglobalunion.org/news/wada-governance-review-a-missed-opportunity-for-urgently-needed-reform/; Grit Hartmann, "Tipping the Scales of Justice: The Sport and Its 'Supreme Court'" (November 2021), 47–8, available at: www.playthegame.org/media/fmxi0jgx/tipping-the-scales-of-justice-the-sport-and-its-supreme-court.pdf.

[108] See e.g. Jelena Dokic and Jessica Halloran, *Unbreakable* (Penguin Random House Australia, 2017).

and one male, who are appointed by the fifteen elected members of the ITF Board.[109] These positions are currently held by former Grand Slam winning professionals Mary Pierce (France) and Mark Woodforde (Australia).[110] Both are more accurately considered former players who can provide their own perspectives from their playing and career experiences. Their legal and political accountability is not to the players, but to the fifteen elected members of the Board. Together, they hold less than 12 percent of the voting rights in the ITF Board.

4.1.2 The ATP

The ATP describes itself as: "[t]he global governing body of men's professional tennis. We entertain a billion fans and showcase the game's greatest players on its greatest stages."[111] The ATP is governed by a nine-member Board of Directors, which consists of a Chairman, four "Player Representatives" (international, Americas, Europe and "at-large") and four "Tournament Representatives."[112] In this way, the current ATP governance model is not unlike the ATP's proposal as a player union to settle the tennis wars in 1973 and which resulted in the creation of the MIPTC, the ATP's predecessor.[113]

The player representatives on the ATP Board are elected by the ATP PAC, which is, in turn, elected by, from and among the players' peers on the ATP Tour to reflect three key cohorts in the player ranks: (1) rankings; (2) geography; and (3) singles and doubles players. Players elected to a specific ranking category are elected by players in that ranking group, while "at-large" representatives are "elected by Division 1 and 2 ATP player members (up to 500 singles and 250 doubles players)."[114] Coaches and alumni players are also represented and are respectively elected by ATP members in those categories. Players are elected for two-year terms, with terms being staggered from 2024, with the aim of enhancing continuity in the membership of the ATP PAC. The 2024 ATP PAC is shown in Table 6.1.[115]

---

[109] ITF Constitution (2025), Art. 11.1, available at: www.itftennis.com/media/2431/the-constitution-of-the-itf-2024-web.pdf.
[110] ITF, "Who's on the Board?" available at: www.itftennis.com/en/about-us/organisation/company-structure/.
[111] ATP, "About," available at: www.atptour.com/en/corporate/about.
[112] ATP, "Board of Directors," available at: www.atptour.com/en/corporate/about.
[113] Evans, *Open Tennis*, 95.
[114] ATP, "New Player Advisory Council Meets in Melbourne" (January 26, 2023), available at: www.atptour.com/en/news/player-advisory-council-meets-in-melbourne.
[115] ATP, "ATP Announces Player Advisory Council for 2024" (January 8, 2024), available at: www.atptour.com/en/news/2024-player-advisory-council.

Table 6.1 *2024 ATP Player Advisory Council*

Member	Player Rankings	Region
Gregor Dimitrov	1–50 singles	Europe
Alexander Zverev	1–50 singles	Europe
Mackenzie McDonald	1–50 singles	North America
Pedro Martinez	51–100 singles	Europe
Dusan Lajovic	51–100 singles	Europe
Wesley Koolhof	1–25 doubles	Europe
Miguel Angel Reyes-Varela	26–75 doubles	North America
Pedro Cachin	At-large	South America
Matthew Ebden	At-large	International
Federico Ricci	Coaches	–
Nicolas Pereira	Alumni	–

The ATP PAC meets several times a year to make recommendations to ATP management and the ATP Board of Directors (especially through the player representatives).[116] Importantly, the ATP PAC's powers are only advisory in nature, the four player representatives on the ATP Board are in the minority and "consistently get out-voted."[117]

The four tournament representatives on the ATP Board of Directors all have significant business interests in the ATP and the business of tennis, including, for example, Herwig Straka and Gavin Forbes.[118] Both Straka, the tournament director of the Vienna Open,[119] and Forbes have simultaneously represented the interests of players, tournaments and the ATP itself. Straka, the CEO and founder of sports business company the e|motion group,[120] has managed his fellow Austrian Thiem.[121] IMG pioneered the multiple representation of clients in the same sporting ecosystem as a business model, with founder Mark McCormack simultaneously contracting tournaments and players to earn healthy commissions from: first, the media and sponsorship agreements negotiated for host tournaments;

---

[116] ATP, "New Player Advisory Council."
[117] Priest, "Working toward Break Point," 954.
[118] ATP, "Board of Directors."
[119] Namit Kumar, "'I Immediately Said It Was the Best Decision' – Dominic Thiem's Former Manager Herwig Straka on Appointment of Galo Blanco," Sportskeeda (October 1, 2021), available at: www.sportskeeda.com/tennis/news-i-immediately-said-best-decision-for mer-manager-herwig-straka-dominic-thiem-s-appointment-galo-blanco.
[120] e|motion group, "Inspiring since 1991," available at: www.emotiongroup.com/en/.
[121] Kumar, "I Immediately Said It Was the Best Decision."

and second, the players' prize money and marketing deals generated from playing in them.[122] Today, IMG's portfolio of tennis properties includes the three ATP Series (250, 500 and 1000), the ATP Next Generation Finals, the four Grand Slam tournaments, a series of ATP tournaments (such as the Miami Open, which it owns) and content properties such as "ATP Uncovered," which provides behind-the-scenes access to players and events.[123] The long-standing IMG Academy recently expanded its "decades-long partnership to nurture emerging tennis talent" with IMG's tennis division, which has managed talents such as Agassi, Djokovic, Osaka, and both Serena and Venus Williams (among many others).[124]

Unsurprisingly, there has been considerable debate and conjecture within professional men's tennis regarding conflicts of interest in the governance of the ATP. In 2021, player John Isner said the "ATP is a broken system" after ATP executive salaries were maintained while prize money was slashed due to the Covid-19 pandemic. "Tennis is run like an intramural sport," Isner said, and "is plagued by conflict and [a] lack of transparency." While "[p]layers and tournaments 'as partners' need to work together," Isner noted the low share of revenue received by tennis players in comparison to players in professional team sports, as well as their inability to share in the asset wealth they help create: "Promoters own assets that appreciate and have infinite time to monetize that asset, whereas the players have a short amount of time to maximize our talents. That's a broken system."[125] The governance debate has pitted player against player.[126] In early 2019, Djokovic and Pospisil, as members of the ATP PAC, were part of a successful effort to remove then ATP chairman, Chris Kermode, who was regarded as too deferential to the

---

[122] Futterman, *Players*, 62–3.
[123] IMG, "Sports Portfolio: Tennis," available at: www.img.com/portfolio/sports/tennis.
[124] IMG Academy, "IMG Academy Expands Decades-Long Partnership with IMG Tennis Division in New Strategic Partnership" (March 28, 2024), available at: www.imgacademy.com/news/img-academy-expands-decades-long-relationship-imgs-tennis-division-new-strategic-partnership; Futterman, *Players*, 143–71; Kurt Badenhausen, "IMG Tennis Business Scores with Osaka, Djokovic and Nishikori," Forbes (March 12, 2019), available at: www.forbes.com/sites/kurtbadenhausen/2019/03/12/img-tennis-business-scores-with-osaka-djokovic-and-nishikori/?sh=231a2cc33785; Forbes, "Profile: WME Sports," available at: www.forbes.com/companies/wme-sports/?sh=4fe2022227b9.
[125] Tennisbuzz, "'The ATP Is a Broken System Plagued by Conflict and Lack of Transparency,' Says John Isner" (February 24, 2021), available at: https://tennisbuzz.net/atp-broken-system-plagued-conflict-transparency-john-isner.
[126] Christopher Clarey, "It Is Time for the ATP to Get Its Act Together," *New York Times* (May 12, 2019), available at: www.nytimes.com/2019/05/12/sports/atp-board-gimelstob.html.

tournaments despite a key vote in 2014 to increase player prize money in a decision split along representative lines. At Wimbledon that year, a meeting of the ATP PAC dissolved, with four members resigning over Kermode's removal and a disputed board seat.[127]

In contrast, the ATP was clear on the question of apparent conflicts of interest in the context of the PTPA. In August 2020, after co-founding the PTPA, Djokovic stepped down as President of the ATP PAC together with PAC members Pospisil, Isner and Sam Querrey,[128] only for Djokovic and Pospisil to be renominated for the ATP PAC elections due in January 2021. In response to the nominations – which Djokovic said were unsolicited and reflective of the "trust and credibility" he and Pospisil enjoyed with the players – the ATP Board cast a vote prohibiting any active player from being a part of the ATP PAC and "any other organisation in the tennis ecosystem."[129] In the end, Djokovic withdrew his nomination. In a statement released on X (formerly Twitter), he said his "first reaction to this nomination was to accept it with the intention that, if elected, [he] would do [his] best to protect player interests *within* the ATP." However, the ATP's "new rule specifies that all members of the newly formed [PTPA] or any association that is deemed as having a 'conflict of interest' cannot be elected as a member of the [ATP PAC]." Accordingly, Djokovic "reluctantly and with a heavy heart" withdrew his name from the list of candidates, noting that "it is extremely important that we do not have conflicts of interest in our sport" and expressing his "hope" that, "going forward, this is not only applied to the formation of new associations at the player level but further applied to *all* levels within the ATP structure."[130] Paul McNamee, a former Grand Slam and Davis Cup winning professional who served also as tournament director of the Australian Open and the Hopman Cup, tweeted that it was with "deep sadness that [he] read that the #1 player in the world is barred from representing his peers … this was never, is not and will never be what

---

[127] Steinberger, "A Few Tennis Pros Make a Fortune."
[128] Matt Fitzgerald, "The ATP in 2021: The ATP Player Council vs. the PTPA," Tennis (December 27, 2020), available at: www.tennis.com/news/articles/the-atp-in-2021-the-atp-player-council-vs-the-ptpa.
[129] "Novak Djokovic Nominated for ATP Players Council But Says Governing Body Are Blocking Him," Eurosport (November 19, 2020), available at: www.eurosport.com/tennis/atp-world-tour-finals/2020/novak-djokovic-nominated-for-atp-players-council-return-but-says-governing-body-are-blocking-him_sto7998797/story.shtml.
[130] Novak Djokovic, X (formerly Twitter) (December 22, 2020) (emphases added), available at: https://x.com/DjokerNole/status/1341094745498632192?s=20.

the organisation ought stand for ... imo [sic] the founders of the ATP, including the late great Arthur Ashe, would be ashamed."[131]

4.1.3 The WTA

The WTA continues to proudly acknowledge its origins in Billie Jean King's struggle to create a players' association for women players, build a professional tour for them and achieve equal opportunity. The WTA is positioned as "the global leader in women's professional sports" and "one of the world's most recognizable and high-profile sports organizations." The WTA Tour today comprises over fifty events, four Grand Slam tournaments, nearly thirty countries and regions, and an estimated global audience of 700 million.[132]

Like the ATP, the WTA's governance structure reflects the labor settlement achieved by women's professional tennis in 1975 with the establishment of the WIPTC.[133] As shown in Table 6.2, the WTA Board of Directors consists of three player representatives, three tournament representatives, one representative of the ITA and the WTA CEO.[134]

Elections are conducted annually by the WTA for members of the WTA Players' Council (PC) which is structured to reflect the WTA player rankings system and include representatives of singles and doubles players. The WTA PC as constituted following elections in 2023 and announced by the WTA on October 3, 2023 is shown in Table 6.3.[135]

Within days of the election, over twenty of the top players on the WTA Tour wrote to the WTA with a series of demands, including higher pay, a more flexible schedule that better considers players' physical and mental health, expanded childcare and official representation on the WTA PC by the PTPA. In response, a WTA spokesperson said that "players have always been equal decision-makers to ensure a strong direction for women's tennis."[136] The WTA refused the players' request for meetings over its demands to be attended by the PTPA

---

[131] Paul McNamee, X (formerly Twitter) (December 22, 2020), available at: https://x.com/PaulFMcNamee/status/1341259069584265218?s=20.
[132] WTA, "About the WTA," available at: www.wtatennis.com/about.
[133] ITF, "Frequently Asked Questions: Governance."
[134] WTA, "WTA Tour Board of Directors," available at: www.wtatennis.com/board-of-directors.
[135] WTA, "WTA Announces 2023 Election Results" (October 3, 2023), available at: www.wtatennis.com/news/3718872/wta-announces-2023-election-results.
[136] Matthew Futterman, 'WTA Facing Rebellion from Numerous Top Players Over Pay and Conditions on Women's Tour', The Athletic (October 31, 2023), available at: https://theathletic.com/5014481/2023/10/30/wta-female-players-letter-push/.

Table 6.2 *2024 WTA Board of Directors*

Member	Representative	Player Rankings/Region
Vanessa Webb	Players	Council Chair, 1–100+ singles and doubles-only representative
Anja Vreg	Players	Top 20 singles
Kurt Zumwalt	Players	21–100+ singles and doubles-only representative
Brandon Burke	Players	Player alternate representative
Adam Barrett	Tournaments	Americas
Peter-Michael Reichel	Tournaments	Europe
Cameron Pearson	Tournaments	Asia-Pacific
Bob Moran	Tournaments	Tournament alternate representative
Steve Simon	WTA CEO	–
David Haggerty	ITF	–
Kris Dent	ITF alternate	–

Table 6.3 *2024 WTA Players' Council*

Member	Player Rankings
Victoria Azarenka	Top 20 member
Caroline Garcia	Top 20 member
Madison Keys	Top 20 member
Jessica Pegula	Top 20 member
Donna Vekic	21–50 member
Daria Saville	51–100 member
Gabriela Dabrowski	21+ and doubles-only representative
Alex Krunic	101+ and doubles-only representative

Executive Director Ahmad Nassar. It was a significant development for both the players and the PTPA, however, which had rightly faced criticism for its initial announcement by Djokovic and Pospisil which included only men on the ATP Tour. Pospisil conceded the "mistake," with Tara Moore, a player reaching out for the PTPA to her fellow professionals on the WTA Tour, having said in 2021 that the male-only launch of the PTPA was a "sore point" with women players and that the

PTPA was a "tougher sell" given that women's tennis was still more lucrative than other female sports.[137]

4.2 Player Rights, Pay and Conditions in Professional Tennis

The rights, pay and conditions of professional tennis players are extensively regulated. In addition to the TADP and the TADC, the principal means of regulation are the respective Rulebooks of the ATP and the WTA which, together, include some 956 published pages.[138] As both are extremely complex – legally and commercially – a thorough analysis is beyond the scope of this chapter. Instead, this section will selectively focus on those aspects of the Rulebooks most pertinent to the pay and working conditions of professional tennis players and, connectedly, their historic, current and future union organizing efforts.

In several key respects, the Rulebooks continue to enshrine pro tennis's first labor settlement of the first half of the 1970s, especially by embedding an independent model of professionalism, limiting player payments to prize money, monopolizing the respective tours and, in turn, creating a monopsonist labor market. The Rulebooks achieve this by providing for a system of work for players that has (at least) five main features: (1) player entry and mandatory terms (which incorporate the Rulebooks into a contract between the ATP or the WTA, on the one hand, and the player, on the other);[139] (2) imposing strict minimum playing commitments (coupled with non-compete restraints);[140] (3) limiting player payments to the forms of prize money, bonuses and other prizes;[141] (4) banning or restricting other forms of player payments

---

[137] Steinberger, "A Few Tennis Pros Make a Fortune."

[138] ATP, 2024 ATP Official Rulebook, available at: www.atptour.com/en/corporate/rule book; WTA, 2024 WTA Official Rulebook, available at: https://photoresources.wtaten nis.com/wta/document/2024/02/12/1a78ea3b-3a70-4847-9951-d59307c2655d/2024-WTA-Rulebook-2-11-2024-.pdf.

[139] 2024 ATP Official Rulebook, s. 1.07(A); 2024 WTA Official Rulebook, II – Player Commitment.

[140] 2024 ATP Official Rulebook, s. 1.07(C) and (D) – a commitment player is one ranked in the "Top 30" as at the previous November and must compete in all ATP World Tour Masters 1000 events, the ATP Finals and four ATP Tour 500 events; s. 1.14(B) imposes restrictions on participating in special events and exhibitions; 2024 WTA Official Rulebook, XVII(E) – Exhibition/Non-WTA Event Rule.

[141] 2024 ATP Official Rulebook. ATP prize money takes the form of: (1) "on-site prize money" payable by tournaments in accordance with the amounts established by the ATP – ss. 3.08(B)(1)(a), 3.09, 3.18(A), 3.20, 3.21, 3.22 and 3.23, and Exhibit J; (2) variable prize money based on tournament profits – ss. 3.17(B), 3.18(B), 3.18(C), 3.20; and (3)

and benefits, including appearance and promotional fees,[142] travel expenses[143] and accommodation expenses;[144] and (5) regulating player publicity, name, image and likeness, including mandating a player license to be granted in perpetuity for the purpose of advertising and promoting tennis events.[145] The established system provides a potentially lucrative form of work for the top-performing and top-ranked players through the combination of prize money and the endorsements players can separately generate through the profile achieved from on-court success. However, the five features – when taken together – leave many players dependent on performance-based prize money for merely basic earnings, needing to generate sponsorship to meet the considerable costs involved in competing on tour, and unprotected in the event of injury or a lack of on-court success. In recognition of this, in late 2023, the ATP announced the three-year pilot of a new and potentially sixth feature of the system of work – ATP Baseline – which aims to provide minimum guaranteed income for the top 250-ranked players, a form of income protection for those players injured on tour and a financial investment in emerging talents in the form of an advance payment to eligible players ranked in the top 125. The ATP expects that about fifty players will receive financial support through the program. Eligibility is "based on a range of criteria," including "a player's ranking, career prize money earnings, and number of events players. Aligned with the purpose of the program, players with more than $15 [million] in career earnings are not eligible."[146]

If a player is to lose his or her ranking, this can have a profound impact on the player's earning potential and position on the tour. Many factors outside a player's control can cause this. The WTA Rulebook includes a "special ranking rule" for players who are unable to compete for a minimum period of twenty-six weeks for reasons such as injury or pregnancy.[147] The case of Simona Halep, however, reveals the fallout that

---

ATP Tour bonus pools, fixed by the ATP – s. 1.07(G) and (H). All other prizes require ATP approval – s. 3.15(A) and (B); 2024 WTA Official Rulebook, IX – Prize Money and XIV – Prize Money Formula.

[142] 2024 ATP Official Rulebook, s. 1.15(A) and (B); 2024 WTA Official Rulebook, XVII(13)(a)(i)(b) – Payment of Personal Expenses.
[143] See 2024 ATP Official Rulebook, s. 3.15(D).
[144] See ibid., ss. 1.20 and 3.09.
[145] See ibid., ss. 1.12(A) and (C), 1.13(A)–(F); 2024 WTA Official Rulebook, VII(A) and (B).
[146] ATP, "'Baseline,' ATP's Pioneering Financial Security Programme for Players" (January 16, 2024), available at: www.atptour.com/en/news/baseline-programme-providing-player-security.
[147] 2024 WTA Official Rulebook, VIII(C).

can occur because of the combined effect of two complex sets of regulations which can run into conflict: the TADP and the rankings system. Halep successfully appealed her four-year doping ban to the CAS, with the suspension reduced to nine months. However, she had already been provisionally suspended and unable to play from August 2022 to March 2024.[148] As a result, the WTA is contemplating another special ranking rule for players impacted by the TADP.[149] This approach reveals that the WTA approaches these issues principally through the norms that have evolved on the tour – of which the rankings system is one – so that the basic rights of players can only be assured in exceptional circumstances and through "special" carve-outs to those norms.

Naomi Osaka's experiences also reveal that the challenges involved affect even the most successful and higher-earning players.[150] Her career has involved a struggle to reconcile her pursuit of a career as a professional tennis player with her advocacy for social justice following the killing of George Floyd, against racism and for her own mental health.[151] These are all internationally recognized human rights. Her experiences as a child athlete also bring to the fore the essential need for the industry to respect child rights, which encompass the right to be protected from "economic exploitation," or from "performing any work that is likely to ... interfere with the child's education, or to be harmful to the child's health or physical, mental, spiritual, moral or social development."[152] Naomi's sister, Mari, retired at 21 after *seven years* on the tour with career earnings of $92,927, an average of little more than $13,000 per year, placing her 1,676th on the career earning list.[153] Mari's career best ranking was 280, but on the day Naomi became number one – January 28, 2019 – it had fallen to 332. A 2013 ITF study estimated that a female player would need to be ranked 253rd or higher to break even

---

[148] CAS, "CAS Upholds the Appeal Filed by Simona Halep and Reduces Her Period of Ineligibility from 4 Years to 9 Months" (March 5, 2024), available at: www.tas-cas.org/en/general-information/news-detail/article/cas-upholds-the-appeal-filed-by-simona-halep-and-reduces-her-period-of-ineligibility-from-4-years-to/. *Halep v. ITIA*, CAS Case 2023/A/10227, Award (March 5, 2024).

[149] Srivathsa Sridhar, "WTA Considering 'Special Rankings' for Players Cleared of Doping," Reuters (March 20, 2024), available at: www.reuters.com/sports/tennis/wta-considering-special-rankings-players-cleared-doping-2024-03-20/.

[150] Osaka ranks 22nd with WTA career prize money earnings of $21,474,174: WTA, "Career Prize Money Leaders" (April 15, 2024), available at: https://wtafiles.wtatennis.com/pdf/rankings/All_Career_Prize_Money.pdf.

[151] Rothenberg, *Naomi Osaka*, 299–304, 314–15, 341, 379, 402.

[152] UN Convention on the Rights of the Child (1989), Art. 32(1).

[153] WTA, "Career Prize Money Leaders."

with minimal travel, lodging, equipment and coaching expenses, although, according to Rothenberg, "most in tennis thought the threshold was actually closer to 120th." In 2018, Mari earned $15,002 in prize money, about 1/400th of Naomi's $6,394,289.[154]

Jelena Dokic writes that "the tour can be a very difficult and lonely place for women," for a number of reasons, especially that most begin at 15 or 16 years of age when still children and "very vulnerable"; most travel "without their parents, especially when they are starting out, because of a lack of finances," and so "just take a coach for their tennis." Dokic – who has revealed that she was physically and emotionally abused by her father Damir in the pursuit of her tennis career – argues that, while she agrees and supports with "[w]omen's rights, gay rights, [and the] call for equal prize money ... we need more people to stick up for the men, women, boys and girls who are being physically and emotionally abused."[155]

Tables 6.4 and 6.5 respectively provide a comparative overview of 2023 prize money earnings on the ATP and the WTA Tours, taking into account the depth of player rankings. For the purpose of the overview, after including all in the top ten and players ranked fifty, rankings have been chosen based on ATP Baseline (the impact of which is also suggested in Table 6.4) and, for the WTA, the ITF's "breakeven research" which highlights rankings 253 and, given Rothenberg's suggestion, 120.[156] Player 300 is included in each table to reflect the stated views of Pospisil on the establishment of the PTPA.[157] The tables highlight the vast discrepancies in prize money between men and women.

5 The PTPA

5.1 *Establishment of the PTPA in 2020 and the Reaction of the "Seven Kingdoms"*

According to Steinberger, writing in 2021: "Tennis is brutally individualistic, and its lopsided economy, in which almost all the rewards go to a select few, inevitably makes collective action difficult if not impossible. It is a sport in which the superstars get most of the money and

---

[154] Rothenberg, *Naomi Osaka*, 266.
[155] Dokic and Halloran, *Unbreakable*, 304.
[156] Rothenberg, *Naomi Osaka*, 266.
[157] Steinberger, "A Few Tennis Pros Make a Fortune."

Table 6.4 *ATP Prize Money 2023 and ATP Baseline*[158]

Money Rank	Player	YTD (US$)	ATP Baseline Amount	ATP Baseline Payment
1	Djokovic, Novak	15,952,044	–	–
2	Alcaraz, Carlos	15,196,504	–	–
3	Medvedev, Daniil	11,548,023	–	–
4	Sinner, Jannik	10,456,264	–	–
5	Rublev, Andrey	6,571,890	–	–
6	Zverev, Alexander	5,643,764	–	–
7	Tsitsipas, Stefanos	5,489,110	–	–
8	Rune, Holger	4,946,875	–	–
9	Hurkacz, Hubert	4,803,644	–	–
10	Fritz, Taylor	4,019,217	–	–
50	Ebden, Matthew	1,199,856	–	–
100	Munar, Jaume	735,698	300,000/ 200,000	Min. Guarantee/ Income Protection
101	Molcan, Alex	729,256	150,000/ 100,000	"
125	Rojer, Jean-Julien	556,209	200,000	Newcomer Investment
175	Melo, Marcelo	323,482	150,000/ 100,000	Min. Guarantee/ Income Protection
176	Zeppieri, Giulio	323,192	75,000/ 50,000	"
250	Cabral, Francisco	176,922	"	"
300	Bellier, Antoine	126,433	n/a	n/a

attention."[159] Ashe and King said pretty much the same, years ago. The world of professional tennis has evolved over a fifty-year period to aggressively reflect the ethos of the player movement, businesspeople and tennis authorities that brought about professional tennis's first labor settlement – an ethos of business, entrepreneurialism, performance,

---

[158] Adapted from ATP, "ATP Prize Money Leaders (US$)"; and ATP, "Baseline."
[159] Steinberger, "A Few Tennis Pros Make a Fortune."

Table 6.5 *WTA Prize Money 2023*[160]

Money Rank	Player	YTD (US$)
1	Sabalenka, Aryna	7,554,653
2	Swiatek, Iga	6,779,686
3	Gauff, Coco	5,976,622
4	Rybakina, Elena	5,097,437
5	Pegula, Jessica	4,320,890
6	Vondrousova, Marketa	4,275,278
7	Muchova, Karolina	2,804,438
8	Jabeur, Ons	2,798,564
9	Kvitova, Petra	2,488,381
10	Sakkari, Maria	2,407,413
50	Begu, Irina-Camelia	835,407
100	Juvan, Kaja	482,339
120	Burrage, Jodie	396,452
253	Riera, Julia	112,929
300	Kessler, McCartney	74,327

vision, risk and growth in a system which pits player against player.[161] But Kramer, Heldman and the commercial pioneers of "Open Tennis" were impresarios, not monarchs. They did not *intend* to create the divisive culture which the game's governors, whether deliberately or otherwise, have subsequently embedded. It was therefore ironic but unsurprising that the "Seven Kingdoms" responded to the establishment of the PTPA with a call for "collaboration, not division," and for the players "to consider and act in the best interests of the sport, now and for the future." Moreover, the tennis authorities reiterated that they "fully support the ATP in its role in representing the best interests of players."[162] Key players concerned that the PTPA would be a divisive influence included Federer and Nadal.[163] Along with four other members

---

[160] Adapted from WTA, "Prize Money Leaders" (November 6, 2023), available at: https://wtafiles.wtatennis.com/pdf/rankings/PrizeMoney/prize_money_2023.pdf.
[161] Arsenault, *Arthur Ashe*, 302–3; King, *Billie Jean King*, 169.
[162] Wimbledon, "Media Statement Regarding Player Representation" (August 29, 2020), available at: www.wimbledon.com/en_GB/news/articles/2020-08-29/media_statement_regarding_player_representation.html.
[163] Roger Federer, X (formerly Twitter) (August 30, 2020), available at: https://x.com/rogerfederer/status/1299774755319422976?s=20.

of the ATP PAC, both wrote to the players on the ATP Tour, expressing concerns over the possible implications of the PTPA, such as the tournaments "going against" the players and possible "fallout both with our careers, income and negativity." In short, Federer and Nadal maintained, "[a] new Player Association cannot co-exist with the ATP."[164] ATP Chairman Andrea Gaudenzi also saw the PTPA as a competing organization and an existential threat to the ATP. "You have," Gaudenzi said, "what other athletes in other sports would strive for – a seat at the boardroom table. That is what players fought for in the creation of the ATP Tour ... It makes no sense why you would be better served by shifting your role from the inside to the outside of the governance structure."[165] Gaudenzi's perspective is important, and raises for discussion whether the players would *in fact* be better and measurably served through external union representation, whether that representation *necessitates* a diminution of the position of the players within the governance of the ATP, and whether the ATP is willing to openly concede *to the players* its historical transformation from a player association to a governing body.

Djokovic and Pospisil – as the founding co-Presidents of the new PTPA – were clear that the "the goal of the PTPA is not to replace the ATP, but to provide players with a self-governance structure that is independent from the ATP and directly responsive to player-members' needs and concerns." Pospisil informed the players that the creation of the PTPA was "the first and most pivotal step" and that "[t]here will be a lot of work in building and perfecting the operations of this association" which will "essentially [have] the same function as a union." Its stated goals include "revenue sharing, disciplinary actions, player pensions, travel, insurance and amenities at tournaments."[166]

Importantly, the reaction of the "Seven Kingdoms" did not in any way acknowledge the trade union rights of the professional tennis players, nor the respective responsibilities of the tennis bodies to respect those rights. At the heart of this is the tension between the position of the players within the existing governance structures of the tennis bodies and the existence of an external and independent player union. While this tension – described immediately by management and some influential players as representing an existential threat – is novel to the world of professional tennis, it is not

---

[164] Ben Rothenberg, "Djokovic and Other Top Men Are Creating a Players' Association," *New York Times* (August 28, 2020), available at: www.nytimes.com/2020/08/28/sports/tennis/tennis-union-men-djokovic.html.
[165] Ibid.
[166] Ibid.

uncommon within international labor relations. In that broader context, by way of contrast, the presence of workers' representatives within management structures are more commonly viewed as threats to the trade union, rather than to management. International labor standards "encourage cooperation on all relevant matters"[167] and "contain explicit provisions guaranteeing that, where there exist in the same undertaking both trade union representatives and elected representatives, appropriate measures are to be taken to ensure that the existence of elected representatives in an enterprise is not used to undermine the position of the trade unions concerned."[168] All parties will certainly need to strategically assess the interaction of both forms of player representation. It is quite wrong, however, for the tennis authorities or leading players to view the emergence of the PTPA in existential terms and jump to the conclusion that all can't coexist.

5.2 The Developing Culture, Governance, Structure and Objectives of the PTPA

The PTPA, established as a not-for-profit corporation in Canada,[169] is "committed to safeguarding and supporting men's and women's professional tennis players worldwide" and has adopted a series of principles "designed as a roadmap for the Association's advocacy work on behalf of all professional tennis players."[170] The "five core tenets" of the principles, which were established in accordance with the WPA's UDPR, are:

1. Take collective action and advocate on behalf of tennis players globally
2. Obtain players' fair share of the business of tennis and terms of participation
3. Optimize and rigorously protect tennis players' rights
4. Safeguard tennis players' welfare and protect players from abuse
5. Advocate for, and contribute to, the best vision and structure of tennis globally[171]

---

[167] ILO Convention No. 135, Art. 5.
[168] ILO, "Compilation of Decisions," 295, para. 1582.
[169] Priest, "Working toward Break Point," 951.
[170] PTPA, available at: www.ptpaplayers.com/; PTPA, "The Professional Tennis Players Association Appoints Eight Players to First-Ever Executive Committee; Unveils Principles to Respect, Protect & Guarantee Fundamental Rights" (January 10, 2023), available at: www.ptpaplayers.com/the-professional-tennis-players-association-appointseight-players-to-first-ever-executive-committee-unveils-principles-to-protect-respect-guarantee-fundamental-rights/.
[171] WPA, Universal Declaration of Player Rights; ibid.

The principles are also designed to squarely address the player versus player dynamic that can be so at odds with the imperative of trade union solidarity. The first principle aims to build a consciousness of trade union rights among the PTPA membership, and incorporates the "collective," "freedom of association" and "the right to organize." It acknowledges that "[t]ennis is predominantly an individual sport, but that should not mean individual players are isolated and divided."[172] The release of the PTPA's principles in January 2023 coincided with the announcement of its inaugural Board, which, as shown in Table 6.6, includes co-founders Djokovic and Pospisil and is comprised with an eye to gender equality and cultural diversity.

The PTPA's articulation of its purpose and principles shows that the developing culture of the PTPA is *not* one that seeks to be embedded in the existing norms of professional tennis, but instead in trade and player unionism, so that new industry norms can be created. The PTPA is well aware that the existing model of player representation in professional tennis has seen many players fall outside the protections of the system, and many fundamental issues of player rights such as abuse have been inadequately addressed, if at all. The PTPA also points to the achievements of player unions in major professional team sports and asks whether the ATP and WTA are offering the world's best tennis players a deal which stands up in comparison. Organizing starts with education, and one of the key themes of the PTPA's communications has been

Table 6.6 *Inaugural PTPA Executive Committee*[173]

Name	Country
Paula Badosa	Spain
Novak Djokovic	Serbia
Hubert Hurkacz	Poland
John Isner	United States
Ons Jabeur	Tunisia
Bethanie Mattek-Sands	United States
Vasek Pospisil	Canada
Saisai Zheng	China

[172] PTPA, available at: www.ptpaplayers.com/.
[173] Ibid.

around the second tenet of its principles – the players' share of the revenue and wealth of the sport. PTPA research indicates that the players' estimated share of revenue at 17.5 percent is very low by comparison to the players in major professional team sports, which are much closer to a 50/50 split. The players' share in tennis is even lower by comparison as in team sports major costs such as coaching, travel, accommodation, medical care and equipment are all borne by management, not by the players from their share.[174] And, as Isner had already pointed out in describing a "broken system," this only takes into account revenue, not the value of assets such as prestigious tournaments that appreciate over the long term.[175]

The creation of the PTPA comes at a historic time for the player union movement, which is undergoing a third wave of organizing.[176] The first wave began in the 1960s, when the PFA – some fifty years after its establishment – won its first major labor disputes over the transfer system and the abolition of the maximum weekly wage.[177] It was towards the end of this wave – which saw the creation of player associations in the major professional sports in the United States and European football – that the ITPA, ATP and WTA were created. The second wave began with the widespread growth of full-time professionalism in many sports with the advent of subscription television in the 1990s, which also saw earlier established player associations reformed, resourced, modernized and globalized. Australian rules football, basketball, cricket, football, Gaelic sports, rugby league and rugby union were among those that reached new levels of organization, which also saw the creation of international player union federations especially in sports such as cricket, football, rugby and on a multi-sport basis at the European and global levels to deal with the increasingly transnational nature of professional sport's labor relations.[178] It was in the midst of this wave that the IMTA was attempted.

The third and current wave is the most sophisticated. Dabscheck estimates over 200 player associations now exist,[179] with 138 based in more than sixty countries representing some 85,000 professional athletes

---

[174] PTPA, "Why Most Tennis Players Struggle to Make a Living," available at: www.youtube.com/watch?v=STff_wOQHn4.
[175] Tennisbuzz, " The ATP Is a Broken System."
[176] Braham Dabscheck, "The Slow and Steady Development of an Industrial Relations of World Sport, 1885–2019" (November 2022) 39 Sport Trad 77, at 80.
[177] Harding, *For the Good of the Game*.
[178] Dabscheck, "Slow and Steady Development," 84–8.
[179] Ibid.

combining under the multi-sport international labor federation, the WPA.[180] In addition to its scale, three key features of the third wave are the organized commitment of the player unions to embed human rights in sport,[181] including athlete trade union rights,[182] the sharing of expertise and knowledge among the unions on key issues such as the holistic personal development and well-being of players,[183] and the embrace of commercialization in the conduct of the business of the players' association so that the players have the resources, financial clout and leverage to match management at the bargaining table. This is being described as "the entrepreneurial era of player unions."[184] Nassar, appointed as the inaugural PTPA Executive Director in August 2022, is one of the era's driving forces, having served as the founding CEO of One Team Partners and President of NFL Players Inc., which he helped grow into one of the largest for-profit marketing and licensing businesses in the world.[185] In 2023, the NFL Players Association (NFLPA) was ranked by License Global as the 24th biggest licensor in the world (The Walt Disney Company was number one), with retail sales of $2.7 billion. A year earlier, NFLPA commercial revenue exceeded $300 million for the first time.[186] One Team Partners aims to maximize the value of athlete name, image and likeness rights, and brings together the group licensing, marketing, media and investing activities of six major player associations, including the NFLPA, the MLBPA and two

---

[180] WPA, "World Players," available at: https://uniglobalunion.org/about/sectors/world-players/; FIFPRO, "Player Associations Benefit from Fruitful WPA #Right2Organize Conference" (May 24, 2023), available at: https://fifpro.org/en/who-we-are/what-we-do/foundations-of-work/player-associations-benefit-from-fruitful-wpa-right2organize-conference/.

[181] WPA, "IOC Must Engage Stakeholders and Add Human Rights to Olympic Charter" (June 7, 2022), available at: https://uniglobalunion.org/news/ioc-must-engage-stakeholders-and-add-human-rights-to-olympic-charter/.

[182] WPA, "#Right2Organise Survey & Report"; WPA, "WADA Governance Review."

[183] WPA, "#PDC22: Developing the Players of Tomorrow" (June 20, 2022), available at: https://uniglobalunion.org/news/pdc22-developing-the-players-of-tomorrow/.

[184] James Emmett and David Cushnan, "The End of Break Point; the Next Big Thing in Track and Field; the Entrepreneurial Era of Player Unions," Leaders Sport Business Podcast (2024), available at: https://podcasts.apple.com/gb/podcast/the-end-of-break-point-the-next-big-thing-in/id1126762453?i=1000649064303&utm_medium=email&_hsenc=p2ANqtz-8_1LLysuBVGfBeAaS5PXYNGbadAt5dzjNZibDlh5bcYzow9avHjrbqSzKojGwL7YL8Djqqm2Z_fTwoVtShi3h5wBCMZw&_hsmi=298434704&utm_content=298434704&utm_source=hs_email.

[185] PTPA, "Our Team," available at: www.ptpaplayers.com/leadership/.

[186] License Global, "The Top Global Licensors 2023," 8–9, available at: https://superbrainheroes.com/wp-content/uploads/2023/10/Global-Licensing-Report-2023-LIC_230727_DE_Copyright_2.pdf.

major groups of women athletes, the Women's National Basketball Players' Association and the US Women's National [Soccer] Team Players Association.[187] To this end, one of Nassar's first initiatives was the raising of $26 million in equity to create the Winners Alliance, which will also serve as the PTPA's for-profit arm.[188] In addition to seeking to maximize through group licensing of the name, image and likeness rights of PTPA members, the Winners Alliance has partnered with the Federation of International Cricketers' Associations (FICA) to "protect and optimize [the] global commercial rights of cricketers."[189]

The creation of the PTPA also comes at a time when professional tennis itself is considering "seismic" change. A "Premier Tour" is under contemplation especially by the four majors, with research by the Boston Consulting Group revealing that 70 percent of tennis fans watched only the four majors, and 80 percent of the sport's revenue comes from the top 10 tournaments, including the majors. A new tour could provide opportunities for the top 300 men and women players and result in equal prize money. The key, according to Tennis Australia CEO Craig Tiley, is for a "transformational way forward" to "become a player-centric and fan-centric proposal."[190] This will necessarily involve professional tennis forging a new labor settlement with its players.

Two key questions arise and will only be answered in the medium term. First, will the PTPA be required to organize and unify the players to attain a level of collective action such as that seen in 1973 when, as player unions, the ATP boycotted Wimbledon and the WTA won equal prize money at Forest Hills? And second, if the PTPA is, will that activism be converted – for the first time in the history of professional tennis – into collective bargaining? Perhaps then, one of the world's greatest sports can successfully replace its Darwinian system with a culture that truly appreciates that players are people first, athletes a distant second, and that they deserve to be genuine partners in the business of the game.

---

[187] One Team Partners, "Who," available at: www.joinoneteam.com/.
[188] Winners Alliance, "Winners Alliance Launched to Serve the Interests of Professional Athletes" (April 4, 2023), available at: https://winnersalliance.com/winners-alliance-launched-to-serve-the-interests-of-professional-athletes/.
[189] Winners Alliance, "FICA and Winners Alliance Forge Historic Partnership to Protect and Optimize Global Commercial Rights of Cricketers" (January 10, 2024), available at: https://winnersalliance.com/fica-and-winners-alliance-forge-historic-partnership-to-protect-and-optimize-global-commercial-rights-of-cricketers/.
[190] Marc McGowan, "It's Not a War: The Seismic Shift about to Hit World Tennis," The Age (March 30, 2024), available at: www.theage.com.au/sport/tennis/it-s-not-a-war-the-seismic-shift-about-to-hit-world-tennis-20240326-p5ffh8.html.

PART 2

Regulatory

7

Access to Justice in Tennis Disputes

ILIAS BANTEKAS

1 Introduction

One must distinguish between regulatory and contract-based disputes in professional tennis. The latter are resolved by reference to the parties' contract, which dictates their obligations, choice of dispute resolution forum (i.e. litigation or arbitration) and the place, as well as the chosen applicable law. Contractual disputes typically arise between players and agents, tournament organisers/player associations and advertisers/sponsors and others. Regulatory disputes concern infractions of rules set out and agreed in advance by the International Tennis Federation (ITF), Women's Tennis Association (WTA), Association of Tennis Professionals (ATP) and, to a lesser degree tournament organisers, to which players and national tennis federations have agreed to adhere. The dispute resolution mechanisms spelt out by these rules are thus obligatory on the parties involved, chiefly players and professional associations and the ITF. Unlike contractual disputes where players negotiate the terms of access to justice in the event of dispute, there is no such possibility on the occasion of regulatory disputes. This chapter will focus mostly on ITF-related mechanisms given that these generate the biggest number of disputes, namely, its internal mechanisms, the Internal Adjudication Panel and the ITF Independent Tribunal. Another sub-section will deal with the relation of these entities with the Court of Arbitration for Sport (CAS), and yet another will explore dispute resolution in the context of the ATP. It should be stated from the outset that since the ITF is the sport governing body (SGB) recognised by the International Olympic Committee (IOC), all doping and integrity (e.g. match-fixing) violations by ATP and WTA players are handled by the ITF and its adjudicatory mechanisms (subject to some exceptions, such as an ATP tour violation). This is why this chapter reserves only a limited amount of discussion to the relevant mechanisms of the WTA and ATP. A small sub-section at the beginning of this chapter will demonstrate the limited role for mediation and alternative dispute resolution (ADR) (other than arbitration) more generally. The role and jurisdiction of the ITF Ethics Commission and of the Independent Panel in the resolution of disputes arising from the ITF Code of Ethics will be explored in detail in Chapter 13 of this volume. Appeals to CAS against decisions from national anti-doping organisations are explored in Chapter 10 of this volume.

While this book was going into production in late 2024, several developments occurred which concern this chapter. First and foremost, the 2025 ITF Constitution has changed the sequence of provisions on dispute resolution analysed here and the pertinent provisions on the jurisdiction of the CAS are more elaborate in comparison to their predecessors. In addition, in 2025, new procedural rules were promulgated for both the Independent Tribunal and the Internal Adjudication Panel. These changes come into effect on 1 January 2025 and hence the authors and editors are unable to incorporate these into the book as the cut-off date was late May 2024. Readers are advised to compare the text in this chapter with the amended constitution and regulations.

2 ADR in Tennis

The regulatory 'disputes' as set out in the introduction concern specific rules-based infractions and hence are not amenable to negotiation and mediation. In any event, the pertinent judicial and quasi-judicial institutions do not enjoy authority to make or accept mediated settlements. Settlements are, however, common in contract-based disputes, chiefly by means of negotiation, irrespective of the stage of the proceedings before the courts or arbitral tribunals. A sphere of disputes which is not discussed in this chapter concerns collective disputes between players and professional tennis associations. Although these are not common, there have existed circumstances where players threatened to boycott a tournament if fundamental concerns were not met. These disputes were resolved through ADR mechanisms without having to resort to litigation.[1] Collective bargaining negotiations and settlements are explored in Chapter 6 of this volume. In addition, there is a limited scope in corruption offences whereby a covered person may in consultation with the International Tennis Integrity Agency

---

[1] See Bradley Raboin, 'Accepting a Double Fault: How ADR Might Save Men's Professional Tennis' (2014) 3 Mississippi Sports L Rev 206; see generally, Ilias Bantekas, 'The Resolution of Professional Tennis Disputes' (2023) 14 JIDS 488.

(ITIA) agree on a sanction in line with the appropriate sanctioning guidelines. This is exceptional, however.

3 Internal ITF Mechanisms

The following sub-section will explore in brief key ITF/ITIA mechanisms set up to undertake on-site investigations and impose sanctions at first instance. The on-site authority of the various ITF/ITIA entities does not strictly pertain to dispute resolution, particularly those dealing with disciplinary sanctions and doping and corruption offences in professional tennis. Their inclusion in this chapter serves to allow readers to achieve a comprehensive and rounded account of the ITF judicial and quasi-judicial architecture. Similar on-site mechanisms exist in the ATP Code.[2] This chapter will not discuss disciplinary actions under the ITF Code of Ethics.

3.1 On-Site Quasi-Adjudicatory Mechanisms

While the Internal Adjudication Panel and the Independent Tribunal remain the two key judicial institutions in the ITF architecture, the ITF has further given authority to certain other entities to administer on-site investigations and impose sanctions. These on-site sanctions typically concern corruption and doping offences, although other welfare violations are not uncommon, and are handed down once a prima facie case has been established by the relevant entity/officer, following an investigation (in the case of corruption) or a doping test.[3] By way of illustration, before the Independent Tribunal can exercise its first-instance jurisdiction over a corruption-related violation, Article I.E.2 of the ITF Women's World Tour Tennis Regulations stipulates that the ITF's anti-corruption hearing official shall have exclusive jurisdiction, in the first instance, over allegations that the Tennis Anti-Corruption Program (TACP) has been breached. This authority is also granted to an Anti-Corruption Hearing Officer (AHO) for breaches of the TACP.[4] For a fuller account and discussion of the AHO, readers are directed to Chapter 10 of this volume.

---

[2] ATP Code, Arts 8.01(G) and 8.03(G), which provide authority for on-site investigations to the Senior Vice-President, Rules and Regulations.
[3] The sanction may well be provisional until a full investigation takes place. See ITIA, 'Six Moroccan Tennis Players Provisionally Suspended', available at: https://itia.tennis/news/sanctions/six-moroccan-players-suspended/
[4] Specifically, TACP (2021), Art. F.3 stipulates that: 'The ITIA may at any time make an application to an AHO for a Provisional Suspension of a Covered Person, including (i)

In addition, the ITF Supervisor possesses authority to make decisions over particular matters. His or her decisions can be challenged by way of appeal to the Panel.[5] The entity of the ITF has granted itself investigative powers in respect of certain types of cases. In accordance with Article VI.C of the ITF Code of Conduct, the ITF has the power to investigate any alleged major offence and it is mandatory for all players and related persons to cooperate fully with such investigation. This may include a request by the ITF to furnish evidence, information or attend a hearing and provide a written statement. Where, as a result of such investigation, there is prima facie evidence that the underlying offence has been committed, the ITF shall refer the matter not to the Panel or the Independent Tribunal, but to its Review Board. Under the same provision the ITF will identify one or more experts who shall be independent of the ITF with a view to re-evaluating the evidence and determine whether 'there is a case to answer'. The Review Board's decision in this regard must be unanimous. Although the Code of Conduct is silent, it is presumed that two avenues are available to concerned parties about the independence of the expert chosen by the ITF to perform this function. The first is to trigger the Panel's supervisory function (described elsewhere below) and the second is by recourse to the courts of the forum (i.e. English courts), whether as a right of access to justice or on the basis of breach of contract (i.e. that the ITF breached its contractual obligation to appoint a suitable expert).

Moreover, the ITF Executive Director possesses authority, among others, to provisionally suspend a player from ITF tournaments in the event of conduct contrary to the integrity of the game.[6] Finally, in accordance with Article 7(a) of the ITF Bylaws, the ITF Board of Directors possesses power to 'investigate and bring a complaint' against a national tennis federation for any violation of the ITF Constitution, rules and regulations and for bringing the game to disrepute or for failure to represent the game adequately in its territory. This prosecutorial function of the Board and any evidence collected therefrom will serve as a basis to further refer the matter either to the

---

before a Notice of Major Offense has been issued, (ii) before a Hearing or (iii) at any time after a Hearing but prior to the AHO's issuance of a written Decision. Provisional Suspensions (and challenges and reviews thereof under this Section F.3) shall ordinarily be determined on written submissions unless the AHO considers an oral hearing necessary.'

[5] ITF Women's World Tour Regulations, Art. I.E.4.
[6] ITF Code of Conduct, Art. VI.B.

International Adjudication Panel or the Independent Tribunal.[7] The Tribunal enjoys authority to suspend the concerned national federation in question from entry into official team competitions, whether provisionally or finally.[8]

4 The Internal Adjudication Panel

Article 9.1(j) of the ITF Bylaws sets forth the Internal Adjudication Panel, the powers and functions of which are spelt out in the Panel's Procedural Rules. The jurisdiction of the Panel and the Independent Tribunal over alleged infractions of ITF rules by professional athletes is grounded in the initial agreement of national tennis federations to abide by such rules governing ITF tournaments. Professional players, as members of national federations, are hence bound by such rules, which in turn provide jurisdiction to the Panel and the Independent Tribunal.

Article 33 of the 2023 ITF Constitution provides for concurrent jurisdiction to both the Panel and the Independent Tribunal in respect of disputes falling within the ITF's Rules of Tennis. The ITF Constitution, however, provides no further information about the Panel. The Procedural Rules of the Panel were promulgated in late 2018 and became effective on 1 January 2019 and form an integral part of the ITF Constitution. The delineation of authority between the Panel and the Tribunal is described in the following sections and sub-sections.

4.1 The Panel's Judicial Function, Jurisdiction and Powers

If the Independent Tribunal was clearly meant to constitute an arbitral institution and its awards subject to the English Arbitration Act of 1996, it is unclear whether a judicial function was conferred also on the Panel. Its Procedural Rules stipulate that it is a standing committee composed of the ITF's Board of Directors.[9] The Board acts by majority to appoint the Panel and has absolute discretion. Although the Panel's Procedural Rules are silent on the selection of Panel members, because Sport Resolutions acts as

---

[7] ITF Bylaws, Art. 7(b).
[8] ITF Bylaws, Art. 7(c). An ITF Extraordinary General Meeting (EGM) unanimously ratified the Board's suspension of Belarussian and Russian tennis federations from ITF memberships and by extension from ITF competitions. See EGM Decision of 9 May 2022, available at: www.itftennis.com/en/news-and-media/articles/itf-member-nations-ratify-suspension-of-russian-tennis-federation-and-belarus-tennis-federation-at-egm/.
[9] ITF Internal Adjudication Panel Procedural Rules, Art. 1.1.

secretariat, in practice the latter compiles a list of potential Panel members and draws from that list. Upon appointment, the Panel possesses authority to: (1) decide any eligibility issue or other dispute[10] under the ITF Rules;[11] (2) authoritatively interpret ITF Rules following a referral by the Board;[12] (3) hear and determine allegations concerning the breach of ITF Rules, but not allegations submitted to the Independent Tribunal;[13] (4) decide whether a suspension of an individual or legal person by a national tennis federation should be recognised by the ITF;[14] (5) have a residual role to hear any other dispute referred to it by the Board;[15] and (6) hear appeals against decisions made by ITF individuals or entities, if such authority is indeed conferred on the Panel by any ITF rule or regulation.[16]

The Panel possesses *kompetenz-kompetenz* power as stipulated under Article 1.4 of its Procedural Rules, and any 'decisions' rendered by it may be 'appealed' to the Independent Tribunal.[17] Although the Panel's Procedural Rules seemingly downplay its powers, it is evident that while it was not meant to serve as an arbitral tribunal, its decisions are binding on the parties and any complaints to the courts can only be brought once the ITF's internal adjudication procedures have been completed. The legal nature of the Panel is similar, although hardly identical to that of so-called expert determination. In construction disputes, it is usual for the parties to resort to expert determination whereby the dispute is submitted to an independent technical expert (chosen from a list pre-agreed by the parties) who determines purely technical issues (not matters of law) and whose decision is final and binding as a matter of contract.[18] The test used by common law courts to distinguish arbitration from expert determination is whether the relevant process was in the nature of a judicial inquiry.[19] In the

---

[10] Ibid., Art. 1.1.1.
[11] The 'ITF Rules' is a broad umbrella encompassing ITF Rules of Tennis, the ITF Davis Cup Regulations, the ITF Fed Cup Regulations, the ITF Pro Circuit Regulations, the ITF Wheelchair Tennis Regulations, the ITF Wheelchair Tennis Classification Manual, the ITF Junior Circuit Regulations, the ITF Junior Team Competitions Regulations, the ITF Senior Regulations, the ITF Beach Tennis Rules, the Code of Conduct for Officials and/or any other rules and regulations of the ITF.
[12] ITF Internal Adjudication Panel Procedural Rules, Art. 1.1.2.
[13] Ibid., Art. 1.1.3.
[14] Ibid., Art. 1.1.4.
[15] Ibid., Art. 1.1.5.
[16] Ibid., Art. 1.2.
[17] Ibid., Arts 1.4 and 6.
[18] *Douglas Harper* v. *Interchange Group Ltd* [2007] EWHC 1834 (Comm); *Union Discount* v. *Zoller* [2002] 1 WLR 1517.
[19] *Age Old Builders Pty Ltd* v. *Swintons Pty Ltd* [2003] VSC 307.

case at hand, the Swiss Federal Tribunal and the European Court of Human Rights (ECtHR), which considered CAS and, finding it to be an independent arbitration system, distinguished it from other processes of adjudication by internal federation bodies.[20]

The Panel's jurisdiction is threefold, namely: (1) as a primary decision-maker; (2) as an appellate entity; and (3) through the exercise of supervisory powers. The Panel serves as a first-instance entity when any dispute falling under Article 1 of its Procedural Rules comes before it for the first time.[21] Its appellate authority arises where the right to appeal a decision made by an ITF individual or entity is authorised under the ITF Rules. All of these three functions/powers of the Panel presuppose that some members possess sound legal qualifications, given that certain determinations require entrenched legal skills and expertise. The judicial function of the Panel is further confirmed by the broad powers conferred upon it by its Procedural Rules. More specifically, it is endowed with the power to conduct relevant investigations;[22] invite persons to make written or oral submissions;[23] and require ITF personnel and entities under the ITF's authority to provide information and documents under their possession, or to attend Panel hearings and offer oral or written statements.[24] These powers are further reinforced by concrete enforcement authority, which is highly unusual for arbitral tribunals as well as expert determination. Under Article 4.3 of its Procedural Rules:

> Failure to cooperate with the Panel (including failure without good cause to comply with a requirement of the Panel within the scope of paragraph 4.2.5 or 4.2.6) shall constitute misconduct, for which the ITF may bring proceedings before the Independent Tribunal to sanction the person or entity involved.

This is unusual because the standard outcome in arbitral and other (non-court) proceedings is an adverse inference,[25] which is sufficient for the parties to generally comply. Moreover, in accordance with Article

---

[20] See e.g. the recent decision of Swiss Federal Supreme Court in *A v. International Biathlon Union*, Case 4A_232/2022 (22 December 2022). See Note available at: www.sportlegis.com/2023/01/12/qualification-of-the-cas-anti-doping-division-and-coexistence-with-the-cas-appeal-division/.
[21] ITF Internal Adjudication Panel Procedural Rules, Arts 4.1.1 and 4.1.2.
[22] Ibid., Art. 4.2.3.
[23] Ibid., Art. 4.2.4.
[24] Ibid., Arts 4.2.5 and 4.2.6.
[25] This is puzzling, since Art. 6.3 of the ITF Independent Tribunal's Procedural Rules expressly states that where a party fails to appear at a hearing or refuses to respond to a question (and by implication to submit requested evidence without justification) the Tribunal may make adverse inferences. The ICC Arbitration Rules take this for granted

5.3.6 of its Procedural Rules, the Panel possesses authority to impose a particular set of sanctions if it finds that ITF Rules have been breached, including cautions, fines, compensation, disqualification, ineligibility or other. The following sub-sections explore the three types of jurisdiction conferred upon the Panel, namely, first instance, appellate and supervisory, by reference to the relevant ITF Rules.

4.1.1 The Panel's First-Instance Jurisdiction

Article I.E.2 of the ITF Men's World Tennis Tour Rules and Regulations (2022)[26] (hereinafter, Men's World Tour Rules) stipulates that the Panel possesses exclusive first-instance jurisdiction over the following matters:

   a) any request for a decision that is entrusted under these Regulations (including the Code of Conduct) to the ITF Internal Adjudication Panel;
   b) any dispute or question about the proper interpretation of these Regulations (including reviewing as appropriate any on-site interpretation by the ITF Supervisor);
   c) any dispute or question about player eligibility arising under these Regulations;
   d) any allegation that a Covered Person has committed a breach of the Welfare Policy;
   e) any allegation that a player, Related Person or other person or entity bound by these Regulations has failed to comply with any other aspect of these Regulations (unless expressly referred elsewhere); and
   f) any other dispute arising out of or relating in any way to these Regulations that is referred to it by the Board.[27]

The Panel's first-instance authority extends also to the determination of requests for change of nationality. The Panel has discretion to decide whether such change is genuine and not intended to circumvent ITF regulations. The Panel may request the player to provide further information regarding this request.[28] The decision of the Panel may be appealed to the Independent Tribunal.[29]

A significant dimension of the Panel's quasi-judicial function relates to what Article IX of the ITF's Code of Conduct misleadingly describes as

---

and make no direction mention. Article 26(2) of the ICC Rules simply endorses so-called default proceedings.
[26] ITF Men's and Women's World Tennis Tour Regulations (2023), available at: www.itftennis.com/media/9100/2023-itf-world-tennis-tour-regulations.pdf.
[27] A verbatim provision is set out in Art. I.E.2 of the ITF World Women's Tennis Tour Rules and Regulations (2022) (hereinafter, ITF World Women's Rules). These have now been replaced with the combined Men's and Women's Regulations, ibid.
[28] ITF World Women's Rules, Art. III.A.2.
[29] Ibid.

reciprocity. Article IX stipulates that the ITF reserves the right to ask the Panel 'to affirm, modify, extend, or reject with respect to any or all ITF World Tennis Tour Tournaments, a suspension or other sanction issued against a Covered Person[30] either by or on behalf of the ITF pursuant to a conduct or disciplinary process under any ITF code or policy or by any other tennis organisation'. Under the particular terms of this process, the Panel has discretion to conduct an investigation or share information with any tennis organisation or other authorities (civil or criminal).

4.1.2 The Panel's Appellate Function

The drafters of Article 6 of the Panel's Procedural Rules thought it wise to conflate several conflicting rules, probably thinking that what they were suggesting was unenforceable under English law. Article 6.7 of the Panel's Procedural Rules stipulates that appellate decisions are final, binding and not subject to any further appeal.[31] It then goes on to say that the parties 'waive irrevocably any right to any form of appeal, review or recourse by or in any court or judicial authority in respect of such [Panel] decisions, in so far as such waiver may validly be made'. It must surely have been evident to the drafters of the Rules that such waiver by contract is unenforceable because it violates a fundamental rule of public policy, namely, that waivers infringing access to (civil) justice are null and void. If the Panel were an arbitral tribunal, then its procedural guarantees would have provided sufficient counterweight against the loss of access to justice provided by the courts; however, because the Panel is not an arbitral tribunal, it provides no such guarantees to the parties before it and hence the parties are not allowed to waive their right to access the courts.

Article 6.7 of the Panel's Procedural Rules goes on to refer to the English Arbitration Act as though it were applicable to proceedings before it. It stipulates that 'for the avoidance of doubt, such a waiver [of the right to claim before the courts] extends to any rights that would otherwise arise under sections 45 and 69 of the [English] Arbitration Act'. Both of these provisions provide the parties with challenges on points of law. Such challenges are exceptional and are of two types: namely, those

---

[30] As defined in Art. XIII of the ITF Welfare Policy.
[31] Such waivers are acceptable as a matter of public policy. See Art. 26.8 of the London Court of International Arbitration Rules, whereby the parties irrevocably waive their right to appeal before state courts or state authorities. Rowan Platt, 'The Appeal of Appeal Mechanisms in International Arbitration: Fairness over Finality?' (2013) 30 J Int Arb 548.

that seek a clarification of an important – and far-reaching – legal issue; and those that seek the correction of a legal mistake made by the tribunal. Applications for the clarification of important legal issues are not challenges per se, but are encompassed here for the purpose of coherency, clarity and completeness. The drafters of Article 6.7 of the Panel's Procedural Rules must have been aware of the likelihood that their reference to sections 45 and 69 were inapplicable. As a result, they introduced a further exception to the original exception (i.e. that the parties waive recourse to the courts) by stipulating that where a party desires (nonetheless) to challenge an appellate decision of the Panel, this shall be submitted to 'the exclusive jurisdiction of English courts, applying English law'.[32]

From a procedural point of view, two types of proceedings are envisaged in Articles 6.5 and 6.6 of the Panel's Procedural Rules: (1) those requiring a fresh re-hearing of the facts in true appellate fashion in order to do justice in the circumstances of a case; and (2) proceedings not requiring a fresh re-hearing of the facts, but instead limited to a 'consideration of whether the decision being appealed was erroneous'.

4.1.3   The Panel's Supervisory Function

The supervisory jurisdiction of the Panel encompasses complaints against any ITF decision that is not susceptible to a first-instance or appellate hearing. In such cases, while not permitted to review the merits of the case, the Panel may uphold the claim if the party making the claim satisfies it that:

> (a) the decision is irrational (i.e., it falls outside the range of what a reasonable person might decide), arbitrary or capricious;
> (b) the decision is based on an error of law (i.e., it is contrary to the ITF Rules, properly construed, or to applicable law); or
> (c) the procedure that was followed in reaching the decision was so unfair as to be contrary to natural justice.[33]

This function is similar, yet hardly the same or comparable, to set aside proceedings in arbitration. Where the composition of the Panel lacks legal expertise, errors of law or unfair processes are not unlikely, even if unintentional. This is a welcome function that is meant to correct gross errors, particularly where the penalties are steep.

---

[32] ITF Internal Adjudication Panel Procedural Rules, Art. 6.8.
[33] Ibid., Art. 4.1.3.2.

5 The Independent Tribunal

The Independent Tribunal's jurisdiction is chiefly found in Article 33 of the ITF Constitution. Paragraph (a) of Article 33 provides for the scope of such jurisdiction, which encompasses all types of disputes arising between: (1) the legal entity of the ITF and one or more of its members (essentially national federations); (2) the ITF and any individual or legal person that does business with the ITF, or which is otherwise involved in any of the circuits or competitions under the aegis of the ITF, 'or that otherwise operates within the sport of tennis'; and (3) one or more members of the ITF.

The ITF Constitution, as well as the Independent Tribunal's Procedural Rules, operate as an agreement to arbitrate in the sense of Article 7 to the UN Commission of International Trade Law (UNCITRAL) Model Law on International Commercial Arbitration, or as terms and conditions appended to ITF contracts with contractors to the same effect (as an agreement to arbitrate). That is precisely why Article 33(b) to the ITF Constitution stipulates that where a dispute between parties under paragraph (a) arises and falls under ITF rules and regulations, the parties are deemed to have accepted the exclusive authority of the Independent Tribunal under its procedural rules and that in turn they have waived the right to litigation or arbitration in another forum. In equal measure, Article 1.3 of the Independent Tribunal's Procedural Rules stipulates that consent to the ITF Rules (in the umbrella sense provided above) serves to confer jurisdiction to the Independent Tribunal, with proceedings seated in London. It is implied that the parties have waived recourse to litigation. Domestic and international courts have unanimously accepted that such waivers do not offend the right to fair trial where the arbitral mechanism in question satisfies fair trial guarantees.[34] It is for this reason that the 'right to a hearing' is expressly recognised in the ITF Rules.[35] Alternatively, where a particular dispute does not fall under the ITF's rules and regulations, the parties are presumed to have accepted the jurisdiction of the CAS, and agree to be bound by the CAS award.[36] Of course, what the parties may not validly do, even voluntarily, is to waive their right to set aside proceedings under the laws of the seat, as this is considered a fundamental procedural guarantee.[37]

---

[34] Ilias Bantekas, 'Equal Treatment of Parties in International Commercial Arbitration' (2020) 69 ICLQ 991, exploring the boundaries of equal treatment in the context of the right to fair trial.
[35] ITF Code of Conduct, Art. VI.C.
[36] ITF Constitution, Art. 33(c).
[37] In X v. ATP Tour, decided by the CAS Appellate Chamber, the duration of the suspension was reduced. More significantly, the tennis player had signed a waiver of the right to bring

It is beyond any doubt that the Independent Tribunal is an arbitral institution in the same manner as other similar institutions. This is clearly spelt out in two relevant instruments. First, the Panel's Procedural Rules emphasise that the Independent Tribunal is an arbitral tribunal, whose proceedings are governed by English law and subject to the English Arbitration Act.[38] This is equally reiterated by Article 1.3 of the Tribunal's own Procedural Rules. Even so, Article 3.2 of the Tribunal's Procedural Rules goes on to say that the primary source of (substantive) obligations is to be found in the ITF Rules and the Tribunal's Procedural Rules, with English law retaining a subsidiary role. Moreover, in the event of conflict, the ITF Rules prevail over those governing the Independent Tribunal. No doubt, this hierarchy makes absolute sense, albeit it needs to be consistent throughout the ITF's various instruments.[39]

Just like other sports tribunals, as well as international criminal tribunals established in the context of transitional justice, the ITF Independent Tribunal has assumed more than just a dispute resolution role. It clearly perceives itself as the guardian of the integrity of the game of tennis and the purity of its image to young athletes and their parents across the globe. In the *Nastase* case, which involved a string of welfare violations, including sexual harassment, assault and racist behaviour, the ITF Tribunal declared that it was:

> conscious of the message whatever sanction is ordered sends to the tennis world and the public more generally in a high-profile sports appeal such as the present one. For example, the Tribunal has regard to what young tennis players in clubs around the world take away from this decision in

setting-aside proceedings against future arbitral awards against the ITF. The CAS was unambiguous in its decision that such waiver agreements are not valid, even if express among the parties, in accordance with Art. 192 of the Swiss (Federal) Private International Law Act (PILA).

[38] ITF Constitution, Arts 7.3 and 7.4; this is also reiterated in Art. I.E.5 of the Men's World Tour Regulations, which emphasises that any dispute arising 'out of or in connection' with the Regulations, including also non-contractual claims, shall be governed and construed in accordance with English law, to the exclusion of English private international law.

[39] See *ITF and Anti-Doping Organization v. Stephane Houdet*, SR/005/2022, at para. 84, where the ITF Independent Tribunal emphasised that the World Anti-Doping Code and the International Doping Tests & Management (IDTM) constitute its general frameworks, with each federation free to construct its own rules as long as they are compliant with these rules (cf. *Coleman v. World Athletics*, CAS 2020/A/7528, at paras 159–60). In the case at hand, it found that the dispute was governed by the ITF Rules and that the Tribunal has recourse to the Tennis Anti-Doping Program (TADP), the IDTM and the TADP Protocol.

terms of what is inappropriate conduct in breach of the applicable rules and what is the appropriate sanction for such conduct.[40]

This so-called 'public purpose' of broader adjudicatory mechanisms,[41] as opposed to narrow arbitral institutions that are client-oriented, as is the case with the ITF Independent Tribunal, is emblematic of its broader function.

5.1 Procedures of the Independent Tribunal

Although elements of the constitution and regulation of the Independent Tribunal may be found in the ITF Constitution and ITF Rules, the Tribunal's Procedural Rules comprise the definitive instrument setting out all procedures before it. It is instructive that the Tribunal's Rules are tailor-made, and its drafters did not rely on model laws. However, this is also a reflection of the complexity underlying ITF dispute resolution processes. It should be pointed out from the outset that the administration and secretarial function of the Tribunal is outsourced to a private non-profit entity, Sport Resolutions.[42] This is an important observation because unlike traditional arbitral institutions, Sport Resolutions has been granted authority to organise a pool of expert arbitrators (known as the Independent Panel) from which independent tribunals are composed. This particular role of Sport Resolutions is in fact expressly stated in the Tribunal's Rules.[43]

Unlike ordinary arbitration whereby the parties are typically allowed to (at least) select an arbitrator of their choice (assuming a three-panel member composition), this is not the case with the Independent Tribunal. Instead, the panel Chairman chooses one to three panel members, including him- or herself, whereupon the Tribunal is constituted with the panel members transformed into arbitrators.[44] It should be stated that the Chairman is a person appointed on a standing basis for a definite amount of time. The parties may challenge the arbitrators on the basis of

---

[40] *Ilie Nastase* v. *ITF*, Independent Tribunal Decision, SR/913/2017, at para. 104.
[41] Ilias Bantekas, 'The Public Interest Perspective of International Courts and Tribunals' (2021) 38 Ariz J Int & Comp L 61.
[42] Its legal status and operations is available at: www.sportresolutions.com. In this sense, Sport Resolutions acts as a secretariat of ITF arbitrations, much like the ICC Council that administers arbitrations on behalf of its clients. Sports Resolutions is a non-profit entity incorporated in the United Kingdom, in the same manner that the ICC is a non-profit chamber of commerce.
[43] ITF Independent Tribunal Rules of Procedure, Art. 1.1.
[44] Ibid., Art. 2.2.

partiality and lack of independence, but other than that they have no other control over the appointment process.[45] The Chairman possesses further authority to consolidate two or more separate proceedings and act as emergency arbitrator.[46] The latter role could have benefitted from more precision in the Rules, particularly since more experienced arbitral institutions have been at pains to elaborate this function in their own rules.[47]

Article 3.5 of the Independent Tribunal's Procedural Rules stipulates that it has both *kompetenz-kompetenz* and inherent powers. Although both of these qualities are *sine qua non* requirements of judicial entities, the latter is limited in accordance with the overall mandate and powers conferred on the entity in question. Certain of the powers enumerated in Article 3.5 are not ordinarily inherent powers of arbitral tribunals. This includes: the power to appoint an expert (independently of the wishes of the parties) and allocate the costs at its discretion;[48] to order a party to make available for inspection a property, document or thing in its possession or under its control;[49] to allow one or more third parties to intervene or be joined in the proceedings.[50] These three powers stand out as being atypical of the powers usually conferred on arbitral tribunals and which generally require the parties' consent and cooperation. This is because these powers are associated with some degree of compulsion and consequences, which is not ordinarily the case in arbitral proceedings. Their atypical character does not in any way denote that they are unlawful, unenforceable or null and void as they do not violate any mandatory laws or offend public policy.

Also atypical is the fact that the Chairman of the Tribunal is given authority to take unilateral action in certain matters without conferring with other members, or at least seeking their opinion. Article 3.6 of the Tribunal's Rules makes the rather unusual statement that 'any procedural rulings may be made by the Tribunal Chairman alone, unless he prefers to have the full independent Tribunal make the ruling in any particular instance'. Although unusual, and undermines the authority of the members

---

[45] Ibid., Arts 2.3–2.6.
[46] Ibid., Art. 2.7.
[47] See e.g. International Chamber of Commerce (ICC) Arbitration Rules, Art. 29 and Appendix V to the Rules, 'Emergency Arbitrator Rules'.
[48] Independent Tribunal Procedural Rules, Art. 2.3(b); by way of contrast, see ICC Arbitration Rules, Art. 25(3), which stipulates that the tribunal can only appoint an expert after consulting the parties, both of which must consent.
[49] Ibid., Art. 3.5(e).
[50] Ibid., Art. 3.5(f); by way of contrast, see ICC Arbitration Rules, Art. 7, which requires consent of the current parties for the joinder of a pertinent claim by a third party.

of the Tribunal and its collegial character, it is not atypical and exists in the CAS framework. Such unilateral authority is also evident in Article 3.7 of the Tribunal's Procedural Rules, which grant authority to the Chairman to issue procedural orders.

In consonance with international standards, Article 6 does not set out an elaborate set of evidentiary rules; Article 6.1 of the Independent Tribunal's Procedural Rules stipulates that 'facts may be established by any reliable means'.[51] The consistent practice of the CAS and other specialised sports tribunals, especially as regards doping and corruption, has created an elaborate body of evidentiary rules that have attained precedential value and which the ITF Independent Tribunal cannot depart from. By way of illustration, the ITF Tribunal has accepted the CAS approach in *WADA* v. *Abdelrahman*,[52] whereby it was held that the standard of evidence tendered has to be persuasive, specific, objective and concrete.[53] As to the burden of proof in doping cases, in following CAS jurisprudence, the ITF Tribunal has held that the literal reading of Article 10.2.3 of the Tennis Anti-Doping Program (TADP) 2020 requires the player to disprove engaging in conduct that he or she 'knew constituted an Anti-Doping Rule Violation' or 'knew that there was a significant risk that the conduct might constitute or result in an Anti-Doping Rule Violation and manifestly disregarded that risk'. This means that the player must not just have not known that the action constituted an ADRV, she or he must also have not known that there was a significant risk.[54] Moreover, other instruments already set out evidentiary rules[55] to which the ITF Tribunal must turn when deciding pertinent cases.[56]

---

[51] This is very close to the language in ICC Arbitration Rules, Art. 25(1), which refers to 'all appropriate means'.
[52] CAS 2017/A/5036.
[53] *ITF and Anti-Doping Organization* v. *Shoshkyna*, SR/262/2020, at para. 78.
[54] Ibid., at para. 124; equally, in agreeing with *Dylan Scott* v. *ITF*, CAS 2018/A/5768, the ITF Tribunal held that should there be a gap in scientific knowledge and that it is not known whether or not a particular proposition is true, and therefore the hypothesis as to source remains unverified, the benefit of the doubt goes against the player, because it is the player that bears the burden of proof on this point.
[55] Pursuant to TADP, Art. 3.1.1, the burden is on the ITF to establish each of the elements of the ADRVs charged 'to the comfortable satisfaction of the hearing panel, bearing in mind the seriousness of the allegation that is made. This standard of proof in all cases is greater than a mere balance of probability but less than proof beyond a reasonable doubt.'
[56] See *ITF and Anti-Doping Organization* v. *Lepchenko*, SR/254/2021, at para. 38, where the ITF Tribunal accepted that where an athlete is unable to identify how a prohibited S=substance entered his or her body, it is very difficult for the athlete to discharge the burden of proof that his or her conduct that led to the positive test was not intentional.

What is, however, controversial is the stipulation in Article 6.2, which suggests that the parties are bound by facts determined by a final court judgment or arbitral award of competent jurisdiction. This is highly problematic and defies elementary notions of justice because many competent courts are autocratic and, in many cases, controlled or heavily influenced by the state or even national sporting federations.

It should be noted that the Independent Tribunal is bound to act fairly without bias. Such an assessment may be made by the competent court as an annulment claim, or as a preliminary/procedural issue during the course of the proceedings. In *Wilander* v. *Tobin*, anti-doping under ITF mechanisms was challenged by Wilander as being unfair. At the High Court, Lord Woolf emphasised the existence of an implied contractual duty of fairness in disciplinary matters administered by the ITF.[57] Failure to do so gave rise to a private cause of action. Such an implied contractual duty must therefore extend also to the Panel.

5.2 The Three Types of Jurisdiction Conferred on the Independent Tribunal

Just like the Panel, the ITF Independent Tribunal possesses jurisdiction to hear disputes at first instance, as an appellate entity and on the basis of a supervisory function. Each of these will be examined in discrete subsections. Without a detailed examination of the ITF Rules, such a task would be meaningless, since the Tribunal's Rules of Procedure do not spell this out.[58] Lack of space precludes us from examining in detail appeals against decisions of the Internal Adjudication Panel, as well as the Independent Tribunal's supervisory function.

5.2.1 The First-Instance Jurisdiction of the Independent Tribunal

As already mentioned, the first-instance jurisdiction of the Independent Tribunal is found in the various ITF Rules. Article I.E.2 of the ITF Men's World Tennis Tour Regulations stipulates that the Independent Tribunal possesses exclusive jurisdiction in the first instance over the following matters:

---

[57] *Wilander* v. *Tobin* [1997] 2 Ll Rep 293, at 299–300.
[58] In fact, Art. 2.1 of the Independent Tribunal's Rules emphasises that the precise contours of its jurisdiction should be sought in the ITF Rules.

a) any request for a decision that is entrusted under these Regulations to the Independent Tribunal;
b) an allegation that a player, Related Person or other person participating on the Men's ITF World Tennis Tour has breached the Tennis Anti-Doping Programme [sic];
c) an allegation that a player or Related Person has committed a Major Offence under the Code of Conduct;
d) any allegation that a Tournament Offence has been committed under the Code of Conduct; and
e) any other dispute arising out of or relating in any way to these Regulations that is referred to it by the Board.

These five grounds of jurisdiction are reproduced verbatim in Article I.E.2 of the Women's World Tour Regulations and it is natural no doubt that the exact same grounds are listed.

In addition, Article 8.1 of the TADP Rules provides that the Independent Tribunal possesses jurisdiction in respect of the anti-doping violations in Article 8 therein. The Tribunal will proceed with the merits of the dispute in accordance with its own Procedural Rules. The Tribunal is convened where a player charged with a pertinent violation disputes all or part of the charge and requests a hearing.[59] Once appointed, the Chair of the Independent Tribunal will convene a preliminary meeting with the ITIA and its legal representatives, and with the player or other person and/or their legal representatives (if any), unless directions are agreed by the parties and approved by the Chair.[60] The purpose of the preliminary meeting is to set the agenda and streamline any procedural issues, although practice suggests that TADP violations are accepted by players, but intent is generally refuted.[61]

The Independent Tribunal further possesses jurisdiction over so-called major offences, in accordance with Article VI.C of the ITF's Code of Conduct. It will be recalled from our analysis in the introduction to this chapter that where there is prima facie evidence of a major offence, the ITF shall convene a Review Board, which in turn will investigate whether a major offence has taken place. Where the Board determines

---

[59] TADP Rules, Art. 8.2.1.
[60] Ibid., Art. 8.3.1.
[61] See e.g. *ITF and Anti-Doping Organization v. Kratzer*, SR/085/2020, where the athlete unsuccessfully argued that she was given the banned substance by an unknown coach of the Chinese Tennis Federation while training abroad. She alleged that the substance must have been in a herbal cream meant to treat a foot irritation.

that a player or related person has a case to answer, the ITF will transmit a notice of charge to the Chairman of the Independent Tribunal. This process will have set out the bulk of the investigation on which the Tribunal will rely, albeit where the player or related person denies the veracity of the charge or the sequence of facts, he or she may seek a full determination of the dispute by the Independent Tribunal. The player or related person must respond to the notice and request a hearing within ten days of receipt of the notice, failing which he or she is deemed to have admitted commission of the major offence.[62] In the event the ITF withdraws the notice of charge, or the player accepts the charges, there shall be no hearing before the Independent Tribunal.[63]

6 Appeals against the Independent Tribunal's Awards to CAS

Article 9.2 of the Independent Tribunal's Procedural Rules allows appeals to the CAS. As a general rule, only first-instance awards of the Independent Tribunal may be appealed to the CAS and not its appellate awards – given that the latter were already the subject of an appeal from a decision of the Panel.[64] Once again, the right to appeal a first-instance award to the CAS must be found in the ITF Rules. Article I.E.4 of the Men's World Tour Rules stipulates that unless otherwise provided: 'c) decisions of the Independent Tribunal (sitting as a first-instance tribunal) may only be challenged by way of appeal to the Court of Arbitration for Sport, as set out in the Independent Tribunal Procedural Rules.'[65] In equal measure, first-instance awards rendered by the Tribunal in respect of major offences shall be appealed to the CAS.[66]

It should be noted that the CAS is governed by its own procedural rules, known as the CAS Code of Sports-Related Arbitration.[67] The CAS operates at both first-instance (ordinary arbitration division) and appellate (appeals arbitration division) levels and further encompasses an anti-doping division.[68] In the case at hand, appeals from the ITF Independent Tribunal to the CAS engage the jurisdiction of the CAS Appellate

---

[62] ITF Code of Conduct, Art. VI.C(d).
[63] Ibid.
[64] See limitations to CAS jurisdiction as outlined in the Independent Tribunal's Procedural Rules, Art. 9.1, explained in detail in sub-section 3.1 of this chapter.
[65] A verbatim provision also exists as Art. I.E.4 of the Women's World Tour Rules (2022).
[66] ITF Code of Conduct, Art. VI.F.
[67] CAS Code (2022), available at: www.tas-cas.org/fileadmin/user_upload/CAS_Code_2022__EN_.pdf.
[68] Ibid., s. 20.

Chamber. The CAS Code includes a set of Procedural Rules. Rule 27 serves as the basis for the jurisdiction of the CAS Arbitral Chamber. It goes on to say that:

> These Procedural Rules apply whenever the parties have agreed to refer a sports-related dispute to CAS. Such reference may arise out of an arbitration clause contained in a contract or regulations or by reason of a later arbitration agreement (ordinary arbitration proceedings) or may involve an appeal against a decision rendered by a federation, association or sports-related body where the statutes or regulations of such bodies, or a specific agreement provide for an appeal to CAS (appeal arbitration proceedings).

The reference or otherwise agreement to arbitrate before the CAS clearly arises in the various ITF Rules, as well as Articles 9.2 and 9.4 of the ITF Independent Tribunal's Procedural Rules. In accordance with Article 9.3 of the Independent Tribunal's Procedural Rules, the deadline for filing an appeal to the CAS shall be twenty-one days from the date of receipt of the decision in question by the appealing party. The decision being appealed will remain in full force, pending determination of the appeal unless the CAS orders otherwise. Once the application has been submitted, it is the CAS Code that prevails from a procedural point of view,[69] albeit the governing substantive law remains the ITF Rules and English law in a subsidiary role.[70]

In closing, it should be emphasised that an appeal against the Independent Tribunal's award is highly unusual from the perspective of transnational arbitral practice. Awards rendered by arbitral tribunals, such as the ITF Independent Tribunal, are not susceptible to further layers of appeal, but only set aside proceedings for failure to observe a closed list of procedural safeguards.[71] An appeal to the CAS against a decision of the Panel or an ITF entity is certainly acceptable, albeit an appeal against a final award does not sit well with the arbitral nature of the ITF Independent Tribunal.

7 ATP Dispute Resolution

As has already been made clear from the introduction, doping and match-fixing (as well as other pertinent regulatory matters) infractions/

---

[69] See Johan Lindholm, *The Court of Arbitration for Sport and Its Jurisprudence: An Empirical Inquiry into Lex Sportiva* (Asser Press, 2019), 35–8.
[70] Independent Tribunal Procedural Rules, Art. 9.4.
[71] See English Arbitration Act, s. 68.

allegations are handled under the aforementioned ITF procedures. As regards anti-doping claims, on-site investigations are administered by the ITIA, the decisions of which may be appealed to the CAS Anti-Doping Tribunal under the same grounds as decisions from the ITF judicial mechanisms. This is specifically mentioned in Article 1.07(2) of the ATP Circuit Regulations. Any other disputes, whether contractual or regulatory, arising from the ATP Rules are subject to those Rules' dispute resolution mechanism.

Under Articles 8.01(G) and 8.03(G) of the ATP Code, authority for on-site investigations is conferred to the Senior Vice-President, Rules and Regulations. Appeals against its decisions are available before the Tribunal established by the ATP's Board of Directors and CEO, in accordance with Article 8.04(K) of the ATP Code. Decisions of the Senior Vice-President concerning major offences may be appealed to the ATP CEO, in accordance with Article 8.05(B) of the ATP Code within five days from the day the decision was rendered. Once the CEO offers the decision on appeal, this is final on the parties.[72] Not all disputes, however, can be resolved under this mechanism. Article 8.07 of the ATP Code provides as follows:

> Any dispute between or among ATP, its Tournaments or its players (with the exception of any dispute relating to or arising out of a change in tournament class membership status) arising out of the application of any provision of this Rulebook which is not finally resolved by applicable provisions of the Rulebook shall be submitted exclusively to the Court of Arbitration for Sport ('CAS') for final and binding arbitration in accordance with CAS's Code of Sports-Related Arbitration. The decision of CAS in that arbitration shall be final, non-reviewable, non-appealable and enforceable. No claim, arbitration, lawsuit or litigation concerning the dispute shall be brought in any other court or tribunal.

8 WTA Dispute Resolution

The WTA's extensive Rulebook[73] sets out a number of obligations on all stakeholders. The enforcement of this body of rules has given rise to three distinct internal organs, each with specific competence. In brief, the Code of Conduct Committee possesses jurisdiction to hear disputes concerning

---

[72] ATP Code, Art. 8.05(B)(5).
[73] The 2024 version of the WTA Rulebook is available at: https://photoresources.wtatennis.com/wta/document/2024/02/12/1a78ea3b-3a70-4847-9951-d59307c2655d/2024-WTA-Rulebook-2-11-2024-.pdf.

alleged violations of the WTA Code of Conduct.[74] The Standards Committee examines disputes in connection with its Standards.[75] Any violations of these Rules which do not specify a process for imposition of a penalty shall be decided by the CEO and such decision of the CEO may be appealed to the Board of Directors.[76] The Board of Directors possesses other quasi-judicial authority, as, for example, in respect of deciding applications for reinstatement of tournament class membership.[77]

Just like the ATP, only disputes arising from the WTA's Rulebook are susceptible to the arbitral mechanism envisaged in section XIX of said Rulebook. Unlike the ATP and the ITF, the WTA has not opted for an internal tailor-made arbitral mechanism. Instead, Article B(2) of section XIX provides that any dispute – save for those arising out of a change in tournament class membership status – that has not been finally resolved by other means provided for in the Rulebook shall be submitted to the American Arbitration Association (AAA). The AAA is an arbitral institution just like the ICC. It is instructive that the parties are restricted to the AAA's Expedited Procedures Commercial Arbitration Rules;[78] that the dispute be heard by a single arbitrator; and that the request be filed with the AAA within twenty-one days from the date the action for the request arose. Where the parties are unable to mutually choose an arbitrator, he or she shall be selected by the AAA in accordance with its own rules.[79] It is a credit to the WTA that while all submissions shall remain confidential, the dispute itself and the findings of the arbitral tribunal and the other three aforementioned internal entities shall be made public.

9   Contractual Disputes and the Role of National Courts

The range of disputes discussed in the aforementioned sections concerned regulatory infractions predicated on the internal rules of the ITF (and its integrity affiliates), the ATP and the WTA. In both professional and amateur tennis, however, a good number of relationships are established by contracts and these are wholly distinct from the rules set out in ITF, WTA and ATP regulations. Such relationship may include player–agent

---

[74] Ibid., s. XVII.
[75] Ibid., s. XVIII.
[76] Ibid., s. I(C).
[77] Ibid., s. XII(G)(b)(ii)(b).
[78] The AAA's Expedited Rules are part of its ordinary rules (Rules E1–E10), available at: https://adr.org/sites/default/files/Commercial%20Rules.pdf.
[79] Ibid., Rule E4.

agreements, agreements between tournament organisers and sponsors/ advertisers, players and sponsors and many others. Any disputes arising from such agreements may be submitted to the most appropriate national court, unless the parties mutually agree to bring the matter before an arbitral tribunal. Moreover, disputes might also arise from an alleged infraction of the law, as is the case with unlawful reproduction of tennis tournaments, as well as similar infractions of intellectual property rights. Given the absence of a contract in the latter cases, the injured party will seek redress from the courts.

The limited available case law indicates that litigation is prevalent, with choice of court clauses favouring English courts, in conjunction with English substantive law as the parties' choice of law in player–agent disputes. The tennis-specific case that stands out is *Zverev* v. *Ace International Group Ltd*, despite the fact that the parties ultimately settled.[80] Although the agent, based in London, had no doubt driven the choice of law clause (the player was not at any time a UK national or resident), in the circumstances of the case, the application of the common law doctrine of restraint of trade turned out to favour the player.[81]

For disputes concerning the contractual liberty of the ITF or ATP/ WTA to remove a tournament from its calendar or relegate it to a lower tier, choice of court clauses vary. In *Deutscher Tennis Bund* v. *ATP Tour Inc.*,[82] two ATP tournaments, namely, Hamburg and Doha (Qatar), had been relegated to a lower tier, which necessarily meant brand depreciation and an inability to attract top tennis players to the tournaments. This in turn had a direct impact on profits. Both tournament organisers challenged their downgrading before US courts. The District Court rejected the arguments, confirming in the process that the ATP can re-organise professional tournaments and relegate one or another to a lower tier without breaching anti-trust rules.[83] Here, the claimants' argument,

---

[80] *Zverev* v. *Ace Group International Ltd* [2020] EWHC 3513 (Ch).
[81] In *Proactive Sports Management Ltd* v. *Rooney* [2011] EWCA Civ 1444, the 17-year-old football star had entered into an image rights representation agency agreement with a company called Stoneygate. The latter agreed to pay a 20 per cent commission to Proactive for the duration of its agreement with Rooney. When a few years later Rooney terminated its contract, the agent sued for breach of contract. The Court of Appeal found the particular terms of the agency agreement unenforceable on several grounds, namely: (1) Rooney at the time was a minor without the benefit of legal advice; (2) the duration of contract was unduly long and certainly far beyond what was customary at the time.
[82] *Deutscher Tennis Bund* v. *ATP Tour Inc.*, 610 F.3d 820 (3d Cir. 2010), cert. denied, 562 US 1064, 131.
[83] Ibid.

unlike *Zverev*, centred on anti-trust violations[84] as well as breach of contract. Ordinarily, and in line with Article 8.07 of the ATP Code, this dispute should have been referred to the CAS. The claimants, however, relied on their anti-trust claim, which is of a public policy nature, to submit the dispute before a US district court.

Other chapters in this volume discuss the role of litigation in tennis disputes, particularly as regards the enforcement of morality clauses,[85] competition claims[86] and intellectual property infractions.[87]

---

[84] See George A. Metanias, Thomas J. Cryan and David W. Johnson, 'A Critical Look at Professional Tennis under Anti-Trust Law' (1987) 4 U Miami Ent & Sports L Rev 57; equally, *Volvo North America Corp. v. Men's International Professional Tennis Council*, 857 F.2d 55 (2d Cir. 1988), one of the earlier cases concerning whether an international tennis federation is susceptible to the Sherman Act, 15 USC § 1 (1982).
[85] See Chapter 4.
[86] See Chapter 12.
[87] See Chapter 3.

8

The ITF, ATP and WTA and the Governance of Global Tennis

MARKO BEGOVIĆ

1 Introduction

The aim of this chapter to is introduce the structure and function of governance in global tennis and to contribute to the wider debate concerning sport-related governance, considering legal, organizational and functional dimensions. Although sport governance has been one of the most researched contemporary topics, the governance landscape in tennis deserves additional attention. The professional nature of tennis has transformed the relationship among its various stakeholders, both externally and internally. Despite the existence of relatively robust governing bodies, players constitute the vehicle of professional tennis, and are more often than not far more important than the states they represent. Professional tennis remains an ambiguous activity straddling not-for-profit entities and the highly commercial and lucrative nature of the sport and related actors.[1] The particular challenge lies in the distribution of power and potential jurisdictional overlap, especially in times of specific external disarray, such as pandemics or war in Europe.[2] Consequently, concern has been raised about the players' representation in decision-making processes and the emergence of unionization, revenue distribution and potential merger of professional bodies in tennis. That said, this chapter represents an overview of the development of professional

---

[1] See Ilias Bantekas, "Is Legitimate Gambling a Threat to the Integrity of Transnational Individual Sport Competitions?" (2024) 25 San Diego Int LJ 23 (demonstrating how the International Tennis Federation has entered into lucrative deals with live data streaming/gambling companies, which has increased manifold the likelihood of match-fixing in the sport).

[2] A key field of contention is the sanction-related power of sports governing bodies and given that in professional tennis there are three potent entities, such power becomes a significant tool of power. See Ilias Bantekas, "Sports Sanctions against Russia through the Court of Arbitration for Sport" (2023) 42 Cardozo Arts & Ent LJ 101.

tennis, particularly highlighting institutional interrelationships framed and directed within a largely corporate and business environment. Further, it focuses on several structural aspects of tennis governing bodies and assesses their organizational and operational relationship through coordinative, collaborative and competitive frameworks.

The contemporary tennis governance is comprised of rather complex institutional interrelationships at the macro-level, as these are shaped by largely corporate and business-style contexts. That said, the focus of this chapter is on the structural aspects of tennis governing bodies and their organizational and operational interdependence. Despite the absence of a singular authority on top, professional tennis governance is structured in the form of a vertical semi-pyramidal organizational ladder. The systematic approach represents a main feature in understanding the complexity between communication, collaboration and competition among the key governing bodies, players, the private sector and other stakeholders.[3] Professional tennis falls within the category of so-called "closed governance structures" with coordinated effort among a variety of entities shaped by on-court competition and commercial activities, all of which are intertwined. To understand the governance of professional tennis, it is important to look at the institutional relationship among key stakeholders. On the one hand, the International Tennis Federation (ITF), the Association of Tennis Professionals (ATP) and Women's Tennis Association (WTA) operate as the sport's dominant stakeholders. The institutional interrelation among these actors is both complex and stable at the same time. On the other hand, the role of athletes, coaches and competition organizations changes over time. In contemporary dynamics, the governance structure of tennis is reshaped primarily toward a species of corporate governance, further infused with bilateral and multilateral arrangements, with the participation of a number of other stakeholders ranging from nation states, companies, media and others. Furthermore, the governance complexity is multiplied by National Sports Federations (NSFs) operating within national geographic boundaries and citizenship/nationality links. Therefore, the interrelation between these actors within the global tennis ecosystem is intertwined with hybrid regulatory frameworks, both contractual and intra-regulatory, as these are generated by state and non-state actors bypassing opposing interests within

---

[3] Ian Henry and Ping Chao-Lee, "Governance and Ethics in Sports" in John Beech and Simon Chadwick (eds), *The Business of Sport Management* (Pearson, 2004), 25.

sport and non-sport-related contexts. The concerted effort is achieved primarily through the interdependence of sport-related entities.

As regards the sport-related context, the ITF exercises a leading governance role. However, due to the importance of the ATP and WTA, especially their engagement and scope of activities, global tennis governance resembles a network rather than a vertical-based organizational structure. The scheduling of events requires concerted effort in order to avoid overlapping and attract broader support, considering the different competences and scope of operations of the ITF, ATP and WTA. To understand this specific institutional and organizational relationship, it is important to elaborate on the role of each of these three global tennis stakeholders in detail. Additionally, NSFs may equally engage in the organization of events that may be part of the ITF/ATP/WTA structure, although in terms of operations, NSFs fully adhere to the ITF regulatory framework if they wish to maintain their membership status and have access to the Olympics. With this in mind, the coordination is particularly important in the relationship with players, including athletes' entourage and tournament organizers. This relationship has evolved mainly due to the excessive commercialization of tennis. The professionalization of tennis has been a historical challenge for the world of tennis and for a larger community, namely, the Olympic Movement.

From the early beginnings of the contemporary Olympic Games in 1896, the friction between the governing body of tennis at that time, the International Lawn Tennis Federation (ILTF), and the International Olympic Committee (IOC) was visible. This was particularly acute mainly in terms of event scheduling, at a time when the Olympic Games in Sweden overlapped with the organization of the Wimbledon tournament in 1912. The second reason is that tennis had long been a highly professionalized sport, and many players demanded appropriate conditions for the organization of the tennis event during the Olympic Games. Third, the ILTF demanded proper planning for the tennis event at the Olympic Games. At that time, the IOC used its dominant role within the Olympic Movement, by adopting the obligatory oath for participating athletes with a view to preserving amateurism. The absence of the ILTF in the preparatory phase of the Olympic Games of 1920 and 1924 in both scheduling and organization is therefore striking, but hardly surprising. Although these tennis events attracted many players, the friction between the IOC and the ILTF was deep, especially as the ILTF insisted on being in charge of the event. The IOC, in turn, insisted on adhering to the core principle of Olympism, namely, amateurism, along with the demand that the ILTF cancel all its major events during the year of the Olympic Games.⁴ The organizers of major events led by the British Lawn Tennis Association decided to reject the IOC's position. In order to maintain its dominant role, the IOC's Executive Board adopted the decision to remove tennis from the Olympic Games.

This decision was approved by the Board during the 27th IOC session. It was clear that the ILTF could maintain its dominant status in the world of tennis, despite the role of the IOC and the significance of the Olympic Games. However, this governance struggle reflected primarily the character of the game of tennis and its opposing organizational philosophies. Despite a renewed application in 1957, tennis was not admitted to the Olympic program, despite the fact that the ILTF revised its rules, by which it sought to maintain a certain degree of amateurism. At the political level, football was not removed from the Olympic program, despite the fact that many football players were in fact fully-fledged professionals. The lack of institutional support for athletes and their specific labor status forced many participants to either move to professional sport or to drop off. At the national level, the NSFs failed to adopt appropriate regulatory frameworks to safeguard athletes effectively. The solution of semi-professional status that would ensure eligibility to participate in amateur competitions was not supported, as the IOC maintained its rigid position on the concept of amateurism. However, the discussions on the governance of tennis and the appropriate balance that needed to be struck between amateurism and growing professionalism under the support from the US Lawn Tennis Association (USLTA) ultimately led to the reintroduction of tennis in the Olympic Games of 1968 in the form of a demonstration sport.⁵ In parallel, while the governing body was under pressure concerning a series of integrity claims, the All England Lawn Tennis Club adopted a decision to allow professional players to compete at Wimbledon.⁶ The changes within the IOC along with geopolitical dynamics led to a rethinking of the concept of amateurism. It resulted in opening a new perspective for cooperation between the

---

⁴ See Matthew P. Llewellyn and Robert J. Lake, "'The Old Days of Amateurism Are Over': The Samaranch Revolution and the Return of Olympic Tennis" (2017) 37 Sport Hist 4.
⁵ See generally, Robert J. Lake and Carol A. Osborne (eds), *Routledge Handbook of Tennis* (Routledge, 2019).
⁶ See Olympic Studies Centre, History of Tennis at the Olympic Games (2017), available at: https://stillmed.olympic.org/media/Document%20Library/OlympicOrg/Factsheets-Reference-Documents/Games/OG/History-of-sports/Reference-document-Tennis-History-at-the-OG.pdf.

IOC and the ILTF. In that respect, the IOC during a session in 1976 recognized the ILTF as the umbrella governing body for tennis. Following the change of status of tennis in 1981, the sport was readmitted to the Olympic program in 1988. This change was dominantly affected by the new developmental direction of the Olympic Movement and global sports.[7]

2 The Governance Structure of Tennis

From its beginning, the governance of tennis was developed between rigid amateurism and uncontrolled professionalism. For many years, the ITF was the dominant governing body in charge of promoting the game of tennis. The ITF is in charge of the administration, structure, organization and promotion of the game of tennis.[8] The Grand Slam tournaments (Wimbledon from 1877, US Open from 1881, Roland Garros from 1891 and the Australian Open from 1905) have been the most prominent tennis events where only amateur athletes were allowed to participate until major changes under the "Open Era" in 1968. Besides its authority to organize the Grand Slam circuit, the ILTF was responsible for the Davis Cup, the Fed Cup, the Hopman Cup and junior competitions. With the diminishing of the boundary between amateurism and professionalism, a number of new actors emerged. This eventuality gave rise to new and different competition formats for men, which signaled an attempt to reduce the dominance of the ILTF. The World Championship Tennis (WCT) and National Tennis League (NTL) were considered as the first promoters in professional tennis, limiting their players' ability to only compete at the ITF's Grand Prix tournaments. It was quickly realized that a coherent competition structure was needed in order to maximize commercialization potential and media exposure. In respect of men's tennis, in 1972, the Association of Tennis Professionals was duly established. First, it was set up to safeguard athletes' rights within the ITF and WCT, which took the dominant role over the NTL. Its creation led to a new ranking system, as

---

[7] Ueberroth cleverly negotiated exclusive licensing deals with a limited number of sponsors such as Coca-Cola, McDonald's and IBM, in the process significantly elevating the value of sport celebrities. See Thomas Boswell, "Ueberroth: Lateral Logic and Forward Motion," *The Washington Post* (September 29, 1984), available at: www.washingtonpost.com/archive/sports/1984/09/30/ueberroth-lateral-logic-and-forward-motion/d58b6388-ee3f-43f3-9cd1-07cce1931326/.

[8] ITF Constitution, available at: www.itftennis.com/media/2431/the-constitution-of-the-itf-2024-web.pdf.

well as registration for tournaments in a manner that enhanced operations and the creation of the Men's International Professional Tennis Council (MIPTC). The composition of the MIPTC reflected the various interests of tennis's major stakeholders: namely, the ITF, the ATP and tournament organizers. The main competence of the MIPTC was to manage tournaments. However, due to the dominance of the ATP, which was reflected in its widespread support from players, a new format competition was created – the ATP Tour. The new format was based primarily on the principle that players and organizers share similar interests, while the ATP and ITF retained their role as the governing bodies responsible for the men's circuit. Further reforms led to the introduction of the Master Series tournaments with a world tour format from 250, 500 and 1000 series. The dominance of the ATP on these reforms reflected a shift toward a complete commercialization of tennis events. The organizational structure and regulatory framework were consolidated, especially in terms of scheduling, ranking system and tournament entry criteria. Moreover, the conferral upon the ATP of capacity to determine the size of particular tournaments resulted in a gradual transition from a mere players' association to a dominant governing body in the men's circuit.

The WTA represents a leading association in professional women's sports, with over fifty worldwide events organized annually. For its operations, the WTA has adopted an annual rulebook.[9] The WTA is the product of the pioneering skills of Billie Jean King, formally established in 1973. Besides King's efforts, one also finds the separate tour known as Virginia Slims that later merged with the USLTA, which originally had its own women's tour. The commercialization of the game of tennis led to the sharp increase in a number of broadcasted tournaments, albeit due to the inequality in prize money, top women players threatened to boycott major events. Nine female players agreed to break away and went ahead to sign a contract with Gladys, thus marking the start of the Virginia Slims Tour with more than a dozen tournaments in the first quarter of 1971. At the same time, the existence of the competing USLTA women's tour prevented all efforts at unifying professional women's tennis. The frictions led to the formation of the Women's International Tennis Federation as the governing body of the Virginia Slims Tour. However, the USLTA used its monopoly status to force female players to adhere to their regulatory framework as

---

[9] The 2024 WTA Rulebook is available at: https://photoresources.wtatennis.com/wta/document/2024/02/12/1a78ea3b-3a70-4847-9951-d59307c2655d/2024-WTA-Rulebook-2-11-2024-.pdf.

a way of forcing them to compete at the Grand Slam events. The solution came in the new framework, which gave rise to the formation of the WTA that jointly with the USLTA worked on creating a unified tour for women's tennis. The main motive behind this effort was to create equality for both sexes in professional tennis, primarily regarding prize money. This goal was achieved in the first decade of the 2000s for tournaments within the Grand Slam circuit. However, the challenge regarding economic imbalance and gender gap remains in other tournaments, with the more opposing voices coming from the men's circuit. This spurred ongoing political debate – between one underlining the importance of gender equality, and others stressing that tennis is professional, commercialized, televised and ultimately a competitive activity organized under market principles.[10] Further, development in both the women's and the men's circuits led to organization of joint events by the ATP and the WTA, which adopted specific provisions within their respective major regulations (rulebooks) in order to maintain autonomy and expand commercial opportunities.[11]

3 Players' Councils

Both professional governing bodies have players' councils that are focused around safeguarding players' rights on and off the court. The ATP Council, with twelve members on board, has the power to influence developments and revision of the ATP Rulebook.[12] The composition of the Council[13] reflects the existing ranking system:

- four players from the top 50 players on the ATP in singles;
- two players from the 51–100 players on the ATP in singles;
- two players below the top 100 on the ATP in singles;
- two players from the top 100 on the ATP in doubles;
- a player alumnus;
- one coach.

---

[10] Isabel Cepeda, "Wage Inequality of Women in Professional Tennis of the Leading International Tournaments: Gender Equality vs Market Discrimination?" (2021) 22 J Int Women's Stud 407–26.

[11] See Bret McCormick, "After Years of Talk, Is Now the Time for the ATP and WTA to Play Doubles?" *Sports Business Journal* (June 29, 2020), available at: www.sportsbusinessjournal.com/Journal/Issues/2020/06/29/Leagues-and-Governing-Bodies/Tennis.aspx.

[12] Amy D. Gibson, "The Association of Tennis Professionals: From Player Association to Governing Body" (2010) 10 J Appl Bus Ec, available at: www.na-businesspress.com/JABE/Jabe105/GibsonWeb.pdf.

[13] See "ATP Announces Player Advisory Council for 2024," ATP Tour (January 8, 2024), available at: www.atptour.com/en/news/2024-player-advisory-council.

The WTA's Council is composed of eight members and differs from the composition of the ATP's Council. It is structured as follows:

- four players from the top 20 players on the WTA in singles;
- two players from the top 21–50 players on the WTA in singles;
- one player from the top 51–100 on the WTA in singles;
- one player ranked in doubles on the WTA.

4 The Relationship between Players and the ATP/WTA

There is an absence of information about the meetings, decisions and plans of the Councils. However, both the ATP and the WTA offer a range of support for a relatively restricted group of players. This support is based on each player's membership and the individual ranking. To be part of the world of tennis, a player must be bound to sport-related regulation. By the mere act of registering, a player is bound to all ITF/ATP/WTA rules, including integrity-related provisions. Moreover, a player must respect and adhere to the World Anti-Doping Code (WADC) and accompanying regulations. Both the ATP and the WTA offer two types of membership (full and associate), which relate to voting in the Players' Council, insurance policy and pension plan. The ATP membership is divided into two divisions: (1) on the date of one's application for membership, the person is ranked in the top 200 in the Pepperstone ATP rankings, or among the top 100 players in the Pepperstone ATP Doubles rankings, and pays ATP dues; (2) on the date of one's application for membership, the person is ranked in the top 500 in the Pepperstone ATP rankings, or among the top 250 players in the Pepperstone ATP Doubles rankings, and pays ATP dues. According to the WTA rules, the annual cost for full membership is set at US $1,000, while for associate membership the cost is US $500. For full membership, the eligibility criteria are based on the ranking system (for a singles player top 150 and for a doubles player top 50), with a minimum of six tournaments played (including ones from the Grand Slam events). As regards associate members, singles players under 750 on the WTA Singles ranking or top 250 on the WTA Doubles ranking must have participated in at least one WTA tournament. Full members possess the right to vote with the opportunity of reappointment in the Players' Councils. In both arrangements, members are entitled to a broad range of medical insurance, while depending on the number of years one has competed in ATP/WTA singles/doubles tournaments and membership status, there is a further entitlement for a pension scheme.[14] In 2023, the ATP announced that it was planning to establish a financial safety net for the top 250 ATP-ranked players. The program is called "Baseline." The first pillar of the program is known as "Guaranteed Base Earnings," which guarantees minimum income levels for the top 250-ranked singles players each season. In case a player's prize money earnings finishes below the guaranteed threshold, the ATP will step in to cover the shortfall. For the 2024 season, these levels are $300,000 (top 100), $150,000 (101–175) and $75,000 (176–250).[15]

For both the men's and women's circuits, the relevant governing bodies adopted a code of conduct that legally binds players to sponsorship and broadcasting deals. For example, on the day of event, players are obliged to undergo a pre-match interview followed by a post-match conference. Exceptions are possible in the case of injury or physical inability to attend. Violation of these rules leads to fines starting from $1,000 and depends on the player's ranking. In addition, the ATP STARS program established in 2008 is aimed at utilizing media and commercial interest in tennis. All players from the main draw are obliged to participate in ATP-sponsored events. If a player fails to participate in the ATP STARS activities, he or she would be subject to a fine depending on his or her ranking. Similarly, for media appearance, dress code has been in almost 150 years in the case of Wimbledon narrowed to all-white uniforms. According to the ATP/WTA regulations, players are obliged to present themselves in a professional manner during tournaments, official practice sites and media appearances. Failure to comply with this rule may lead to a fine or default from the tournament. It is hardly uncommon for a discretionary power to be conferred upon tournament officials (Chair Umpire or Supervisor) by which to order a player to comply with the pertinent rules and regulations.[16] However, in 2023, women are allowed to wear dark-coloured undershorts, departing from the original and strict application whereby players incurred fines. From 2019, the WTA has eased the rules for players, but even so, approval is

---

[14] For the WTA, see Section XI.E. from the WTA Rulebook, available at: https://photoresources.wtatennis.com/wta/document/2022/01/26/125189f7-fe9f-4aaf-8ff4-88973e54bd9a/2022-WTA-Rulebook-1-26-2022-.pdf.

[15] See "ATP Unveils Baseline, a Pioneering Financial Security Program for Players," ATP News Release (August 22, 2023), available at: www.atptour.com/en/news/baseline-financial-security-programme-august-2023.

[16] See ATP Rulebook 2023, Section VIII Code, sub-section L, On-site Offenses/Procedures, available at: www.itftennis.com/media/9098/2023-atp-rulebook.pdf.

needed for some forms of attire, such as footwear. As an alternative, players may submit a sample shoe for approval no later than ninety days from entering a tournament.[17]

5 The Relationship between National Tennis Federations and the ITF

The NSFs and organizations where the Grand Slam events are organized prevailed over time. Before the Open Era, the dominance of some amateur-oriented NSFs was strong and decisive in terms of national ranking systems and representation, with players forced to adhere to the rules if they desired to participate in both national and international events. There are currently 213 NSFs under the global governing body, the ITF. Out of these 213, 160 possess voting rights. These rights are divided between different member classes (B and C) of participants. According to the ITF Constitution, the following classes enjoy "exclusive voting rights":

- Class B – five leading NSFs (Australia, Great Britain, France, Germany and the United States) with twelve votes;[18]
- Class B – fourteen NSFs with nine votes;
- Class C – NSFs with seven, five, three and one votes.

Besides the NSFs endowed voting rights, there are fifty-three member federations from within Class C without voting rights. NSFs are structured within a framework of continental federations or confederations as follows:

- Asian Tennis Federation;
- Central American and Caribbean Tennis Confederation;
- Confederation of African Tennis;
- Oceania Tennis Federation;
- South America Tennis Confederation; and
- Tennis Europe.

The conferral of voting rights clearly concerns the NSFs' capacity to participate and influence the AGM of the ITF and its overall operations. The membership procedure is twofold. NSFs need to prove their ability

---

[17] See WTA Rulebook 2023, Section VII, Player responsibilities/on-court rules and procedures, sub-section C, available at: www.itftennis.com/media/9258/2023-wta-rulebook.pdf.
[18] See ITF Constitution, Art. 11, available at: www.itftennis.com/media/2431/the-constitution-of-the-itf-2024-web.pdf.

to operate in their geographical territory of origin. This requires that they are following that country's legislative framework. Second, concerning the NSF's organizational capacity, the ITF will grant membership status in accordance with the applicable criteria. A two-thirds majority of the Council at the AGM is needed to grant membership status. As per Class B, the Council shall adopt an appropriate resolution in accordance with Article 3 of the ITF Constitution, by which it grants particular NSFs membership status.

A potential member is obliged to present all relevant details related to the development of the game of tennis for its respective territory.[19] As per Class B requirements, the Board of Directors assigns an envoy or representative to visit the applicant with a view to submitting an appropriate report. The procedure includes the ITF's Council adopting the resolution at the AGM. According to the ITF Constitution, the Council may take a range of actions against NSFs, including suspension and expulsion from their membership where they are responsible for damaging the image of the ITF (and the game of tennis) or failing to comply with the ITF's rules.[20]

6   Contemporary Governance Setting and Challenges

In accordance with Article 10 of the ITF Constitution, the ITF is organized and registered as a limited liability company under the laws of the Commonwealth of the Bahamas, but retains its headquarters in London. This is unusual, because the vast majority of sports governing bodies are organized in the form of non-profit entities.[21] In the contemporary setting, the three main governing bodies of global tennis continue to operate in a rather concerted manner. Despite their autonomous competences, as a result of their business orientation, their mutual interaction without conflict reflects their desire for functional sustainability. The latter is particularly important for scheduling purposes despite the possible opposing interests. Although not impactful as before the Open Era, the ITF is considered as the sole sports governing body in the world of tennis. As an important part of policymaking, the ITF adopts the Rules of Tennis.[22]

---

[19] See ibid., Arts 3.g and 11.
[20] See ibid., Art. 4.
[21] Art. 1 of the FIFA Statute stipulates that FIFA is a foundation (non-profit) under Swiss law and in equal measure Art. 15.1 of the Olympic Charter emphasizes that the IOC is a non-profit association under Swiss law.
[22] The latest, 2025, version is available at: www.itftennis.com/media/7221/2025-rules-of-tennis-english.pdf.

These rules are subjected to the review of the Rules of Tennis Committee that further recommends revisions (when needed) to the ITF's Board of Directors. Besides the President, the composition of the Board includes:

- fourteen individuals elected in accordance with Article 21 of the ITF Constitution; and
- two Athlete Representatives (one from each sex) appointed by the elected members of the Board of Directors in accordance with Article 21 of the ITF Constitution.

Members, excluding the President, are elected by Class B members during the AGM for a term of four years. There is a clause that limits terms for not more than twelve years in total. A member may be removed by the Council by a two-thirds majority resolution adopted by the Board of Directors. The ITF adopts and/or updates on a yearly basis the ITF Rules of Tennis aimed at setting up a framework for the organization of competitions under the predictable format of play, as well as maintaining the traditional character and integrity of the game of tennis. In ensuring the consistency of rules with possible changes (e.g. technological ones), the ITF appoints the Rules of Tennis Committee to monitor, evaluate and prepare when needed recommendations to the AGM as the authority in charge for making any changes to the ITF Rules of Tennis. These rules are issued by a Ruling Board appointed by the President of the ITF.[23] The Chairperson of a Ruling Board determines the appropriate procedure for review/hearing if and when necessary.

The Board of Directors appoints the ITF International Adjudication Panel to decide any eligibility issues related to decisions under the ITF Rules of Tennis, the ITF Davis Cup Regulations, the ITF Fed Cup Regulations, the ITF Pro Circuit Regulations, the ITF Wheelchair Tennis Regulations, the ITF Wheelchair Classification Manual, the ITF Junior Circuit Regulations, the ITF Junior Team Competitions Regulations, the ITF Senior Regulations, the ITF Beach Tennis Rules and the Code of Conduct for Officials.[24] The competence of the Panel is broad and includes interpretation of the ITF Rules, determining possible breaches thereof, hear/determine appeals made by other governing bodies under the ITF

---

[23] See ITF Rules of Tennis, Appendix XI, Procedures for Review and Hearings on the Rules of Tennis, available at: www.itftennis.com/media/4421/2021-rules-of-tennis-english.pdf.
[24] See Chapter 4 of this volume for a discussion on the jurisdiction of the ITF's International Adjudication Panel.

Rules and propose changes to the ITF Rules before appropriate governing entities.[25]

According to the ITF Constitution, the ITF Code of Ethics is set to ensure that the game of tennis and governing structures are governed in accordance with the highest standards of ethics and integrity.[26] The Director of the ITF, the ITF President, its CEO and any person serving on an ITF committee or commission are obliged to adhere to the ITF Code of Ethics.[27] The ITF Ethics Commission was formed in 2019 to ensure compliance with principles of integrity and ethics under the ITF Code of Ethics. The major governing bodies in the world of tennis, the ITF, ATP and WTA, along with related bodies and stakeholders, are bound and must comply with the Code of Conduct for Officials. The Code is issued and could be revised by major governing bodies, contributing to the shared responsibility, network-based and complex governance structure.

There were steps between 2008 and 2009 to establish an appropriate anti-corruption body (Tennis Integrity Unit, TIU). However, in order to address wider challenges associated with integrity and ethics in a more autonomous manner, the International Tennis Integrity Agency (ITIA) was established by the ITF, ATP, WTA, the Australian Open, French Open, US Open and Wimbledon. The ITIA adopted two programs, the Tennis Anti-Corruption Program (TACP) for tackling corruption and the Tennis Anti-Doping Program (TADP) for ensuring a clean game of tennis.

The composition of the main decision-making body of the ATP, its Board of Directors, besides encompassing a chairperson, includes three players' representatives and three tournament representatives. The ATP Players' Council elects players' representatives. The composition of the ATP Tournament Council includes thirteen members of organizers from the regions of the Americas, Europe and the International Group of tournaments. The WTA's Board of Directors is composed of a chairperson, and three players' and three tournaments' representatives, in addition to the WTA CEO and an ITF representative. The

---

[25] See Art. 1 of the Procedural Rules Governing Procedures before an Internal Adjudication Panel convened under ITF Rules, available at: www.itftennis.com/media/5989/2019-procedural-rules-itf-iap.pdf.
[26] See Chapter 12 of this volume for a discussion of ethical issues and adjudication thereof in the context of the ITF.
[27] ITF Constitution, Art. 8. The ITF Code of Ethics is available at: www.itftennis.com/media/7246/2023-itf-code-of-ethics-english.pdf.

composition of the WTA Tournament Council includes nine members, three each from the regions of the Americas, Europe and Asia-Pacific. The recent emergence of players' associations/union(s), such as Djokovic's Professional Tennis Players Association (PTPA) established in 2020, disrupted the supremacy of the ATP and caused tensions. The tension between players and the ATP, in particular, are not new; however, its financial challenges for players are multiplying, thus giving rise to yet another challenge to the existing governance ecosystem in tennis. The level of mistrust was obvious during Djokovic's attempt to run for the ATP's Players' Council. He was not allowed to run because he is a member of the PTPA. The ATP initiated a campaign to prevent players from joining the PTPA. Despite these frictions, 250 players are members of the PTPA, thus signaling the need for necessary changes. In parallel, the ATP is under discussion on possible streamlines of reforms in order to improve players' conditions. As a result, the Baseline financial security system was launched, which, as already explained, aims to enable tennis professionals at the lower end of the rankings to make a fair income. The program aims to provide base salaries, compensate players in the case of injury and provide financial support for newcomers. Within the proposed system there are three levels of support, depending on ranking (up to 250 on ATP) and threshold earnings.

From 2019, both professional governing bodies have been discussing the potential of taking their cooperation to another level. The main motive behind this is related to utilizing media and commercial interests in a number of joint events. However, their respective positions are significantly apart, with the ATP focusing on media, while the WTA plans to achieve equal compensation with their male counterparts by 2033. That said, there are a number of challenges to be resolved before proceeding to a potential merger, as both actors have their own sponsorship and broadcasting deals. In addition, the involvement of investment companies is taking pace. While the WTA accepted a proposal from CVC Capital Partners to sell 20 percent of their media rights from WTA Ventures, the ATP rejected the same proposal.[28] Similarly, the ATP announced it will organize the NEXT Gen in Saudi Arabia. While questioning a potential merger, the PTPA addressed another governance challenge – the relationship with betting authorities. The PTPA suggested that 50 percent of

---

[28] "WTA Announces Partnership with CVC Capital," Reuters (March 7, 2023), available at: www.reuters.com/lifestyle/sports/wta-announces-partnership-with-cvc-capital-2023-03-07/.

revenues from betting sponsorship deals with tournament organizers should be awarded to athletes.[29]

6.1 Commercialization, Corruption and Financial Governance Challenges

The challenges and potential disruptions to the existing governance structure are closely aligned with the concept of autonomy of sport. The first reference on autonomy is found in the Olympic Charter of 1949. The rationale behind this was an attempt to prevent the omnipresence of state aspirations to utilize the Olympic Games for non-sporting objectives. The number of corruption scandals and widespread negative phenomena (e.g. doping) questioned the place and scope of sports autonomy. Further, the *Bosman* ruling added another perspective to sport governance, formulating limits to such autonomy as sport became more professional and intertwined with the commercial sector.[30] Later, the IOC adopted its Basic Universal Principles of Good Governance as an attempt to lower external pressure. Despite this and similar actions, the spread of corruption (e.g. FIFA)[31] and institutional doping scandals (e.g. McLaren Report)[32] confirmed the need for external involvement aimed at supervising governance and limiting autonomy. The Olympic Movement, the IOC and International Sports Federations (ISFs) jointly with governments founded the World Anti-Doping Agency (WADA) in order to eliminate doping in sport. Reforms to sport arbitration and further involvement of intergovernmental organizations (e.g. European Union or Council of Europe) culminated in the erosion of autonomy of governing bodies.

---

[29] Adam Addicott, "Novak Djokovic Calls for Changes to Tennis' Partnerships with Betting Companies," Ubitennis (September 22, 2023), available at: www.ubitennis.net/2023/09/novak-djokovic-calls-for-changes-to-tennis-partnerships-with-betting-companies/.

[30] *Union Royale Belge des Sociétés de Football Association ASBL v. Jean-Marc Bosman, Royal club liégeois SA v. Jean-Marc Bosman and Others and Union des Associations Européennes de Football (UEFA) v. Jean-Marc Bosman*, Case C-415/93, ECLI:EU:C:1995/463.

[31] Brian W. Bean, "FIFA – Where Crime Pays" in M. Breuer and D. Forrest (eds), *The Palgrave Handbook on the Economics of Manipulation in Sport* (Palgrave, 2018), 281; Mark Pieth, "'Governing FIFA: Concept, Paper and Report," cited in Roger Pielke, "How Can FIFA Be Held Accountable?" (2023) 16 Sport Manag Rev 258.

[32] The McLaren Report is available at: https://ita.sport/resource/mclaren-independent-investigator-report-to-the-oversight-and-integrity-commission-of-the-international-weightlifting-federation/.

The term "governance" has been exploited and is ambiguous at the same time. Although there are different definitions, governance may be defined as the manner through which organizations are regulated, steered, navigated and controlled. This term emerged in the Olympic Charter emphasizing the importance of its own operations. One of the fundamental principles served as a foundation for the development of the Basic Universal Principles of Good Governance. As indicated, this framework reflects the necessity to maintain the concept of political neutrality.[33] The updated version from 2022 is based on Recommendation 14 of Olympic Agenda 2020+5.[34] Specific emphasis is given to compliance with the Olympic Charter, the WADC and the Olympic Movement Code on the Prevention of the Manipulation of Competitions.[35] This effort was mostly involuntary. The rationale behind it represents numerous governance issues associated with major sports organizations that feed the public's interest. That said, governance in sport-related organizations has become a major topic for practitioners, policymakers, academia and the broader public.[36]

The changes toward commercialization have led to the exposure of sport to negative phenomena reflected in numerous corrupt practices resulting in deteriorating legitimacy.[37] Consequently, all major ISFs, including the ITF, needed to introduce a number of governance-related rules to respond

---

[33] See Basic Universal Principles of Good Governance within the Olympic Movement, Preamble, para. 1, available at: https://stillmed.olympics.com/media/Documents/Beyond-the-Games/Integrity/Bonne-Gouvernance-EN.pdf; see also Ilias Bantekas, "Political Neutrality of International Sports Federations: Compatible with Fundamental Rights of Athletes?" (2024) 34 Fordham IP, Media & Ent LJ 193.

[34] The 2020+5 Agenda is available at: https://olympics.com/ioc/olympic-agenda-2020-plus-5.

[35] The 2016 version of the Code is available at: https://stillmed.olympic.org/Documents/Commissions_PDFfiles/Ethics/olympic_movement_code_on_the_prevention_of_the_manipulation_of_competitions-2015-en.pdf.

[36] See Mathieu Winand and Christos Anagnostopoulos, *Research Handbook on Sport Governance* (Edward Elgar, 2019).

[37] On commercialization, see Trevor Slack and Ben Hinings, "Planning and Organizational Change: A Conceptual Framework for the Analysis of Amateur Sport Organizations" (1987) 12 Canadian J App Sport Sci 185–93; Trevor Slack and Ben Hinings, "Understanding Change in National Sport Organizations: An Integration of Theoretical Perspectives" (1992) 6 J Sport Manag 114–32. On integrity, see Arnout Geeraert, Michael Mrkonjic and Jean L. Chappelet, "A Rationalist Perspective on the Autonomy of International Sport Governing Bodies: Towards a Pragmatic Autonomy in the Steering of Sports" (2015) 7 Int J Sport Pol & Politics 473–88; Jean L. Chappelet, "Autonomy and Governance: Necessary Bedfellows in the Fight against Corruption in Sport," Transparency International, Global Corruption Report: Sport (2016), available at: https://transparency-france.org/wp-content/uploads/2018/02/2016_GCRSport_EN.pdf.

to growing public pressure. For the world of tennis, as a result of its complexity, the challenge was more demanding as all three major bodies are in charge of their own events. The complexity is further fueled by the fact that their relationship with NSFs and tournament organizers seems to be blurred, as was the case with the suspension of Russian and Belarussian tennis players from competing at the Wimbledon Championship in 2022.[38] Although an organizational clarity and division between ITF and ATP/WTA operations seems to be in place, the organization of the Davis Cup has presented a major challenge – first, for scheduling the event, and second, for the recent emergence of the ATP event called the ATP Cup. Interestingly, top players were not keen for both the Davis Cup and the ATP Cup to be on their schedules, albeit the ATP remained resolute to proceed with the event. It was founded in 2018, as a response to the change of the Davis Cup format. However, after 2022, the ATP Cup was abolished, with a new event emerging involving both the ATP and the WTA – the United Cup.[39] It is a mixed-gender event with two singles men's and two singles women's events, plus a mixed doubles match. It consists of a round-robin format of competition, with eighteen countries qualifying based on the following criteria:

- six countries qualify based on the ATP ranking;
- six countries qualify based on the WTA ranking; and
- six countries qualify based on the combined ATP/WTA ranking.

The second challenge to the current governance structure requires a transformation of players' associations and their relationship with other stakeholders. The ATP is a global non-stock corporation in charge of the professional circuit, including scheduling and organizing professional tennis events. The ATP's competence includes adopting and implementing the ATP ranking system for players and tournaments. Although Grand Slam tournaments and the Davis Cup are governed by the ITF, these tournaments employ the ATP raking system for entry and seeding. In return, the ATP agreed not to organize events that could

---

[38] Ray Siladitya. "Wimbledon Bans Russian and Belarusian Tennis Players – Here's Who's Affected," Forbes (April 20, 2022), available at: www.forbes.com/sites/siladityaray/2022/04/20/wimbledon-bans-russian-and-belarusian-tennis-players–heres-whos-affected/?sh=28bc19062499.

[39] The United Cup is a first joint event of the ATP and the WTA organized in Australia prior to the Australian Open, with 500 points for individual players from both the ATP and the WTA. The points make this event different from the existing Hopman Cup, which is rather seen as an exhibition event.

conflict with ITF events and include the latter in the ranking system. The Grand Slam tournaments are mandatory for professional players, and the ITF will not organize an event that conflicts with the ATP Finals. This is particularly important due to the technical demand in announcing weekly ranking lists based on players' performance during an entire year as it constitutes the basis for entry into tournaments and consequently impacts the allocation of prize money. Therefore, the ATP, with its monopoly on the ranking and organization of professional tennis events, may decide to upgrade or downgrade tournaments. The ATP's decision to downgrade certain tournaments has been challenged before the courts. The importance of the ruling in *Deutscher Tennis Bund* v. *ATP Tour, Inc.* was that it confirmed that by joining the ATP, NSFs are bound by its regulatory framework, save of course if the ATP or other tennis entity is violating anti-trust legislation by enforcing a monopoly. In addition, the judgment recognizes that under applicable legislation, the Board of Directors may adopt/amend/revise the ATP Rulebook.[40] However, the ATP governance mechanism does engage wider consultation as part of the Board of Directors operations. Recently, these consultations resulted in addressing the question of financial accountability and transparency, concluding the need for a 50/50 profit-sharing formula for players and organizers. These changes reflect the growing commercialization of tennis, resulting in prolonged and more televised games, was well as the introduction of new technologies and diversified engagement by major sponsors.[41] Echoing business opportunities, the format for the specific number of ATP Masters 1000 events has been changed from 56-draw to 96-draw, further extending these tournaments from eight to twelve days, enabling more opportunities for the ATP as a circuit promoter, and for tournament organizers, players and sponsors.[42]

That said, the Board of Directors represents a specific form of governance, as indicated earlier, reflecting both the nature of organizational and regulatory evolution of professional tennis, facilitating as

---

[40] *Deutscher Tennis Bund* v. *ATP Tour, Inc.*, 610 F.3d 820 (3d Cir. 2010).

[41] See, in particular, Francesca Jenner, "Innovation in Tennis Brings Opportunities and Challenges – Francesco Ricci Bitti," *Horizon Magazine* (June 30, 2014), available at: https://ec.europa.eu/research-and-innovation/en/horizon-magazine/innovation-tennis-brings-opportunities-and-challenges-francesco-ricci-bitti; Robert Demir and Sten Söderman, "Strategic Sponsoring in Professional Sport: A Review and Conceptualization" (2015) 15 Eur Sport Manag Q 271.

[42] Five tournaments have been the subject of these changes: Mutua Madrid Open from 2023, Internazionali BNL d'Italia from 2023, Rolex Shanghai Masters from 2023, National Bank Open from 2025 and Western & Southern Open from 2025.

well an institutional arrangement between players and tournament organizers. Consequently, both actors share responsibility on policy-making and implementation, although from both parties, there have been growing voices, especially players, speaking up about the lack of adequate representation. In particular, achieving coordination between key stakeholders serves only to multiply business opportunities, whereas players have been underrepresented and underpaid, among other challenges.[43] The complex governance interrelation was magnified during the Covid-19 pandemic.[44] Besides tennis events being cancelled or postponed, the restructuring scheduling, organizational rules and procedures have been the subject of major changes.[45] However, these challenges resulted in a greater coordinating effort that led to a more coherent short-term policy toward protecting players' interests.[46] The main features of this unique governance structure were based on collaborative efforts and cooperation among a variety of different stakeholders. Furthermore, the game was shaped around professionalization and commercialization as major drivers, resulting in the continued growth of the game over time and balancing rules, format and schedules favoring the commercial nature of the sport. However, revenue sharing, heterogeneity of stakeholders and their engagement in decision-making bodies remains one of the major impediments to the stability of governance bodies.

---

[43] Saul J. Shrom, Jennifer Cumming and Sarah-Jane Fenton, "Lifestyle Challenges and Mental Health of Professional Tennis Players: An Exploratory Case Study" (2022) 21 Int J Sport Exerc Psychol 1.

[44] The Covid-19 pandemic had severe effects on sport-related industry at both national and international levels. For more, see Marko Begović, "Effects of COVID-19 on Society and Sport National Response" (2020) 27 Manag Sport Leis 241.

[45] "Expert Insights: Tennis Players' Struggles during COVID-19," Western News, Western Communications, Western University (May 31, 2021), available at: https://news.westernu.ca/2021/05/expert-insights-tennis-players-struggles-during-covid-19/; Kelsey Slater and Jim Watkins, "Tennis Players' Responses to Covid-19 and the Global Pandemic's Impact on Professional Tennis Governance" in Paul M. Pedersen, Brodey J. Ruihley and Bo Li (eds), *Sport and the Pandemic* (Routledge, 2020), 146–56; Toru Ishihara, Nicolas Robin, Takashi Naito et al., "Effects of the COVID-19 Pandemic on Professional Tennis Players' Match Statistics: A Large-Scale Population-Based Study" (2022) 32 Scand J Med Sci Sports 1516; Matthew Futterman, "How Tennis and Djokovic Are Pushing against the U.S. Covid Vaccine Rule," *New York Times* (March 6, 2023), available at: www.nytimes.com/2023/03/06/sports/tennis/djokovic-biden-miami-open-covid-vaccine.html.

[46] "Governing Bodies Join Forces to Answer Players' Cry for Financial Help," Reuters (April 18, 2020), available at: www.reuters.com/article/sports/governing-bodies-join-forces-to-answer-players-cry-for-financial-help-idUSKBN21Z2E0/.

7 Epilogue

There are currently three major initiatives at the table for wider discussion – namely, reshaping the profit-sharing formula, the merger of professional associations and ATP's Baseline program. Contrary to football, these discussions are limited and related to internal processes within existing organizational structures, with a possible outcome being the granting or decentralization of power and responsibility with a view to achieving unique organizational and operational interdependence. This reflects a continuous interplay between political legitimacy and institutional governance focusing on the manner in which power is being practiced, and the scope of the influence within a given regulatory framework that facilitates to some extent the prevailing corporate governance. The democratic deficit within global tennis was manifested during the unionization process, especially during the formation of the PTPA.[47] Quickly, the ATP dislocated its focus from a number of challenges, including the devastating effects of the pandemic, to supress such developments because of their potential impact on existing governance that is already complex and, in some cases, proved to be uncoordinated or fragmented. This was particularly obvious following the Russia–Ukraine war, when the All England Lawn Tennis and Croquet Club (AELTC), organizer of the Wimbledon tournament, decided in concert with the LTA to unilaterally ban Russian/Belarussian tennis players from participating in 2022. With support from the UK government, the LTA declined entries to Russian/Belarussian athletes to take part in any UK tennis event. The official holder of the Grand Slam circuit, the ITF and both professional associations failed to apply their own regulations, except for removing points from all categories for competition, including the ATP/WTA imposing fines on the LTA/AELTC. This confirms the limited authority and enforcement of rules over particular tournament organizers, cumulatively confirming a deficit of contemporary tennis governance and the need for comprehensive reforms.

---

[47] Patil Swarali, "Pro Tennis Needs an Organization That Advocates for Players' Health, Safety and Prize Money," The Conversation (November 2020), available at: http://theconversation.com/pro-tennis-needs-an-organization-that-advocates-for-players-health-safety-and-prize-money-149203.

9

Safeguarding in Tennis

An Enforceable Duty of Care

ILIAS BANTEKAS

1 Introduction

High-profile scandals, chiefly involving coaches,[1] have served as the catalyst for legislative change and the promulgation of robust safeguarding policies with a focus on vulnerable persons, chiefly children, and disabled athletes. In 2001, the United Kingdom extended the scope of the National Society for the Prevention of Cruelty to Children (NSPCC) by the introduction of a Child Protection in Sport Unit.[2] In 2008, AusAID became the first bilateral donor to implement a Child Protection Policy,[3] with a view that funding is only provided to sports organizations that implement robust safeguarding policies. In 2012, UNICEF adopted a set of International Safeguards for Children in Sport,[4] and a working group was set up as a follow-up mechanism. Despite the significance of safeguarding for children in sport, the subject has received very little attention in the legal literature. This may, of course, be due to the fact that the well-being of children is also the subject matter of specific criminal laws[5] and human rights standards pertinent to children, chiefly as articulated by the Convention on the Rights of the Child

---

[1] See Hadley Freeman, 'How Was Larry Nassar Able to Abuse So Many Gymnasts for So Long?' *The Guardian* (26 January 2018), available at: www.theguardian.com/sport/2018/jan/26/larry-nassar-abuse-gymnasts-scandal-culture.
[2] Available at: https://thecpsu.org.uk.
[3] The Policy is available at: www.dfat.gov.au/international-relations/themes/child-protection/child-protection#:~:text=The%20Department%20of%20Foreign%20Affairs,prevent%20child%20exploitation%20and%20abuse.
[4] Available at: https://downloads.unicef.org.uk/wp-content/uploads/2014/10/International-Safeguards-for-Children-in-Sport-version-to-view-online.pdf.
[5] Elisabeth St Pierre, Sylvie Parent and Nadine Deslauriers-Varin, 'Exploring the Modus Operandi of Coaches Who Perpetrated Sex Offences in Canada' (2022) 13 Front Psychol 1; Ingunn Bjørnseth and Attila Szabo, 'Sexual Violence against Children in Sports and Exercise: A Systematic Literature Review' (2018) 27 J Child Sex Abus 365.

(CRC),[6] as well as Article 30 of the Convention on the Rights of Persons with Disabilities (CRPD).[7] Even so, all these laws are focused exclusively on child–adult relationships; are unconcerned with the particular sporting context; fail to consider the well-being of adults; and, equally, do not account for all those situations that pose a likelihood of 'harm' to athletes in their future life without the intervention of any criminal conduct. The latter category includes 'burn out', no alternative career transition upon termination of a sporting career, health and safety concerns on the court, child-to-child abuse, bullying and others.

It should be stated from the outset that there is an extensive body of rules on safeguarding generated by tennis academies and clubs, and the International Tennis Federation (ITF) has promulgated a Safeguarding Children Policy,[8] and another for adults.[9] The Women's Tennis Association (WTA) released a Safeguarding Code of Conduct on 26 December 2024, at a time when this book was already in production.[10] Hence, this late-December 2024 development will not be discussed here. The Association of Tennis Professionals (ATP) has drafted an instrument, but has not promulgated a discreet safeguarding code, and as far as this author is aware such a process is ongoing.[11] There is also a good number of general safeguarding codes,[12] as well as others that are tennis-specific and generated

---

[6] See, in particular, CRC, Art. 19, emphasising that everyone has the responsibility to protect all children from all forms of harm, abuse, neglect and exploitation, and Art. 31, confirming every child's right to participate in play and recreational activities.

[7] Ilias Bantekas, 'The Right of Access to Sport and Recreation for Disabled Persons under International Law: What Does It Really Entail?' (2022) 45 Loy LA Int & Comp L Rev 157 (discussing CRPD, Art. 30 and arguing that states are obliged to facilitate access to sporting opportunities to persons with disabilities and by implication safeguard their well-being and welfare).

[8] ITF Safeguarding Children Policy 2023, available at: www.itftennis.com/media/4458/itf-children-safeguarding-policy-2023.pdf.

[9] ITF Safeguarding Adults Policy 2023, available at: chrome-extension://efaidnbmnnnibp cajpcglclefindmkaj/https://www.itftennis.com/media/4457/itf-adult-safeguarding-pol icy-2023.pdf.

[10] The Code is available at: https://wtafiles.wtatennis.com/pdf/publications/2025-WTA-Safeguarding-Code.pdf. It should be noted, however, that the WTA has a safeguarding policy in place with required safeguarding education for anybody seeking a credential.

[11] In 2021, the ATP appointed ATP Tour Director of Safeguarding, while later this year the ATP received an Independent Safeguarding Report.

[12] A good example is offered by the US Center for Safesport's Code for the US Olympic and Paralympic Movement (2023), available at: https://uscenterforsafesport.org/wp-content/uploads/2023/09/2023-SafeSport-Code.pdf, which provides an elaborate definition of all the conduct prohibited in the safeguarding context.

by national tennis associations.[13] Safeguarding policies and codes are further supplemented – and superseded where in conflict – with national legislation. Such legislation may be sport-specific, such as the US Protecting Young Victims from Sexual Abuse and Safesport Authorization Act of 2017, upon which the USTA Safe Play Handbook is predicated, as well as others of a more general nature aiming to protect children athletes from abusive behaviour.

In order to avoid a legalistic approach to the subject by squeezing into a relatively short chapter an abundance of rules from a variety of instruments, the chapter relies principally on ITF and WTA instruments. Space constraints sadly dictate that the analysis is not exhaustive, the aim being to provide an overall perspective of the legal aspects of safeguarding. The chapter adopts a broad definition of safeguarding, which encompasses all aspects of the safety and well-being of tennis players, whether children or adults, the enforcement of which is incumbent on all tennis professionals and tennis institutions enjoying a direct relationship with players. This duty is not exhausted by one stakeholder (e.g. the ITF or an academy) on account of the fact that another stakeholder (e.g. a parent) enjoys a closer relationship with a particular player. It should be understood that safeguarding obligations are not ethical duties, at least in the sense of largely personal decisions about what is good or bad; rather, as will be explained, they are concrete duties imposed by law or contract on the pertinent stakeholders.

2   Safeguarding as a Duty of Care

It is by no means an easy task to locate the legal premise of this duty of safeguarding.[14] However, it is important for the purposes of this discussion to do so because one needs to be aware of the consequences for a stakeholder's failure to uphold the requisite safeguarding standards. The law requires that those entrusted with a 'duty of care' over others must exercise such duty to the best of their abilities and by considering the

---

[13] See e.g. US Tennis Association (USTA) Safe Play Handbook, which was the first comprehensive safeguarding code in the tennis sphere, available at: www.usta.com/content/dam/usta/2021-pdfs/Safe%20Play%20Handbook%20051420%20-%20updated%20Center%20reporting%20number.pdf; Tennis Australia Safeguarding Children Code of Conduct, available at: www.tennis.com.au/wp-content/uploads/2023/10/TA-Safeguarding-Children-Code-of-Conduct-12-Oct-2023.pdf; Lawn Tennis Association (LTA) Safeguarding Children Policy and Procedure 2023, available at: www.lta.org.uk/498128/siteassets/about-lta/file/lta-safeguarding-children-policy.pdf.

[14] See Jack Anderson and Neil Partington, 'Duty of Care in Sport: Time for a Sports Ombudsman?' (2018) 1 Int Sports L Rev 3.

best interests of the protected person. The law does not always spell out all such relationships (i.e. parent–child or teacher–child), but there are tests to ascertain these. In the English case of *Donoghue* v. *Stevenson*, Lord Aitkin set out the contours of 'good neighborliness' as follows:

> You must take reasonable care to avoid acts or omissions which you can reasonably foresee would be likely to injure your neighbor. Who then in law is my neighbor? ... Persons who are so closely and directly affected by my act that I ought reasonably to have them in contemplation as being so affected when I am directing my mind to the acts or omissions which are called in question.[15]

This is a test for tort-based liability and not a mere reference to expected ethical conduct lacking enforcement. Common law and civil law jurisdictions have further elaborated this duty on sports coaches and by extension also to academies – as a direct tort liability based on a duty of care, or alternatively on the basis of vicarious liability. By way of illustration, in *Shone* v. *British Bobsleigh and Skeleton Association* (BBSA), it was held that the BBSA, through the actions of its coaches, 'owed the claimant [athlete] a duty to take reasonable care of her safety [ultimately resulting in injuries]. ... The BBSA owed a duty of care to the claimant to take all reasonable actions to ensure she was reasonably safe in the course of her activities on the bobsleigh run, in accordance with the prevailing standard of reasonable practice.'[16] While the duty of care for sports professionals is extensive, the standard is hardly an impossible one. It is based on a test of reasonableness.[17] The various rules set out by tennis clubs and the ITF effectively clarify and contextualise what is reasonable in the realm of a tennis relationship. While no doubt such rules do not bind the courts about what is *in fact* reasonable,[18] they do give rise to general principles and at the very least provide concrete guidelines to the club, coaches and other stakeholders about their duties of care. However, such duty is clearly broader than said rules and injured players and their families may well argue for broader tort-based liability. Article 14 of the ITF's Safeguarding Policy for Children correctly adopts the trust-based model of the duty to care, as follows: '[T]o address the risk of sexual abuse perpetrated by adults exploiting an imbalance of power

---

[15] *Donoghue* v. *Stevenson* [1932] AC 562, at 580.
[16] *Shone* v. *British Bobsleigh Ltd* [2018] 5 WLUK 226, at paras 2 and 4.
[17] Neil Partington, *Coaching, Sport and the Law: A Duty of Care* (Routledge, 2021), 29–39.
[18] See e.g. Art. 1 of the ITF's Safeguarding Policy for Children, whose definition of 'safeguarding' is significantly narrower than that suggested in the introduction to this chapter. It chiefly focuses on abuse, harassment, violence and exploitation.

over a child or young person, the ITF applies the "Relationship of Trust" doctrine. This covers relationships between a covered person who cares for, advises, supervises, trains or supports any child participating in any tennis activity.' This model is unconcerned with the age of consent to engage in sexual relations. Any covered person engaging in sexual activity with a child athlete (i.e. below the age of 18) is considered to be in breach of the ITF's Safeguarding Policy.[19] This has also long been part of the WTA's Safeguarding Code of Conduct, as contained in its Rulebook. This model is in line with the laws of most countries. In 2022, the United Kingdom's 2003 Sexual Offences Act was amended to include a new Article 22A, which extends the 'position of trust' to include any adult that regularly coaches, teaches, trains, supervises or instructs a 16- or 17-year-old in sport. This category of people is presumed to be aware of the power imbalance they hold over children and are under a duty not to use this for personal advantage or gratification.

3 The Sporting Context of Abuse

Sexual, physical and emotional abuse, as well as violence, are the most prevalent safeguarding concerns in sports, most often perpetrated by sports professionals in a position of trust against children athletes. The cultural context of abuse is predicated upon the unequal and discriminatory power differentials across a range of social and individual factors. It has been reported that on average, 40 to 50 per cent of athletes have experienced some degree of mild harassment to severe abuse during their lifetime in organised sport.[20] On average, 44–75 per cent of athletes have experienced psychological abuse by stakeholders in sports settings.[21] Sexual abuse is particularly pervasive and in a study conducted on 159 cases of sexual abuse in sport-related contexts, 98 per cent of the perpetrators were coaches or sports personnel.[22] Significantly, research demonstrates that elite young athletes are more likely to be sexually assaulted and abused than their lower-level counterparts.[23]

---

[19] ITF Safeguarding Policy for Children, Art. 14.
[20] Tine Vertommen, Nicolette Schipper-van Veldhoven, Kristien Wouters et al., 'Interpersonal Violence against Children in Sport in the Netherlands and Belgium' (2016) 51 Child Abuse Negl 223.
[21] Ibid.
[22] Ibid.
[23] Kari Fasting and Trond S. Sand, 'Narratives of Sexual Harassment Experiences in Sport' (2015) 7 Qual Res Sport Exerc Health 573.

It is no accident that the International Olympic Committee (IOC),[24] UNICEF[25] and the European Union,[26] among many others, have adopted several instruments, reports and guidelines in order to counter sexual and other types of abuse in the sporting context. All of these instruments emphasise the close link between elite athletes and their coaches – as well as other stakeholders – which is easily manipulated, thus mandating increased safeguarding by all covered persons.

4 Safeguarding in Child–Adult Relationships in Tennis

The following sections focus on safeguarding in child–adult relationships. The various sub-sections explain the pioneering contribution of the WTA but go on to analyse safeguarding in this context on the basis of the ITF Policy.

4.1 The WTA's Pioneering Safeguarding Role

The WTA's contribution should not be underestimated. The WTA conducted its first formal review of the unique needs of young women participating in elite international professional tennis in 1994. The independent body which conducted that groundbreaking first study and made its attendant recommendations continues to oversee WTA initiatives relating to healthy and safe participation of WTA athletes. The WTA's Age Eligibility Rule (AER) and Player Development Program (PDP), which will be explored in more context in a subsequent section of this chapter, are designed to identify and ameliorate the stressors in professional tennis, improve athlete career longevity and enhance player

---

[24] IOC, 'Safeguarding Athletes from Harassment and Abuse in Sport: Toolkit for IFs and NOCs' (2018), available at: https://stillmed.olympics.com/media/Document%20Library/OlympicOrg/IOC/What-We-Do/Promote-Olympism/Women-And-Sport/Boxes%20CTA/IOC_Safeguarding_Toolkit_ENG_Screen_Full1.pdf; IOC Guidelines for International Federations and National Olympic Committees Related to Creating and Implementing a Policy to Safeguard Athletes from Harassment and Abuse in Sport, available at: https://olympics.com/athlete365/app/uploads/2020/12/IOC_Guidelines_for_IFs_and_NOCs.pdf.

[25] UNICEF, 'Protecting Children from Violence in Sport', available at: www.oroplataybronce.com/wp-content/uploads/2017/01/violence_in_sport-Unicef.pdf.

[26] European Union, 'Safeguarding Children in Sport Report' (2019), available at: https://op.europa.eu/en/publication-detail/-/publication/03fc8610-e4c2-11e9-9c4e-01aa75ed71a1; European Commission, 'Study on Gender-Based Violence in Sport' (2016), available at: https://sport.ec.europa.eu/sites/default/files/gender-based-violence-sport-study-2016_en.pdf.

safety and well-being. Two further extensive formal reviews (in 2004 and 2014, respectively) clearly demonstrated the effectiveness of these initiatives since their inception in 1995. The WTA has successfully decreased premature retirements (players leaving the Tour at or before the age of 21) and increased players' career length. In recognition of the need to enhance the safeguarding of WTA players, the WTA convened a Safety and Security Task Force in 2006 to review its procedures and policies relevant to that area. That year-long review process identified critical components necessary to enhance athlete health and safety. Accordingly, key elements were implemented, including a robust augmentation of the Code of Conduct, clear complaint and violation procedures, instigation of an educational and training program for WTA personnel, players and Player Support Team members, all designed to specifically address and prevent abuse and harassment. Additionally, the safeguarding role was included as part of a restructuring of responsibilities of the former Athlete Assistance position. It is also worth noting that with the addition of a formal safeguarding position at the WTA, a mandatory safeguarding education course was introduced in 2023 for anyone seeking a WTA credential that provides access to player-protected areas as part of the WTA's Credential Eligibility System. That system itself was designed to improve and centralise the information of anyone with access to the WTA environment, along with ensuring (through the safeguarding education course) that those individuals also understood their obligations under the WTA Code of Conduct, as well as when and how to report suspected misconduct to the WTA.

The view of the WTA is that safeguarding incorporates the whole of the WTA environment, as safeguarding is not limited to a specific dynamic. Player safety has always been a priority, not only under the WTA Rulebook, but it has also been augmented by the introduction of a formal safeguarding policy.

4.2 The ITF Safeguarding Policy for Children

The asymmetry in maturity between a child athlete and its coaches, medical professionals, club/academy/federation administrators and potentially other tennis stakeholders raises the likelihood of abuse, whether sexual, physical or mental. This includes sexual grooming, rape, manipulation with the aim of enhancing one's abilities through the use of banned substances, match-fixing and even less innocuous conduct but no less harmful, such as preventing a child athlete from focusing on his or her studies or inflicting upon a child a sense of unworthiness and contempt. While some of the aforementioned conduct clearly constitutes a violation of criminal laws (e.g. rape, grooming, integrity), what is the status of chastisement (and punishment intended to improve a child's sporting performance) that is prohibited, albeit not necessarily criminal?[27] The answer to this important question lies in the foundational and customary principle of the 'child's best interests', as enshrined in Article 3 of the CRC. According to this principle, any decision, judgment, action (e.g. contract) or law (legislative or administrative) concerning children is enforceable only if it is in the best interests of the child.[28] The application of the 'best interests' principle under Article 3(2) of the CRC must take into account 'the rights and duties [of the child's] parents, guardians or other individuals legally responsible'. A child's best interests must be assessed on an individual basis by the courts and administrative authorities, and hence pertinent decisions must be reasoned as to their effects and outcomes on the particular child.[29] According to the European Court of Human Rights (ECtHR), the best interests of the child comprise two limbs: maintaining family ties (except where the family has proved particularly unfit); and ensuring the child's development within a sound environment, such as would not harm his or her health and development.[30]

A particular dimension of the best interests principle is its direct application to entities and institutions other than the courts or the state. Private entities and institutions are not immune from the application of this principle in their dealings with children. Although such an obligation is not conferred on private entities, states parties to the CRC, International Covenant on Civil and Political Rights (ICCPR) and CRPD are obliged to incorporate such obligation in their domestic laws on the basis of which

---

[27] See above Section 2 of this chapter for a discussion of the extension of the 'trust relationship' in the English Sexual Offences Act.
[28] According to CRC, Art. 3(1), 'the best interests of the child shall be a primary consideration'. Article 2 of the Optional Protocol to the CRC (Communications Procedure) setting out the general principles guiding the functions of the Committee stipulates that the Committee on the Rights of the Child (CtRC) 'shall be guided by the principle of the best interests of the child'. Under Art. 3(2) of the Optional Protocol, the CtRC 'may decline to examine any communication that it considers not to be in the child's best interests'.
[29] See *Y. B. and N. S. v. Belgium*, CtRC Views, UN Doc. CRC/C/79/D/12/2017 (5 November 2018), at para. 8.3.
[30] See *Neulinger and Shuruk v. Switzerland* (2012) 54 EHRR 31, at para. 136; see generally Michael Freeman, *Commentary on the UN Convention on the Rights of the Child: Article 3* (Brill, 2007), and, in the digital context, CtRC, General Comment 25 (2021) on children's rights in relation to the digital environment, UN Doc. CRC/C/G/25 (2 March 2021), at paras 12–13.

private entities are obliged to apply the welfare principle. For the purposes of this chapter, such an obligation extends to all private tennis stakeholders because of their relationship of trust with children athletes. It should be stated that because a parent endorses an unhealthy child–adult relationship out of financial greed or sport favouritism, this does not mean that the duty of care of incumbent tennis stakeholders is discharged; quite the contrary, identifying abusive parents is a continuous and integral part of such a duty.[31]

Article 5 of the ITF's Guidelines Policy for Children sets out its core principles as follows:

- The welfare of every child and young person is of paramount importance.
- Safeguarding is everyone's responsibility.
- All children, regardless of colour, race, nationality, ethnic or national origin, age, gender, sexual orientation, disability or religion have the right to protection from harassment, abuse, violence, exploitation and poor practice.
- All children have the right to participate, enjoy and develop through tennis, in a safe and inclusive environment, free from all forms of harassment, abuse, violence, exploitation and poor practice.
- Children should feel safe, respected and valued in all our activities and engagement.
- All Covered Persons must be alert to the signs of abuse and neglect and report their concerns to ensure that children receive effective protection.

What is important in this statement is the ITF's acknowledgement that all covered persons, as stakeholders and as gatekeepers, are incumbent with a duty of care that includes a threefold dimension: (1) provision of actual care; (2) a preventive duty; and (3) a concrete reporting duty. It is instructive that Article 6 of the ITF Policy refers to a 'culture of embedding of reporting concerns and aims to create a culture of vigilance', as well as 'promote safe environments'.

4.3 The ITF's Monitoring Process

A key element of the ITF's safeguarding is its safer recruitment policy,[32] and its commitment that persons recruited by it to work with children

---

[31] See Art. 4 of the ITF Children's Safeguarding Policy, which encompasses parents and legal guardians among the group of persons 'covered' by the Policy.

[32] The ITF does not seem to have publicised such a policy, so it is the opinion of this author that the ITF's own declaration of such a policy is not in the formal published sense, but as part of its overall safeguarding policy.

are appropriately qualified for that role. This includes rigorous background checks prior to a job offer being made.[33] The ITF has established the office of the Safeguarding Manager and each ITF event is equipped with a Designated Safeguarding Officer (normally the Tournament Supervisor), who is responsible for receiving reports and ensuring timely processing, whether internally or with national police authorities. At the time of writing, the ITF's Safeguarding Manager, Gary Bye, was a former law enforcement officer, thus demonstrating the kind of skills required to undertake a thorough investigation of harmful conduct against athletes, alongside a capacity to engage with victims and alleged perpetrators, as well as effectively collaborate with police authorities. The Safeguarding Manager has overall responsibility for background checks, training and the enforcement of the ITF's policy, among other duties.[34] Where an allegation injurious to the welfare of a child athlete occurs and concerns a covered person at an ITF tournament:

> ... the ITF will encourage and support the relevant National Association and/or Regional Association to investigate and resolve the allegation in the first instance by implementation of the applicable local safeguarding policies and procedures. In the absence of such policies and procedures, or for any of the reasons stated at section 22 below, the ITF will assume jurisdiction to ensure that all safeguarding concerns are investigated and sanctioned as appropriate.[35]

One of the more persistent safeguarding issues concerns child athletes' accommodation while away from home in tournaments. Most families cannot afford a separate accommodation for their child and their coach (whose expenses are typically covered by the family) and a large part of sexual abuse arises as a result of shared accommodation between children and adults. Article 12(9) of the ITF's Safeguarding Policy for Children makes it clear that children are under no circumstances to share accommodation with persons above the age of 18 and if they are to be hosted by families, appropriate background checks are to be made in advance. This is no doubt welcome, but does not eliminate situations of children athletes being sent to tournaments by parents unable to afford travel and accommodation expenses for themselves, for which a distinct investigation should be required. The ITF has not set out any requirements for

---

[33] ITF Children's Safeguarding Policy, Art. 10.
[34] Ibid., Art. 11.
[35] Ibid., Art. 12(4).

parents and legal guardians to notify the ITF of accommodation arrangements, nor is there a mechanism for verification.[36]

Article 15 of the ITF Safeguarding Policy for Children contains a long list of conduct that is not allowed by covered persons or those in a position of trust. This list has been carefully thought out and the drafters should be commended because they tackle not simply abusive behaviour, but also situations that while not abusive or illegal may, nonetheless, lead to grooming. One in particular stands out. Article 15 (B)(xi) stipulates that covered persons and those in a relationship of trust:

> [or those who] have authority, supervision or control over any Child [must not] (a) engage in personal electronic communication with that Child, or (b) have that Child as a 'friend' or 'follower' within personal social networking sites and apps, in either case, unless an arrangement approved by the Child's parent/legal guardian is in place and *all* communications are copied to the Child's parent or legal guardian.[37]

Besides abuse, harassment, violence and sexual exploitation,[38] the ITF's Safeguarding Policy for Children adds 'poor practice', 'neglect' and 'emotional abuse'[39] to the list of conduct that is unacceptable and which constitutes a violation of the Policy, even if not an infraction of the law. Poor practice is conduct that is not immediately harmful, but which could cause harm in the future and sets a poor example.[40] Examples of poor practice include 'failing to provide safe training or competition environments, not paying due care and attention to players during participation, inappropriate use of the Internet and online communication or social media apps and platforms, working with children while under the effects of drugs or alcohol, smoking, swearing or acts of aggressive behaviour in front of children'. Research has shown that grooming of child athletes by covered persons through their social

---

[36] It is not clear to this author that the World Tennis Tour Juniors Organisational Requirements cater for this eventuality. Available at: www.itftennis.com/media/11469/2024-itf-world-tennis-tour-juniors-organisational-requirements.pdf.

[37] Emphasis added.

[38] Celia H. Brackenridge, 'He Owned Me Basically ...': Women's Experience of Sexual Abuse in Sport' (1997) 32 Int Rev Sociol Sport 115; Celia H. Brackenridge, Daz Bishopp, Sybille Moussalli et al., 'The Characteristics of Sexual Abuse in Sport: A Multidimensional Scaling Analysis of Events Described in Media Reports' (2008) 6 Int J Sport Exerc Psychol 385.

[39] See Charlotte L. Wilinsky and Allyssa McCabe, 'A Review of Emotional and Sexual Abuse of Elite Child Athletes by Their Coaches' (2020) 10 Sports Coach Rev 84.

[40] ITF Safeguarding Policy for Children, Art. 16.

media platforms is prevalent.[41] Covered persons also have a duty to meet a child's basic physical and psychological needs. Article 16 defines this type of neglect as failing to:

- Provide adequate food, clothing and shelter (including exclusion from home or abandonment);
- Protect a child from physical and emotional harm or danger;
- Ensure adequate supervision (including the use of inadequate caregivers);
- Ensure access to appropriate medical care or treatment.

It may also include neglect of, or unresponsiveness to, a child's basic emotional needs. In elite tennis and sporting environments, psychological and emotional neglect may be exacerbated by adverse reaction from key covered persons (such as coaching staff or parents) to a player's perceived poor performance.

This is a good example of a duty incumbent chiefly on parents and caregivers, with a corresponding duty on the ITF to monitor compliance and report abuses. It is well reported that a good deal of parents have invested much of their earnings and personal time to develop a talented offspring who subsequently loses interest in the sport or under-performs. Abuse against children in this context is hardly unusual. In equal measure, parents, guardians and other covered persons may inflict 'emotional abuse' on children. This is defined in Article 16 of the ITF's Safeguarding Policy as 'persistent emotional maltreatment of a child such as to cause severe and persistent adverse effects on the child's emotional development'. It should be pointed out that where emotional abuse, poor practice and neglect take place, in addition to such conduct constituting an affront to the ITF Policy, they may also give rise to custody arrangements by child protection authorities and the courts because of their negative impact on the child in question. The reports compiled by the ITF Safeguarding Manager and its staff will certainly help national authorities in reaching their decision. Article 16 of the ITF's Safeguarding Policy for Children lists further conduct that is unacceptable and which will be reported to the national authorities. This includes grooming[42] – which has been touched upon in other sections of this chapter – bullying,

---

[41] Jimmy Sanderson and Melinda R. Weathers, 'Snapchat and Child Sexual Abuse in Sport: Protecting Child Athletes in the Social Media Age' (2020) 23 Sport Manag Rev 81.
[42] See Helen Owton and Andrew C. Sparkes, 'Sexual Abuse and the Grooming Process in Sport: Learning from Bella's Story' (2017) 22 Sport Educ Soc 732.

radicalisation and extremism, and female genital mutilation, as well as modern slavery and child exploitation.

Training of all staff and a culture of reporting should alert all covered persons when abuse is taking place. But how does one detect it in the face of silence, especially from victims? Article 18 of the ITF's Safeguarding Policy provides a list of key indicators for identifying abuse and poor practice, while Article 19 sets forth a 'listening culture' within the ITF as an integral component of identification and prevention. Articles 20 to 24 of the ITF Safeguarding Policy make it clear that all covered persons and the organisation as a whole have an obligation to report any infraction to the ITF or the police and that the ITF is under an obligation to investigate, report to the authorities and protect whistleblowers from any adverse impact.

5 Safeguarding for Future Harm

A particular concern that is hinted (i.e. poor practices) in the ITF Safeguarding Policy but not highlighted enough is the likelihood of future harm to children. Indeed, the majority of talented tennis players train long hours, engage in several long-distance trips in any one year (and hence spend many hours travelling) and as a result fail to keep up with their academic pursuits. This is further fuelled by family and tennis professionals. When the child is either burnt out or ultimately realises that a professional career is not feasible, the family is already in significant debt and the child has no fall-back plan.

The question then arises whether the future welfare of child tennis players should be a concern for the ITF, WTA and ATP and top-flight tennis academies and whether this should constitute a recognisable duty of care.[43] In the opinion of this author, the answer is self-evident. All three entities would be rendered meaningless and generate no profit without the struggle of junior players to make it into the professional circuit. Top professional players do not just happen; they are part of a process involving intense competition at the junior ranks and it is because of this competition with other players through the course of multiple years that they later achieve stardom. Simply using those other players to create the tennis stars of tomorrow and in the process deprive them of future prospects is as bad as all the evils that safeguarding aims to

---

[43] Harmonisation and joint education efforts have been in place; that said, there are jurisdictional issues as the WTA and ATP cannot take jurisdiction over matters that arise at ITF events.

eradicate. It is for this reason that the WTA Rulebook sets out in its section X a series of Age Eligibility Rules (AERs) which, among others, require 'minimum educational requirements' for children participating in its pro-path phase: 'Each player must submit to the WTA an official certificate from her country of legal residence verifying that she is meeting or has met her country's minimum educational requirements. A player must submit updated documentation annually until she reaches 18 years of age.'[44] The same requirement is demanded in respect of the WTA's introductory phase,[45] and during the rookie phase players must participate in educational programmes offered by the WTA's PDP.[46] Female players who succeed to the elite phase are required to undergo several education programmes, crucially including fundamental financial planning and career development.[47] Even players ranked in the top 100 of the WTA rankings, and who are below 18 years of age, must not only attend the WTA's mandatory courses, but equally provide evidence that they are meeting their countries' minimum educational requirements.[48] It is no accident that the vast majority of WTA-ranked players are multilingual, with many pursuing a university degree. A longitudinal study commissioned by the WTA aptly demonstrated that:

> Adolescent athletes participating in the WTA after the combined AER/ PDP initiative had longer career durations, higher probabilities of 10-year and 15- year careers, and decreased risk of premature retirement compared with those participating prior to AER/PDP. Organisational practices that encompass both education and competition regulation can positively affect career longevity related to improving athlete well-being.[49]

While this is a splendid example of preventing future harm to junior tennis players, it does not account for the fate of other junior players at the lower tiers of the game. It would be extremely impactful if the ITF, WTA and ATP used some of their resources with a view to collaborating with national tennis federations to create similar programmes and set out minimal educational requirements for their top 100 (or more) nationally ranked players.

---

[44] 2024 WTA Rulebook, s. X(B)(2)(b)(ii).
[45] Ibid., s. X(B)(3)((b)(ii).
[46] Ibid., s. X(B)(4)(b)(iii). A brief overview of the WTA's Development Program is available at: www.wtatennis.com/player-development.
[47] WTA Rulebook, ibid., s. X(B)(5)(b)(v).
[48] Ibid., s. X(B)(6)(a).
[49] Carol L. Otis, Brian Hainline, Christopher Harwood et al., 'Differences in Career Longevity before and after Implementation of the Women's Tennis Association Tour Age Eligibility Rule and Player Development Programs: A 25-Year Study' (2022) 56 Brit J Sport Med 1.

Top-flight tennis academies should play a major role in this development and assume the development role required.

There is also a worrying trend of doping among children in a variety of sports settings. The latest World Anti-Doping Agency (WADA) report did not single out tennis, as opposed to weightlifting, swimming and athletics, but it did highlight six areas of concern arising from doping in junior categories, namely: trauma, isolation, impact, pressure, ignorance and abandonment.[50] This should be a safeguarding concern for the International Tennis Integrity Agency (ITIA). Given the absence of anti-doping control in the majority of junior tennis tiers, it is very difficult to have an overview of the prevalence of doping among children tennis players.[51] While it might be difficult, from an ethical, financial and logistical perspective, to undertake doping controls in national junior circuits, there is little doubt that tennis stakeholders can and should educate parents, players, clubs and tennis professionals on a mandatory basis.

6 The Safeguarding of Adult Athletes

The ITF's Safeguarding Policy for Adults is modelled on its equivalent policy for children.[52] In order to avoid overlap, this section will explore only notable differences. Article 4 of the Adults' Policy emphasises that in the adult context safeguarding refers to 'vulnerability to risk or harm'. Risk and vulnerability are considered interchangeable, and each is dependent on personal circumstances, such as disability, poverty, homelessness, domestic violence and others. Unfortunately, however, despite two articles on the likely risks to disabled tennis players, the Adults' Policy is an almost verbatim iteration of the Children's Policy and is hardly personalised to the plight of adult players.[53] This is, in the opinion

---

[50] WADA, 'Operation Refuge: An Examination of Doping among Minors' (24 January 2024), 7, available at: www.wada-ama.org/sites/default/files/2024-01/wada_public_report_-_operation_refuge_24jan.pdf.

[51] See allegations by a 12-year-old Romanian star player who alleged that she was provided with enhancing substances during her training at the Mouratoglou Academy. Available at: https://as.ro/tenis/dezvaluiri-explozive-de-la-academia-mouratoglou-li-se-dau-sporti vilor-substante-unii-nu-sunt-prinsi-ca-stiu-cand-sa-le-ia-374118.html (in Romanian).

[52] See also LTA Safeguarding Adults at Risk Policy and Procedure 2003, available at: www.lta.org.uk/498128/siteassets/about-lta/file/lta-safeguarding-adults-policy.pdf, which mainly emphasises the protection required by adults with disabilities.

[53] The introduction of cyber bullying, 'mate crime' and forced marriage in Art. 19 of the Adults' Policy is unconvincing as a meaningful distinction, as these are more likely to affect children than adults.

of the author, a disappointing effort that very much ignores the real problems faced by young adult tennis players and aims to confirm the ITF narrative that organised gambling in the lower tiers of the sport is good for the game of tennis.[54]

It has been demonstrated elsewhere that adult tennis players who are unable to make a living from prize money (i.e. mid- and lower-tier ranked athletes) are susceptible to match manipulation where organised gambling has been introduced at these lower tiers.[55] By way of illustration, in March 2021, the ITF announced the results of a match-fixing investigation against two Nigerian tennis players. One was ranked 986 and the other was not ranked at all; yet their matches were amenable to betting by the ITF and the two had gone on to bet on their own games.[56] The Independent Tennis Integrity Review pressed the point that:

> A comparison of the costs and available prize money for players at the Lowest Level of professional tennis – ITF men's and women's $15 k or $25 k events – underscores this point. The ITF's review in 2014 demonstrated that the average costs of playing professional tennis, excluding coaching, were $38,800 for men and $40,180 for women. On the other hand, the winner of a singles tournament at that level is unlikely to receive more than $4,000. As a result, a player at that Lowest Level[57] would need to win at least ten tournaments in a year just to break even, without any accounting for coaching. By comparison, at the ATP World Tour level, the loser in a first-round singles event will typically earn over $10,000.[58]

This is hardly a surprising outcome. If the ITF is serious about the safeguarding of adult players, apart from abuse and violence, it has to confront the evils of integrity and manipulation of the game as a matter of

---

[54] See Ilias Bantekas, 'Is Legitimate Gambling a Threat to the Integrity of Transnational Individual Sport Competitions?' (2024) 25 San Diego Int LJ 23 (demonstrating how the ITF has entered into lucrative deals with live data streaming/gambling companies, which has increased manifold the likelihood of match-fixing in the sport).

[55] See William Ralston, 'The Fixer, the Cheat and the Corruption Crisis in Global Tennis', Financial Review (8 July 2022), available at: www.afr.com/companies/sport/the-fixer-the-cheat-and-the-corruption-crisis-in-global-tennis-20220701-p5aydc; Simon Cambers, 'Organized Crime Has Already Infiltrated Tennis Says Security Expert', *The Guardian* (25 November 2014), available at: www.theguardian.com/sport/2014/nov/25/organised-crime-tennis-security-expert.

[56] ITIA, 'Two Nigerian Tennis Players Banned for Life for Match Fixing Offences' (11 March 2021), available at: www.itia.tennis/news/sanctions/two-nigerian-tennis-players-banned-for-life-for-match-fixing-offences/.

[57] The 'Lowest Level' is made up of ITF men's and women's $15,000 and $25,000 events. The 'Mid-Level' is made up of ATP Challenger, ITF women's $60,000–100,000 and WTA $125,000 events.

[58] Independent Review of Integrity in Tennis (19 December 2018), para. 85.

safeguarding also. The Independent Review of Integrity in Tennis emphasised in its 2018 report that:

> the imbalance between prize money and costs is foremost among the several circumstances that render professional tennis vulnerable to breaches of integrity. The vast majority of nominally professional players, of whom there are as many as 14,000, are unable to make a living through competition. While players ranked in the top 100, and possibly down to around 150, can generally earn a living from prize money and sponsorships, at the lower rungs of the sport the available money is small and the costs are high. An ITF review in 2014 determined that the 'break even' point – the ranking where a player earned as much money from professional tennis as he or she spent on costs – was 336 and 253 in the worldwide rankings for men and women, respectively.[59]

An additionally egregious practice plaguing the adult professional game is the use of social media to inflict fear, distress and mental harm. Professional players are public figures and are 'easy' prey for malicious users. The ATP and WTA have a duty, as far as possible, to protect their prized assets from such harmful practices, and recently the AI-powered tool Matrix was pioneered with a view to monitoring players' public-facing social media for abusive and threatening content.[60]

7   Health and Safety as a Safeguarding Duty

The safeguarding policies of the ITF refer to health and safety in very general terms. The regulation of health and safety is undertaken at national level through general or specific legislation. In the United Kingdom, for example, the Health and Safety Act at Work of 1974, as updated, regulates the responsibility of employers towards employees and third persons while working or being present at their work premises, or using work-related equipment. For the purposes of this section of the chapter, sections 2 and 3 of the 1974 Act stipulate that employers are under a continuous duty to ensure, so far as is reasonably practicable, the health, safety and welfare at work of all their employees and any other person present at their place of work. An important part of this legislation is the duty to train all employees in health and safety matters. It is clear

---

[59] Ibid., para. 84.
[60] 'Tennis Players to Get Protection from Online Abuse through New Monitoring Service', Associated Press (20 December 2023), available at: www.tennis.com/baseline/articles/tennis-players-social-media-online-abuse-protection-threat-matrix-service-ai-signify-group.

that health and safety legislation is of paramount importance in the safeguarding of adult and children tennis players. The Lawn Tennis Association's Coach Qualification Health and Safety Policy emphasises that: 'All individuals have a legal responsibility, as stated under section 7 of the Health and Safety at Work Act 1974, to do everything practicable to prevent an accident or injury to themselves and to others.'[61] Clubs, academies and national associations, tennis professionals acting as consultants or any other entity operating tennis or training facilities, whether privately owned or leased, are charged under the law with ensuring as far as practically possible that all equipment and facilities are safe and do not pose a health hazard. A violation of this duty gives rise to criminal liability and possible tort claim by the person suffering an injury.

8 Consequences for Failure to Meet Safeguarding Obligations

There is nothing in the safeguarding policies examined thus far explaining the legal consequences for failure to meet the stated safeguarding obligations, save for the LTA health and safety policy which refers to consequences arising from statute. The ITF frames the pertinent duties twofold: (1) situations that implicate criminal and child welfare laws, which give rise to a criminal investigation on the part of the territorial state against the alleged perpetrators; and (2) duties that do not fit in category (1), but whose legal implications are somewhat vague. The relevant safeguarding policies may, but not necessarily, give rise to tort-based liability, as well as contractual liability. By way of illustration, the sexual grooming of a child athlete is clearly a criminal offence and the accused will undergo a criminal prosecution to determine his or her culpability. However, this process does not address the potential liability of the club, the national federation or the pertinent sport governing body (e.g. the ITF) for their failure to detect the offence and protect the athlete. If the law treats the relationship between these three entities and the victim athlete as one entailing a concrete duty of care, failure to execute this duty to the best of their abilities gives rise to liability in tort and perhaps also criminal liability.

If the prospect of tort-based liability for stakeholders is remote, chiefly because such a duty is not predicated in common law or statute, then the pertinent safeguarding policy may serve as a contract between the athlete

---

[61] The LTA Policy is available at: www.lta.org.uk/4a29b3/siteassets/roles/coaches/file/lta-health-and-safety-policy.pdf.

and the institution that has produced the policy. Where the policy is framed as an *offer* made by the institution to the athlete and the latter *accepts* it tacitly or expressly and both form a *common intention* that the institution is bound to adhere to its terms, then such terms are contractual in nature. In the case of the ITF Safeguarding Policy for Children, the *offer* is clear in Article 2, which reads: 'The International Tennis Federation (ITF) is *committed* to safeguarding all children participating in tennis tournaments, events, projects and programmes that it delivers or sanctions and rejects all forms of harassment, abuse, violence and exploitation' (emphasis added). It is absurd to suggest that welfare policies simply express hortatory principles which the institution is not bound to enforce, especially where the policy in question uses language suggesting commitment. The very fact that the ITF, in addition to its express commitment, has set up the post of Safeguarding Manager subject to elaborate procedures furnishes proof of its commitment to the terms of the Safeguarding Policy. If the institution fails to adhere to the terms in its policy, it is in breach of said policy and the victim may seek recognition of this breach, as well as damages, financial or moral, if these are proven. It is of no significance that the institution might argue that its safeguarding policy is not a contract, especially if its terms are such that leave no doubt about its contractual nature. It is unclear if the ITF Safeguarding Policies constitute 'ITF Rules', which in turn confer authority on the ITF's Internal Adjudication Panel and Independent Tribunal. If this is not the case, an aggrieved athlete can raise a civil claim before the courts against the institution in breach of the contract/policy and seek damages.

In practice, safeguarding-based claims are predicated on the law of torts where there exists an extensive array of duties of care,[62] and hence contract-based claims are extremely rare. This author is not aware of aggrieved athletes making contract-based claims, as explained in this section, against institutions for failure to adhere to their safeguarding policies.

9 The Boundaries of Safeguarding Duties

The various safeguarding policies explained in this chapter concerned abusive conduct, criminal offences or poor practices against tennis players, whether children or adults. They did not in any way discuss

---

[62] Partington, *Coaching, Sport and the Law*, 87–121.

equivalent conduct by tennis athletes against non-athletes. It seems fair that safeguarding rules do not apply in such circumstances, chiefly because this does not give rise to a relationship of trust in the sporting context – save where one athlete is being abusive to another athlete. The welfare of the victim, non-athlete, can be adequately remedied by the laws on domestic violence, or violence against one's person. Even so, when allegations of domestic violence against Alexander Zverev emerged, the ATP was quick to institute a 'safeguarding investigation', the aim of which was to make wide-ranging recommendations to 'ensure safeguarding is embedded across all aspects of ATP organisational activity. Topics covered include prevention, reporting and investigation of abuse, disciplinary measures, policy statements, event safety, training, information sharing, collaboration with other bodies of tennis and the appointment of dedicated safeguarding leads.'[63] By January 2023, at which time the investigation was completed and Zverev exonerated due to a lack of evidence, the ATP's press statement made no reference to safeguarding whatsoever and instead justified the investigation on the basis of the ATP's On-Site Offenses or Player Major Offenses rules.[64] It is clear that the ATP reversed its original thinking that the incident in question pertained to safeguarding and went on to dismiss such a notion.

But what of other sports professionals, particularly agents, who enter into agency or advertising agreements with tennis players in a manner that is contractually abusive or is otherwise in violation of restraint of trade rules?[65] Agents owe fiduciary duties to their clients upon entering into the agency agreement, these being contractual and statutory,[66] as well as common law-based. Good faith and loyalty are among these. In addition, prior to entering the agreement, the agent negotiating with a child, or even an adult athlete, must make truthful representations. Besides this contractual realm, however, it is obvious to this author that other stakeholders have a duty to address unequal and unhealthy/predatory athlete–agent relationships as part of their ordinary safeguarding commitments.

---

[63] ATP Tour News Release, 'ATP Receives Independent Safeguarding Report: Zverev Investigation Announced' (4 October 2021).
[64] See ATP Tour News Release, 'Zverev Investigation Completed' (31 January 2023).
[65] Ilias Bantekas, 'Professional Tennis and Restraint of Trade in the English Common Law' (2023) 22 Va Sports & Ent LJ 1.
[66] E.g. the US Sports Agent Responsibility and Trust Act of 2004 and the Uniform Athlete Agents Act.

10

Integrity in Tennis

Doping, Match-Fixing and Other Corruption Offenses

ROSS BROWN, JAMIE SINGER AND LILY ELLIOTT

1 Introduction

Tennis, like all sports, takes the maintenance of integrity in all its events with the utmost seriousness. Tackling the issues of corruption and doping, which this chapter focuses on, has been a cornerstone of the approach adopted by the governing bodies of tennis for a significant period. Corruption issues, where a player, coach or official might contrive some or all of a match in a variety of ways for a financial return were first investigated by the Tennis Integrity Unit (TIU) in 2009 and managed under the Tennis Anti-Corruption Program (TACP). The International Tennis Federation (ITF) has dealt with doping matters for far longer under the Tennis Anti-Doping Program (TADP). In December 2020, the International Tennis Integrity Agency (ITIA) was formed. It is a private company limited by guarantee and without share capital with a registered office in the United Kingdom. The ITIA is an operationally independent organization with the aim of addressing integrity issues in tennis. On January 1, 2021, it took over responsibility for investigating and prosecuting corruption matters from the TIU and took over responsibility for investigating and prosecuting doping matters from the ITF a year later.

The ITIA employs over forty individuals and is led by a CEO, currently Karen Moorhouse. There are significant teams investigating breaches of the TACP and TADP, analyzing data and addressing education. The ITIA is overseen by the Tennis Integrity Supervisory Board, which has nine members and is independently chaired by Jennie Price CBE. Of those members, four are from each of the tennis governing bodies in membership of the ITIA, being the ITF, the Association of Tennis Professionals (ATP), the Women's Tennis Association (WTA) and the Grand Slam Board (as the umbrella body for the four Grand Slam tournaments). The remaining five, including the non-executive chair, are independent of the sport of tennis, ensuring that the ITIA's decision-making is as independent as it possibly could be. Funding for the ITIA is received from the governing bodies.

2 Anti-Doping

The concept of anti-doping is an evocative one. The vast majority of professional athletes, together with all stakeholders in sport from governing bodies, sponsors, fans and others, are firmly opposed to doping. It is cheating and it should have no place in professional sport. Sport is, of course, based upon the principles of fairness and equality. If one athlete seeks to change that through artificially enhancing their own performance, then the basic concepts of sport that so many love will start to break down. It is, therefore, natural that there must be rules to regulate the doping of athletes, and hopefully dissuade them from doping in the first place. Sport has dealt with anti-doping issues before harmonization of the international approach, with the incorporation of the World Anti-Doping Agency (WADA) in November 1999 to regulate anti-doping on a global basis. The WADA brought a consistency to how athletes were held to account and sanctioned. The Prohibited List was born, which set out what the Prohibited Substances were (and the related Prohibited Methods). It categorized them – some were more serious than others, some had legitimate uses, while others did not. It is scientific and technical in nature, making it complicated for all.

In order for the WADA to address this complexity, its rules were necessarily lengthy and detailed. The World Anti-Doping Code itself is currently over 150 pages long. There are several supporting regulations known as International Standards encompassing all areas of anti-doping which also run to hundreds of pages when taken together. This results in a complex but necessary set of harmonized rules for both the regulators and the athletes, as well as a significant amount of case law.

2.1 Legal Framework

In common with other international federations, the ITF is a signatory to the Code and is accountable to the WADA for its compliance with the Code in terms of how it regulates anti-doping within tennis. It does so through the TADP. The ITF has delegated all aspects of doping control and education to the ITIA.[1] This means that the ITIA is responsible for the entirety of the anti-doping process from testing through to results management, which ultimately involves the prosecution of individuals alleged to have committed an Anti-Doping Rule Violation (ADRV).

The TADP principally applies to players, with the term defined on a broad basis.[2] There are other individuals/entities that are subject to the TADP,[3] but for the purposes of this chapter, the focus is on players. The TADP and the International Standards set out the anti-doping offenses before addressing the entire anti-doping process that an individual might be subject to, from the act of providing a urine or blood sample; what happens if that sample is found to contain a prohibited substance; and the legal process that would then follow to establish whether that individual should have a sanction imposed upon them.

2.1.1 The Anti-Doping Offenses

The two most common violations under the TADP are "presence" and "use" of a prohibited substance, or a prohibited method under Articles 2.1 and 2.2 of the TADP.[4] For the purposes of this chapter, the focus will be on prohibited substances. These are strict liability offenses which put a personal responsibility on any player to ensure that they do not commit an offense.[5] It is not, therefore, necessary in most situations to prove intent, fault, negligence or knowing use on the player's part in order to establish an ADRV; nor is lack of intent, fault or knowledge a defense to an ADRV.[6] The usual starting point is that in most cases where there is an Article 2.1 charge brought, a charge will also be brought under Article 2.2.

---

[1] See TADP 2025, Art. 1.1.7.
[2] "Player" is defined by reference to TADP, Art. 1.2.6, which includes any individual who has an association with the ITF or any national association, as well as any individual who has participated in professional tennis. This provision also addresses how players become subject to the jurisdiction of the TADP.
[3] In particular, a "player support person," which is also broadly defined as "any coach, trainer, manager, agent, team staff, official, nutritionist, medical or paramedical personnel, parent or any other Person working with, treating or assisting a Player who is participating in or preparing for sports Competition."
[4] TADP, Art. 2.1 states that an ADRV is committed by the "presence of a Prohibited Substance or any of its metabolites or markers in a Player's Sample." TADP, Art. 2.2 states that an ADRV is committed by the "use or attempted use by a player of a prohibited substance or a prohibited method."
[5] See TADP, Art. 2.1.1.
[6] Ibid.

The only circumstances where presence or use is established but there is no ADRV is where: (1) the presence or use is in accordance with a therapeutic use exemption[7] (so to address a legitimate medical need); and/or (2) the prohibited substance or prohibited method[8] related to a period where the relevant individual was out-of-competition, with such substance or method only being prohibited in-competition. The WADA publishes the Prohibited List[9] on an annual basis and that document determines what constitutes a prohibited substance or a prohibited method.

2.1.1.1 Presence An ADRV is often established under Article 2.1 simply by virtue of a prohibited substance (or its metabolites or markers[10]) being detected in a blood or urine sample provided by an athlete – namely, the testing of the sample results in a positive result, known as an Adverse Analytical Finding (AAF). The exception to that is where a prohibited substance is a threshold substance, meaning that an AAF will only arise if a specific quantity of the prohibited substance is detected, with those quantities being set out in the Prohibited List. A good example is asthma medication, where use of a certain amount is accepted as treating a legitimate condition, but going above the threshold suggests abuse of that product for performance-enhancement reasons.

2.1.1.2 Use An ADRV under Article 2.2 usually follows on directly from an Article 2.1 violation. If "presence" is established, then it is assumed that a player "used" the prohibited substance, and received some benefit from it, whether or not that use was intentional, and irrespective if the benefit was significant or not.

---

[7] A therapeutic use exemption (TUE) permits "a player with a medical condition to use a prohibited substance or prohibited method," albeit subject to conditions.
[8] A prohibited substance refers to any "substance, or class of substances, so described on the Prohibited List," being a list produced annually by the WADA, with a prohibited method defined by reference to the Prohibited List as well.
[9] The Prohibited List 2025 is available at: www.wada-ama.org/sites/default/files/2024-09/2025list_en_final_clean_12_september_2024.pdf.
[10] A metabolite is defined as "any substance produced by a biotransformation process," which essentially refers to a substance produced during the process of metabolism in the body. A marker is defined as a "compound, group of compounds or biological variable(s) that indicate the use of a prohibited substance or prohibited method."

2.1.1.3 Other ADRVs
There are nine other ADRVs under the TADP, addressed at Articles 2.3 to 2.11. These predominantly relate to circumstances where: (1) a player is seeking to avoid the doping control process in some way; or (2) a player/player support person is assisting another player in committing (or covering up) an ADRV.

Those ADRVs are (in summary):

1. Evading, refusing or failing to submit to sample collection (Article 2.3).
2. Whereabout failures, including missed tests and filing failures in a 12-month period (Article 2.4).
3. Tampering with any part of doping control (Article 2.5).
4. Possession of a prohibited substance or a prohibited method (Article 2.6).
5. Trafficking in any prohibited substance or prohibited method (Article 2.7).
6. Administration of a prohibited substance or a prohibited method with variation depending on whether the administration is out-of-competition or not (Article 2.8).
7. Complicity (Article 2.9).
8. Prohibited association with an individual serving a period of ineligibility (Article 2.10).
9. Acts that discourage or retaliate against reporting to anti-doping authorities (Article 2.11).

ADRVs under Articles 2.3 and 2.5 to 2.8 have the same starting point of a four-year ban when considering the appropriate sanction being imposed. The presence and use of ADRVs are potentially considered as serious. Articles 2.9 and 2.11 have a lower starting point of two years, but with scope for a four-year ban or higher. Articles 2.4 and 2.10 have a maximum sanction of two years. There is a significant body of case law (both from tennis and other sports) that considers many of these ADRVs. However, Articles 2.3 to 2.11 are beyond the scope of this chapter, where the focus is on the substantial detail available regarding ADRVs under Articles 2.1 and 2.2.

2.2 Proceedings

Once a sample has been taken from a player, it will be transported to a WADA-accredited laboratory for testing for any prohibited substance, on an anonymous basis. If a prohibited substance is detected in a player's

A sample, an AAF will be reported to the Results Management Authority, which is usually either a national anti-doping organization or the relevant domestic or international federation. As above, in tennis, it is the ITIA that is tasked with responsibility for results management. This responsibility has been delegated by the ITF.

An AAF does not mean that a player has committed an ADRV, but rather gives rise to the need for the ITIA to investigate. The first step the ITIA may take is to appoint a review board which will consider several issues,[11] including whether the player has a TUE in place, which would adequately address an AAF so that the matter would go no further.

2.2.1 Notice

Assuming the review board finds no reason not to, the ITIA would then issue a Notice.[12] That document will address various issues, including: (1) the alleged ADRV(s); (2) the relevant facts/evidence; (3) whether a provisional suspension[13] is to be imposed; (4) the possible sanction the player may face; and (5) what the player must do next. As to point (5), the Notice will also set out the principal rights that the player has, including the right to the laboratory documentation package relating to the AAF and the right for the player to have their B sample analyzed, as well as attend that analysis. The two other key steps are that the player will be invited to provide an explanation of why their A sample tested positive for a prohibited substance and be asked if they want to admit or deny that they have committed an ADRV.

2.2.2 Charge Letter

The ITIA will review the player's explanation and the results of any B sample analysis. The ITIA may also elect to investigate the matter, including conducting interviews with a player and any other relevant individuals (such as members of the player's coaching and support teams). At the conclusion of its review/investigation, the ITIA will decide whether the player should be charged with one or more ADRVs. If the player is to be charged, a Charge Letter will be sent.[14] Like the Notice, it will include the alleged ADRV(s) and the relevant facts/evidence. It will also confirm the Consequences the ITIA will seek, which is principally

---

[11] See TADP 2025, Art. 7.4.2.
[12] Ibid., Art. 7.4.4.
[13] See ibid., Art. 7.12, for how provisional suspensions are imposed and challenged.
[14] See TADP 2025, Art. 7.13.

the period of ineligibility,[15] and the timeframe for a response. Here, the player will need to set out clearly the option they would like to pursue. They can:

1. Admit the ADRV(s) and accede to the Consequences specified in the Charge Letter.[16]
2. Admit the ADRV(s), but seek to mitigate the Consequences by attempting to agree a sanction with the ITIA.[17]
3. Admit the ADRV(s), but seek to mitigate the Consequences and request that they be determined at a hearing.[18]
4. Deny the ADRV(s) and have the charge and Consequences determined at a hearing.[19]

In the event of the ADRV(s) being admitted and Consequences acceded to, the ITIA will promptly issue a reasoned decision to confirm the outcome.[20]

2.2.3 Hearing

Where an individual requests that the charge and/or Consequences are to be determined at a hearing, the matter will be referred to an Independent Panel, comprised of lawyers, and medical and technical experts.[21] The Chair of the Independent Panel will select an Independent Tribunal, made up of three individuals with a legally qualified Chair, to determine the matter.[22] Once convened, the Chair of the Independent Tribunal will convene a preliminary meeting to set a hearing date and a timetable leading up to that date, along with addressing any other pre-hearing issues.[23] The principal directions to be agreed will be for the parties to exchange witness evidence, whether factual or expert, and a written brief setting out their position on the charges in light of the evidence.

---

[15] See the definition of Consequences for the full list, which can include disqualification of results, public disclosure and the payment of costs.

[16] Where the Charge Letter asserts a period of Ineligibility of four or more years, the player may seek a reduction in their sanction for an early admission in accordance with TADP 2025, Art. 10.8.1. See also Art. 7.13.3.

[17] See the Case Resolution Agreement process under TADP 2025, Art. 10.8.2, something that also requires the approval of the WADA. In the well-publicised CAS proceedings of *WADA v. Jannik Sinner, the ITIA and the ITF*, the parties agreed a case resolution agreement in February 2025. See also TADP 2025, Art. 7.13.3.2.

[18] See TADP 2025, Art. 7.13.3.3.

[19] Ibid., Art. 7.13.3.4.

[20] Ibid., Art. 7.14.2.

[21] Ibid., Art. 8.1.

[22] Ibid., Art. 8.2.

[23] Ibid., Art. 8.3.

The starting point is that an in-person hearing will be held in London, in English and will be confidential.[24] The player has the right to be present and to speak at the hearing, as well as being legally represented.[25] The Independent Tribunal will aim to issue its decision within fourteen days, albeit longer is often needed. That decision will address, as needed, whether an ADRV has been committed and, if so, what the Consequences should be (being, principally, what the period of ineligibility for the player should be), as well as confirm that there is a right of appeal.[26] As to costs, and subject to the Independent Tribunal's view, the starting point is that the ITIA will bear the costs of convening the hearing and each party will then bear its own costs.[27]

Given the strict liability nature of the offenses under the TADP, it is most likely that a hearing will not address the question of liability and will only address the appropriate Consequences. For example, in the "presence" charges being considered here, the presence of a prohibited substance in a player's sample is sufficient for liability to be found. Therefore, the battleground at hearings is usually around the period of ineligibility issued and the extent to which that can be reduced, or even eliminated, under the TADP. All matters pertaining to the Independent Tribunal are explained in detail in Chapter 7 of this volume.

2.3 Sanctions

In Article 2.1 or 2.2 concerning "presence" and "use," the starting point for a player's period of ineligibility, assuming it is a first offense, will be four years.[28] However, it is possible that a four-year period may be significantly reduced or even eliminated by various means. The Independent Tribunal may consider two key questions in order to determine the appropriate period of ineligibility:

1. Whether the player acted with intention in committing the ADRV. If so, no further steps are required, and the period of ineligibility will stay at four years. If the player did not act intentionally, the four-year starting point will be reduced to a two-year starting point.[29]

---

[24] Ibid., Art. 8.4.3.
[25] Ibid., Art. 8.4.5.
[26] Ibid., Art. 8.5.2.
[27] Ibid., Arts 8.5.3 and 8.5.4.
[28] Ibid., Art. 10.2.1.
[29] Ibid., Art. 10.2.2.

2. Assuming that the player was successful on the question of intention, the period of ineligibility may be reduced further, or eliminated entirely, depending on the level of fault. The player will need to establish that one of the concepts of "no fault or negligence" or "no significant fault or negligence" applies to their circumstances.

While the burden of proof is on the ITIA to establish that an ADRV has taken place,[30] since the strict liability concept exists and ADRVs are usually admitted, it is the questions of intention and fault that are most important. As regards those questions, the burden of proof usually, but not always, falls upon the player.

2.3.1 Intention

The first issue to consider when addressing intention in "presence" and "use" cases is whether the prohibited substance is a specified substance or a non-specified substance. Various substances are identified as such on the Prohibited List. Broadly, a specified substance is one where there may be a legitimate reason for a player to be using it, such as medication for treating a condition like asthma. A non-specified substance is one for which there is no therapeutic need and hence there is no legitimate reason for its use, such as an anabolic steroid. This distinction is important since:

1. for a non-specified substance, the burden of proof is on the player to prove that an ADRV was not intentional;[31]
2. for a specified substance, the burden of proof is on the ITIA to prove that an ADRV was intentional.[32]

If the player can meet their burden of proof in the first example, or the ITIA cannot meet its burden in the second example, the period of ineligibility will decrease from four years to two. In the rest of this chapter, the focus will be on the question of intention as regards non-specified substances, as that is where it is more likely that a player and the ITIA will be in dispute. There is a presumption that an ADRV in these circumstances was intentional, and the four-year starting point is

---

[30] See ibid., Art. 3.1.1, which addresses the "comfortable satisfaction" standard of proof and confirms it is "greater than a mere balance of probability [51%] but less than proof beyond a reasonable doubt [75%]." In percentage terms, it is generally considered to be around a 66 percent likelihood.
[31] See TADP 2025, Art. 10.2.1.1.
[32] Ibid., Art. 10.2.1.2.

justified, given such substances have a significant potential to enhance sporting performance and do not have relevant and/or legitimate therapeutic benefits.[33] That presumption has been consistent in Court of Arbitration for Sport (CAS) jurisprudence for at least twenty years.

The term "intentional" is used with the aim of identifying players engaging in conduct that they knew constituted an ADRV or knew that there was a significant risk that the conduct might constitute an ADRV and manifestly disregarded that risk;[34] or, in more simple terms, players who are cheating. There are two ways in which a player might establish a lack of intention to commit an ADRV:

1. The way envisaged by the TADP, and by far the more common, is for a player to identify the source of the prohibited substance found in the AAF and then use that to explain why they were not acting intentionally.
2. Despite not identifying the source, the player can demonstrate there is some other good reason to justify a finding that they were not acting intentionally.

2.3.2 Identifying the Source

The TADP is derived from the Code, which makes it clear that the expectation for an athlete seeking to establish a lack of intention is that they will usually be expected to establish the source of the prohibited substance.[35] The onus is on the athlete.[36] The starting point when interpreting the TADP and CAS jurisprudence is that establishing the source will entail the identification of a particular product, such as a medication or a supplement, or some other item that provides a clear rationale for that product/item being the source.[37] There is a logic to this,

---

[33] *Dylan Scott v. ITF*, CAS 2018/A/5768, at para. 128.
[34] See TADP 2025, Art. 10.2.3.
[35] Comment 58 to Art. 10.2.1.1 of the Code states that: "While it is theoretically possible for an Athlete or other Person to establish that the anti-doping rule violation was not intentional without showing how the Prohibited Substance entered one's system, it is highly unlikely that in a doping case under Article 2.1 an Athlete will be successful in proving that the Athlete acted unintentionally without establishing the source of the Prohibited Substance."
[36] *Jose Paolo Guerrero v. FIFA and WADA v. FIFA and Guerrero*, CAS 2018/A/5546 and 5571, at para. 65(i), which states: "It is for the athlete to establish the source of the prohibited substance, not for the antidoping organisation to prove an alternative source to that contended for by the athlete."
[37] *WADA v. International Weightlifting Federation & Yenny Fernanda Alvarez Caicedo*, CAS 2016/A/4377, at para. 52, which states: "CAS and other cases make clear that it is not

since knowing specifically how a prohibited substance was ingested permits the relevant arbitral body to draw a conclusion as to whether this was intentional or not. If the nature of the player's conduct is unknown, then it is difficult to assess whether the conduct was intentional.[38]

Therefore, establishing that something is possible is not sufficient to establish source.[39] Instead, "concrete evidence"[40] is required in a manner that permits an arbitral body to carry out a full analysis on a player's explanation of their AAF. That is why it is rare for an athlete to disprove intention without identifying a specific source or the "means of ingestion,"[41] something requiring a degree of specificity. Where a particular medication, supplement or other product is identified as containing a prohibited substance, there must be evidence to support that

sufficient for an athlete merely to protest their innocence and suggest that the substance must have entered his or her body inadvertently from some supplement, medicine or other product which the athlete was taking at the relevant time. Rather, an athlete must adduce concrete evidence to demonstrate that a particular supplement, medication or other product that the athlete took contained the substance in question."

[38] *Roberto La Barbera v. International Wheelchair & Amputee Sports Federation*, CAS 2010/A/2277, at para. 35: "The CAS has constantly repeated that the requirement of showing how the Prohibited Substance got into the Athlete's system must be enforced quite strictly since, if the manner in which a substance entered an athlete's system is unknown or unclear, it is logically difficult to determine whether the athlete has taken precautions in attempting to prevent such occurrence."

[39] See *Guerrero*, at para. 65(ii), which states that "establishing that a scenario is possible is not enough to establish the origin of the prohibited substance."

[40] See *Caicedo*. See also *Ihab Abdelrahman v. Egyptian Anti-Doping Organization, WADA v. Ihab Abdelrahman & Egyptian Anti-Doping Organization*, CAS 2017/A/5016 and 5036, at para. 125, which states that "in order to disprove intent, an athlete may not merely speculate as to the possible existence of a number of conceivable explanations for the AAF" and "then further speculate as to which appears the most likely of those possibilities to conclude that such possibility excludes intent." Reference is then made to significant consistent CAS jurisprudence on this topic. Another relevant case is *Iannone v. FIM*, CAS 2020/A/6978; *WADA v. FIM & Iannone*, CAS 2020/A/7068, at para. 134, which again refers to "concrete and persuasive evidence."

[41] See *UKAD v. Buttifant*, SR/NADP/508/2016, at para. 33, where it was stated that "we consider it will be a rare, possibly very rare case, where the athlete will be able to satisfy the burden of proof as to intent without establishing the likely means by which the Prohibited Substance entered his system." On appeal in the same case, at para. 31, it was held that: "It is only a rare case that the athlete will be able to satisfy the burden of proof that the violation of article 2.1 was not intentional without establishing, on the balance of probabilities, the means of ingestion."

conclusion.[42] Explanations based solely on speculation, clean anti-doping records and protestations of innocence will not be sufficient.

2.3.3 Other Good Reason

It is clear from the drafting of the TADP and the Code that it is not a mandatory requirement to establish source in order to establish a lack of intention. However, it is also clear from CAS jurisprudence that, factually, these will be rare and exceptional cases. A player must pass through the "narrowest of corridors" to be able to do so.[43]

In recent years, a few CAS awards have sought to widen the narrow corridor concept, even if marginally. Relevant awards widening the concept have preferred to consider: (1) the science; (2) the totality of the evidence; (3) common sense; and (4) the credibility of the relevant athlete.[44] However, other recent CAS awards have reinforced the traditional view.[45] Whichever analysis is used, it is clear that this route for a player discharging their burden to demonstrate a lack of intention remains an exceptional one.

2.3.4 Fault

The concept of fault is only relevant in non-specified substance cases where the player has managed to discharge their burden to prove a lack of

---

[42] *WADA v. CADC & CSF & Kaskova*, CAS 2019/A/6213, at para. 65: "In the proceedings before the CADC the Athlete submitted that the only way the prohibited substance could have entered her body was through the use of the food supplement Ginseng Kianpi Pil ... She could not submit the product for testing, as she did not have it any more but furnished statements from her mother and colleagues of her father, a report on the care provided to her father, a written consultation from a toxicologist and website screenshot of Ginseng Kianpi Pil ('Ginseng'). There is no proof of purchase, no information as to the specific type of supplement used, by whom it is produced, etc. and the Athlete did not disclose Ginseng Kianpi Pil on the doping control form submitted by her. The documents submitted by the Athlete did not substantiate her contention that she did use that product or that it was contaminated with metandienone."

[43] *Mauricio Fiol Villaneuva v. FINA*, CAS 2016/A/4534, at para. 37, which states that: "the Panel can envisage the theoretical possibility that it might be persuaded by an athlete's simple assertion of his innocence of intent when considering not only his demeanour, but also his character and history ... That said, such a situation would inevitably be extremely rare. Even on the persuasive analysis of Rigozzi, Haas et al, proof of source would be 'an important, even critical' first step in any exculpation of intent. Where an athlete cannot prove source it leaves the narrowest of corridors through which such an athlete must pass to discharge the burden which lies upon him."

[44] *WADA v. Swimming Australia, Sport Integrity Australia & Shayna Jack*, CAS 2021/A/7579 and 7580, at para. 157.

[45] See *Iannone*, at para. 134, where two precursor cases to *Jack*, ibid., were considered as "outliers."

intention. At this stage, the starting point for a player's period of ineligibility is two years. That period can be reduced further, or even eliminated entirely, where the player can:

1. Establish that he or she bears no fault or negligence in respect of the ADRVs. If so, the period of ineligibility shall be eliminated.[46]
2. Establish that he or she bears no significant fault or negligence.[47] If so, the period of ineligibility shall be, at a minimum, a reprimand and no period of ineligibility. At a maximum, two years of ineligibility depending on the degree of fault shall be imposed.

2.3.5 No Fault or Negligence

The player must demonstrate that "they did not know or suspect, and could not reasonably have known or suspected even with the exercise of utmost caution" that they were committing an ADRV. In the majority of situations, the player "must also establish how the Prohibited Substance entered their system."[48] The latter quote sets out an initial threshold that an athlete "must" establish before going further. This is a mandatory requirement from which there is no discretion to depart and refers to the question of identifying the source addressed above in relation to the concept of intention.[49] This requirement entails that some specifics are needed, such as the name of the relevant product, how it was ingested and when, among others.[50] This is an important pre-condition[51] for the

---

[46] See TADP 2025, Art. 10.5.
[47] Ibid., Art. 10.6.1. While Art. 10.6.2 also provides the possibility of No Significant Fault or Negligence, that use of that provision is far less common and beyond the scope of this chapter.
[48] Both quotes taken from the definition of "No Fault or Negligence" in the TADP 2025.
[49] This is different from the concept of intention, where proving source is important, but not mandatory.
[50] See *FINA & WADA* v. *Marco Tagliaferri*, CAS 2008/A/1471 and 1486, at para. 9.5.2, which states that it was not established "how, and because of what surrounding circumstances" the Prohibited Substance came to be in the athlete's system. See also *I* v. *FIA*, CAS 2010/A/2268 – para. 130 of which states that: "As a consequence of the Appellant's failure to prove the objective element of the route of ingestion, the subjective element of fault does not fall for consideration." See also *ITF* v. *Mariano Puerta*, ITF Independent Anti-Doping Tribunal Award (December 21, 2005), available at: www.5rb.com/wp-content/uploads/2013/10/Maria-Puerta-Tribunal-ITF-21-Dec-2005.pdf, para. 57 of which quotes *ITF* v. *Jamie Burdekin*, ITF Independent Anti-Doping Tribunal Award (April 4, 2005) – para. 76 of which states that a player must "show what the factual circumstances were in which the substance entered his system, not merely the route by which it entered his system."
[51] See *WADA* v. *Darko Stanic & Swiss Olympic Association*, CAS 2006/A/1130 – para. 30 of which states: "Obviously this precondition is important and necessary otherwise an

obvious reason that an arbitral body cannot properly analyze whether a player is at fault for the presence of a prohibited substance if it is unknown how it got into the player's system. It is not, therefore, sufficient to make general assertions as to what the source might have been.[52] However, if a player has discharged their burden in proving a lack of intent, they are likely to have done so through the identification of a source. Hence, in practice, this threshold can often be overcome.

If this is so, consideration of the "utmost caution" test is required. A player must demonstrate to an arbitral body that they have fully complied with that duty. This means that they must show that they have made every conceivable effort to avoid taking a prohibited substance and that the substance got into their system despite all due care on their part. As a result, the "utmost caution" test is a very high standard to overcome.[53] The global anti-doping system is premised on the basis of strict liability. If a prohibited substance is in a player's system, then that player bears personal responsibility for that outcome. It is only on the basis of an exceptionally good reason, on an objective rather than a subjective basis, that a player may circumvent strict liability. It is, therefore, incumbent upon players to take all steps that they can to ensure a prohibited substance is not present in their system. It is their fundamental duty under the TADP and the Code.[54]

---

athlete's degree of diligence or absence of fault would be examined in relation to circumstances that are speculative and that could be partly or entirely made up. To allow any such speculation as to the circumstances in which an athlete ingested a prohibited substance would undermine the strict liability rules ... thereby defeating their purpose."

[52] See *UKAD* v. *Catana*, UK Anti-Doping Tribunal Award (unreported) – para. 6.5 of which states that: "the Respondent's contention is that the Prohibited Substance in question must have entered his system by being ingested through contaminated supplement. The Respondent has provided no more than a list of supplements that he has taken. He has not indicated which one or more of the supplements he considered was contaminated, nor has explained how such contamination might have occurred. He produces no scientific or other evidence that any supplement taken by him is or was in fact contaminated ..." See also *Roberto La Barbera* v. *IWAS*, CAS 2010/A/2277: "One hypothetical source of a positive test does not prove to the level of satisfaction required that such explanations are factually or scientifically probable. Mere speculation is not proof that it did actually occur."

[53] See *ITF* v. *Stefan Koubek*, ITF Independent Anti-Doping Tribunal Award (2005) – para. 79 of which referred to the "utmost caution" test and described it as being a "very high standard which will only be met in the most exceptional cases." A subsequent CAS appeal affirmed that decision.

[54] See *Robert Kendrick* v. *ITF*, CAS 2011/A/2518, at para. 10.14.

The phrase often used is a player making "every conceivable effort" to avoid a prohibited substance being present in their system.[55] However, this does not mean that it is impossible to succeed with a no fault or negligence defense – great care is needed, but there remains an avenue where a player may have been able to have done more, but such a step was not considered necessary in the relevant circumstances. A player is responsible for the acts and omissions of others around them, whether friends and family, members of the backroom staff at their club or members of the support team they surround themselves with.[56] Examples where a no fault or negligence defense has been successful include the following:

1. A player had a TUE in place for the use of a terbutaline inhaler for his asthma. He asked a doctor at an ATP event for some more, but the doctor provided a salbutamol inhaler in error, for which the player had no TUE. It was held that there was no way that the player could have known about that error.[57]
2. A player ingested cocaine after kissing a woman who had taken cocaine herself. It was held that it was not reasonable to expect anyone to know that it was possible to be contaminated with cocaine in such circumstances.[58]

Even so, a no fault or negligence defense was unsuccessful where a player was found to have some fault despite being unaware that the prohibited substance ingested was in a glass of water that his wife had used to take some medication and then used the same glass. There were no other clues from the flavor, odor or color of the water ingested.[59]

---

[55] *Hans Knauss v. FIS*, CAS 2005/A/847, at para. 7.3.1, where it states that athletes must demonstrate that they have "made every conceivable effort to avoid taking a prohibited substance." Mr. Knauss did actually take significant steps, such as proving that he reviewed the label and the packaging of the supplement he took and that he had written to the distributor of the supplement and obtained their written certification that no prohibited substance was contained within it. However, that was not enough to satisfy the "every conceivable effort" test since Mr. Knauss could have done more – such as having the supplement tested or simply not having taken it at all and avoiding the consequential risk.
[56] *Sara Errani v. ITF*, CAS 2017/A/5301, at para. 198, where it is stated that Ms. Errani's "responsibility includes that she is responsible for the behaviour of her entourage, be it her coaches, medical staff etc" and then at para. 199, that the "degree of fault exercised by the Athlete's mother is to be imputed to the Athlete herself."
[57] *ATP v. Perry*, ATP Anti-Doping Tribunal Award (2005).
[58] *ITF v. Richard Gasquet*, CAS 2009/A/1926.
[59] *Puerta v. ITF*, CAS 2006/A/1025.

A common defense to many anti-doping proceedings is that a supplement was contaminated with a prohibited substance, without the player's knowledge. However, the Code is clear that contaminated supplements are not sufficient to justify a finding of no fault of negligence.[60]

2.3.6 No Significant Fault or Negligence

In order to demonstrate that they are entitled to a reduction in their sanction under the concept of no significant fault or negligence, a player must establish that "their fault or negligence, when viewed in the totality of the circumstances and taking into account the criteria for no fault or negligence, was not significant ...." Again, the player "must also establish how the prohibited substance entered their system."[61] The same points set out in this no fault or negligence section above regarding this threshold apply again.

Since this chapter is focused on ADRVs for non-specified substances, the most likely reason for a no significant fault or negligence defense to apply is in relation to "contaminated products."[62] In such cases, the player must establish that they meet the definition of no significant fault or negligence, as well as that the prohibited substance detected came from a contaminated product.[63] Given that a player will likely have established that there was a contaminated product in order to discharge their burden on the question of intention, this threshold may again not be a difficult one to overcome. However, if a player discharged their burden without proving source, then they would not be able to achieve a reduction under no significant fault or negligence as they would not have proven that the prohibited substance came from a contaminated product nor, therefore, how it entered their system. Assuming that threshold can be overcome, the principal debate will be around the first quoted passage from the definition. The no fault or negligence definition

---

[60] See the Code comment to Art. 10.5: "They will only apply in exceptional circumstances" and "No Fault or Negligence would not apply in the following circumstances: (a) a positive test resulting from a mislabelled or contaminated vitamin or nutritional supplement (Athletes are responsible for what they ingest (Article 2.1) and have been warned about the possibility of supplement contamination ...)."
[61] Both quotes taken from the definition of "No Significant Fault or Negligence" in the TADP 2025.
[62] See TADP 2025, Art. 10.6.1.2.
[63] This is defined as a "product that contains a Prohibited Substance that is not disclosed on the product label or in information available in a reasonable internet search" in the TADP 2025.

is expressly mentioned and hence the "utmost caution" test will be relevant again.[64] This means that exceptional circumstances are again required for an athlete to show their fault was not significant. The standard is therefore high, but CAS jurisprudence is also clear that the two concepts are distinct and by implication the standard is not as high as it would have been for no fault or negligence.[65]

Given the definition of fault in the TADP, there is both an objective and a subjective element to the consideration of no significant fault or negligence, with the objective assessment of fault usually being the more important. That assessment will involve a review of the steps that a player took prior to ingesting the prohibited substance. There are "clear and obvious" precautions[66] that a player should take,[67] all of which serve as a useful guide.[68] However, every case will turn on its own facts and while precedent can be, and often is, very instructive, it will not replace an analysis of the merits of the particular circumstances relevant to the case at hand, particularly the risk factors present that a player could, or perhaps should, have been aware of.[69] For example, a player using

---

[64] The comment in the Code relating to Art. 10.6.1.2 includes: "It should be further noted that Athletes are on notice that they take nutritional supplements at their own risk. The sanction reduction based on No Significant Fault or Negligence has rarely been applied in Contaminated Product cases unless the Athlete has exercised a high level of caution before taking the Contaminated Product."

[65] See *Knauss*, at para. 7.3.5, which states that the standard "must not be set excessively high." In *Maria Sharapova v. ITF*, CAS 2016/A/4643, there is similar wording at para. 84, which states that No Significant Fault or Negligence is "consistent with the existence of some degree of fault and cannot be excluded simply because the athlete left some 'stones unturned.' As a result, a deviation from the duty of exercising the 'utmost caution' does not imply per se that the athlete's negligence was 'significant.'"

[66] See *Knauss*, at para. 17, which describes some of the "clear and obvious precautions any human being would take" in the circumstances of that case.

[67] In *Marin Cilic v. ITF*, CAS 2013/A/3327, at para. 74(aa), some of the standard precautions are set out, which are: "The athlete could always (i) read the label of the product used (or otherwise ascertain the ingredients), (ii) cross-check all the ingredients on the label with the list of prohibited substances, (ii) make an internet search of the product, (iv) ensure the product is reliably sourced and (v) consult appropriate experts in these matters and instruct them diligently before consuming the product."

[68] *WADA v. Hardy & USADA*, CAS 2009/A/1870, at paras 117 and 118, confirms that "a reduced sanction based on 'no significant fault or negligence' can be applied where the athlete establishes that the cause of the positive test was contamination in a common multiple vitamin with no connection to prohibited substances . . ." and "the fact that an adverse analytical finding is the result of the use of a contaminated nutritional supplement does not imply per se that the athlete's negligence was 'significant.'"

[69] Even *Cilic* itself acknowledges, after setting out the precautions that could be taken, at para. 75, that "an athlete cannot be reasonably expected to follow all of the above steps in every and all circumstances."

a basic nutritional supplement from a reputable retailer, with arguably more limited risk factors, may be held to a lower standard than a player obtaining a bodybuilding supplement from an unlicensed operator where the degree of risk may well be perceived as higher.

A subjective assessment will then follow with an arbitral body to consider the player's departure from the expected standard in light of their personal circumstances. Common factors cited by players as reducing their degree of fault include (lack of) experience and (minimal) exposure to or understanding of anti-doping education (e.g. in the case of newer professional players) and the reason for using the contaminated product in the first place. If a factor does not explain why the player's behavior departed from the expected standard, then it will not be relevant for the purposes of no significant fault of negligence. Examples include previous good character, a clean anti-doping record and a lack of any intention to enhance performance.[70] Examples of where no significant fault or negligence defenses were accepted include:

1. Where it was held that there was no reason why a player should have been concerned by a herbal tea and drinking it without attempting to ascertain further details about what it was or where it came from.[71]
2. Where a player ingested glucose tablets purchased by his mother on the advice of a pharmacist.[72]
3. Where a player accidentally ingested medication meant for her mother through cross-contamination in food preparation.[73]
4. The player who drank from his wife's water glass referred to above.

Should an arbitral body conclude that a player's degree of fault was not significant, it is then necessary to consider what the appropriate reduction ineligibility period should be. The starting point for this consideration is the *Cilic* case and the case law that followed it. In *Cilic*, the CAS Panel established three categories of fault to the possible sanction range of zero to twenty-four months – with "light" fault at zero to eight months, "normal" fault at eight to sixteen months and "considerable" fault at

---

[70] In *Jack*, at para. 133, it was stated that "there is at least clear consensus at the following level of generality: speculations, declarations of a clear conscience, and character references are not sufficient proof."
[71] *Hipperdinger v. ATP*, CAS 2004/A/690, at para. 45.
[72] See *Cilic*.
[73] See *Errani*.

sixteen to twenty-four months.[74] All of these were based, of course, on an analysis of the merits of the player's circumstances.

Subsequent case law has suggested an amended version of that approach with the three categories reduced to two, with "light" fault incurring a zero-to-twelve-month ban and "normal" fault incurring twelve to twenty-four months.[75] This is on the basis that "considerable" fault is the equivalent of "significant" and the level of fault must not be significant in order for a reduction to be possible.

2.4 Appeals

The ITIA and the player both have a right of appeal against several types of decisions.[76] In addition, the relevant national anti-doping organizations and the WADA provide appeal rights, as do the International Olympic Committee and the International Paralympic Committee in certain circumstances pertaining to their major events.[77] An appeal by an international-level player[78] may be lodged to the CAS,[79] in accordance with the TADP and CAS Rules.[80] An appeal by the player must be made within twenty-one days of the date of receipt of the reasoned decision to be appealed by the appealing party.[81] The ITIA have a longer time period to appeal,[82] with the WADA having further time still.[83]

Appeals are heard by the CAS on a "de novo" basis, meaning the parties are free to run the same arguments as they did before the first-instance tribunal, or raise any new arguments that they wish. Effectively, it is a re-trial. Usually appeals are heard by a panel of three arbitrators, with one selected by each party and a president appointed by the CAS. A sole arbitrator is possible if the parties agree. The standard process is that the appealing party will have to file a statement of appeal and various

---

[74] See *Cilic*, at para. 70.
[75] See *Errani*, at para. 194.
[76] See TADP 2025, Art. 13.2.
[77] Ibid., Art. 13.2.3.
[78] This term refers to any "Player who enters or participates in more than one Covered Event (whether in qualifying or the main draw," so, in practice, captures the vast majority of professional tennis players.
[79] See TADP 2025, Art. 13.2.1.
[80] The CAS Rules are available at: www.tas-cas.org/fileadmin/user_upload/CAS_Code_2023__EN_.pdf. See Rules R47–R59 in particular.
[81] See TADP 2025, Art. 13.8.1.1.
[82] Ibid., Art. 13.8.1.2.
[83] Ibid., Art. 13.8.1.3.

initial material required by the CAS in order to commence the appeal. The appealing party must then file an Appeal Brief and accompanying evidence within a ten-day period, albeit this timeframe can often be extended (a common occurrence in anti-doping proceedings which are often technical and predicated on scientific considerations). The responding party will then have an opportunity to present an Answer Brief with accompanying evidence within a twenty-day period, although that is also often extended.

3 Anti-Corruption

While there are corruption risks associated with betting in almost all sports, there are three factors in tennis which create certain vulnerabilities justifying tennis's robust and early response to the threat of betting-based competition manipulation. First, tennis is, primarily, an individual sport. If one player is corrupted, they can clearly influence the outcome of any match they play. Contrast this with a team sport, say football, where influencing the outcome of a match is far more difficult since you may need to corrupt more players (or the referee), meaning that corrupt acts on the football pitch are more likely limited to spot fixing (unless they involve the referee or possibly the goalkeeper). Second, tennis is not profitable for many individuals trying to make their way up the significant pathway to the elite level of the sport. It is very expensive to compete with numerous outgoings for players, including coaching, travel and accommodation costs, and prize money is limited at the lower levels.[84] These developing players will generally need support from their national federation, club or private sponsorship. Only players in the top 200 or so of either the ATP or WTA tours are likely to turn a profit from their prize money and it is really only a ranking in the top 100 that will start to earn a player more significant sums.[85] That is a stark reality for one of the most popular global sports. Contrast this with football, where the Premier

---

[84] On the ITF World Tour, the total prize money for events is $15,000 or $25,000, meaning that many players will not earn enough to cover their costs of attending the event.

[85] This January 2023 ESPN article gives a helpful account of the challenges players face in funding a professional tennis career, from around a ranking of 100 and lower. D'Arcy Maine, "Why Am I Here, Playing for Literally $6? The Stunning Financial Reality of Pro-Tennis," ESPN (January 17, 2023), available at: www.espn.com/tennis/story/_/id/35414286/the-stunning-financial-reality-high-cost-pro-tennis. The ATP has recognized the challenges and is now trialing a three-pillar strategy called Baseline, with the first pillar being a "Minimum Guarantee" to ensure players in the top 250 of the ATP rankings earn at least $75,000 in a year. See Chapter 6 of this volume for an elaborate discussion.

League in England can sustain over 500 professionals at any one time earning, on average, over £3 million a year.[86]

Therefore, as tennis players at the lower end of the sport seek to move up the rankings or where they are on the way down, they may struggle to afford their professional lifestyles. The philosophy of the tennis pyramid is entirely merit-based in that players who do not win sufficiently eventually work their way down and out of the professional level of the sport based on their decreasing ranking and their places are taken by emerging players on the way up. This structure may make a small minority of players vulnerable to corruption as they struggle to cling on to evaporating opportunity and financial rewards. While the vast majority of players will say no to a corrupt approach, the financial pressures alongside other personal factors mean a small number may succumb and say yes.

Third, there is huge appetite for online betting on tennis, including point-by-point in-play betting. Those markets exist right down to the lower rungs of professional tennis where male and female players ply their trade on the ITF World Tennis Tour. There are hundreds of ITF World Tennis Tour events per year,[87] meaning numerous events and hundreds of matches taking place every week, with betting markets available for the matches in all of those events. A combination of a small cohort of potentially vulnerable players and available betting opportunities mean the risk of corruption is real.

3.1 Legal Framework

The TACP is the instrument that governs the approach of tennis to issues of corruption.[88]

3.1.1 Jurisdiction

If an individual is caught by the definition of the term "Covered Person" in the TACP, then he or she is subject to the jurisdiction of the TACP,

---

[86] See this article from *The Guardian* referring to a 2019 Global Sports Salary Survey: Sean Ingle, "Average Annual Salary of Premier League Players Tops £3m for First Time," *The Guardian* (December 23, 2019), available at: www.theguardian.com/football/2019/dec/23/premier-league-salaries-manchester-city-nba-barcelona#:~:text=The%20average%20salary%20for%20a,of%20English%20football's%20top%20fli.

[87] See the ITF website for a list of all tournaments in 2025 for men: www.itftennis.com/en/tournament-calendar/mens-world-tennis-tour-calendar/?categories=All&startdate=2025; and women: www.itftennis.com/en/tournament-calendar/womens-world-tennis-tour-calendar/?categories=All&startdate=2025-04.

[88] See s. A of the TACP 2025 for a summary of the purpose of the TACP.

and of the Anti-Corruption Hearing Officers, who will determine any proceedings. "Covered Person" is a broad term[89] relating to a number of individuals, ranging from obvious ones such as players/coaches/officials through to less obvious ones such as player agents and family members who receive accreditation as part of a player's entourage.

The initial mechanism to ensure that a player is subject to the TACP and is made aware thereof is the International Player Identification Number (IPIN) and the equivalent "player zone" registration for the ATP and WTA tours. All players seeking to register with professional events will be issued with an IPIN (or ATP/WTA player zone registration) and as part of doing so they are required to confirm that they will comply with the TACP (and the TADP and other regulations as well). The IPIN/player zone registration is renewed on an annual basis. There is also an annual approval of the Player Welfare Statement, which also includes a confirmation regarding awareness of, and compliance with, the TACP. A similar process exists for coaches, officials and others. In addition, all players, as well as coaches/officials and others, are required to undertake the mandatory Tennis Integrity Protection Programme (TIPP), which provides details of the TACP, gives real-life examples and asks questions of the user. The TIPP must be completed every two years. This is supplemented by in-person education at events delivered by the ITIA education team.

3.1.2 Governing Law

The governing law of the TACP is the law of the US state of Florida,[90] reflecting that the ATP and the WTA are both Florida-based organizations where the TACP was originally developed prior to the incorporation of the ITIA. However, the starting point is the language of the TACP itself, which means that many cases can progress with limited, or any, reference to Florida law. On appeal at the CAS, Swiss law may also become relevant. One exception to this concerns the admissibility of evidence. Rather than being constrained by Florida law, an AHO is not bound by the judicial rules of any jurisdiction regarding evidence.

---

[89] See the definition at s. B.9 of the TACP 2025 and the consequential definitions of "Player," "Related Person" and "Tournament Support Personnel" at ss. B.27, B.30 and B.38, including the timeframes within which an individual may be subject to those defined terms. Section C1 is clear that "All Players, Related Persons, and Tournament Support Personnel shall be bound by and shall comply with all of the provisions of this Program and shall be deemed to accept all the terms set out in herein ..."

[90] See TACP 2025, s. K.2.

Instead, the facts related to an alleged Corruption Offense can be established by any reliable means, which an AHO can determine.[91] This includes the use of inference,[92] a necessity in many cases the ITIA brings where the evidential picture is often incomplete; this is natural, given that an individual committing corruption offenses is unlikely to simply admit to their conduct and provide the relevant evidence.

3.1.3 Burden/Standard of Proof

The burden of proof is upon the ITIA to prove its case. It must do so to the standard of the "preponderance of the evidence"[93] – that is a Florida law term akin to the "balance of probabilities" standard under English law. In simpler terms, the ITIA's case must be more likely than not to be true for it to succeed, often expressed as being tantamount to a 51 percent threshold.

3.1.4 Hearings

There are two principal parts to the process which may culminate in a hearing of charges before an AHO. The first is not addressed by the TACP. That is the investigatory phase. The ITIA employs various investigators supported by individuals with expertise in areas such as betting markets or intelligence to obtain the maximum available evidence. Once an investigation has been completed and the investigator considers that there are grounds for charges under the TACP to be brought, the matter is passed to the ITIA's legal function. If it is agreed that charges should be issued, there follows a typical process common to most regulatory proceedings of this nature,[94] particularly within the sport's disciplinary field:

1. A Notice of Major Offense[95] will be issued to the relevant covered person. This will set out[96] the corruption offenses alleged to have been committed by reference to the relevant sections of the TACP, the facts upon which the allegations are based, the potential sanctions and the covered person's entitlement to have the matter determined at

---

[91] Ibid., s. G.3.d.
[92] In *ITIA v. Baptiste Crepatte*, AHO McLaren stated at para. 57 that "it is possible to find a breach of the TACP without direct evidence" subject to any inferential evidence meeting the required standard of proof. The decision can be found at: www.itia.tennis/media/amcldxbh/decision-of-aho-mclaren-player-b-crepatte-corrected-_redacted.pdf.
[93] See TACP 2025, s. G.3.a. Section G.3.b refers to limited situations where the burden of proof may fall upon the covered person. Where it does, the standard is again the preponderance of the evidence.
[94] See, in particular, TACP 2025, ss. G.1 and G.2.
[95] See ibid., ss. B.23 and B.25.
[96] Ibid., s. G.1.a.

a hearing. The covered person will be asked whether they admit or deny the charges.
2. If there is an admission, the parties will set out their position as to an appropriate sanction and the AHO will decide, often without the need for a hearing.
3. If there is a denial, the parties will agree on directions for the case to proceed to a hearing, which the AHO will approve.
4. Those directions will include provision for (1) the parties to exchange any relevant documents they intend to rely upon at the hearing, (2) filing of written witness or expert evidence and (3) filing written submissions setting out their position.[97]
5. The parties will then attend a hearing where witnesses will be heard and questioned, and further oral submissions made.

The AHO will consider the evidence before preparing a written decision[98] to confirm whether or not a corruption offense has been committed and, if so, what the appropriate sanction should be. The AHO will aim to issue that decision within fifteen business days of the hearing. There are also separate mechanisms whereby the ITIA and the covered person can agree a sanction in line with the Sanctioning Guidelines (as to which, see below) or, in the case of more minor breaches (such as betting on others' matches or participating in a betting advertisement), the ITIA can issue a sanction itself which is appealable to an AHO.

3.1.5 Appeals

The Covered Person and the ITIA have a right of appeal.[99] As with the TADP, an appeal is made to the CAS in accordance with both the terms of the TACP and the CAS Rules. An appeal must be made within twenty business days[100] from receipt of the decision by the appealing party. The basis of the appeal is the same as set out in the anti-doping section above.

3.2 Corruption Offenses

The TACP 2025 contains eighteen corruption offenses,[101] with the bulk of those offenses targeting match-fixing in some form, but also those likely to

---

[97] Ibid., s. G.1.g.ii.
[98] Ibid., ss. G.4.a and G.4.b.
[99] Ibid., s. I, with s. I.1 setting out what types of decisions may be appealed.
[100] Ibid., s. I.4.
[101] Ibid., ss. D.1.a–D.1.r.

influence or have inside information about matches. The common theme underlying the vast majority of corruption offenses is the relevance of the global, and usually online, betting industry. The fact that a betting market exists for almost every professional tennis match that is played is crucial to the existence of match-fixing, since it is there that the individuals who seek to corrupt covered persons have an incentive to do so.[102]

In almost every instance of a covered person who acts in breach of the TACP, such as by losing a match deliberately or umpires entering the wrong scores into the device they use to score matches, a link to the betting markets exists. The basic methodology is that a player agrees with a third party to lose a point, game, set or match and the third party then places bets on the agreed outcome occurring, so earning a profit through a successful bet. The player will then receive a fee for their role. The global betting industry is, therefore, crucial to the ITIA's efforts to tackle match-fixing in tennis. It is often the first line of defense since betting operators will observe the bets placed on the betting markets they offer with the aim of spotting any bets that raise suspicions of match-fixing. That is primarily for their own commercial purposes, but, where they do so, a "match alert" is raised and ultimately sent to the ITIA. The reporting of match alerts is predicated in memorandums of understandings between the ITIA and certain licensed betting operators that provide for the sharing of this information.[103] This enables the ITIA to investigate and without the provision of match alerts the fight against corruption in tennis would be much more difficult, since the only other main source of intelligence that results in an investigation being commenced around match-fixing is information coming directly from covered persons. While this method relies on covered persons complying with their reporting obligations under the TACP, there can often be a natural reluctance to report potential offenses. Match alerts from betting operators are, therefore, vital.

Following an investigation by the ITIA, match alerts, and the underlying betting data, may be supplemented by information from covered persons in interviews, social media exchanges,[104] open-source research,

---

[102] See Ilias Bantekas, "Is Legitimate Gambling a Threat to the Integrity of Transnational Individual Sport Competitions?" (2024) 25 San Diego Int LJ 23.

[103] The ITIA does not have memorandums of understanding with all licensed betting operators. That is not realistic given the number that exist, particularly from jurisdiction to jurisdiction. There are also a huge number of unlicensed betting operators with whom there is no relationship.

[104] It is common for covered persons involved in breaches of the TACP to try and avoid sharing social media exchanges, since that is where the most incriminating evidence usually lies.

checks on the levels of education on the TACP of the covered person being investigated and ITF records. At the conclusion of an investigation, the ITIA will make a decision as to whether the available evidence is sufficient to allege that the relevant covered person may have committed a corruption offense, so whether there is a case to answer. If so, a Notice of Major Offense will be prepared, which will set out what the alleged breaches of the TACP are and the process described above will commence. Some of the key corruption offenses are considered in the remainder of this section.

3.2.1 Betting Offenses

It is an offense under section D.1.a of the TACP 2025 for a covered person to bet upon tennis[105] and it is an offense under sections D.1.b and D.1.q for a covered person to facilitate, encourage or promote betting.[106] A prohibition on betting on the sport in which an individual competes is common across all sports. That is because of the obvious conflict of interest between a participant being involved in a match/event in which they may have a specific interest in its outcome and betting on that match/event, which could, of course, detract from the event's integrity. It is often the case that covered persons who bet on tennis do so in ignorance of the TACP requirements. It is unlikely that standalone betting offenses would incur a sanction of over a one-year ban and a limited fine.

3.2.2 Fixing a Match

Match-fixing strikes at the very heart of any sport and certainly poses a huge threat to the integrity of tennis. The draw of competitive sport for participants and for its audience (and therefore also for sponsors, broadcasters and other stakeholders) lies largely in the uncertainty of outcome of any event. It has often been described as a "cancer" by numerous courts, tribunals and academics, with the following statement from a CAS Panel being a typical comment: "The Panel has to remind itself that match-fixing ... and the like are a growing concern, indeed a cancer,

---

[105] TACP 2025, s. D.1.a reads: "No Covered Person shall, directly or indirectly, Wager on the outcome or any other aspect of any Event or any other tennis competition."

[106] TACP 2025, s. D.1.b reads: "No Covered Person shall, directly or indirectly, facilitate, encourage and/or promote Tennis Betting," with several examples then given. Section D.1.q reads: "No Covered Person, whether personally or via another arrangement or legal entity, may endorse, be employed, sponsored and/or otherwise engaged by a Tennis Betting Operator."

in many major sports ... and must be eradicated. The very essence of sport is that competition is fair; its attraction to spectators is the unpredictability of its outcome."[107]

It is, therefore, an offense under section D.1.d of the TACP 2025 to contrive the outcome of an Event.[108] It is also an offense under section D.1.n to attempt to fix a match (or commit any corruption offense), with section D.1.d having also been held to address an attempt.[109] This is the most common section for match-fixing offenses. It can be used to capture any circumstances in which a covered person deliberately seeks to fix all or part of a match, through losing specific points, games, sets or the match itself. A typical methodology for a section D.1.d offense is as follows:

1. An individual makes contact with a player who it is believed may be vulnerable to a corrupt approach. That contact can be directly from someone outside of tennis,[110] but it is often made through a middleman,[111] commonly a player themselves, known to both the player and the corruptor. The approach may be in person, but is often through apps such as WhatsApp or Telegram.[112]
2. A financial offer is presented in relation to the outcome of the match, or more often, a particular part of the match. It is very common for individuals fixing a match to have the chance to go on and win that match.[113]

---

[107] *Oleg Oriekhov v. UEFA*, CAS 2010/A/2172, at para. 78.
[108] TACP 2025, s. D.1.d reads: "No Covered Person shall, directly or indirectly, contrive the outcome, or any other aspect, of any Event."
[109] TACP 2025, s. D.1.n reads: "No Covered Person shall, directly or indirectly, attempt, agree, or conspire to commit any Corruption Offense." See *ITIA* v. *Jules Okala*, TACP AHO Decision, available at: www.itia.tennis/media/2b1p1tnb/jules-okala-decision-1-12-22_redacted.pdf, for a case where an attempt to fix resulted in liability. This principle has also been approved at the CAS in *Daniel Köellerer* v. *ATP and Others*, CAS 2011/A/2490.
[110] See *ITIA* v. *Mick Lescure*, TACP AHO, available at: www.itia.tennis/media/r4wlujj2/mick-lescure-aho-decision-1-12-22_redacted.pdf.
[111] See *ITIA* v. *Timur Khabibulin*, TACP AHO Decision and *ITIA* v. *Sanjar Fayziev*, TACP AHO Decision. The cases are available at: www.itia.tennis/media/gqrjeguj/aho-decision-on-sanction-itia-v-khabibulin_redacted.pdf and www.itia.tennis/media/thbjv52s/aho-decision-on-sanction-itia-v-fayziev_redacted.pdf, respectively.
[112] See *ITIA* v. *Mick Lescure* and *ITIA* v. *Timur Khabibulin*.
[113] There is a logic to that, of course – earn money for winning a match and making the next round while simultaneously earning money for losing an aspect of that match such as a service game.

3. There is sometimes a negotiation, but usually the offer is simply accepted or declined. If there is a middleman, the offer will often include a smaller sum for their role.[114]
4. If the offer is accepted, the corruptor will make arrangements for the relevant bets to be placed. This is almost always achieved by using online betting operators and often multiple ones in several jurisdictions. Depending on the nature of the bet and where the odds may be most beneficial, the bets may be placed pre-match or during the match (but before the part of the match relevant to the bet).
5. The player will then carry out the agreed fix on-court, with the easiest way to lose on purpose being to ensure service games are lost through double faults. The player will likely play normally for any part of the match not affected by the agreed fix.
6. If the fix was successfully carried out, payment is usually made using money transfer services, such as MoneyGram or Western Union,[115] or more modern app-based equivalents such as Neteller or Skrill.[116] Those payments are often made to family/friends of the player by associates of the corruptor,[117] to disguise the payments to some extent. Sometimes, payments are made in cash.

The level of sophistication of the individuals making corrupt offers to players is varied. However, at its most sophisticated level, one individual running an organized criminal network successfully fixed hundreds of matches over several years with numerous covered persons and a vast number of bettors at his disposal, earning millions of Euros in the process.[118] There have been other examples of well-organized betting syndicates sitting behind the corruptor/middleman/covered person relationship.[119]

There is no need for a financial return to be proven in order to demonstrate liability under section D.1.d. This is important as it reflects

---

[114] See *ITIA v. Simohamed Hirs*, TACP AHO Decision, for an example of how the offers are presented, available at: www.itia.tennis/media/c4acx1rl/simohamed-hirs-sanctioned-28-07-21_redacted.pdf.
[115] See *ITIA v. Sanjar Fayziev*.
[116] See *ITIA v. Jules Okala*.
[117] Again, see *ITIA v. Sanjar Fayziev* for an example of both.
[118] The individual was an Armenian national based in Belgium called Grigor Sargsyan. He was often known as the "Maestro" among other nicknames. See Kevin Sieff, "The Maestro: The Man Who Built the Biggest Match-Fixing Ring in Tennis," *The Washington Post* (2023), available at: www.washingtonpost.com/world/interactive/2023/tennis-match-fixing-itf-grigor-sargsyan/.
[119] See *ITIA v. Timur Khabibulin*.

the practical reality of match-fixing that the arrangements can often go wrong. One example may arise where a covered person changes their mind or carries out the fix incorrectly. Another is where betting operators may identify concerns with the betting being observed from a particular match and refuse to pay out. It would be wrong if covered persons were found not liable in those circumstances. A financial return is, however, relevant to an applicable sanction (see below).

3.2.2.1 Facilitating Others to Fix a Match

It has been often held, both before AHOs and at the CAS, that while all match-fixing offenses are serious, the most serious offense is where one covered person corrupts another to fix a match,[120] particularly someone who otherwise may not have fixed a match. The same methodology as set out in the previous section might apply, but with the covered person in question this time being either the corruptor or, more likely, the middleman. This concept is addressed by sections D.1.e to D.1.g and section D.1.o of the TACP 2025.[121]

3.2.2.2 Umpires Fixing a Match

There is little difference between why players fix matches and why an umpire might do so – it is again the availability of betting markets and a desire for financial gain that makes a minority of umpires equally vulnerable to corruptors as some players. The primary means for an umpire to fix (accepting that in lower-level matches without line judges they can also make intentionally erroneous line calls) arises from the way in which they enter the score into the electronic device used when they are officiating a match. Those scores feed into the global betting markets and inform betting operators of the events on court so that it is known whether bettors have been successful in their bets.

However, if an umpire is corrupt and either (1) delays entering the correct score or (2) deliberately enters the wrong score, bettors with knowledge of the umpire's actions in advance can place bets knowing they will be successful. Those actions are prohibited under section D.1.m of the TACP 2025 with liability found in various cases,[122] and previously

---

[120] See *ITIA v. Franco Feitt*, TACP AHO Decision, available at: www.itia.tennis/media/0ehcf1dj/franco-feitt-sanctioned-12-04-2021-aho-decision_redacted.pdf.

[121] TACP 2025, s. D.1.e reads: "No Covered Person shall, directly or indirectly, facilitate any Player to not use their best efforts in any Event." Sections D.1.f and D.1.g broadly relate to the receipt of money and the offer/provision of money. Section D.1.o covers more serious concepts of soliciting and inciting others to commit corruption offenses.

[122] One example is *ITIA v. Edvinas Grigaitis*, TACP AHO Decision, available at: www.itia.tennis/media/nfbhgble/decision-itia-v-grigaitis-final__redacted.pdf.

have been held to be a breach of section D.1.d as well, on the basis that their conduct contrives "an aspect of an event."[123]

3.2.3 Failure to Report

Aside from information from betting operators, the other main source of intelligence leading to ITIA investigations is the disclosure by a covered person. All covered persons have a reporting obligation under section D.2 of the TACP 2025 in certain circumstances. Typical examples include a disclosure that a covered person had been approached to fix a match,[124] or that they have a suspicion that another covered person is committing a corruption offense.[125] This is an important provision given the challenging nature of the task facing the ITIA. It does not have the investigatory powers that law enforcement authorities have, so is limited to the powers under the TACP – which are not as robust. As a result, the ITIA is reliant on third parties working with them to assist, and often instigate, their investigations.

Covered persons are the most important third party since they are the direct recipients of corrupt approaches and can explain the nature of the approach, how the proposed scheme might be carried out and any others that may be involved. This evidence is potentially of more value than the match alerts that the ITIA might receive from a betting operator, which are ultimately a step removed from the actual moment a breach of the TACP is taking place. It is, therefore, very important for covered persons to adhere to their reporting obligations under the TACP rather than simply ignore these.[126]

3.2.4 Failure to Cooperate

In a similar way to the reporting obligations on covered persons, there is also an obligation to "cooperate fully" with investigations of the ITIA;[127] with that obligation arising out of a very similar rationale to the need for reporting obligations. Given the "full" nature of the obligation to

---

[123] See *ITIA v. Majd Affi, Abderahim Gharsallah and Mohamed Ghassen Snene*, TACP AHO Decision, available at: www.itia.tennis/media/xtbdkyw1/affi-snene-gharsallah-decision-4-7-22-aho-mulcahy_redacted.pdf.
[124] See TACP 2025, ss. D.2.a.i and D.2.b.i.
[125] Ibid., ss. D.2.a.ii and D.2.b.ii.
[126] Note that there are few decisions focusing on non-reporting alone, as it is often a charge that sits alongside more serious match-fixing charges. However, the largest sanction for standalone non-reporting offenses is twenty months for a chair umpire who failed to report two separate corruption offenses.
[127] TACP 2025, s. F.2.b.

cooperate, a covered person is required to do several things, including being a part of ITIA investigations, answering questions posed by investigators, attending hearings, preserving evidence and complying with demands[128] for information, such as providing phones, betting records and bank statements for analysis, as well as access to social media accounts. Failure to do so could be deemed a failure to cooperate under the TACP.

There is no limitation on the sanction that may be imposed if liability is found for non-cooperation offenses, a necessity if such an offense is to have any practical impact.[129] Clearly, a covered person should not view a failure to cooperate as a possible alternative to admitting to more serious offenses such as match-fixing.

3.2.5 Other Offenses

There are several other offenses set out at section D of the TACP. They include offenses relating to: (1) the provision of inside information (sections D.1.h and D.1.i); (2) benefits around a tournament (sections D.1.c, D.1.j, D.1.k and D.1.l); (3) conspiracy (sections D.1.n and D.1.o); and (4) associating with a related person who is, among other things, serving a period of ineligibility under the TACP (section D.1.r).

3.3 Sanction

Where a covered person is found to have committed one or more corruption offenses, it is highly likely that they will then receive a sanction. There are two principal aims underlying the sanctioning process. First, in the context of a specific covered person, to impose a reasonable and proportionate sanction upon that individual that reflects the offenses committed and the seriousness of their conduct. Second, the sanction should serve as an effective deterrent to other covered persons such that the risk of future offending by others is decreased and the overall integrity of the sport is protected as far as possible. Against this background, it is no surprise that there is a broad range of available sanctions. For the most serious offenses, usually match-fixing offenses, the maximum sanction available is a lifetime ban

---

[128] See ibid.
[129] In *ITIA* v. *Juan Carlos Saez*, the CAS upheld a sanction of eight years and a $12,500 fine imposed by an AHO primarily for non-cooperation offenses. The press release is available at: www.itia.tennis/news/sanctions/cas-upholds-sanction-for-juan-carlos-saez/. At the time of writing, the award was unreported.

from tennis, a $250,000 fine and the repayment of any sums earned that relate to a corruption offense.[130] There have been numerous lifetime bans[131] imposed, but the maximum fine has rarely been awarded.[132]

Since 2021, the starting point has been the ITIA's Sanctioning Guidelines.[133] The aim of this instrument is to set out key principles relevant to sanctions and a scheme for calculating an appropriate penalty fairly and consistently. It was produced following a review of the outcomes from over ten years of precedents, with the trends then incorporated into the Sanctioning Guidelines. As the name suggests, the Sanctioning Guidelines offer guidance only. They are meant as a framework. An AHO is not bound by the Sanctioning Guidelines, so need not rigidly apply them, and may depart from the standard process set out where he or she considers it appropriate to do so. The starting point for the ITIA is that it is required to adhere to the Sanctioning Guidelines.

There are several stages to applying the Sanctioning Guidelines. The first is "Determining the offense category," where an AHO must assess the level of culpability of a covered person and the impact their actions have had upon tennis. Culpability is split into categories A, B and C, with impact split into categories 1, 2 and 3. A1 is the most serious and C3 is the least serious.

Category A relates to covered persons who have demonstrated a "high degree of planning or premeditation," have been "initiating or leading others to commit offenses" and have committed "multiple offenses over a protracted period of time." Categories B and C reflect the same concepts, but reduced levels of seriousness – so little planning, just one offense and so on. Category 1 relates to covered persons who have committed TACP offenses other than D.1.a, D.1.b, D.1.q, or D.2 (i.e. offenses which are considered to be more major), caused a "significant, material impact on the reputation and/or integrity of the sport," currently hold a "position of trust/responsibility within the sport," such as an umpire, and have received

---

[130] See TACP 2025, ss. H.1.a(i) and (iii) and H.1.b(i) and (iii).

[131] There are forty-seven TACP cases with a lifetime ban imposed currently listed on the ITIA website, available at: www.itia.tennis/sanctions/.

[132] See *ITIA* v. *Karen Khachatryan*, where the maximum sanction was awarded. The press release can be found at: www.itia.tennis/sanctions/. However, note the CAS cases of Gleb and Vadim Alekseenko, which reduced the $250,000 fine imposed by an AHO on each of them to $25,000 each. The press release can be found at: www.itia.tennis/news/sanctions/cas-upholds-lifetime-ban-alekseenko-brothers/.

[133] A copy of the current set of Sanctioning Guidelines is available at: www.itia.tennis/anti-corruption/policies/.

a "relatively high value of illicit gain." Again, categories 2 and 3 reflect the same concepts, but reduced levels of seriousness.

Having assessed these two factors, the second step for an AHO is assessing the "Starting point and category range." Each of the nine possible outcomes for culpability and impact, from A1 to C3, have a starting point and range attributed to them. The starting point for A1 is a lifetime ban (interpreted as being a thirty-year period), but with the range going as low as a ten-year suspension. Contrast this with C3, where the starting point is a three-month suspension, but the range is between an admonishment and a six-month suspension.

The AHO's discretion in their approach means that they can assess covered persons as sitting between categories; in this manner, a covered person may have characteristics of B1, but also of B2. The starting points for each are a ten-year suspension and a three-year suspension, respectively. AHOs may, therefore, consider that the starting point for this covered person should be somewhere in between, so around six-and-a-half years. The AHO will then consider whether there are factors existing in the case of the particular covered person that justify moving the suspension higher or lower, within the category range, to reflect the seriousness of the identified conduct. Aggravating factors include previous sanctions, impeding ITIA investigations and having significant levels of education in the TACP. Mitigating factors include genuine remorse, a threat of harm to the covered person or their family, age/experience and lack of education in the TACP.

Step 3 considers whether a covered person has admitted their conduct which was in breach of the TACP and the stage at which they did so. The earlier the admission, the greater the reduction is likely to be, up to a maximum of 25 percent from the otherwise applicable sanction. Step 4 considers whether there are other factors which may merit a reduction in sanction, with the specific example of substantial assistance[134] being given. Note that in some cases, substantial assistance is given after a sanction is imposed, in which case an AHO will consider in a separate process whether there should be a reduction in sanction in light of the substantial assistance provided. Finally, Step 5 requires consideration of whether it is appropriate to impose a fine upon a covered person, with the likelihood of a fine, and the size of that fine, increasing with the seriousness of the conduct and broadly based on the

---

[134] See TACP 2025, s. B.34, which refers to "substantial assistance" as "assistance given by a Covered Person to the ITIA that results in the discovery or establishing of a corruption offense by another Covered Person."

number of major offenses the covered person was found liable for. There is a table with a scale of fines to give guidance to an AHO. Many covered persons may not have the financial means to pay fines, so AHOs can take that into account in the quantum of the sanction and the ability to order installments.

There are several types of offending which have been categorized as A1, with many of those offending being subject to a lifetime ban (or, if not, a very lengthy suspension):

1. Covered Persons who have repeatedly fixed multiple matches over a protracted period of time.
2. Covered Persons who have sought to corrupt other covered persons and convince them to fix professional tennis matches. As above, this has generally been considered the most serious of the match-fixing offenses.
3. Umpires who fail to uphold their role in managing the integrity of the game through deliberately entering the wrong score into the devices used to score professional tennis matches, or delaying that entry, to benefit third parties operating in online-betting markets.

11

Regulating On-Court Tennis Indiscipline

BEN LIVINGS

1 Introduction

Rules are a defining and indispensable feature of sports. As Vamplew writes: 'It is rules that differentiate one sport from another. It is also rules that distinguish the sophisticated games of sport from the more naïve ones of play.'[1] A sport's rules dictate by whom and how it is played; they seek to ensure that the on-field contest is free from corrupting influences such as doping or match-fixing; and they set standards of behaviour that players – and indeed others involved in the sport – must conform to, both on and off the field of play.

Among other purposes, and depending on the sport, the rules are in place to protect the participants' safety, ensure fair competition, and maximise the sport's enjoyment and entertainment value for those participating and spectating. The latter function is particularly important in tennis, a sport which places an emphasis on player decorum to maintain its character and aesthetic appeal to participants, spectators and sponsors. Lake describes tennis as 'a sport characterized and self-regulated by an unwritten code of sportsmanship and restrained gentlemanly behavior since its inception in the mid/late nineteenth century'.[2] As Lake points out, 'key aspects of the traditional code of conduct were modelled on British amateur ideals'.[3] The historical development of tennis was grounded in its middle-class roots, and the behavioural and aesthetic expectations of the sport continue to reflect this: 'The cultural expressions of upper-class taste sought by the most aspirational upper-middle-class players had a lasting impression upon the sport. From its very beginnings, principally because of its noble heritage ...

---

[1] Wray Vamplew, 'Playing with the Rules: Influences on the Development of Regulation in Sport' (2007) 24 Int J Hist Sport 843, at 843.
[2] Robert J. Lake, 'The "Bad Boys" of Tennis: Shifting Gender and Social Class Relations in the Era of Năstase, Connors, and McEnroe' (2015) 42 J Sport Hist 179, at 181.
[3] Ibid.

and also due to its earliest upper-class enthusiasts, lawn tennis attracted those seeking to improve their social positions.'[4]

This chapter looks at the rules governing participant behaviour that are contained in the International Tennis Federation (ITF) World Tennis Tour Code of Conduct (hereinafter, the 'Code').[5] The Code is the principal basis for disciplinary action in tennis,[6] with some variations where a matter falls under the jurisdiction of the Association of Tennis Players (ATP), the Women's Tennis Association (WTA) or the organisers of the four Grand Slam tournaments, with each having their own 'Rulebooks'.[7] The Code augments and operates alongside the ITF's 'Rules of Tennis',[8] which 'constitute and define what counts as playing' tennis.[9] Foster refers to the rules of the game as '*lex ludica*', the composition, adjudication and enforcement of which are matters almost entirely within the control of a given sport's governing bodies. The Court of Arbitration for Sport (CAS), for example, does not generally accept appeals or otherwise interfere in disputes over the interpretation and enforcement of these rules.[10] Sports governing bodies therefore form a kind of 'private government',[11] and the ITF enjoys great power in the devising, promulgation and enforcement of its rules, including the Code.[12]

---

[4] Robert J. Lake, *A Social History of Tennis in Britain* (Routledge, 2014), 17.
[5] The Code is available at: www.itftennis.com/media/8955/world-tennis-tour-code-of-con duct.pdf. This chapter does not investigate the procedural issues, which have been considered by the author elsewhere: Ben Livings and Karolina Wlodarczak, 'Procedural Fairness in the International Tennis Federation's Disciplinary Regime' (2020) 18 Ent & Sports LJ.
[6] The Code is 'the exclusive basis for disciplinary action', except for integrity matters falling under the jurisdiction of the TACP or TADP, available at: www.itftennis.com/media/ 8955/world-tennis-tour-code-of-conduct.pdfchrome-extension://efaidnbmnnnibp cajpcglclefindmkaj/https://www.itftennis.com/media/11558/grand-slam-rule-book-2024-f3.pdf.
[7] The Rulebooks are available at: www.itftennis.com/en/about-us/governance/rules-and-regu lations/?type=tour-regulations; www.atptour.com/en/corporate/rulebook; and www.wtaten nis.com/wta-rules.
[8] Rules of Tennis (2025), available at: www.itftennis.com/media/7221/2025-rules-of-ten nis-english.pdf.
[9] Christoph Lumer, 'Rules and Moral Norms in Sports' (1995) 30 Int Rev Sociol Sport 263.
[10] Ken Foster, 'Lex Sportiva and Lex Ludica: The Court of Arbitration for Sport's Jurisprudence' (2006) Ent & Sports LJ 1.
[11] Stewart Macaulay, 'Private Government' in David Campbell (ed.), *Stewart Macaulay: Selected Works. Law and Philosophy Library* (Springer, 1986).
[12] Cisneros states that 'these are rules which are imposed rather than consented to'. Ben Cisneros, 'Challenging the Call: Should Sports Governing Bodies Be Subject to Judicial Review?' (2020) 20 Int Sports LJ 18, at 23.

2 The Code

The 'Rules of Tennis' acknowledge the need to strike a balance between maintaining tradition and the development of the sport. This is set out explicitly in the 'objectives' cited in Appendix XIII, which state that the ITF is committed to:

 a. Preserving the traditional character and integrity of the game of tennis.
 b. Actively preserving the skills traditionally required to play the game.
 c. Encouraging improvements, which maintain the challenge of the game.
 d. Ensuring fair competition.[13]

This idea of '[p]reserving the traditional character and integrity' while 'encouraging improvements' is therefore central to the regulation of tennis. The Code is a key means to achieving this; its purpose is set out in Article I(A) as follows: 'The International Tennis Federation promulgates this Code of Conduct ... in order to maintain fair and reasonable standards of conduct by players, Related Persons, Covered Persons and the organisers of Men's and Women's ITF World Tennis Tour tournaments, and to protect their respective rights, the rights of the public and the integrity of the Sport of Tennis.'[14]

Serious integrity breaches are beyond the scope of the Rules of Tennis or the Code (and of this chapter).[15] Until 2021, the ITF (in conjunction with the WTA, ATP and Grand Slams) oversaw the Tennis Integrity Unit, which administered the integrity rules related to doping, match-fixing and other forms of corruption. From 2021, this is the responsibility of the International Tennis Integrity Agency (ITIA), which describes itself as 'an independent body established by the international governing bodies of tennis to promote, encourage and safeguard the integrity of professional tennis worldwide'.[16] To this end, the ITIA administers the Tennis Anti-Corruption Program (TACP) and the Tennis Anti-Doping Program (TADP). Breaches of the integrity rules can have serious consequences for the offender, including large fines and lifetime bans from participation in the sport. Because of this, there are appeals mechanisms in place, which involve independent tribunals and the potential for an

---

[13] Rules of Tennis (2025), Appendix XIII.
[14] ITF World Tennis Tour Code of Conduct, Art. I(A), available at: www.itftennis.com/media/8955/world-tennis-tour-code-of-conduct.pdf.
[15] This is covered in more depth elsewhere in this book, specifically Chapter 10.
[16] ITIA, available at: www.itia.tennis/.

appeal to the CAS. It should be noted that the behaviours captured by these codes may also comprise criminal offences.

Contravention of the Code can lead to the imposition of penalties. These range from in-game sanctions (warnings, points penalties, forfeiture of games or even matches) to (usually more severe) out-of-game punishments, such as fines, disqualification from tournaments, suspensions or even participation bans. Although this chapter is concerned primarily with on-court player misconduct, it is important to note that the applicability of the Code goes well beyond this, both in terms of the conduct it captures and the 'covered persons' who are subject to it. This breadth of application can be seen in the case of Ilie Năstase, who was punished in his capacity as Romanian Fed Cup captain for misconduct in the build-up to and during a home tie against the Great Britain team in April 2017 in Constanta, Romania.[17] The misconduct comprised: a comment made in relation to Serena Williams's pregnancy that the ITF alleged was 'unethical, unprofessional, unacceptable, offensive, derogatory, and may be interpreted as racist'; repeated and unwelcome sexual advances towards GB team captain Anne Keothavong; alleged intimidation of the GB players;[18] repeated abuse of the media; repeated accusations of umpire bias during the match; and abusive language directed at the umpire and the GB team.[19]

At a hearing before the ITF Internal Adjudication Panel (IAP) in July 2017, Năstase was found guilty of several breaches of the Fed Cup Welfare Policy, which reproduced in identical language the behavioural standards set out in the ITF Code of Conduct's Welfare Policy.[20] The IAP imposed a fine of $10,000 and a two-part suspension. The first part of the suspension applied to Năstase's attendance at ITF events and was for one year and eight months. The second part of his suspension related more narrowly to his 'acting in an official capacity' at ITF-sanctioned events and was for the longer duration of three years and eight months. Năstase appealed the decision of the IAP to the Independent Tribunal, which upheld the original decision, but altered the penalty. The fine was doubled (from US$10,000 to US$20,000), but both periods of suspension were reduced by around eight months, to one year and three years, respectively.

---

[17] *Ilie Năstase v. ITF*, Independent Tribunal Decision, SR/913/2017.
[18] This is the only charge that was held not to be substantiated.
[19] *ITF v. Năstase*, at paras 5 and 35–116.
[20] Ibid.

2.1 Code Violations

Năstase's case demonstrates the breadth of application of the Code, but this chapter is centrally concerned with the regulation of players' on-court behaviour. The type of conduct that might lead to sanctions is captured in the following list of common Code violations:

- Audible Obscenity
- Visible Obscenity
- Racket Abuse
- Ball Abuse
- Verbal Abuse
- Physical Abuse
- Coaching
- Time Violations
- Dress Code Violation
- Failure to Give Best Effort
- Unsportsmanlike Conduct

In-game violations are punished according to the 'point penalty schedule' set out in Article IV(R) of the Code.[21] According to this, a player's first offence during a match will result in a 'warning'. Subsequent Code violations will result in a 'point penalty', then a 'game penalty'. Any further violations may result in default for the offending player, meaning that the player will be disqualified from the match and victory awarded to the opponent. The decision as to whether to impose a default rests with the 'ITF Supervisor'.[22] A sufficiently serious Code violation can result in a player receiving an 'Immediate Default', even where this is the first Code violation of the match.[23] Importantly, the Code sets out that decisions made under the point penalty schedule or to declare a default are 'final and unappealable'.[24]

2.1.1 Physical Violence

The Code provisions listed above are concerned primarily with maintaining the aesthetic and fairness of the competition. A study of junior tennis players that looked at the prevalence and causes of norm-breaking behaviours found that norm-breaking behaviours were a stress response to an

---

[21] Many Code violations also attract a monetary fine.
[22] Art. IV(S).
[23] Ibid.
[24] Art. IV(R).

individual psychological crisis.[25] By far the most common manifestations were 'behaviours directed toward property' (37 per cent of the incidents) and 'self-directed verbal behaviours' (33 per cent of the incidents). There is relatively little concern for interpersonal physical violence. The Code violation of 'physical abuse' is defined as 'the unauthorised touching of an official, opponent, spectator, or other person'. The relevant offence entails 'the unauthorized touching of any official, opponent, spectator, or other person within the precincts of the tournament site'.[26] In his study of the prevalence and types of violence that manifest in different sports, Guilbert notes that interpersonal physical violence is rare in tennis.[27] The format and nature of the sport preclude it, since the opponents are separated by a net and the sport does not involve contact between them. In an exceptional example of causing injury through physical violence, in 2012, at the Queen's Club Championships, David Nalbandian injured a line judge by frustratedly kicking an advertising board into the judge's shin and drawing blood. Code violations that involve physical violence are more likely to be captured under the offences of 'abuse of ball', 'abuse of racquet or equipment' or 'unsportsmanlike conduct'.

The Code sets out the offence of 'abuse of balls' as follows: 'Players shall not violently, dangerously or with anger hit, kick, or throw a tennis ball within the precincts of the tournament site except in the reasonable pursuit of a point during a match.' This is defined as 'intentionally hitting a ball out of the enclosure of the court, hitting a ball dangerously or recklessly within the court or hitting a ball with negligent disregard of the consequences'.[28] The most notorious and heavily punished offences involving such behaviour arise out of those relatively rare instances where a ball is hit in anger or frustration and ends up striking another person.

In 1995, Tim Henman became the first player to be disqualified from Wimbledon in the Open era after hitting a ball in anger which struck a ball girl. More recently, Denis Shapovalov hit chair umpire Arnaud Gabas in the eye with a ball he struck in anger after losing his serve to Great Britain's Kyle Edmund during a Davis Cup match in 2017. Although it was clear that Shapovalov did not intend to hit Gabas, referee

---

[25] Ronit Hanegby and Gershon Tenenbaum, 'Blame It on the Racket: Norm-Breaking Behaviours among Junior Tennis Players' (2001) 2 Psychol Sport Exerc 117.
[26] Art. IV(H).
[27] Sèbastien Guilbert, 'Sport and Violence: A Typological Analysis' (2004) 39 Int Rev Sociol Sport 45.
[28] Art. IV(I).

Brian Earley declared an immediate default of Shapovalov for unsportsmanlike conduct.[29] More recently still, Novak Djokovic was disqualified from the 2020 US Open in similar circumstances after unintentionally hitting a line judge with a tennis ball. In each of these cases, the players were deemed to have engaged in 'unsportsmanlike conduct' and were defaulted from their respective matches.

'Abuse of racquet or equipment' is defined in the Code as 'intentionally and violently destroying or damaging racquets or equipment or intentionally and violently hitting the net, court, umpire's chair, or other fixture during a match out of anger or frustration'. Violations of this aspect of the Code are punished relatively frequently. Malis and Michalica describe the application of this rule as 'clear', and set out the purpose of it: 'The purpose of this rule is to emphasize the historical legacy of this game and its ethos, which includes subtle non-aggressive manifestations, and therefore deliberately smashing things such as rackets is a social offense against good morals. The purpose of the rule is to sanction inappropriate behavior on the court.'[30] The approach is seemingly approved by sponsors. In 2017, racquet manufacturer Yonex reportedly inserted clauses into the contracts that it held with players using its equipment, meaning that the players would incur a financial penalty for abusing Yonex racquets. The move was to allow Yonex to maintain a 'clean image'.[31]

The examples given above illustrate potentially serious breaches of the Code, and some even resulted in physical harm to the victim. Although there are rare occasions in tennis where frustration or aggression do result in violence, the offences contained in the Code are not primarily concerned with keeping the players (or indeed officials, spectators or anybody else in close proximity) physically 'safe'. The violence exhibited in each of these incidents constituted an egregious breach of the Code, not just because of the minor danger posed to the respective victims, but also because it violated the norms of the sport's aesthetics.

---

[29] 'Updated ITF Statement Regarding Denis Shapovalov' (6 February 2017), available at: www.daviscup.com/253005?channel=daviscupnews.

[30] Jiri Malis and Tomas Michalica, 'Why Carlos Ramos Was in Compliance with His Duty and USTA and WTA Are Wrong in the Case of US Open 2018 Women's Final' (2023) 17 Sport Ethics Philos 9 (references omitted).

[31] Michael Chammas, 'Nick Kyrgios' Racquet Manufacturer Yonex Starts Fining Its Players for Smashes', SMH (2 January 2017), available at: www.smh.com.au/sport/tennis/nick-kyrgios-racquet-manufacturer-yonex-starts-fining-its-players-for-smashes-20170120-gtvgx8.html.

This percolates through all levels of tennis, as Lake discovered in his auto-ethnographic study of a suburban London tennis club. What Lake refers to as '[t]he club's code of behavioural etiquette' encouraged members to adopt behaviours in keeping with the spirit of tennis, and to avoid overt displays of aggression. Lake ties these expectations to the traditions born of the historical development of the sport: 'These standards rooted in history were cherished to protect tennis from unsavoury influences like over-aggression, petulance and dishonesty ... deferential treatment was expected from those lower in the social hierarchy, and signs of disrespect or ignorance to these behavioural standards were felt as collective assaults on the club's established value-system.'[32] As Lake makes clear in the excerpt above, the transgressions can be physical, but they can also manifest in other ways, such as verbally or through gestures or other actions.

2.1.2 Audible Obscenity, Visible Obscenity and Verbal Abuse

The offences of 'audible obscenity', 'visible obscenity' and verbal abuse' seek to minimise the verbal and psychological forms of violence that Guilbert describes as common features of tennis.[33] When it comes to obscenity, the offences proscribe the use of 'profane' language and obscene gestures. As noted above, this is often self-directed, and a result of frustration,[34] with players seemingly unable to restrain themselves.[35] Since the offence of 'audible obscenity' covers 'the use of words commonly known and understood to be profane and uttered clearly and loudly enough to be heard by the Court Officials or spectators', those willing to be creative with their swearing may escape punishment. This has caused some controversy, insofar as it privileges those who do not speak English or use well-known expletives from other languages.[36]

The offence of 'verbal abuse' makes it clear that it is not just particular words that will invite a Code violation, but the way in which they are directed at somebody. One of the most notorious examples of a player being punished for this type of behaviour occurred during a third-round

---

[32] Robert J Lake, '"They Treat Me Like I'm Scum": Social Exclusion and Established-Outsider Relations in a British Tennis Club' (2013) 48 Int Rev Soc Sport 112, at 121.
[33] Sèbastien Guilbert, 'Sport and Violence: A Typological Analysis' (2004) 39 Int Rev Sociol Sport 45.
[34] Hanegby and Tenenbaum, 'Blame It on the Racket', 117.
[35] Christopher Clarey, 'Where Four-Letter Words Lead to Four-Figure Fines', *New York Times* (3 June 2015), available at: www.nytimes.com/2015/07/01/sports/tennis/at-slam-events-players-prefer-other-four-letter-words.html.
[36] Ibid.

match at Wimbledon in 1995 between Jeff Tarango and Alexander Mronz. Tarango was given a Code violation for 'audible obscenity' by the chair umpire Rebeuh after he told the crowd to 'shut up'. Tarango challenged Rebeuh over whether this was sufficient to amount to 'obscenity' and asked for the supervisor to attend. The supervisor did attend, but did not overturn the Code violation warning. When Rebeuh sought to resume play, Tarango refused, shouting at the umpire: 'You are the most corrupt official in the game, and you can't do this.' This earned Tarango a further Code violation for 'verbal abuse', at which point Tarango 'threw a pair of tennis balls to the ground, grabbed his bag and became the first player in Wimbledon history to walk out in the middle of the game'.[37] Leaving the court without permission meant that Tarango was defaulted.[38] In what was the most surprising and shocking aspect of the episode, Tarango's wife Benedicte Tarango came onto the court and slapped Rebeuh twice across the face.

3   Indiscipline and the Rising Popularity and Commercial Success of Tennis

Two observations should be made about the misconduct of Jeff Tarango described above. First, it was out of character; he had not received a Code violation before the events described above, and he never did in his subsequent tennis career. Second, it came at or towards the end of the high point of bad behaviour in tennis. In the 1970s and 1980s, tennis had witnessed the outspoken and iconoclastic antics of players such as John McEnroe, Jimmy Connors and Ilie Năstase. Lake notes that these three players, whom he refers to as the 'bad boys' of tennis, were also apt to be crowd favourites, and thus an inevitable crowd draw.[39] The increasing popularity of tennis brought commercial opportunities, and what Lake refers to as 'the commodification of "bad boy" tennis' was at least partly responsible for the increasing popularity of the sport in the 1970s and 1980s.[40]

---

[37] J. A. Adande, 'Tarango, Wife Aim Volleys at a Chair Umpire', *The Washington Post* (1 July 1995), available at: www.washingtonpost.com/archive/sports/1995/07/02/tarango-wife-aim-volleys-at-a-chair-umpire/84673f7f-0075-4861-8aef-e8da6bda0b5a/.
[38] See Art. IV(N) of the current iteration of the Code.
[39] Lake, *A Social History of Tennis in Britain*.
[40] Ibid., 186.

3.1 The Influence of Sponsors

The increased popularity of tennis made it commercially attractive, and the amount of money in tennis has increased markedly in the Open era. The relative wealth enjoyed by modern tennis comes principally from sponsors and the sale of broadcast rights, and the sums involved are significant. For instance, the sponsorship deal entered into by the Australian Open with its principal sponsor, Kia, is worth AU$107 million in the five years up to 2028 (Kia has been the main sponsor of the Open since 2002).[41] In addition, in November 2022, the Open signed a $500 million, five-year broadcasting deal with the Australian broadcaster Nine, covering broadcast rights from 2025 until 2029.[42]

Sponsors engage with tennis (and other sports) because of a perceived alignment between their brand and the sport,[43] and in the belief that it will positively affect their business. Research shows that bad behaviour and ill-discipline on the part of athletes can harm the interests of sponsors;[44] the move by the manufacturer to penalise players who smash Yonex racquets reflects this concern. Yonex did not comment publicly on its decision, and it is rare for sponsors to issue public statements about concerns within a sport. However, there have been other instances where misconduct has clearly affected sponsorship arrangements in tennis. For example, major sponsors Nike and Tag Heuer cut ties with tennis player Maria Sharapova (at the time the world's highest paid female athlete) when she admitted testing positive to the banned drug meldonium in 2016.[45] Misconduct can also affect the sponsorship of sports organisations: after unruly behaviour by the US team in the Davis Cup final against Sweden in 1984, sponsor Louisiana-Pacific Corporation threatened to withdraw its support unless the US Tennis

---

[41] Sam Buckingham-Jones, 'Kia Signs Record $107m Deal with Tennis Australia', Financial Review (10 January 2023), available at: www.afr.com/companies/media-and-marketing/kia-signs-record-107-million-deal-with-tennis-australia-20230110-p5cbka.
[42] Edmund Tadros and Gus McCubbing, 'Tennis Australia-Nine Seal Record $425m Deal', Financial Review (11 November 2022), available at: www.afr.com/companies/media-and-marketing/nine-seals-australian-open-deal-for-425m-20221111-p5bxdo.
[43] Kia, 'Australian Open', available at: www.kia.com/au/discover-kia/sponsorship/australian-open.html.
[44] Qi Ge and Brad R. Humphreys, 'Athlete Off-Field Misconduct, Sponsor Reputation Risk, and Stock Returns' (2021) 21 Eur Sport Manag Q 153; Christopher Knittel and Victor Stango, 'Celebrity Endorsements, Firm Value, and Reputation Risk: Evidence from the Tiger Woods Scandal' (2014) 60 Manag Sci 21.
[45] Jessica Elgot, 'Nike and Tag Heuer Cut Ties with Maria Sharapova', *The Guardian* (8 March 2016), available at: www.theguardian.com/sport/2016/mar/08/nike-and-tag-heuer-cut-ties-with-maria-sharapova.

Association put in place a code of conduct.[46] A contemporary newspaper reported the principal concern of this development: 'Rule One is that they must "act with courtesy and civility towards competitors, officials and spectators".'[47]

There is a tension here. Governing bodies and sponsors purport to desire sport that is free from indiscipline in all its many forms, but sport must be engaging in order to appeal to its audience. As the experience of tennis in the 1970s and 1980s suggests, some forms of indiscipline may add to the allure of a sport and heighten its value as entertainment. Writing of the appeal of aggression and violence in sport, including tennis, Bryant, Zillmann and Raney state: 'The extant evidence clearly indicates that increased player aggressiveness enhances spectators', especially male spectators', enjoyment of watching sports contests . . . and . . . commentary that stress[es] hostility and animosity between opponents can cause spectators to perceive play as more violent than it is and also can result in greater enjoyment for spectators.'[48] During a particularly tempestuous second-round match between John McEnroe and Ilie Năstase at the US Open in 1979, chair umpire Frank Hammond defaulted Năstase and awarded the match to McEnroe after issuing numerous warnings to Năstase for delaying play. The resultant crowd disturbance was later described by Năstase as 'total chaos' and led to the police being called.[49] In order to quell the discontent, tournament director Bill Talbert and tournament referee Mike Blanchard removed Hammond as umpire, with Blanchard taking his place in the chair. Blanchard revoked the default and reinstated Năstase, and the match was allowed to continue.[50] The lesson that McEnroe learned was clear; as he wrote in his autobiography: 'the rules of tennis are eternally flexible and . . . promoters generally were loath to spoil a crackling good show by booting a crowd-pleasing marquee name'.[51]

---

[46] Lake, *A Social History of Tennis in Britain*, 190.

[47] Sally Jenkins, 'USTA Sets Rules for Davis Conduct: Outbursts in Series with Sweden Seen Principal Impetus for Action', *The Washington Post* (15 January 1985), available at: www.washingtonpost.com/archive/sports/1985/01/16/usta-sets-rules-for-davis-conduct/ee14e661-d5a3-4578-90b9-13c3d8520ed0/.

[48] Jennings Bryant, Dolf Zillmann and Arthur A. Raney, 'Violence and the Enjoyment of Media Sports' in Lawrence Wenner (ed.), *MediaSport* (Routledge, 1998), 265.

[49] Ilie Năstase, *Mr. Năstase: The Autobiography* (CollinsWillow, 2005), 235.

[50] Jane Gross, 'Hammond Concedes He Lost Control', *New York Times* (1 September 1979), available at: www.nytimes.com/1979/09/01/archives/hammond-concedes-he-lost-control-persuaded-to-return-hammond-cedes.html.

[51] John McEnroe, *Serious* (Time Warner Paperbacks, 2002), 190.

4 Adjudication and Enforcement

Reinstating Năstase was an egregious example, but it illustrates the point that adjudication and enforcement of the Code can be as important as its substantive contents.[52] Studies have suggested that 'home advantage' could contribute to inconsistent decision-making by tennis officials,[53] and this potential for bias extends to disciplinary matters.[54] As I have written elsewhere, popular opinion and media representations of players may influence the disciplinary action taken in relation to certain players:

> [T]he governing body is likely to be sensitive to popular opinion, as viewed through the lens of media characterisations and representations, which can be a significant spur to decisive action. This may lead to calls for greater punishment, including on the basis of a participant's past conduct and reputation. A recent comparison between the relative treatment of Australian professional players Nick Kyrgios and Daria Gavrilova suggested that 'crowd favourite' Gavrilova received considerably less opprobrium than Kyrgios for more serious disciplinary infractions.[55]

The significance of enforcement practices independent from the substantive rules has importance beyond any implicit bias on the part of the officials. Some of the Rules of Tennis are routinely broken without any consequence for the offending players. For instance, a study of Grand Slam matches by Kolbinger, Großmann and Lames found that time rule violations occurred in relation to 58.5 per cent of serves (i.e. beyond the 20 seconds permitted between points), with only 0.1 per cent of these violations penalised by the umpire.[56]

As long as it is applied consistently, this deviation from the law on the books is unlikely to prove controversial. But the appropriateness of 'temporal variance' in sport, whereby different rules are enforced in different ways at different points in a match, is more divisive. Berman discusses temporal variance in the application of the 'foot fault' rule in the 2009 US Open semi-final match between Serena Williams and Kim

---

[52] Fred d'Agostino, 'The Ethos of Games' in William J. Morgan and Klaus V. Meier (eds), *Philosophic Inquiry in Sport* (Human Kinetics, 1995).
[53] Fabian Wunderlich, Carla Corten, Philip Furley et al., 'Home Advantage in Tennis Exists Independent of Competition Level, Gender and COVID-19 Restrictions: Evidence from German Team Tennis Competitions' (2022) 2 Int J Sport Exerc Psychol 1.
[54] Chris Goumas, 'Home Advantage and Referee Bias in European Football' (2014) 14 Eur J Sport Sci 243.
[55] Livings and Wlodarczak, 'Procedural Fairness'.
[56] Otto Kolbinger, Simon Großmann and Martin Lames, 'A Closer Look at the Prevalence of Time Rule Violations and the Inter-Point Time in Men's Grand Slam Tennis' (2019) 5 J Sport Anal 75.

Clijsters. In this match, Williams was penalised for a foot fault by stepping over the baseline when serving. In arguing with the chair umpire about this, Williams was given a Code violation which ultimately resulted in her losing the match. For Berman, a minor infraction such as a foot fault should not be called at crucial points in a tennis match.[57] For Standen, however, this variance in the enforcement of the rules is never appropriate.[58]

5 The Case of Grunting

The practice and treatment of 'grunting' in tennis has also proven a controversial topic in recent decades. Aside from often-expressed aesthetic objections to grunting, there are legitimate sporting reasons to be concerned about the practice. Although some studies point to grunting as a useful – even necessary – technique in tennis,[59] other research shows that it could affect the opponent's anticipation of the ball trajectory, and that this could confer an unfair competitive advantage over the opponent.[60] This is potentially contrary to Rule 26 of the Rules of Tennis, which provides: 'If a player is hindered in playing the point by a deliberate act of the opponent(s), the player shall win the point', going on to say that an unintentional hindrance will result in a replay of the point. In addition to potentially being captured under the Rules of Tennis, grunting could also fall foul of Article IV(L) of the Code, as an example of 'unsportsmanlike conduct'.

Grunting has been happening in tennis since at least the 1970s, with Jimmy Connors a noted practitioner, but it became something of a 'moral panic' when young female players like Monica Seles started grunting in the late 1980s. The noises made by Seles during her 1992 Wimbledon

---

[57] Mitchell N. Berman, 'Let 'Em Play: A Study in the Jurisprudence of Sport' (2011) 99 Geo LJ 1325.

[58] Jeffrey Standen, 'Foot Faults in Crunch Time: Temporal Variance in Sports Law and Antitrust Regulation' (2014) 41 Pepp L Rev 349.

[59] Dennis G. O'Connell, Martha R. Hinman, Kevin F. Hearne et al., 'The Effects of "Grunting" on Serve and Forehand Velocity in Collegiate Tennis Players' (2014) 28 J Strength & Cond Res 469; Dennis G. O'Connell, Jacob F. Brewer, Timothy H. Man et al., 'The Effects of Forced Exhalation and Inhalation, Grunting, and Valsalva Maneuver on Forehand Force in Collegiate Tennis Players' (2016) 30 J Strength & Cond Res 430.

[60] Florian Müller, Lars Jauernig and Rouwen Cañal-Bruland, 'The Sound of Speed: How Grunting Affects Opponents' Anticipation in Tennis' (2019) 14 *PLoS One*, available at: https://link.gale.com/apps/doc/A582459966/HRCA?u=unisa&sid=googleScholar&xid=4a01ae70.

semi-final win over Martina Navratilova led to complaints from her opponent and negative media coverage for Seles,[61] and prompted a newspaper report that read: 'Few would deny that the sound of Seles is one of the least aesthetic features of the sport. Though far removed from John McEnroe's obscenities, Seles's constant stream of exclamations, a cross between 'Je t'aime' and Tarzan, is offensive to the ears of spectators and opponents alike.'[62] For many, this juxtaposition of sexualisation (the reference to the Serge Gainsbourg and Jane Birkin song 'Je t'aime') and masculinisation (the reference to Tarzan) illustrates the gendered and sexist nature of the debate about grunting in tennis. Stahl suggests that 'efforts to police the sound reinscribe weakness onto femininity', and that this 'weakens her performance for the pleasure of the spectators and the neutralization of a competitive advantage'.[63]

Grunting continues to be a point of contention. During Wimbledon in 2009, the loud grunts of Portuguese player Michelle Larcher de Brito drew attention and complaints from both spectators and opponents. Although there was significant discussion about the possibility of implementing measures to control excessive grunting, Larcher de Brito was not formally penalised for her grunting.[64] Three years later, the WTA announced that it was working with the Grand Slam tournaments and the ITF to 'drive excessive grunting out of tennis'.[65] Despite considerable attention devoted to the subject, and the potential to use both the Rules of Tennis and the Code to combat it, no prominent player has been disciplined for grunting. There are no records of the hindrance rule being used as a response, nor are there any recorded instances of a player being given a Code violation for grunting.

---

[61] John Roberts, 'Grunt and Graf in Way of Seles Dream: The Determination of Monica Seles Came over Loud and Clear as She Beat Martina Navratilova Yesterday', *The Independent* (2 July 1992), available at: www.independent.co.uk/sport/tennis-wimbledon-92-grunt-and-graf-in-way-of-seles-dream-the-determination-of-monica-seles-came-over-loud-and-clear-as-she-beat-martina-navratilova-yesterday-1530972.html.

[62] Ibid.

[63] Anita Stahl, 'Somaesthetics of the Grunt Policing Femininity in the Soundscapes of Women's Professional Tennis' in Andrew Edgar (ed.), *Somaesthetics and Sport* (Brill, 2022), 142; cf. Tony Manfred, 'No, Wanting Women's Tennis Players to Stop Screaming All the Time Doesn't Make You Sexist', Business Insider (26 June 2012), available at: www.businessinsider.com/grunting-womens-tennis-isnt-sexist-2012-6.

[64] 'Larcher de Brito Cuts down on Volume at Wimbledon', Tennis.com (23 November 2009), available at: www.tennis.com/news/articles/larcher-de-brito-cuts-down-on-volume-at-wimbledon.

[65] See 'WTA Aims to Phase out Grunting', Essential Tennis, available at: www.essentialtennis.com/wta-aims-to-phase-out-grunting-tennis/.

6 Changes to the Rules

As Lumer notes, sports' rules and their enforcement are constantly evolving to meet the expectations of players and others: 'The rules of the various sports games are reformed constantly in practice ... or formally by the respective sports association. Usually, the reason for such reforms is raising social or moral desirability of the games: to make them more exciting or to adapt them to the individual preferences.'[66] Given its adherence to tradition, it is perhaps unsurprising that rule changes in tennis are a relative rarity, but developments in relation to on-court coaching and the Wimbledon dress code are recent standout examples where amendments have been made.

6.1 Coaching

Tennis is unusual in strictly limiting player–coach interaction during a match. In the football codes, for example, the coach, or indeed the whole coaching staff, can often be seen shouting instructions to the players during play. In tennis, however, the coach has been a more or less silent observer. The reasons for the restrictions are ostensibly competition-based; Malis and Michalica explain: 'Tennis is an individual sport, and the fact that coaching during a match is forbidden increases the pressure on the player themselves, thereby supporting the individual philosophy of the sport.'[67] Permitting coaching during play arguably impinges on the individuality of the sport and introduces the possibility of unfairness; the availability of on-court coaching would deleteriously affect those lower-ranked players who cannot afford to have a coach present at their matches.

The extent of on-court coaching in tennis is unclear, but it was widely believed to be common practice at all levels of the sport.[68] In the wake of Serena Williams receiving a warning during her fourth-round match against Naomi Osaka at the US Open in 2018, Williams's coach Patrick Mouratoglou suggested that the practice was ubiquitous. He stated that Osaka's coach Sascha Bajin had been coaching Osaka during the same match (a claim denied by Bajin).[69] If this is true, and on-court coaching

---

[66] Lumer, 'Rules and Moral Norms', 275.
[67] Malis and Michalica, 'Why Carlos Ramos Was in Compliance', 8.
[68] Steve Tignor, 'Has Tennis Figured out Its On-Court Coaching Problem, or Shown That It'll Never Be Solved?' Tennis.com (5 September 2023), available at: www.tennis.com/news/articles/has-tennis-figured-out-on-court-coaching-problem-never-solved-us-open-gauff.
[69] 'Mouratoglou: I Coached Serena from Stands', Tennis Now (September 2018), available at: www.tennisnow.com/Blogs/NET-POSTS/September-2018/Mouratoglou-I-Coached-Serena-From-Stands.aspx.

was ubiquitous, it was relatively rarely punished at the highest level: for instance, in 2018, 'a total of 22 code violations for coaching were awarded at all four Grand Slams'.[70] Because of its seeming prevalence and the relative infrequency with which it was detected or punished, the banned practice posed a problem in relation to detection and enforcement.

The rules around coaching have been relaxed in recent years, with a trial taking place from 2020 on the WTA Tour and from 2022 on the ATP Tour. Players and coaches have offered a range of opinions on the changes.[71] Some years before the advent of the trials, Mouratoglou suggested that the officially proscribed practice is endemic and that lifting the ban would help to popularise the sport, stating: 'Seeing and hearing the coaches and players talking to each other personalises the sport and brings out their characters.'[72] For Malis and Michalica, the relaxation of the rules was a necessary change: 'We believe that the change in coaching rules that the WTA has made in 2022 is a step in the right direction (ATP Tour 2022). It is a departure from the individual philosophy of the sport, but we do not see a better solution under the circumstances.'[73]

6.2 *Wimbledon*

Another recent change to the Code (as it applies in its amended form to the Wimbledon tournament[74]) relates to the famously strict clothing requirements that pertain to those participating at Wimbledon. Wimbledon has a reputation as the most conservative of the major tennis tournaments, possessing a 'stuffiness' that led to Andre Agassi refusing to play at the tournament in the late 1980s.[75] Central to its traditional

---

[70] Malis and Michalica, 'Why Carlos Ramos Was in Compliance', 7.
[71] Ben Miller, 'Tennis Coaching Rules: What Can Players and Coaches Do from Off-Court and Is In-Game Coaching Allowed?' The Sporting News (26 August 2024), available at: www.sportingnews.com/au/tennis/news/tennis-coaching-rules-court-game/gylwoan0ijaxlvlwgf5q4tf6.
[72] Alan O'Brien, 'Serena Williams Coach Patrick Mouratoglou Calls for On Court Coaching to Be Allowed', *The Independent* (18 October 2018), available at: www.independent.co.uk/sport/tennis/serena-williams-coach-patrick-mouratoglou-interview-us-open-2018-on-court-coaching-a8590651.html.
[73] Malis and Michalica, 'Why Carlos Ramos Was in Compliance', 9.
[74] 'About Wimbledon: Clothing and Equipment', available at: www.wimbledon.com/en_GB/about_wimbledon/clothing_and_equipment.html.
[75] Richard C. Crepeau, 'Andre Agassi' (2006) On Sport & Society 716. This conservatism seemingly lives on in the suburban tennis clubs of England. See Lake, 'They Treat Me Like I'm Scum'.

aesthetic has been its insistence on all-white playing attire,[76] and numerous players have fallen foul of the dress code requirements. For instance, in 2017, Venus Williams was reportedly asked to change her pink bra after it became visible under her white top during play.[77] In 2023, however, Wimbledon introduced a significant change to its dress code, allowing female players to wear dark-coloured undershorts beneath their all-white outfits. This change was undertaken to address concerns about competing while menstruating.[78]

6.3 Changes in Adjudication and Enforcement Practices

The changes to the coaching rules and the Wimbledon dress code are relatively rare examples of substantive rule changes. More subtle, but no less important, are shifts in the interpretation and enforcement of the written rules. To pick two examples in the realm of tennis, there have been observable changes in relation to race and mental health. These are areas in which the approach of the tennis authorities has clearly been affected by changing social mores, and perhaps with an eye on the views and desires of the sponsors.

6.3.1 Race

Tennis has largely moved past the overt racism experienced by black players such as Althea Gibson and Arthur Ashe.[79] However, opinions are divided on the extent to which positive change has been achieved. Leppard describes sport as essentially a 'white space'; he states that '[t]he punitive treatment of black players in the world of sports demonstrates the continuation of racism albeit less overt'.[80] Leppard asserts that 'athletes of colour like Venus and Serena Williams have continued to face racism throughout their careers which highlights that the world of tennis remains a white space despite the work of trailblazers'.[81]

---

[76] See 'About Wimbledon: Clothing and Equipment'.
[77] Patrick Sawer, 'Venus Williams Changes Bright Pink Bra Mid-Match after Breaching Wimbledon's "All White" Rule', *The Telegraph* (3 July 2017).
[78] See 'About Wimbledon: Clothing and Equipment'.
[79] Yven Destin and Ervin Dyer, 'The Legacies of Tennis Champions Althea Gibson, Arthur Ashe, and the Williams Sisters Show the Persistence of America's Race Obstacles' (2021) 13 Race Soc Probl 195.
[80] Tom R. Leppard, 'Athlete Activism and the Role of Personal and Professional Positionality: The Case of Naomi Osaka' (2022) 57 Int Rev Sociol Sport 1214, at 1215.
[81] Ibid., 1219.

Tredway offers a similarly trenchant account of the racism faced by players such as Serena Williams, and offers an account of how this colours how she is perceived:

> Serena is very successful in a sport that is underpinned by the upper-class and white milieu in which it was formed. Her outbursts have been understood in the popular discourse as violent not because they were more vehement than others, because they were not, but ... because Serena has been positioned differently in women's tennis, both historically and currently, than her White counterparts. These outbursts trigger a heightened perception of violence as compared to similar outbursts by White tennis players because Serena is not viewed as possibly the greatest tennis player to have ever played the sport, but as a Black woman and Black women are perceived to be violent.[82]

For Tredway, this has had real implications for how the rules are interpreted and enforced when it comes to Williams's conduct:

> The rules, however, have not been regularly interpreted for other players in the ways that they were interpreted for Serena, if ever. In this sense, Serena is forced to play competitive tennis by different rules (because the rules are interpreted differently for her) than others in women's tennis. Her outbursts are how she highlights this rift in the disciplinary domain of the matrix of domination, as anyone would who was treated unfairly. What, then, is different about Serena in the world of women's tennis? It seems too obvious to state that it is her race; however, that is the primary difference between Serena and the other players.[83]

As the pre-eminent female player of her generation, Serena Williams has clearly had a significant impact on tennis, and it is arguable that this is comparable to the male players of the 1970s and 1980s in the way that she has changed perceptions about the women's game, and the place of women of colour in tennis. Malis and Michalica point to the contrasting treatment of Serena Williams in the 2009 and 2018 US Open as evidence that the tennis authorities are 'influenced by American society's greater sensitivity to gender issues' and point to this as having a direct and positive effect on the operation of the rules.[84]

Tredway argues that the Williams sisters have 'normalised' a previously incongruent 'Black aesthetic and performance' that has paved the way for

---

[82] Kristi Tredway, 'Serena Williams and (the Perception of) Violence: Intersectionality, the Performance of Blackness, and Women's Professional Tennis' (2020) 43 Ethn Racial Stud 1563, at 1564.

[83] Ibid., 1577.

[84] Malis and Michalica, 'Why Carlos Ramos Was in Compliance', 3.

others to follow;[85] she points to players like Madison Keys, Coco Gauffe and Taylor Townsend as benefitting from, and continuing, this.

6.3.2 Mental Health

The experiences of Naomi Osaka also illustrate developments in the relationships between players, tournament organisers and spectators. Osaka sees herself as an activist advocating for change as a woman of colour on the tour,[86] but she has also been at the forefront of mental health awareness. At the 2021 French Open, Osaka declared that she would not be engaging with the media during the tournament, claiming that the interactions were deleterious to her mental health. Osaka then refused to attend the post-match press conference after her first-round victory over Patricia Maria Tig. The French Tennis Federation fined Osaka US$15,000 and threatened her with expulsion. This was later compounded by threats of further fines and expulsion from other Grand Slam tournaments.[87] After Osaka withdrew from the event, she was met with messages of support from her national federation, major sponsors and high-profile figures within and outside of tennis.[88]

The negative reaction to their punitive approach seemingly led to significant backtracking on the part of the tennis authorities, with statements issued on behalf of the four Grand Slam tournaments offering 'support and assistance' to Osaka.[89] Although her experience was not explicitly cited as inspiration, in 2023, Roland-Garros implemented an 'anti-online harassment and hate speech tool'. This measure used artificial intelligence software to protect players from online abuse, and its implementation tacitly acknowledged the obligations of the tennis authorities amid a shifting understanding, appreciation and prioritisation of mental well-being.[90]

---

[85] Tredway, 'Serena Williams', 1571.
[86] Leppard, 'Athlete Activism'.
[87] 'Statement from Grand Slam Tournaments Regarding Naomi Osaka', Roland-Garros (30 May 2021), available at: www.rolandgarros.com/en-us/article/statement-from-grand-slam-tournaments-regarding-naomi-osaka.
[88] 'Naomi Osaka: Grand Slams Want "Meaningful Improvements" & to "Advance Mental Health"', BBC (1 June 2021), available at: www.bbc.com/sport/tennis/57323649.
[89] Ibid.
[90] Jean-Baptiste Baretta, 'Roland-Garros 2023: Players to Get Social Media Protection', Roland-Garros (22 May 2023), available at: www.rolandgarros.com/en-us/article/roland-garros-2023-players-social-media-protection-bodyguard.

12

Compatibility of Selected ATP Rules with EU Economic Law

KATARINA PIJETLOVIC

1 Introduction

Sports governing bodies (SGBs) are normally entities in a position of regulatory monopolies that simultaneously occupy the dominant position on the organisational market for their sport. The conflict of interest created by such conflation of regulatory and commercial functions enables them to use their regulatory powers to protect their commercial dominance by imposing various market restrictions on actual and potential commercial rivals, players and investors. Unlike many other sports, the restrictive regulatory rules that govern professional tennis have never been tested under the European Union's competition and free movement laws. The reasons for this can be traced back to the culture of compliance resulting from the inadequate governance standards, including issues with representation, transparency and accountability. The same reasons are the likely culprit behind the adoption and maintenance of Association of Tennis Professionals (ATP) restrictions on the economic activity of some groups of stakeholders in the tennis industry. Such regulatory restrictions emanating from SGBs are not necessarily illegal in the EU law order: the analytical framework supplied by the *Meca-Medina* case in competition law,[1] and the functionally equivalent *Gebhard* case[2] concerning freedom of movement, can be utilised by private regulators to defend their prima facie illegal rules, rendering them compliant if they satisfy certain requirements. To benefit from these judicially constructed justifications, rules that impede economic

---

[1] *David Meca-Medina and Igor Majcen* v. *Commission*, Case C-519/04 P, EU:C:2006:492.
[2] *Reinhard Gebhard* v. *Consiglio dell'Ordine degli Avvocati e Procuratori di Milano*, Case C-55/94, EU:C:1995:411.

activity must be intended for the attainment of legitimate objectives in the public interest, inherent in, and proportionate to those objectives.

This chapter will test two distinct ATP rules for their compliance with EU competition law and free movement as set out in the Treaty on the Functioning of the European Union (TFEU or the Treaty) and elaborated in the jurisprudence of the Court of Justice of the European Union (CJEU or the Court). They include rules and practices that restrict access to the market for tournament organisers and therefore hinder additional commercial opportunities for players, and discriminatory distribution of wild-card entries for the professional tennis tournaments. Before diving into the analysis, we will first address relevant governance issues to briefly explain the regulatory environment that enabled the adoption of the restrictive rules in the first place. The applicable legal framework and the main case law will then be detailed and lead into the discussion on the legality of the two selected ATP rules.

2 Good Governance Standards in Light of EU Law and Policy

Monopolistic private regulation stands in contrast to the competitive private regulation in which multiple private regulatory schemes compete for members on the basis of price and quality. Tennis belongs to neither of these categories. It is governed neither by a single global regulator, nor multiple regulators competing for members on the same segment of the market. As commented by Begović, 'global tennis governance resembles a network rather than a vertical-based organizational structure'.[3] The ATP, Women's Tennis Association (WTA) and the International Tennis Federation (ITF) have split the areas of regulatory competence and market among themselves, but closely cooperate on issues such as the international tennis calendar, ranking system and criteria concerning entry to tournaments. The European Council recognised the independence of SGBs and their right to organise themselves through appropriate associative structures in the way they see fit.[4] However, this right is not unfettered: in EU sports law and policy, it is conditional upon respect for law and principles of good governance, including transparency, democracy, accountability and proper representation of all affected

---

[3] For more details, see Chapter 8 of this volume.
[4] 'Declaration on the Specific Characteristics of Sport and Its Social Function in Europe, of which Account should be taken in Implementing Common Policies', Doc. 13948/00, Annex to the Presidency Conclusions, Nice (hereinafter, 'Nice Declaration').

stakeholders.[5] The European Union's emphasis is therefore not on the form of the organisational model, but on the standards of governance that exist within the chosen model in its internal dimension, and the respect for law in its external dimension.[6]

One of the very central aspects of any governance structure is the composition of its main decision-making boards. It is surprising that there are no (publicly available) rules specifying the composition, procedure and powers of the various ATP bodies. When it comes to tennis governance, the lack of transparency surrounding deliberations and agenda of the decision-making bodies makes any independent governance report, and therefore any criticism of the system, difficult. This may well be one of the reasons for the chronic lack of external scrutiny by the media and certainly explains why many players do not truly understand the tennis governance ecosystem and willingly accept the rules that might be working to their own detriment. The reference to their 'privilege' instead of right to participate and vote in the ATP, as enshrined in Rule 1.21 of the ATP Rulebook, is illustrative of the role they are assigned to play in the governance of their sport. In the ATP, while players are its most important stakeholders, they do not have a decisive influence. The ATP Players Advisory Council, which consists of nine current players, a coach and an alumni player, is given a consultative rather than a decision-making role.[7] This is seemingly compensated by the fact that the Council has the power to elect its representatives to the ATP Tour Board of Directors. The Board of Directors is composed of all-white male members. It consists of four player representatives and four tournament representatives, and in case of a voting tie between these two groups, the Chairman casts a decisive vote.[8] The current Chairman of the ATP, Andrea Gaudenzi, also serves on the Board of Directors of the ATP

---

[5] See Commission Staff Working Document, 'The EU and Sport: Background and Context, Accompanying Document to the White Paper on Sport', COM(2007) 391 final, para. 4.1, and Communication from the Commission to the European Parliament, the Council, the European Economic and Social Committee, and the Committee of the Regions, 'Developing the European Dimension in Sport' COM(2011) 12 final (18 January 2011).

[6] Katarina Pijetlovic, 'The European Football Competition Model (under Stress)' in Robby Houben (ed.), *Research Handbook on the Law of Professional Football Clubs* (Edward Elgar, 2023), 66.

[7] See 'ATP Announces Player Advisory Council for 2024', available at: www.atptour.com/en/news/2024-player-advisory-council.

[8] Previously, there were three player representatives on the Board: a former tournament director, former executive and agent at IMG, and one former tennis player who worked as a tennis commentator. This entrenched the tournament dominance at the ATP.

Media (the global sales, broadcast production and distribution arm of the ATP World Tour rights) and the ATP Data Innovations. The latter is a joint venture between the ATP Tour and ATP Media initiated by Gaudenzi in his first term as ATP Chairman, to manage and commercialise data including betting, media and performance. This represents a glaring conflict of interest in favour of the tournaments under the aegis of the ATP Tour Board of Directors.

Finally, it must be noted that the top players, as well as players from Europe and North America, are overrepresented in the ATP Players Advisory Council, while other groups are significantly underrepresented. An alternative design idea for the governance of men's tennis is to separate the tournament and player representative bodies altogether and engage in collective negotiations between the two parties, with equally strong bargaining positions.[9]

Whereas the EU economic provisions do not directly address the internal structure of the undertakings, the external economic effects of the rules governing the internal dimension of private regulation are subject to competition law scrutiny.[10] The poor governance standards in either case usually produce unfair or badly designed regulatory measures that negatively affect the economic activity of some of its participants. Against this background, we will now turn to the organisational market and applicable TFEU provisions and jurisprudence before evaluating the compliance of the two selected ATP rules with the legal demands set out therein.

3 Access to the Organisational Market for Rival Tennis Tours under Competition Law

3.1 Blocking Rivals from Accessing the Organisational Market

The organisational market in sports is important in terms of economic opportunities for investors, athletes and organisers alike. It consists of the market for organisation of sporting events that is connected to the upstream market (i.e. the supply market composed of everything and

---

[9] The establishment of the Professional Tennis Players Association (PTPA) is a good first step towards such a structure – see www.ptpaplayers.com.
[10] The biased board structures contributed to the Court's finding of illegal restrictions in API – *Anonima Petroli Italiana SpA and Others* v. *Ministero delle Infrastrutture e dei Trasporti and Others*, Joined Cases C-184/13–C-187/13, C-194/13, C-195/13 and C-208/13, EU:C:2014:2147, against a transport regulator.

everyone required to stage the competition) and the downstream market (i.e. the market for the exploitation of sporting rights through the sales of broadcasting and media rights, sponsorship rights, ticketing and merchandising).[11] It is worth emphasising that only the services of top-ranked athletes are not substitutable – they belong to a segment of the service market with a very low degree of cross-elasticity. The governing bodies that fulfil a dual function of being both regulators and organisers of competitions are in a position to block the entry of rivals to the organisational market by adopting a number of restrictive regulatory measures.

There are essentially three discernible methods.[12] One method is to make an entry to the market conditional upon obtaining the prior approval of the governing body.[13] Such approval is usually very difficult to obtain on paper or in practice, and even the mere existence of an improperly designed prior authorisation system can discourage any potential competitor from applying. The second method is to adopt the restrictions intended to block a competitor from accessing the supply market. Restrictive regulatory measures can be addressed to players and officials, threatening them with severe sanctions (such as fines or suspensions) if they join any unapproved alternative competition, which is usually enough to dissuade them from participating.[14] There is not much that SGBs can legally do if the alternative competition is organised in accordance with law and does not endanger any legitimate sporting objective of public interest, so this method may be viewed as a safety net for SGBs designed to block any 'rebel' organisers who decide to ignore the prior authorisation requirement. SGBs have control over uniform international ranking systems and point awards, and any competition that is not integrated into that system will face additional difficulties in attracting athletes. Finally, blocking access to the exploitation market can be achieved in many ways, chiefly by using both regulatory and commercial power. Governing bodies usually set the international calendar and

---

[11] Alexander Egger and Christine Stix-Hackl, 'Sports and Competition Law: A Never-Ending Story?' (2002) 23 Eur Comp L Rev 81–91, at 85.

[12] Katarina Pijetlovic, 'European Model of Sport: Alternative Structures' in Jack Anderson, Richard Parrish and Borja Garcia (eds), *Research Handbook on EU Sports Law and Policy* (Edward Elgar, 2018), 332–4.

[13] For an illustration, see *European Super League v. SL v. Fédération internationale de football association (FIFA) and Union of European Football Associations (UEFA)*, Case C-222/21, EU:C:2023:1011, discussed below.

[14] For an illustration, see *International Skating Union v. European Commission*, Case C-124/21 P, EU:C:2023:1012, discussed below.

are in a position to reserve attractive venues and broadcasting slots for their own competition. In the *FIA case*,[15] the regulator prohibited promoters from using circuits for races that presented a competitive threat to Formula One, and broadcasters were subjected to a fine in the amount of 50 per cent of their agreement if they aired a rival race.

3.2 Applicable EU Legal Framework

When private regulators engage in market-blocking practices, this necessarily raises legal concerns from the point of view of EU competition law, in particular Articles 101 and 102 of the TFEU on the prohibition of cartels and abuse of dominant market position, respectively. Any agreement between two or more undertakings[16] can be caught within the scope of the prohibition of Article 101(1) of the TFEU if it affects trade between EU Member States and has 'as its object or effect the prevention, restriction or distortion of competition' on the market. The concept of undertaking is interpreted broadly and includes sports associations such as the ITF and ATP. In addition to agreements, unilateral decisions and practices of the undertakings are also included in the scope of Article 101(1) of the TFEU to prevent them from evading competition rules on account of the form (i.e. a collective structure) in which they coordinate their conduct in the market.[17] Article 102 of the TFEU that prohibits abuse of dominant position on the market is aimed at the unilateral conduct of dominant undertakings. Sports associations not only commercially dominate the organisational market, but also control entry to it via their private regulatory powers. The conflict of interest brought about by such conflation of regulatory and commercial powers is not per se illegal under EU law; rather, there exist specific legal parameters under which such regulatory power can be exercised.

The formation of cartels and abuses of dominant position that constitute prima facie breaches of competition law may escape the designation of illegal restrictions on economic activity if they satisfy the conditions of

---

[15] Notice published pursuant to Art. 19(3) of Council Regulation No. 17 concerning Cases COMP/35.163 – Notification of FIA Regulations, COMP/36.638 – Notification by FIA/FOA of agreements relating to the FIA Formula One World Championship, COMP/36.776 – GTR/FIA and Others (2001/C 169/03).

[16] Defined as any entity engaged in economic activity, regardless of its legal status and the way in which it is financed. See *Höfner and Elser* v. *Macotron GmbH*, Case C-41/90, EU:C:1991:161, at para. 21.

[17] Opinion of Mr Advocate General Léger delivered on 10 July 2001 in *Wouters and Others* v. *Algemene Raad van de Nederlandse Orde van Advocaten*, ECLI:EU:C:2001:390.

the *Meca-Medina* test. Accordingly, any prima facie cartel or abusive measure will not breach competition law if it is adopted to attain a legitimate objective in the public interest (as opposed to private commercial interests); is inherent in the pursuit of the said objective; and is proportionate (i.e. it is capable of attaining the said objective and there are no less restrictive means available).[18] The legitimate objectives of sporting rules are usually perceived as necessary for the 'organisation and proper conduct of competitive sport',[19] such as the protection of athletes' health, the safety of spectators and participants, training and recruitment of young players, integrity of sport (e.g. match-fixing), ensuring a uniform and consistent exercise of a given sport, providing equal opportunities for all athletes, etc. The broad *Meca-Medina* test was applied to the rules of sports associations that control access to the organisational market in the judgments rendered in *European Super League (ESL)* and *International Skating Union (ISU)* in December 2023 by the CJEU. Prior to these two cases, the matter was addressed at EU level[20] only by the largely outdated EU Commission's *FIA* decision,[21] adopted prior to *Meca-Medina*, and the Court's ruling in the *MOTOE* case, decided under Article 106 of the TFEU, in conjunction with Article 102.

In *MOTOE*, the Court elaborated on the governance standards expected of SGBs that operate a prior authorisation system and simultaneously participate as undertakings on the organisational market. Because such conflict of interest allows private regulatory monopolies in sport to 'distort competition by favouring events which they organise or those in whose organisation it participates',[22] the Court's presumption was against the intent of SGBs in their role as market gatekeepers. In other words, the conflated regulatory and commercial functions afford a high degree of probability that SGBs will use their regulatory power to favour own events by, for instance, imposing discriminatory licensing terms, blocking third parties from access to the organisational market or

---

[18] *Meca-Medina*, at para. 42.
[19] Commission Communication, 'Developing the European Dimension in Sport', at para. 4.2; and Commission Decision of 8 December 2017 in *International Skating Union's Eligibility Rules (ISU)*, Case AT.40208, (2017) 8240 final.
[20] At the Member State level there were relevant decisions by national courts and competition authorities in pursuit of the enforcement of TFEU, Arts 101 and 102.
[21] While the restrictions identified in *FIA* remain relevant today, it is outdated for administrative remedies and justification purposes and will not be addressed further.
[22] *Motosykletistiki Omospondia Ellados NPID (MOTOE)* v. *Elliniko Dimosio*, Case C-49/07, EU:C:2008:376, at paras 51–2.

rendering such access commercially unattractive. The Court's presumption here is sound: empirical evidence strongly suggests that in the conflict of interest between safeguarding public interests and private commercial interests, commercial considerations will ultimately shape the actions of private regulators.[23] The *MOTOE* judgment therefore placed emphasis on procedural safeguards in the exercise of SGBs' gatekeeping functions, highlighting that the power of prior control must be made subject to 'restrictions, obligations and review'. A risk of abuse of regulatory power created by the conflation of regulatory and commercial functions will only be accepted insofar as SGBs are subjected to an appropriate standard of control.

ISU[24] involved two Dutch professional speed skaters who launched a challenge against the ISU eligibility rules.[25] The rules provided that skating or officiating in a non-authorised event rendered a person ineligible to participate in ISU activities and competitions up to a maximum period of one's lifetime, including the ISU Congress, the ISU events (such as the ISU World Cup and the ISU Speed Skating Championship), Olympic Winter Games, and other competitions, exhibitions and tours within the purview of the ISU. The threat of lifetime bans was enough to dissuade complainants and all other skaters from participating in alternative Icederby competitions that offered attractive financial packages and other benefits. Unable to secure skaters' services, Icederby was forced to abandon the organisation of its competitions.[26] Following the legal challenge before the EU Commission by the speed skaters, the ISU revised its rules to impose a sliding scale of sanctions, but the changes were cosmetic and inadequate to address competition concerns.

Not surprisingly, the ISU lost the case. In applying the *Meca-Medina* test, a series of legitimate objectives were put forth by the ISU, including protecting the integrity of speed skating from the risks associated with betting, the protection of health and safety in an inherently dangerous sport, the protection of the good functioning of the international calendar and the protection of uniform rules of sport. However, the specific content of the ISU eligibility rules backed up by severe sanctions

---

[23] Tim Bartley, *Rules without Rights: Land, Labor, and Private Authority in the Global Economy* (Oxford University Press, 2018).

[24] The *ISU* complaint was first filed before the EU Commission (administrative enforcer), the decision of which was appealed before the General Court (lower EU-level court) before finally being appealed in the CJEU ('the Court' – the supreme EU court).

[25] ISU General Regulations (2014), Rule 102(2)(c).

[26] *ISU*, Case AT.40208, at paras 67–9.

predestined them to fail the inherency requirement for the purposes of the *Meca-Medina* test. Even if they had been deemed inherent, the penalties imposed on skaters, including a five-year ban, were bound to fail for being 'manifestly disproportionate', particularly in light of the short careers of professional skaters.[27]

After the Court's judgments in *MOTOE* and *ISU*, the results of the European Super League (ESL)[28] legal challenge against UEFA were largely predictable. Article 49 of UEFA's Statutes[29] endowed UEFA with the sole jurisdiction to organise and abolish cross-border competitions in Europe, while all other competitions required its prior approval. The dispute ensued when UEFA refused to authorise a semi-closed ESL competition and threatened the participating clubs with bans from their lucrative domestic competitions. This threat was sufficient to block the ESL project.[30] UEFA's status as a regulatory body with power to exercise gatekeeping functions at the entry point to the organisational market in European football was confirmed by the Court as legitimate. The idea of leaving the public interests in the hands of private commercial entities, such as ESL, that have no responsibility over the sport was never seriously entertained by the Court – managing SGBs' conflict of interest by imposing the proper standards of governance in the exercise of their regulatory/gatekeeping functions was always the preferred option. In *ISU*, the General Court confirmed that the licensing requirements imposed by SGBs through a prior authorisation system must be clearly defined, non-discriminatory, objective, transparent, verifiable, reviewable and proportionate, and must be capable of ensuring effective access to the relevant market for the organisers of alternative events.[31] In *MOTOE*, the Court insisted that a system of undistorted competition can be guaranteed only if equality of opportunity is secured between all economic operators on the market.[32]

---

[27] *International Skating Union* v. *European Commission (ISU)*, Case T-93/18, EU:T:2020:610, at paras 92–3.
[28] *ESL*.
[29] UEFA Statutes (2024), available at: https://documents.uefa.com/v/u/07zyuoc_69TV_sHbFYvA2w.
[30] Even though other reasons were publicly advanced by the clubs ('we listened to our fans'), it was UEFA's threats and UK government interference that made the difference. Fan-based official opposition to ESL was publicly known prior to the ESL short-lived breakaway attempt.
[31] *ISU*, Case T-93/18, at paras 88, 118 and 129. See also *Ordem dos Técnicos Oficiais de Contas*, Case C-1/12, EU:C:2013:127, at para. 99.
[32] *MOTOE*, at para. 51.

The principles set out in this line of jurisprudence were confirmed and applied in the *ESL* case. Accordingly, UEFA was criticised for not having a procedural and substantive framework for its system of prior control, and for enforcing Article 49 of its Statutes through equally unpredictable and arbitrary sanctions, which rendered the system incompatible with EU competition law requirements. Apart from the obligation in Article 49 to obtain UEFA's prior approval, no guidance was provided to third-party organisers on how to submit the application; how many months in advance it should be submitted; what requirements should the aspiring third-party organisers fulfil to get the approval; what the sanctions for non-compliance are; and many others. Properly developed frameworks with a clear and complete set of rules serve as a safeguard that should, at least in theory, eliminate the risk of abuse of dominant position and arbitrary decisions. A notable novelty of the *ESL* judgment was confining the scope of the *Meca-Medina* justification and making it available only for those rules that restrict competition 'by effect'. For more severe 'by object' restrictions under Article 101 of the TFEU and equivalent rules which 'by their very nature' breach Article 102, only economic efficiency defence is available to SGBs. This is the category in which the Court placed UEFA's inadequately designed prior authorisation system and therefore limited the defences available to economic efficiency arguments.[33]

3.3 Rules 1.07, 1.14 and 8.05A(2)(e) of the ATP Rulebook

After briefly discussing the applicable legal parameters in EU competition law, it is not difficult to discern a number of potential legal issues in the manner that the ATP controls the organisational market in men's professional tennis. Rules 1.07 and 1.14 of the ATP Rulebook[34] are ostensibly designed with the purpose of protecting the commercial value involved in the ATP's own competitions by making it impossible for an alternative tour to appear on the market. Rule 1.07C designates top 30 players in the ATP rankings as 'commitment players'. The commitment for these players relates to obligatory participation in all of nine ATP Tour Masters 1000 tournaments, at least four ATP Tour 500 tournaments, one of which must be entered following the US Open,

---

[33] *ESL*, at paras 183–8.
[34] See 2024 ATP Official Rulebook, available at: www.itftennis.com/media/11553/2024-rulebook-atp.pdf.

and the Nitto ATP Finals (applicable only for top 8 players).[35] It is further clarified that the Monte Carlo Masters 1000 will be included in the minimum requirements for the ATP 500 category for commitment purposes. Should a player fail to comply with these commitments, he or she is labelled as not 'being in good standing with the ATP' under Rule 10.7F, which carries a wide range of sanctions, reprimands and lost benefits. This includes ineligibility to participate as a main draw entry in the following ATP season, loss of retirement programme benefits and 'the privilege to actively participate, including voting, in ATP governance'.[36] In practice, Rule 1.07 obliges the commitment players to enter at least twelve ATP tournaments, and top 8 players must also enter Nitto ATP Finals. Players are also obliged to play four Grand Slam tournaments that are integrated in the ATP tournament calendar and ranking system. Additionally, they might represent their country in the Davis Cup, which is also integrated in the ATP system. Depending on one's success in individual and Davis Cup events, a player may end up playing in up to twenty different events in one season that take up to twenty-seven weeks in the annual calendar.

The ATP Board of Directors' strategic '30-year plan' (adopted in 2021 and rebranded as 'OneVision') consolidated the existing market dominance and exclusivity of the ATP Tour events, increased the ATP calendar footprint by expanding the ATP Masters 1000 events and further tied in the services of the top players.[37] Preparations specific for the mandatory tournaments, which often involve playing other ATP tournaments, travelling and early arrivals to tournaments to get adjusted to the surface, time zone and weather conditions, must be factored into this formula. It adds about five to six extra weeks to the schedule of a top 30 player, amounting to up to thirty-four weeks. Tennis has a short four-week off-season. Such a schedule effectively requires a playing/participating time of thirty-eight weeks out of a fifty-one-week year. Top 10-ranked players usually play around twenty-one or twenty-two tournaments per season

---

[35] Rule 1.07D.
[36] Provided by a combination of Rule 1.21B and Rule 1.07F.
[37] The architect of the plan was Andrea Gaudenzi in his role of Director of ATP Media, right before he became Chairman of the ATP Tour. The players were not properly consulted and informed – see Samuel Gill, 'Statement PTPA/Djokovic: 'We Are Not Saying 30 Year Plan or ATP Is Bad, We Just Want More Clarity', Tennisuptodate.com (25 June 2021), available at: https://tennisuptodate.com/tennis-news/statement-ptpadjokovic-we-are-not-saying-30-year-plan-or-atp-is-bad-we-just-want-more-clarity.

on average[38] and prefer to mentally rest, practice and spend time with family for the remaining thirteen weeks of the year, rather than travel and compete. Tennis is extremely demanding not just in terms of its physicality, but also because tournaments are spread all over the globe, time zones and ATP Tour competition calendar. Some players in the top 30 will play a few more tournaments, but these will normally be ATP 500 or ATP 250 category events as no other alternatives are normally available.[39]

The remaining thirteen weeks of the year are subject to further restrictions and leave little space for the rival individual competitions, let alone a viable alternative tour.

Rule 1.14(1)B, explicitly designated as 'restrictions', provides a combination of temporal and geographical limitations that additionally prevent the participation of commitment players in alternative events:

- during the weeks of nine ATP Tour 1000 events, 13 ATP Tour 500 events, and ATP Nitto Finals;
- within 30 days before or after any of the above-listed tournaments, and during any of the 38 ATP Tour 250 tournaments, if the alternative event is located either within 100 miles/160 kilometres, or within the same market area of the city of any of the ATP tournaments (as determined by the ATP CEO).

Infringement of these rules carries penalties described as 'Major Offense Conduct Contrary to the Integrity of the Game' set out in Rule 8.05A(2)(e). Accordingly, a player is liable to a fine of up to US$250,000 and/or a suspension from play in the ATP Tour or ATP Challenger Tour tournaments for a period of up to three years.

3.4 Legality of the Rules 1.07, 1.14 and 8.05A(2)(e) and Reinforcing Practices under EU Competition Law

3.4.1 Restrictions

The ATP is highly likely a dominant undertaking[40] in the market for the organisation of professional tennis competitions. It has the largest calendar and broadcasting footprint; purchases players' services for more than

---

[38] As per information accessed on 31 March 2024, available at: www.atptour.com/en/rankings/singles.

[39] Ultimate Tennis Showdown (UTC) started during the Covid-19 pandemic as an exhibition that is not integrated into the ATP ranking or calendar. It stages only three events per season, each lasting only two to three days. It is not a competitive threat to the ATP Tour. For UTS tournaments, see www.uts.live.

[40] Regardless of the revenue distribution in which the ATP is second to the Grand Slams.

12 COMPATIBILITY OF ATP RULES WITH EU ECONOMIC LAW   275

half a season; holds a monopoly over ranking points and the annual tennis calendar; and possesses regulatory powers. The Grand Slams and the ITF use the ATP system for entry and seeding – in return, the ATP includes their tournaments in its calendar, awards ATP ranking points for their tournaments and agrees not to organise events that could conflict with them.[41] This arrangement between the long-established entities could be classified as a horizontal supply-and-market-sharing cartel under Article 101(1) of the TFEU that limits investments, markets and development of the sport. The OneVision plan on the ATP website confirms the relationship between these entities and stipulates that 'at times, we find ourselves competing rather than collaborating' before highlighting the need for a shared governance and operating model, aggregation of media and data rights, and working together towards a shared vision.[42] The ATP, Grand Slams and ITF can also be viewed as undertakings that are in a collectively dominant position on the market for organisation of professional men's tennis events (where they collectively hold a monopoly) and purchasing players' services (where they collectively amount to monopsony).

Regardless of the precise form in which the restrictions were adopted, Rules 1.07 and 1.14, as enforced by sanctions under Rule 8.05A(2)(e), and reinforced by tournament licensing practices, and arrangements with Grand Slams and the ITF, reserve many big markets and geographic areas in the world exclusively for the ATP Tour, leaving only insufficient space in the calendar and geographic markets for staging an individual event in which organisers may hope for the participation of some of the top 30 players. Access to this group of players is important for the commercial viability and success of any alternative venture. Hence, there is no doubt that the combination of those ATP rules and practices constitute prima facie restrictions on the players' economic opportunities, investments and third-party organisers. Counterintuitively, it is less of a restriction for the financially well-off top 30 players to whom the commitment rules are specifically addressed, than for the lower-ranked players who are free to play in any alternative tournament or tour. But without the top 30 players, it is difficult to stage a financially viable alternative for lower-ranked players, as there are no opportunities for investments, innovation or market development outside the established structures. Only around 100 or 150 top male players in the world, out of

---

[41] See Chapter 8 of this volume.
[42] Available at: https://onevision.atptour.com/onevision/phase-two.

thousands playing in ATP Tour, ATP Challenger Tour and ITF-level tennis, can earn a living from their profession. Occupying an empty space in the calendar and staging an exhibition that is neither included in the ATP calendar nor given ranking points will not attract the interest of the top 30 tennis players unless the investors are ready to incur significant losses by offering attractive appearance fees and prize money. This might happen on a one-off basis, but will not create an alternative tour, or sufficient number of individual competitions to provide options on a regular basis. Even if it did, the top 30 players would still be obliged to participate in ATP and Grand Slam events for most of the year.

A standard way to enter the market for the organisation of professional men's tennis tournaments is to obtain a licence for one of the ATP tournaments that is already integrated into the ATP calendar and assigned classification and ranking points. Instead of competing with the ATP Tour, aspiring entrants can become a part of it. No transparent and objective licensing requirements or procedures have been clearly specified as required by the *ISU* and *ESL* judgments, and there is no system of 'restrictions, obligations and review' in case of rejection as required by *MOTOE*. Moreover, the ATP's OneVision plan has granted thirty-year licences and category protection to ATP 1000 Masters tournaments, and fifteen years to ATP 500 tournaments. This extremely lengthy period is coupled by three related restrictions:

- the contractual promise to licence-holders to restrict the number of licences for both categories;[43]
- a prohibition on participation fees and the introduction of a maximum level of prize money that tournaments can offer, which amounts to a hard-core price-fixing cartel[44] and prevents intra-brand competition; and
- an exclusivity protection for ATP Masters 1000 events that no other ATP Tour competition will be staged at the same time.[45]

Thus, players who are not qualified for the ATP 1000 Masters tournaments by virtue of their ranking, or as wild-card entries, do not have any Tour-level competition for the duration of the Masters event. For

---

[43] See George Patten, 'Grading Each Potential New Masters 1000 Venue', Lob & Smash (24 February 2024), available at: https://lobandsmash.com/posts/grading-each-potential-new-masters-1000-venue.
[44] ATP Regulations (2024), Exhibit J.
[45] *Super Slam Ltd* v. *ATP Tour Inc.*, Complaint filed in Delaware District Court dated 15 July 2021.

example, in the 2024 ATP Tour calendar, there are only two Masters tournaments scheduled in March. The ATP envisaged one additional ATP 1000 Masters (on grass) and up to three ATP 500 category tournaments to be added in the future, but did not specify the procedure or substantive rules by which they should be selected – the decision is left entirely to the discretion of the ATP. The idea of an ATP Super Tour is currently on the table, whereby the Grand Slam and ATP 1000 events overshadow other categories of tournaments.

While each of the identified restrictions should be subject to a separate legal evaluation, they reinforce one another, provide overall context in which they operate, and generate a cumulative foreclosure effect on the market for the organisation of tournaments and provision of players' services.

3.4.2 Legitimate Objectives and Proportionality

Whether the restrictions created by the described rules and practices can be classified as 'object' or 'effect' restrictions will not be the subject of discussion here. It is presumed that they restrict competition by effect and that the *Meca-Medina* justification framework applies. Under that framework, the ATP can mount arguments fitting the broad justification of 'organisation and proper conduct of competitive sport'. Specifically, for a good functioning of the ATP Masters 1000 events, it might be necessary to secure the participation of the best players in the world to preserve the sporting value and qualitative status of the ATP Masters events, and to afford them a certain degree of exclusivity. The establishment of a uniform international calendar and preventing overlaps between events are certainly in the public interest and fall within the regulatory competence of sports governing bodies.[46] As held by the Advocate General in *MOTOE*: 'It may make sense to prevent clashes between competitions so that both sportspersons and spectators can participate in as many such events as possible.'[47] However, by insisting on calendar exclusivity, the ATP blocks all players not eligible for Masters tournaments from the international calendar for the duration of ninety days per season, with this being a disproportionate restriction on their participation in the market as service providers.[48] With specific reference to the ATP 250 tournament, if played elsewhere in the world, it would not

---

[46] *ISU*, at para. 219.
[47] Opinion of AG Kokott in *MOTOE*, delivered on 6 March 2008, at para. 94.
[48] The claim can also be made under Art. 56 of the TFEU on the freedom to provide services.

present a competitive threat to the Masters 1000 on the exploitation market, apart from perhaps domestic broadcasting rights, which are negligible. An overlap in the calendar would not matter for any legitimate sporting or commercial purpose. Moreover, even without Rules 1.07, 1.14 and 8.05A(2)(e), ATP Masters-level tournaments can be expected to attract most of the top 30 players on the basis of their prize money and ranking points. They already possess the status of superior tournaments by their very classification, and there are no other tournaments for the players to enter when Masters events are staged. With this in mind, Rules 1.07 and 1.14 appear unnecessary, while their enforcement by Rule 8.05A (2)(e) providing for a possible three-year ineligibility ban and US$250,000 fine is disproportionate even with regard to participation in any future exhibition outside the ATP calendar.

The ATP can argue that long-term licences for ATP 500 and 1000 categories encourage investments and improvement of its flagship competitions and contribute to the organisers' financial stability. A counterargument could be persuasively made that while propping up these competitions, it discourages investments by ATP 250 organisers because they cannot be upgraded to the higher category for a very long period of time. Also, the length of the protection for the licence-holders is manifestly disproportionate. In general, vertical agreements that exceed five years are considered disproportionate for most types of investments – considering the position of the parties to the agreement and the overall market set up in the case at hand, it is certain that the length of licences would fail to satisfy the proportionality limb of the *Meca-Medina* test. In sports broadcasting cases, the EU Commission considered three years of exclusivity as an upper limit,[49] following which the new tender should be published with open, transparent, objective and non-discriminatory criteria. Consequently, the duration of licences should be no longer than five years, while the exclusivity afforded to ATP Masters 1000 tournament organisers should be made less exclusive.

Limits on the maximum prize money per category of tournament and a prohibition on participation fees might well be intended to protect the hierarchy between the different categories. Players would possibly choose to participate in ATP 250s if offered higher financial rewards than ATP 500 tournaments. A requirement that ATP 250 tournaments do not exceed a certain threshold of prize money ensures good

---

[49] See Commission Decisions in COMP/37.398, UEFA Champions League, OJ 2003 L291/25; Case COMP/C-2/38.173, Joint Selling of Media Rights to the FA Premier League, OJ C 2006/868 final; and Decision COMP/C.2/37.214, Joint selling of the media rights to the German Bundesliga, OJ 2005 L134/46.

functioning of ATP 500 events and is thus reasonable. However, there seems to be no reason why the maximum prize money limit should also apply to ATP 500 events. ATP Masters 1000 events are unlikely to be affected even if mandatory top 30 participation and exclusivity are removed from the equation. As stated above, due to the ranking points awarded, top players would likely choose on their own to participate in most Masters events to the exclusion of other tournaments staged at the same time. Any limitation on prize money for reasons linked to protecting the good functioning of the ATP Tour should be limited to ATP 250 events.

Setting a limit on the number of ATP 1000 Masters and ATP 500 tournaments does not appear unusual or unreasonable – all sports have different categories of competitions, and it would dilute the value and quality of the flagship tournaments and the whole tour if licences were issued in unlimited numbers. This argument could work if the ATP reviews the process of awarding licences and creates a procedural framework for clearly defined, non-discriminatory, objective, transparent, verifiable, reviewable and proportionate criteria. Additionally, a need for mainstreaming is apparent from the inconsistent Masters tournament lengths and number of participants. The status of the Monte Carlo tournament is confusing as it is Masters 1000 in name, but ATP 500 in quality – and commitment players are exempted from obligatory participation, but can use it for one of the four obligatory ATP 500s. In the *ESL* case, had UEFA's threat of sanctions against the alternative league taken place within the properly designed procedural framework and contained detailed substantive rules designed according to *ISU* and *MOTOE* criteria, it would have likely been found to be compatible with EU law. The lack of procedural framework for otherwise legitimate ATP rules could therefore prove fatal if challenged.

4   Wild Cards under the Lens of Article 56 of the TFEU on the Freedom to Provide Services

4.1   Wild Cards in Tennis

According to Rule 7.12 of the ATP Rulebook, wild cards are players who have not qualified for a tournament, but are nevertheless awarded entry to the main draw. Because invitations to wild cards are extended 'at the sole discretion of the tournament', the issue of discrimination between players of different nationalities in the implementation of Rule 7.12 could have been easily foreseen.[50] Tournaments have generally drafted policies on wild-card entries to enable the participation of star players returning from injuries, young (mostly local) talents and local players who have not earned their place in the draw on the basis of objective ranking-based criteria. This often prevents the participation in important tournaments of more deserving players. The ITF has an equivalent provision, namely, Rule V(I),[51] and Grand Slam tournaments are subject to Rule Z(2)(b) on wild cards.[52] The French Tennis Federation policy awards most of the wild cards for the Roland-Garros entries specifically to players from France.[53] Likewise, the US Open and Australian Open also issue most of their wild-card entries to local players. Within the framework of the agreement that the French Tennis Federation has with the US Tennis Association (USTA) and Tennis Australia, one ATP and one WTA player from the United States and Australia are to be awarded a wild card for the main Roland-Garros draw. The favour is returned by Tennis Australia and USTA when they organise their Grand Slam tournaments.[54] ATP tournaments of various categories, many of them in the European Union, implement a similar system of preference for local players. It is therefore no surprise that the highest number of wild-card entries in the history of tennis were awarded to Andy Murray from the United Kingdom (fifty-four WCs).[55] The highest number of wild-card entries up until the age of 25 were awarded to three players from the United States: Ryan Harrison (thirty-four WCs), followed by Donald Young (twenty-seven WCs) and Jack Sock (twenty-two WCs), which is far above the average number of wild-card invitations extended to players from other countries. Players from France and Australia also received a disproportionate number of wild-card invitations before the

---

[50] See e.g. the Lawn Tennis Association wild-card policy 2024, stipulating that wild cards are a privilege for British players, available at: www.lta.org.uk/48ceb8/siteassets/pro-players/lta-wild-card-policy-2024.pdf.

[51] ITF World Tennis Tour Men's and Women's Regulations 2024, available at: www.itftennis.com/media/11861/2024-wtt-regulations.pdf.

[52] Official Grand Slam Rulebook 2024, available at: www.itftennis.com/media/11558/grand-slam-rule-book-2024-f3.pdf.

[53] See Roland-Garros News Item, 'RG 2020 Wild Cards: How Does It Work' (27 November 2019).

[54] According to Lev Akabas, 'Slam Wild-Cards Serve as a Lifeline – If You're French, Aussi, or a Yank', Sportico (29 August 2023): 'the reciprocal wild card agreement is primarily a strategy to provide their own players with money and experience, not necessarily to produce likely winners. In the three non-Wimbledon majors, out of more than 100 reciprocal wild cards in the past decade, none have advanced past the third round.'

[55] Zlatko Vodenicharov, 'Andy Murray Breaks Record as He Receives Unexpected Wildcard for 2023 Qatar Open', Tennis Infinity (19 February 2023).

age of 25.⁵⁶ In 2023, the US Open reported that out of forty-three American players in the main draw of the 2023 US Open, eleven received wild cards.⁵⁷ In other words, players from Grand Slam organising countries that also host some other big tennis tournaments top the wild-card charts. All big tournaments are organised in markets of several countries to the exclusion of others. Hence, ATP Rule 7.12 and equivalent Grand Slam and ITF rules enable discrimination between players on the basis of nationality as they delegate the selection of wild cards to the discretion of the tournament organisers, instead of employing objective criteria based solely on players' ranking.⁵⁸ Wild cards cannot make 'a journeyman into a superstar', but they can boost a player from, for example, the top 200 to the top 100. For tour players, this can make a substantial difference.⁵⁹

4.2 Legal Evaluation of Wild Cards under Article 56 of the TFEU

In *Deliège*, decided under Article 56 of the TFEU on freedom to provide services, the CJEU analysed the legality of selection rules which limited the number of participants in high-level international competitions.⁶⁰ Deliège was a judoka who failed to achieve the necessary qualification criteria and was not selected by her country to participate in high-level international tournaments. The Court here first considered the limitation on a number of participants as 'inherent in the conduct of an international high-level sports event, which necessarily involves certain selection rules or criteria being adopted'.⁶¹ However, the Court also implied that any such limitations must be proportionate and emphasised that the adoption of one system over another 'must be based on objective criteria unconnected with the personal circumstances of the athletes' – in other

---

⁵⁶ See Tennis Abstract statistics, available at: https://tennisabstract.com/reports/wildCardRecipients.html.
⁵⁷ US Open News Item, 'Who Are the Americans Who Received 2023 US Open Wild Cards?' (27 August 2023).
⁵⁸ This could include, for example, awarding a tournament wild-card entry to talented young players based on their worldwide ranking.
⁵⁹ Jeff Sackman, 'Tennis Abstract' (25 March 2018), available at: www.tennisabstract.com/blog/category/wild-cards.
⁶⁰ *Christelle Deliège v. Ligue francophone de judo et disciplines associées ASBL, Ligue belge de judo ASBL, Union européenne de judo and François Pacquée*, Joined Cases C-51/96 and C-191/97 [2000] ECR I-2549.
⁶¹ Ibid., at para. 64.

words, it must be non-discriminatory.[62] It is therefore important to note that selection rules allowing nationality-based discrimination, such as Rule 7.12 of the ATP Rulebook, cannot benefit from the *Deliège* exception. Had the issue been about national tennis federations selecting their players for representation in international competitions (such as the Davis Cup or the Olympic Games), the exception to nationality-based discrimination laid down in *Walrave* and *Donà*[63] would become applicable and there would be no need to seek further legal guidance.

The proper legal test for Rule 7.12 lies in the functional equivalency of the *Meca-Medina* test under competition law; a standard objective justification framework set out by the Court in *Gebhard*[64] and made famous in the sporting context by the *Bosman* case.[65] It provides that only proportionate restrictions (on freedom to provide services in case of wild cards) pursuing a legitimate aim compatible with the TFEU and justified by pressing reasons of public interest are compatible with free movement provisions.[66] While giving a chance to compete at a higher level to young tennis talents could be seen as beneficial to encourage them to practise and propel them into high-level tennis (legitimate aim in the public interest), it is hard to find any legitimate justification for favouring local players (direct discrimination is, by default, disproportionate). The fact that local spectators want to see their own players is not convincing. In *Bosman*, the arguments that clubs should have a quota on foreign players to enable the public to identify with their favourite teams and to ensure that they effectively represented their countries when taking part in cross-border club competitions did not persuade the Court.[67] Tennis tournaments are visited by people from all around the globe, and the worldwide audience tunes in to watch tennis on TV channels and various other media platforms. It is also unconvincing to argue that organisers of the tournaments should have a right to offer an advantage to their own players. National associations from countries across the globe invest in their youth and help develop talents who later go on to participate in Grand Slam, ITF and ATP

---

[62] Ibid., at para. 65.
[63] *Walrave and Koch* v. *Union Cycliste Internationale and Others*, Case 36/74, ECLI:EU:C:1974:140; and *Gaetano Donà* v. *Mario Mantero*, Case 13/76, EU:C:1976:115.
[64] *Gebhard*, at para. 37.
[65] *Union Royale Belge Sociétés de Football Association ASBL* v. *Jean-Marc Bosman, Royal club liégeois SA* v. *Jean-Marc Bosman and Others and Union des Associations Européennes de Football (UEFA)* v. *Jean-Marc Bosman*, Case C-415/93, ECLI:EU:C:1995:463.
[66] Competition and free movement laws can be applied simultaneously, and conclusions are identical under the *Meca-Medina* and *Gebhard* tests.
[67] *Bosman*, at paras 121–37.

tournaments. They are the sole reason those tournaments exist. Several national associations from big markets that profit from their countries' organisation of the most important tennis tournaments do not even share their revenues with global tennis, and the system of vertical or horizontal solidarity is weak in tennis. Players from privileged countries in the tennis world[68] already reap the benefits of this ecosystem because their associations, which are involved in the organisation of the biggest tournaments, receive significant funds from those tournaments that are made up of foreign players who are the products of investments of foreign tennis associations. This means better infrastructure, funds to travel to tournaments in junior and professional tours, paid coaches, better sponsorship opportunities, etc. Players from many other countries are facing tougher career trajectories and reduced career prospects, and there is no equality of opportunity. The wild-card system thus appears to be a part of a broader arrangement that favours tournament-organising countries/national associations, which in turn favours local players in multiple ways.

5 Recapitulation

The key legal concerns regarding the organisation of sporting competitions and provision of professional player services usually stem from the governance structures in which SGBs, with or without a small segment consisting of top contestants, dominate the decision-making process. The rules that emerge from such process are usually heavily tilted in favour of their dominant members. Within the ATP structures, it appears that players – particularly those ranked outside the top 100, as well as players outside Europe and North America – are not properly represented. Without the ability to represent one's interests in the governance scheme, there is no ability to improve one's position in the tennis ecosystem. It has been suggested that the two rules discussed in this chapter merely reflect those broader governance issues. Not many professional players would agree to have a wild-card system left to the discretion of tournament organisers, as it inherently enables discrimination. Likewise, most professional players would welcome an opportunity to participate in the alternative tournaments that offer better financial incentives and benefits, especially if they were integrated into the ATP

---

[68] On its website, the ITF refers to the USTA, Tennis Australia, French National Federation and the All England Lawn Tennis & Croquet Club and Lawn Tennis Association as '[f]our of the ITF's leading National Associations'. Available at: www.itftennis.com/en/itf-tours/grand-slam-tournaments.

ranking point system, or have a sufficient number of ATP tournaments throughout the year that compete on prize money. The legal criteria laid down in *ESL*, *ISU* and *MOTOE* apply to all SGBs, including the ATP, when it comes to blocking an entry to the organisational market. These cases carry a clear signal from the CJEU that performing regulatory functions by non-public entities entails responsibilities to comply with law and implement good governance standards in terms of the practices, substantive rules and procedural regulations they adopt. Prioritising private commercial goals over public interests, discriminating between players or treating them unfairly might eventually produce a system-changing lawsuit. The best chance for any private regulator to remain unchallenged is to make a genuine effort to improve accountability, transparency, democracy and equal representation of all affected stakeholders on their decision-making boards.

13

The Regulation of Ethics in the ITF's Governance

ILIAS BANTEKAS

1 Introduction

It may not be apparent in what manner a discussion of ethics will add value to this book and its specialist subject matter. Indeed, non-ethics experts are usually surprised when they realise the range of issues left untouched by normative-based regulation. It is also surprising to learn that ethical rules are no less normative, as are their consequences. This chapter aims to fill the ethical gap that was not touched upon in other chapters in this book. The chapter's focus shall be restricted to the extensive ethical regulation of the International Tennis Federation (ITF) and hence will not examine equivalent developments in national tennis federations, the Women's Tennis Association (WTA) or the Association of Tennis Professionals (ATP).[1] Given the limited length of the chapter, we shall not cover the 2024 ITF Code of Conduct for Officials, which jointly covers ITF, ATP, WTA and Grand Slam Board. Unlike the ITF Code of Ethics, which applies 'at all times', the Code of Conduct applies during official tennis duties.[2] It is hoped that based on the analysis offered in this chapter, readers will be able to appreciate ethical rules in all tennis entities.

The chapter concentrates on the various ethical duties set out in the ITF Code of Ethics[3] and the consequences that arise from their breach. As will be demonstrated, these duties are of a contractual nature and by extension their breach entails breach of contractual consequences in the form of prescribed sanctions. The chapter goes on to show that while

---

[1] Chapter VIII of the 2024 ATP Official Rulebook, available at: www.itftennis.com/media/11553/2024-rulebook-atp.pdf, titled 'The Code', contains a significant amount of provisions of legal and ethical value. The distinction between the two is unclear and the term 'ethics' is not mentioned anywhere in the Rulebook.
[2] Available at: www.itftennis.com/media/2511/2024-code-of-conduct-for-officials.pdf. There are several ethical rules in this Code.
[3] The Code was adopted in 2019 and slightly amended in 2023. It is available at: chrome-extension://efaidnbmnnnibpcajpcglclefindmkaj/https://www.itftennis.com/media/7246/2023-itf-code-of-ethics-english.pdf. The most notable additions in the 2023 version were references to WTA and ATP employees regarding duties of loyalty and disclosure.

the Ethics Commission enjoys the right to investigate alleged breaches of the Code and impose sanctions where the official in question does not contest the findings of the investigation or the sanction, where the official denies the charges or the sanction, the matter is referred to the ITF's Independent Tribunal. The Ethics Commission further enjoys authority to assess whether candidates comply with the ITF's Candidacy Rules.

2 What Are Ethics and Are They Different from Law?

Ethics or ethical conduct is generally conduct that is fair and serves the best available outcome under the particular circumstances. While there is a body of ethical rules that guide social life and inter-personal relations in a non-binding manner (i.e. lying or cheating on one's spouse), many ethical rules have found their way into the regulatory realm. Tax professionals, certified accountants and lawyers are subject to ethical rules as part of their profession, whether nationally or internationally.[4] To understand why this is so, it is perhaps instructive to briefly examine the key justifications for the regulation of lawyers, namely: the *cynical*, the *client protection* and the *public interest* perspectives. In one of the major reviews of the legal profession in England and Wales in 2004, Sir David Clementi identified the roles justifying regulation of the legal profession, namely: access to justice, maintenance of the rule of law, protection of consumer interests, promotion of healthy competition among well-trained lawyers and promotion of a public understanding of citizens' rights.[5]

Such ethical rules with defined consequences arise for most professional fields, regardless of their classification as regulated 'professions' or not.[6]

There are several models of regulation for the professions and it is assumed that these models apply also to non-recognised professions,

---

[4] For instance, the American Institute of Certified Public Accountants (AICPA) subjects its members to standards contained in the AICPA Code of Professional Conduct, available at: https://pub.aicpa.org/codeofconduct/Ethics.aspx; see also the AICPA Statements on Standards for Tax Services No. 1–7, available at: www.aicpa.org/content/dam/aicpa/inter estareas/tax/resources/standardsethics/statementsonstandardsfortaxservices/downloada bledocuments/ssts-effective-january-1-2010.pdf.

[5] See David Clementi, Review of the Regulatory Framework for Legal Services in England and Wales: Final Report (2004).

[6] See Austin Sarat, 'The Profession versus the Public Interest: Reflections on Two Reifications' (2002) 54 Stanford L Rev 1491. The EU Directive on Recognition of Professional Qualifications, 2005/36/EC, defines liberal professions as 'those practiced on the basis of relevant professional qualifications in a personal, responsible and professionally independent capacity by those providing intellectual and conceptual services in the interest of the client and the public'.

such as the executive, judicial or governing entities and persons of sports governing bodies.[7] These models consist of: *rules-based*, enforced by a regulatory body; *outcomes-based*, which relies significantly on personal discretion to achieve fair outcomes (premised on consequentialism and rule-consequentialism); *self-enforcement*, in the sense that a profession develops ethical rules and procedures that must meet the approval of a regulator; and *competitive regulation*, which is grounded on enhanced regulation following consultation with the profession.[8]

In practice, the professions have been allowed to self-regulate attendant ethical issues and considerations and the same is true with regard to sports governing bodies through so-called *lex sportiva*.[9] While self-contained entities such as the ITF can devise their own internal ethics rules, the creation of a coherent body of transnational ethical rules is more complex and requires consistent practice over time. A good example is illustrated by the regulation of the impartiality of arbitrators in international arbitral proceedings. While originally an ethical standard whose breach entailed the ridicule of the impugned arbitrator and loss of future work, it is now a hard rule in all arbitral statutes. Article 12(1) of the UNCITRAL Model Law on International Commercial Arbitration[10] posits a general principle in this sense by demanding that an arbitrator 'shall disclose any circumstances likely to give rise to justifiable doubts as to his impartiality or independence. An arbitrator, from the time of his appointment and throughout the arbitral proceedings, shall without delay disclose any such circumstances to the parties unless they have already been informed of them by him.' All institutional rules encompass relevant ethics provisions, in addition to more detailed ethical codes, such as the American Association of Arbitration (AAA) Code of Ethics for Arbitrators and the International Bar Association (IBA) Rules of

---

[7] For a sociological perspective, see Andrew Abbott, *The Theory of Professions* (University of Chicago Press, 1998).
[8] Jonathan Herring, *Legal Ethics* (Oxford University Press, 2016), 76.
[9] See Antoine Duval, 'Transnational Sports Law: The Living Lex Sportiva' in Peer Zumbansen (ed.), *The Oxford Handbook of Transnational Law* (Oxford University Press, 2021), 493; and Lorenzo Casini, 'The Making of a Lex Sportiva by the Court of Arbitration for Sport' (2011) 12 German LJ 1317. Both articles emphasise that the particular status of the institutions forming the international sports order renders its regulatory ambit transnational in nature, albeit in synergy with national laws.
[10] The 2016 version of the Model Law is available at: https://uncitral.un.org/sites/uncitral.un.org/files/media-documents/uncitral/en/19-09955_e_ebook.pdf.

Ethics for International Arbitrators.[11] Although it is expected that arbitrators must be impartial and independent, lest the award be set aside under the *lex arbitri* or refused enforcement at a later stage, there is no single internationally accepted standard of impartiality.[12] As a result, while ethical issues are largely driven by institutional codes of conduct which prescribe, among others, the extent of disclosure and possible conflicts of interest, the ultimate arbiter of such issues are the courts of the seat. These in turn are not averse to relying on the standards adopted in institutional rules.[13]

There are several theories about the nature of ethical rules and the expected conduct of human actors. We will mention just two here with the aim of facilitating the discussion. *Deontology* pays less attention to the consequences of one's actions[14] and elevates one's adherence or application to a set of rules. Thus, a deontologist will be justified to act immorally if the action is backed by rules, as is the case with lawyer–client confidentiality. Such rules-based confidentiality justifies adherence even if a client's actions are otherwise illegal. Virtue ethics suggests that unless a person is born virtuous, virtue has to be acquired through acquiring the right habits, in which case both the socio-economic environment and the legal system play important roles in forming a virtuous person.[15] The keen reader will perhaps distil many of these theories in the ITF's Code of Ethics.

---

[11] Mini codes of ethics may also be found in some multilateral treaties, such as Annex 14(c) of the EU–Korea FTA and the code of conduct prescribed for persons sitting on dispute settlement panels under chapters 19 and 20 of NAFTA.

[12] English courts are generally in agreement that the appropriate test for impartiality is that of 'real possibility of bias', as per the judgment in *AT&T Corp.* v. *Saudi Cable Co.* [2000] 2 Lloyd's Rep 127; the IBA Rules of Ethics, on the other hand, provide that prospective arbitrators should disclose all facts or circumstances that may give rise to 'justifiable doubts' as to their impartiality; Art. 3(1) of the Portuguese Chamber of Commerce Code of Ethics introduces an 'absolute' impartiality test.

[13] US courts rely heavily, for example, on the AAA/ABA Code of Ethics for Arbitrators in Commercial Disputes in order to decide issues of independence and impartiality. See *Merit Insurance Co.* v. *Leatherby Insurance Co.*, 714 F.2d 673 (7th Cir. 1983); *Brandeis Instel Ltd* v. *Calabrian Chemicals Corp.*, 656 F.Supp. 160 (SDNY 1987); *Reeves Brothers, Inc.* v. *Capital-Mercury Shirt Corp.*, 962 F.Supp. 408 (SDNY 1997).

[14] See the ethical theory of consequentialism: Pe Bryne, 'Consequentialist Moral Theory' in *The Philosophical and Theological Foundations of Ethics* (Palgrave Macmillan, 1999); Paul Zwier, 'The Consequentialist/Nonconsequentialist Ethical Distinction: A Tool for the Formal Appraisal of Traditional Negligence and Economic Tort Analysis' (1985) 26 BCL Rev 905.

[15] Herring, *Legal Ethics*.

3 The ITF's Substantive Ethical Rules

As will become evident in this section, the ITF's Ethics Rules concern integrity-related conduct by officials in governance, administrative or official positions (e.g. investigators, umpires). As such, they exclude integrity-related infractions committed by athletes and coaches, all of which are dealt under discreet rules and subject to the jurisdiction of the ITF's judicial entities.[16] The point of reference for our discussion is the ITF's Code of Ethics (hereinafter, the Code). It expressly builds on the International Olympic Committee (IOC) Code of Ethics[17] and best practice.

3.1 Covered Persons

In accordance with Article 1.3 of the Code, its provisions are applicable to so-called 'officials', as follows:

1.3.1. each person serving as a director of the ITF, or of any subsidiary or associated company of the ITF (an Associated Company) from time to time (each, a Director);
1.3.2. the President and the Chief Operating Officer of the ITF (each, an Officer);
1.3.3. each person serving as a member of a committee, commission, taskforce or working party of the ITF or any Associated Company, and each person appointed to represent the ITF or any Associated Company on a committee, commission, taskforce or working party of another body (each, a Committee Member); and
1.3.4. each person who is a candidate for election or appointment as a Director or Officer or Committee Member (a Candidate), provided that while such persons are only Candidates (and not a Director or Officer or Committee Member), the only substantive requirements in this Code that are applicable to them are the requirements set out at Articles 2.6.2 and 2.8.

The Code is concerned with the ITF's integrity and its credibility towards its various stakeholders. The Code applies as a contract between the ITF and its officials because their actions are subject to the jurisdiction of the ITF Ethics Commission irrespective if the

---

[16] See Chapter 4 of this volume on the dispute resolution mechanisms of the ITF.
[17] IOC Code of Ethics 2023, available at: https://olympics.com/ioc/code-of-ethics.

impugned action also befalls the authority of the host state's (forum) criminal or labour courts.[18]

All of the obligations incumbent upon ITF officials are subject to a test of knowledge, intention, recklessness or negligence.[19] Given that these standards of knowledge require different standards of proof in criminal proceedings, as opposed to civil proceedings, it must generally be assumed that evidence with a probative value suffices so long as procedural fairness prevails.

3.2 Basic Obligations

The ITF Code of Ethics distinguishes between general 'basic' obligations, which are meant to guide all actions of ITF officials, and other more specific obligations. Article 2.1 of the Code puts forth the following basic obligations:

2.1.1. [maintain the] highest standards of honesty and integrity;

2.1.2. respect for human rights … [including] human dignity; non discrimination … on grounds of race, color, sex, gender, sexual orientation, language, religion, political or other opinion, national or social origin, disability, or any other unlawful ground; and not committing any form of harassment or abuse of any person, whether physical, professional, sexual, psychological or otherwise;[20]

2.1.3. respect the Olympic principles of autonomy from government interference and political neutrality … and;

2.1.4. refrain at all times … from any fraudulent or corrupt act, or [acts] that bring or risks bringing the ITF or the sport of tennis into disrepute.[21]

---

[18] ITF Code, Art. 1.6.

[19] Ibid., Art. 2.

[20] See ITF Ethics Commission Decision against Evgeniy Zukin. Decision of the ITF Ethics Commission (25 July 2022) (hereinafter, *ITF Ethics Commission v. Zukin*), available at: www.itftennis.com/media/8735/itf-ethics-commission-decision-zukin-25-july-2022-publication.pdf. Slapping another official during dinner (i.e. outside official ITF duties) was found to be a breach of this provision. It should be noted that this Decision was appealed to the Independent Tribunal and a final award was issued on the matter in late December 2024, which partially upheld the findings of the Ethics Commission. *Evgeniy Zukin v. ITF*, SR/076/2024 (10 December 2024), available at: www.sportresolutions.com/assets/documents/241210_-_Zukin_v_ITF_Ethics_Commission_-_Decision_%28Amended%29_1.pdf.

[21] Ibid., equally bringing the ITF and the game of tennis into disrepute.

These basic obligations are meant to apply 'at all times', that is, regardless as to whether the official is acting in an official or private capacity. The private lives of ITF officials are inextricably interwoven with their professional dimension by reason of contract.

3.3 Other Substantive Duties and Obligations

A key duty of officials is that of 'undivided loyalty' to the ITF.[22] This entails that in the execution of their duties, officials must always act in the interests of the ITF, its members and tennis as a whole.[23] In addition, where there is an apparent, actual or potential conflict of interest,[24] the official in question must make a full disclosure to the ITF without delay.[25] This duty is of a continuing nature and in respect of Directors in particular an annual disclosure statement is required, while other officials are bound to do so every two years.[26] Any covered person subject to a conflict must excuse him- or herself from a meeting even if the conflict has been registered in a disclosure statement.[27] Conflicts of interest may not only give rise to a breach of the employment contract, but also constitute infractions under the criminal law of the forum, in addition to claims of compensation under the law of torts.[28]

Bribery and corruption are particularly singled out in Article 2.3 of the Code. Officials must not directly or indirectly solicit, accept or offer any form of undue remuneration, commission or concealed benefit or

---

[22] ITF Code of Ethics, Art. 2.2.
[23] Ibid., Art. 2.2.1.
[24] The ITF Ethics Commission issued in 2021 a simplified 'Guide to Conflict of Interest Declarations' to assist officials in avoiding conflicts and filing their disclosure statements, available at: www.itftennis.com/media/7245/ethics-commission-conflict-of-interest-guidance-english.pdf.
[25] ITF Code of Ethics, Art. 2.2.2.
[26] In Decision of the ITF Ethics Commission against Iva Majoli (3 August 2022) (hereinafter, *ITF Ethics Commission* v. *Majoli*), available at: www.itftennis.com/media/8678/itf-ethics-commission-decision-majoli-3-august-2022.pdf, an official had been repeatedly asked to complete her conflicts of interest declaration and failed to respond. The Commission noted that: 'The reason for ensuring that conflicts are declared prior to or during any meeting of an ITF Committee, Commission or Taskforce is that a conflict of interest calls into question whether a decision, a vote, or the work of an Official is truly in the interests of the ITF or whether that decision furthers the interest of that Official, their family and associates, and/or their employer. Any doubt as to the motivations of an Official can undermine the integrity of the ITF's work.'
[27] ITF Code of Ethics, Arts 2.2.2.1–2.2.3.3.
[28] This is in fact envisaged in Art. 2.9 of Appendix 1 to the ITF Code of Ethics.

service, nor misuse their position for private aim.[29] It is equally prohibited to accept any kind of bribe or improper payment in order to influence decision-making[30] within the ITF or any associated company. A particular form of corruption arises where an ITF official interferes with the integrity of the bidding process in order to accrue financial benefit for himself or others.[31]

Article 2.4 of the Code imposes on all officials a strict duty of confidentiality, whether for personal gain or otherwise. This duty is always subservient to the requirements of local law, particularly in the determination of unlawful acts,[32] and it is of credit to the ITF that this is explicitly stated in Article 2.4.2 of the Code.

The duty not to violate the integrity of ITF competitions is paramount to the basic duties of officials. It requires that officials do not influence the course or result of a tennis match or event with a view to achieving an advantage for themselves or others, or otherwise engage in any action that may undermine the integrity of a competition.[33] In addition, ITF officials must not in any way facilitate or assist in the breach of ITF integrity rules (doping, match-fixing).[34]

Any person, whether an existing official or other, who is in the process of campaigning for election to the Board of Directors of the ITF (candidates) must abide by the ITF candidacy rules and those who are not candidates must respect the candidacy process.[35] This is not a straightforward ethical rule because candidates who are not already ITF officials are not ordinarily bound by the ITF Code in the contractual manner that other officials are. The same is true of non-candidates (who are equally non-officials) interfering with the integrity of candidates. Candidacy rules are set out in Appendix 4 to the ITF Code of Ethics (hereinafter, Rules of Candidates). Key obligations include: (1) refraining from sending official campaign material prior to the public announcement of all ITF candidates; (2) conducting one's campaign with dignity and respect for opponents; (3) avoiding exerting improper influence over the process; (4) refraining from seeking or using financial, political or other support from any regional association or

---

[29] Echoes Art. 15 of the 2003 UN Convention against Corruption.
[30] See ibid., Art. 18 (trading in influence).
[31] ITF Code of Ethics, Art. 2.7.
[32] In 2019, the European Union adopted Directive 2019/1937 through the EU Parliament and the Council, On the Protection of Persons Who Report Breaches of Union Law, OJ L 305/17 (16 November 2019) (hereinafter, Whistleblower Directive).
[33] ITF Ethics Code, Art. 2.5.1.
[34] Ibid., Art. 2.5.2.
[35] Ibid., Art. 2.6.

other ITF partner or supplier; (5) refraining from soliciting or accepting any benefits with the aim of using one's influence upon election; (6) refraining from receiving or offering improper hospitality gifts; and (7) duly disclose any gifts received to the Ethics Commission. Article 14 of the Rules of Candidates stipulates that:

> unless in the ordinary course of their business as an existing Official, [officials shall] not receive individual or special support or services from the ITF, or ITF staff, including any consultants, agents or advisors engaged by the ITF (or their related or connected affiliates), beyond general administrative support and services provided to ensure that candidacies are conducted in a fair, open and consistent manner.

In a case decided in 2010 (and when Article 16 of the 2023 Code was Article 14 of the 2019 version of the Code), the incumbent ITF President was running for re-election and solicited the services of a private consultancy firm. The Commission interpreted the relevant provision as being:

> intended to prevent the ITF from providing favourable services to any particular Candidate or Candidates. It is also intended to ensure that Candidates who are also ITF Officials are not able to exploit their position within the ITF to gain favourable services from the ITF. The scope of Article 14 extends beyond ITF staff, to 'any consultants, agents or advisors engaged by the ITF'. If a consultant, agent, or advisor is not engaged by the ITF, it does not fall within the scope of Article 14.[36]

Given that the consultancy firm in question was not engaged by the ITF at the same time, the Ethics Commission did not find a violation of Article 14 and proceeded to dismiss the case.[37] It should be noted that the Ethics Commission issued a statement in March 2019 by which to clarify the Candidacy Rules.[38]

---

[36] Ethics Commission Decision, Art. 14 Candidate Rules (15 July 2019) (*ITF Ethics Commission Re. Art. 14 Candidate Rules*), available at: www.itftennis.com/media/2336/decision-regarding-matters-raised-in-relation-to-article-14-of-the-rules-for-candidates-in-the-2019-itf-presidential-elections-15-july-2019.pdf.

[37] See also Ethics Commission Decision, Art. 12 Candidate Rules (15 July 2019) [*ITF Ethics Commission Re. Art. 12 Candidate Rules*], available at: www.itftennis.com/media/2335/decision-regarding-matters-raised-in-relation-to-article-12-of-the-rules-for-candidates-in-the-2019-itf-presidential-elections-15-july-2019.pdf, which concerned allegations that a candidate for elections participated in a public event to support his campaign without making such forum available to other candidates. The allegation was not proven and the case was dismissed.

[38] Available at: www.itftennis.com/media/6261/itf-ethics-commission-statement-candidacy-rules-2019-elections.pdf.

In order for the ITF to achieve integrity in all of its functions and operations, it is imperative that all of its officials cooperate and report anything that comes to their attention. This obligation is set out in Article 2.8 of the Ethics Code, according to which officials must without delay report 'any information they have that a reasonable person would consider might evidence or otherwise reflect' any form of infraction of the Code, especially if instigated by a non-ITF official. This obligation entails that disclosure shall be made to the ITF Ethics Commission, unless exceptionally the official in question considers in good faith that the issue is best dealt under another discreet ITF procedure. The duty to cooperate entails that officials do so 'truthfully, fully and in good faith', including by answering any questions and providing access to any information, data and/or documentation; as well as by ensuring that they do not obstruct, prevent, delay or otherwise interfere with or frustrate any investigation. This duty further entails that officials do not make a report in bad faith, with malicious intent or other improper purpose.

4 The ITF Ethics Commission

The relatively large volume of integrity infractions by athletes and coaches and the low number of ethical violations by ITF officials has necessitated their diffusion to two distinct bodies. Whereas the ITF's judicial entities entertain infractions of ITF/International Tennis Integrity Agency (ITIA) regulations by athletes and coaches, the ITF's Ethics Commission possesses jurisdiction over the conduct of its 'officials'. While this bifurcation is consistent with the practice of sports governing bodies experiencing large volumes of violations, those with smaller volumes do not set up a discreet ethics commission and hence generally subsume ethical disputes within the jurisdiction of an existing judicial entity. By way of illustration, the Badminton World Federation's (BWF) Independent Hearing Panel (IHP) is its key dispute settlement body in respect of intra-governance and regulatory/ethical disputes. Under the terms of Article 7.5.1 of the BWF Judicial Procedures, it possesses authority over: (1) *integrity and ethics disputes* as these arise under the BWF Code of Ethics;[39] and (2) alleged breaches of the BWF Code of Conduct in respect of

---

[39] BWF Code of Ethics, available at: https://system.bwfbadminton.com/documents/folder_1_81/Statutes/CHAPTER-2—ETHICS/Section%202.1%20-%20Code%20of%20Ethics.pdf.

actions or omissions by electoral candidates[40] and elected officials.[41] It also encompasses alleged infractions arising from the BWF Code on the Prevention of Manipulation of Competitions and the BWF Para Badminton Classification Regulations in respect of intentional misrepresentation.[42] As the chapter will go on to demonstrate, the ITF's Independent Tribunal does exercise authority over ethical breaches, but only above a specific threshold.

It should be stated from the outset that while the ITF Code of Ethics confers jurisdiction on the Commission to investigate any infraction of the duties set out in the previous section, where the impugned official entertains a grievance against this process, he or she may ultimately resort to the English courts.[43] The case would be different where the ITF Constitution or other instrument conferred authority over such issues on the ITF's other judicial organs. As we go on to show, where an impugned official does not admit a violation under investigation by the Commission, the Chair may among other options refer the case to the ITF's Independent Tribunal, in accordance with Article 4.3 of Appendix 1 to the ITF Code of Ethics. In the event that such dispute is ultimately referred to English courts, they are bound to construe the Code in accordance with English law.[44]

Appendix 1 to the ITF Code of Ethics establishes the Ethics Commission and sets out its mandate. The Commission is an independent body.[45] This in no way suggests that it is a judicial entity or an arbitral

---

[40] BWF Candidates for Election Code of Conduct, available at: www.badmintonpanam.org/wp-content/uploads/2018/04/2.2.1-Candidates-for-Elections-Code-of-Conduct-01062017.pdf.

[41] BWF Code of Conduct for Elected Officials, available at: www.badmintonpanam.org/wp-content/uploads/2021/01/2.2.2-CC-Elected-Officials-Effective-Date-19-July-2020.pdf.

[42] In 2017, the BWF set up an External Judicial Experts Group under Art. 31.1.4 of the 2017 version of the BWF Judicial Procedures to hear doping and ethics-related disputes (also referred to as the Doping Hearing Panel), but with the coming into effect of the current Constitution and Judicial Procedures, this entity has been effectively abolished. See https://corporate.bwfbadminton.com/news-single/2017/07/13/experts-to-judge. It did, however, entertain a few cases, such as *BWF* v. *Kate Jessica Foo Kune*, Decision 2019/04 (21 October 2019). The BWF appealed the decision to the Court of Arbitration for Sport (CAS) and as a result decided to refer future doping cases to the CAS. BWF-related anti-doping cases have been delegated under Art. 8.1.1 of the BWF's Anti-Doping Regulations to the CAS Anti-Doping Division, which it now has authority over first-instance hearings or waivers thereof and decision-making powers. The BWF Anti-Doping Regulations are available at: https://extranet.bwf.sport/docs/document-system/81/1466/1468/2.3.%20Anti-Doping%20Regulations.pdf.

[43] ITF Code of Ethics, Art. 4.4.
[44] Ibid.
[45] Ibid., Art. 1.1, Appendix I.

tribunal. It simply means that it is independent from other officials or entities within the ITF and that it is under no circumstances subservient to their authority or influence.[46] Even so, the ITF Board appoints the Chair, following which the Chair appoints other members, at least three of whom (inclusive of the Chair) must have a legal background.[47] No member may be removed other than for 'just cause'. The need for enhanced legal expertise aptly demonstrates that the ITF Code of Ethics has effectively been transformed into the species of legal ethics one finds at lawyers' bar associations and which bring about legal consequences. In short, these ethical duties are effectively binding duties. The Commission is aided by a Legal Secretary, to whom all communications are directed.[48] The Commission is tasked with oversight of elections and/or appointments to the Board of Directors. This function is both regulatory (i.e. approval of candidate rules) and adjudicatory, particularly in respect of candidate eligibility,[49] or concerning its determination as to whether an ethical duty has been breached.

4.1 Investigations

Any person or entity may file a complaint concerning potential violations of the Code.[50] Upon receipt, the Chair may request further information from the complainant.[51] Where the Chair considers that the complaint is not frivolous or malicious and hence warrants investigation, an independent (from the ITF) investigator shall be appointed.[52] In practice, investigators are members of the Commission.[53] Even so, the investigation is led by the Chair of the Commission and as such it may be instigated *proprio motu* without grounds even in the absence of a complaint (e.g. by an anonymous complaint).[54] The Chair may at any

---

[46] See ibid., Art. 1.4.
[47] Ibid., Art. 1.2.
[48] Ibid., Art. 1.3.
[49] Ibid., Art. 1.7.
[50] Ibid., Art. 2.1. In the case against Evgenyi Zukin, the complaint was filed by Tennis Europe Board of Management. See Decision of the ITF Ethics Commission (25 July 2022), available at: www.itftennis.com/media/8735/itf-ethics-commission-decision-zukin-25-july-2022-publication.pdf.
[51] Ibid., Art. 2.3.
[52] Ibid., Art. 2.5.
[53] By way of illustration, Jack Anderson was tasked to investigate allegations against Evgeniy Zukin. See Decision of the ITF Ethics Commission (25 July 2022).
[54] ITF Code of Ethics, Arts 2.6 and 2.7.

stage of the investigation approach an impugned official and after explaining how they may have breached the Code ask whether said official wishes to admit the breach. Admission culminates in termination of the investigation and imposition of sanctions, which if accepted by the impugned official will lead to a written decision that is binding on the parties and final.[55] If the impugned official does not admit the violation, the Chair may initiate or continue the investigation, make a finding or refer the case to the ITF's Independent Tribunal, in accordance with Article 4.3 of Appendix 1 to the ITF Code of Ethics. It is not improbable that the issue in question involves a criminal, administrative or other offence of the forum. In this case, the Chair may refer the matter to the relevant authorities, or if it is already under investigation therein, the Commission may pause its own investigation until the local authorities conclude theirs.[56]

The investigation is not kept confidential from the parties. Rather, where this is initiated by the Chair of the Commission, the parties must be informed of the alleged violations, as well as 'the materials on which the Chair has relied in deciding that the matter warrants investigation'.[57] In all other respects, the proceedings are confidential and the same is true in respect of information arising from the investigation.[58] The investigated party may be represented by legal counsel at its own expense and make written submissions.[59] The investigator may seek evidence from any source, within or outside the ITF,[60] and if during the course of the investigation evidence arises concerning violations by other officials, the Chair may decide to expand the scope of the investigation.[61] Upon conclusion of the investigation, the investigator shall make a comprehensive report with the available evidence and provide an assessment of culpability along with a recommendation as to whether the matter should be dealt with by the plenary of the Commission.[62]

---

[55] Ibid., Arts 2.8 and 2.8.1.
[56] Ibid., Art. 2.9.
[57] Ibid., Art. 3.1.
[58] Ibid., Art. 9.1. Exceptionally, the Ethics Commission may publicise relevant information in order to inform the public, avoid reputational damage to the official and protect the integrity of the game, in accordance with ibid., Art. 9.2.
[59] Ibid., Art. 3.3.
[60] Ibid., Art. 3.4.
[61] Ibid., Art. 3.5.
[62] Ibid., Art. 3.6.

4.2 Decision Following the Investigator's Report: Aggravated and Non-Aggravated Breaches

The Chair of the Commission has several options following receipt of the investigator's report. Depending on the sufficiency of the evidence and whether this meets the standard of proof, the Chair may request further investigation, dismiss the case,[63] proceed to a finding or otherwise refer the case to the ITF's Independent Tribunal.[64] Where the Chair accepts that a breach has occurred, it may issue a warning, a reprimand or a fine of US$20,000 and/or a suspended period of ineligibility if it reckons that a higher and more aggravated sentence is disproportionate to the violation. The impugned official has twenty-one days from receipt of the decision to appeal it to the Independent Tribunal,[65] which shall sit as an appellate panel.[66] If no appeal is filed, the Commission's decision becomes final and binding.[67] It should be made clear that because the Commission is not an arbitral tribunal or a court, its decisions are binding as a matter of contract. This is best described as a species of expert determination, as is the case with the Independent Hearing Panel of the BWF.[68]

Where the Chair considers that the violations are of a more serious nature, a written notice of charge will be served on the investigated official.[69] This shall advise the person that they have a case to answer, set out the provisions alleged to have been violated, in addition to the evidence relied upon and the sanctions sought by the Commission.[70] More importantly, the investigated person will be informed that in respect of serious breaches it is not the Commission that will adjudicate the dispute, but the Independent

---

[63] In ITF Ethics Decision against Bernard Guidicelli (16 November 2020) [*ITF Ethics Commission* v. *Guidicelli*], available at: www.itftennis.com/media/4294/itf-ethics-commission-decision-on-complaint-against-bernard-giudicelli.pdf, it was held that the official in question was only negligent and had not intentionally lied on his resume. The Commission decided to publish the decision in accordance with Art. 9.2.2. of its Code of Ethics in order to correct damaging information and avoid the spread of rumours.
[64] ITF Code of Ethics, Art. 4.1.
[65] Ibid., Art. 4.2.
[66] Procedural Rules Governing Proceedings before an Independent Tribunal Convened under ITF Rules, Art. 9, available at: www.itftennis.com/media/5989/2019-procedural-rules-itf-iap.pdf.
[67] ITF Code of Ethics, Art. 4.2, Appendix 1.
[68] See Ilias Bantekas, 'The Dispute Resolution Mechanism of the Badminton World Federation: Sui Generis Expert Determination?' (2024) 20 South Carol J Int Law & Bus 1.
[69] According to Art. 7.1 of Appendix 1 to the ITF Code of Ethics, no notice charging an official with breach of the ITF Ethics Code may be sent more than twelve years after the date on which the breach is alleged to have occurred.
[70] ITF Code of Ethics, Arts 4.3.1–4.3.4, Appendix 1.

Tribunal, sitting as a first-instance body.[71] This is an important development because the Independent Tribunal has the status of an arbitral tribunal and its awards are binding in accordance with the 1996 English Arbitration Act.

4.3 The Suspensive Effect of the Notice of Charge

Where a notice of charge has been issued, the Commission *may* provisionally suspend the official from all official duties.[72] Article 4.4.1.1 goes on to add a layer of complexity by suggesting that where the provisional suspension is aimed at a Director, this shall be done in accordance with the laws of the Bahamas and the ultimate decision taken by the Board of Directors. This is clearly done because the ITF is incorporated as a commercial entity in the Bahamas and any action affecting its corporate governance must be consistent with the law of that country.

Provisional suspensions may be resisted by written application to the Independent Tribunal under Article 3.5 of the Tribunal's Procedural Rules.[73] The only admissible grounds by which to contest the suspension are that:

    a. the charge(s) has/have no reasonable prospect of being upheld, e.g., because of a patent flaw in the case against the Official; or
    b. other facts exist that make it clearly unfair, in all of the circumstances, to impose a provisional suspension prior to a full hearing on the merits of the charge(s) against the Official. This ground is to be construed narrowly, and applied only in exceptional circumstances.[74]

In every other respect, the Independent Tribunal shall follow its prescribed rules and procedures and its Chairman shall determine whether an oral hearing is required in the circumstances of the case.[75]

5 Recourse to the Independent Tribunal and CAS

The procedure provides ample opportunities for non-contentious resolution.[76] The official has fourteen days to respond to the notice of

---

[71] Ibid., Art. 4.3.5.
[72] Ibid., Art. 4.4, Appendix 1.
[73] Ibid., Art. 4.4.2.
[74] Ibid.
[75] Ibid., Art. 4.4.3.
[76] A significant incentive for the official is that if he or she loses its case the likelihood that the tribunal will order the payment of costs is very high. This includes the expenses of the Independent Tribunal, in addition to possible fines. See ibid., Art. 6.4.

charges. Where the official admits the charges and consents to the proposed sanctions, this will be recorded by the Chair of the Commission in a published decision.[77] Where the official disputes the findings of the investigation and/or the sanctions, the case is referred to the Independent Tribunal.[78] In the event that the official does not offer a reasoned submission to the charges, it is presumed that he or she has not only waived his or her right to a hearing, but also accepted the charges. Consequently, the Commission will confirm the breaches in a public decision.[79]

Article 5.3 of Appendix 1 to the ITF Code of Ethics emphasises that while proceedings before the Independent Tribunal are brought in the name of the ITF, the prosecuting party is the Ethics Commission. The latter may act on its own or instruct legal counsel to act on its behalf.[80] Exceptionally, if the official and the Ethics Commission so agree, the case may be referred directly to the CAS, the award of which will be subject to no further appeal.[81]

The decisions of the Independent Tribunal may be appealed by the official or the Commission *solely* to the CAS, just like all other decisions of this entity.[82] In the event of an appeal by the official, the respondent will be the ITF and not the Commission.[83] Appeals against the decisions of the Independent Tribunal are referred to the jurisdiction of the CAS:

> save that the appeal will only take the form of a *de novo* hearing where that is required in order to do justice (for example, to cure procedural errors at the hearing of first instance). In all other cases, the appeal will not take the form of a *de novo* hearing but instead will be limited to consideration of whether the decision of the Independent Tribunal that is being appealed was erroneous.[84]

5.1 *Sanctions*

Sanctions are a necessary component of any value system, whether this is normative or ethical. Without appropriate and proportionate sanctions,

---

[77] Ibid., Art. 5.1.1.
[78] Ibid., Art. 5.1.2.
[79] Ibid., Art. 5.2.
[80] Ibid., Art. 5.3.
[81] Ibid., Art. 5.5.
[82] Ibid., Art. 5.4.
[83] Ibid.
[84] Ibid.

the goals of the Code of Ethics could never be achieved. Article 6.1 of Appendix 1 to the ITF Code of Ethics stipulates that any of the following sanctions may be imposed:

> 6.1.1. a warning as to future conduct (i.e., a reminder of the substance of the provision of the Code of Ethics that has been infringed, together with a threat of sanction in the event of further infringement);
> 6.1.2. a reprimand (i.e., an official written pronouncement of disapproval);
> 6.1.3. a fine in an amount proportionate to the breach;
> 6.1.4. an order of reimbursement or restitution;
> 6.1.5. removal of any award or other honour previously bestowed by the ITF;
> 6.1.6. removal from office, or suspension from office for a specified period;
> 6.1.7. disqualification from acting as a Director and/or as an Officer and/or as a Committee Member and/or as a Candidate for a specified period (of up to a lifetime); and/or
> 6.1.8. any other sanction(s) that may be deemed appropriate and proportionate.

The appropriate sanction shall be imposed by taking into regard all relevant factors, including the seriousness of the breach, the need to protect the integrity of tennis, deterrence, the existence of mitigating or aggravating circumstances and others.[85] In the case against Evgenyi Zukin, although it was found that the impugned official had slapped a colleague in public, the Commission acknowledged that the incident had taken place a few days following the Russian invasion of Ukraine (Zukin was a Ukrainian national) and hence the official was emotionally charged and there was evidence that his sincere apology had been accepted by the victim of his outburst. The Commission proceeded to impose a warning and a reprimand.[86] In the case against Iva Majoli, where the officer in question failed following several requests to complete her conflicts of interest declaration, the Ethics Commission considered that the appropriate sanction was a suspended period of ineligibility during which time Ms Majoli would not be permitted to participate in the ITF Coaches Commission.[87]

---

[85] Ibid., Art. 6.2.
[86] See above note 20 for the Decision.
[87] ITF Ethics Commission Decision against Majoli, *ITF Ethics Commission v. Majoli*.

6 The Elections and Eligibility Panel

The Ethics Commission enjoys authority over the eligibility of candidates for election to the various positions within the ITF. The Chair and two other Commission members will form a sub-group with oversight of elections and/or appointment to the Board of Directors. This sub-group is known as the Elections and Eligibility Panel.[88] Its functions are:

> 1.9.1. to approve the Candidate Rules and issue updates to those Candidate Rules from time to time (the Candidate Rules as currently in force are set out at Appendix 4);
>
> 1.9.2. without prejudice to the procedures detailed in Article 3 to 6 of this Appendix, to ensure Candidates comply with the Candidate Rules;
>
> 1.9.3. to monitor and where necessary adjudicate upon (i) the eligibility of Candidates, and (ii) the ongoing eligibility of members of the Board of Directors (including the President) following their election or appointment, pursuant to Articles 19(c)(iii) and 21(l) of the ITF Constitution and in accordance with the provisions of Article 9 of this Appendix 1; and
>
> 1.9.4. to ensure the proper administration of all tasks relating to elections and/or appointments to the Board of Directors (including the President) in collaboration with the ITF (as more fully set out in the Commission's Terms of Reference).

In certain other sports governing bodies, this task, as well as/or the broader function of assessing applicants, is performed by so-called vetting bodies.[89]

Where the Commission is tasked with assessing the eligibility of candidates who have been the subject of criminal convictions, the Ethics Commission is once against transformed into the Eligibility Panel. These issues are regulated by the ITF Constitution, particularly Articles 19(c)(iii) and 21(k) thereof. The role of the Commission is to determine whether the criminal conviction of an ITF official should result in the post becoming vacant.[90] The mere conviction of an ITF official does not automatically entail their dismissal from office. Indeed, the impugned official may plead their case by providing relevant documents and attend a hearing in inquisitorial proceedings if the

---

[88] ITF Code of Ethics, Art. 9.1, Annex 1.
[89] BWF Constitution, Appendix II, available at: https://extranet.bwf.sport/docs/document-system/81/1466/1467/BWF%20Constitution%20-%20May%202023.pdf.
[90] ITF Code of Ethics, Art. 8.1, Annex 1.

Commission so determines.⁹¹ The Commission shall determine the case by simple majority and provide reasons. Its decision shall be final without recourse to appeal. Its determination, however, can be subject to challenge as a decision of the Board of Directors, in accordance with the ITF Constitution's provisions on internal arbitration (i.e. through the Independent Panel) and recourse to the CAS (ordinary arbitration procedure).⁹²

⁹¹ Ibid., Art. 8.2.
⁹² Ibid., Art. 8.3.

INDEX

ADR in tennis: *see also* collective bargaining
  collective disputes between players and professional tennis associations, 148
  rules-based infraction, reasons for exclusion, 148
  settlement by negotiation (contract-based disputes), 148
  TACP jurisdiction in respect of corruption, 230: *see also* corruption
Agassi, Andre, 128, 259
agency (player-agent relations)
  introduction, 23–4
  historical background
    commercial returns, 26
    earlier focus on individual sports (golf, tennis etc), 25
    extension of services to a wide gamut of tennis-related projects, 26
    IMG/Proserv, 25–7
    increase in the number of agents, 26
    predominance of popular team sports, 24–5
    sparcity of the literature, 24
  agency statistics
    EU survey (2009), 28
    governing factors, 28
    a niche and static sector, 28
    US market, 28 n.30
  contracts: *see* agency (player-agent relations (contracts))
  roles
    contract representation, 27
    managerial and administrative services, 27
    maximisation of revenues, 27–8
  types of agency
    agents' backgrounds, 27
    'all-inclusive agencies, 27
    'bespoke' firms, 27
    player-led agencies, 27
    services provided by specialist firms, 27
agency (player-agent relations (contracts)), 36–41
  overview (a broad consensus), 36–7
  civil law jurisdictions
    French/German practice, 37
    good faith principle, 37
    mandates, 32
    special rules applicable to agency contracts, 37
  common law jurisdictions
    Burleson v. Earnest, 38
    conflict of interests, 38
    good faith obligation (fiduciary relationship), 37–8
    good faith obligation (in general), 37
    Imageview Management v. Jack, 38
agency (player-agent relations (legal interests arising from)), 38–41
  conflicts of interest, 38–40
    examples, 39
    Lendl, 39
    MITPC conflict of interests rule/*Volvo*, 40
    reasons for expansion of the problem, 39–40
  restraint of trade issues: *see also* restraint of trade
    Volvo, 40
    Zverev, 6, 40–1, 55, 96–9, 127, 136, 168–9

INDEX

agency (regulation of agencies/agents) (domestic rules), 29–36
    from no *lex specialis* to close regulation, 29, 34–5
    mixed model (USA), 33–4
        applicability of the general rules of obligation, 33
        Miller-Ayala Act, 34
        Revised Uniform Athlete Agents Act (2015), 30
        UAAA model rules (limitation to student athletes), 33–4
        UAAA model rules (states' varying implementation of), 34
    no *lex specialis* (British practice)
        absence of statutory provision/LTA regulation, 29
        applicability of laws relating to self-employed workers/businesses, 30
        common law of agency, 30
    no *lex specialis* (German/Netherlands practice), 30
    specific legislation/regulation (French practice)
        Code du sport provisions on sports agency, 30–1
        FFT good practice obligations/professional conduct regulations, 31–2
        FFT membership exam/conditions of integrity, 31
        FFT status as a Sports Agent Commission, 31
    specific legislation/regulation (Italian practice), 32–3
        FITP conditions of integrity, 32–3
        FITP exam requirement/qualifying test, 32
        Legge 27 dicembre 2017 (registration with CONI/FITP), 32–3
        obligation to respect CONI Code, 33
        restriction of operation to registered agents/sanctions, 32–3

agency (regulation of agencies/agents) (transnational rules) (ITF/ATP/WTA), 35–6
    contractual basis/contractual enforcement, 36
    transnational character, 36
    lack of specific applicability to agents, 35
    sanctions, 36
    standards of behaviour, 35–6
Alcaraz, Carlos, 122, 136
ambush marketing, 59–60: *see also* sponsorship agreements (IP rights) (key provisions), ambush marketing
anti-doping (introduction)
    concerns over doping in child athletes, 204
    doping as a breach of fairness and equality, 211
    early efforts to control, 211
    establishment of WADA (1999)/Prohibited List, 211
    on-site anti-doping investigations, 165–6
    WDAC, a complex but necessary set of harmonized rules, 211
anti-doping rules (TADC/CAS/ITF jurisprudence)
    Abdelrahman, 100, 161, 220 n.40
    Burdekin, 222 n.15
    Buttifant, 220
    Caicedo, 219, 220
    Catana, 223
    Cilic, 227–8
    Dylan Scott, 100 n.46, 218–19
    Errani, 224, 228
    Gasquet, 224
    Guerrero, 219, 220
    I, 222 n50
    Iannone, 220 n.40, 221
    Jack, 221, 227
    Kaskova, 220–1
    Kendrick, 223
    Knauss, 224, 226
    Koubek, 223
    Lepchenko, 100 n.48, 161

anti-doping rules (cont.)
  Perry, 224
  Puerta, 222 n.50, 224
  Roberto La Barbera, 220, 223 n.52
  Sharapova, 226 n.65
  Shoshkyna, 100, 161
  Stanic, 222 n.51
  Suarez, 101
  Tagliaferri, 222
  Villaneuva, 221
  X, 100 n.49
applicable law
  overview, 9
  broadcasting rights agreements (Rome Convention), 61
  building a new role, 43
  CAS appeals, 165
  design rights (WIPO Hague System), 54
  the dilemma, xxxiv
  domain name complaints (UDRP), 66
  interacting possibilities, 1–2
  ITF Independent Tribunal, 158
  tennis governance, 1, 2–4, 9–11
Ashe, Arthur, 25–6, 110–14, 119–21, 129–30, 136, 260
ATP
  ATP PAC
    advisory powers, limitation to, 127
    composition, 126–7, 176
    election/eligibility, 126
    Federer as president, 121
    term of office, 126
  ATP-ITF relationship, 10, 174–5
  Board of Directors, 10, 126
    composition, 10, 126
  Board of Directors (Player Representatives)
    election, 126
    outnumbering, 126
  Board of Directors (tournament representative)
    multiple representation of clients and interests, 127–8
    significant business interests, 127
  criticism of (conflicts of interest), 128–30
    ousting of Kermode, 128–9
    treatment of PTPA, 129–30
  establishment (1972), 174
    from mere players' association to dominant governing body on the men's circuit, 175, 274–5
    full commercialisation of tennis events, 175
    impact on the organization of professional tennis, 174–5
    as a non-profit entity, 10
    original purpose (safeguarding of players' interest within the ITF and WCT), 174
  responsibilities
    ATP tour tournament, 7–8, 10, 174–5
    as the global governing body of men's professional tennis, 126
ATP (dispute resolution)
  appeals
    disputes for determination by CAS, 166
    major offences (ATP CEO), 166
    on-site investigations (ATP Tribunal), 166
  applicability to all non-doping claims arising from the ATP Rules, 165–6
  authority for on-site investigations, 166
  excluded disputes, 166

Becker, Boris, 72 n.10
brand investment: *see also* personal branding
  sponsorship deals, 43–4
broadcasting rights agreements, 60–2
  applicable law (Rome Convention (1961)), 61
  commercial importance to sports organizations, 60
  complexities
    multiple territories/type of rights and media, 61

INDEX

significant variations between
  national IP laws, 61
piracy issues
  importance of effective legislation,
    monitoring and
    enforcement, 61
  loss of revenue, 61
  theft of identity/personal data, 61
Sky Sports deal with ATP and WTA
  (2023), 60–1

CAS: *see also* anti-doping rules (TADC/
  CAS/ITF jurisprudence)
appeals against
  Independent Tribunal awards,
    164–5
  ITIA decisions, 166
applicable law (procedure vs
  substance), 165
arbitration proceedings
  CAS as an independent arbitral
    body, 152–3
  as compulsory arbitration, 17 n.49
  CAS Code, amendment (2005), 148
  case law, universality as binding
    precedent, 6, 100
  Abdelrahman, 100
composition
  criticism of, 125
fair trial obligations (ECHR 6(1)), 17:
  see also fair trial obligations
  (ECHR 6(1))
FIFA's recognition of, 5 n.15
headquarters (Lausanne), 5 n.15
jurisdiction
  ATP disputes, 166
  basis for, 128, 164–5
  challengeable decisions of the
    IOC, 124
  disputes involving Olympic
    Games participants, 124
  ITF recognition of, 124
  WADC appeals, 5, 124
procedure (appeals), 228–9: *see also*
  TADP Procedural Rules in
  numerical order, 13.2
  (appealable decisions), 228
applicable law (CAS Code), 165

deadline for filing, 165
effect of appeal on the
  decision, 165
limitation of challenge to set-aside
  proceedings, 165
proportionality and fairness
  requirement, 100–1
restraint of trade, relevance, 100–1
structure
  anti-doping division, 5 n.15
  as appellate forum, 5
  first-instance arbitration, 5
Casals, Rosie, 115
collective bargaining, 12–14
commercialization of IP rights: *see also*
  broadcasting rights agreements;
  merchandising agreements;
  sponsorship/endorsement
  agreements
overview, 56
company name complaints, 67: *see also*
  IP rights (enforcement action)
Connors, Jimmie, 80, 244, 252, 256
contract-based disputes (domestic
  court litigation)
introduction
  examples of contractual
    agreements, 147, 167–8
  limited resort to, 168
  parties' right to determine dispute
    resolution mechanics, 147, 168
  preference for litigation/English
    law/courts, 168
  regulatory disputes distinguished,
    16–17, 147, 168
choice of court (ITF or ATP/WTA
  liberty to change the status of a
  tournament), 168
  *Deutscher Tennis Bund v. ATP
    Tour Inc.*, 168–9
choice of law, 168
  Rooney, 168 n.81
  Zverev, 168
copyright
duration
  artistic, musical, dramatic and
    literary works, 54
  broadcasts, 54

copyright (cont.)
    sound recordings, 54
    purpose, 54
    scope of protection
        areas of particular interest to the tennis industry, 54
        lack of international harmonization, 54
        limitation to the expression of an idea, 54
        UK Copyright, Designs and Patents Act 1988, 54
corporate capture, 18
corruption
    TACP jurisdiction, 230
Court, Margaret, 115

damages or account of profits (IP infringements), 68
Davis Cup
    IOC and, 15
    ITF Regulations, 16
    ITF responsibility for, 10, 11
    players' interests and, 13
design rights
    particular importance in the sports industry, 53
    purpose, 53
    registered designs
        applicability of the WIPO Hague System, 54
        duration, 54
        eligible designs, 54
        EU Council Regulation No. 6/2002 on Community Designs, 54
        UK Registered Designs Act 1949, 54
    unregistered design protection
        EU Council Regulation No. 6/2002 on Community Designs, 53
        UK Copyright, Designs and Patents Act 1988, 53
digital developments/applications, 42–3
    digital trainers, 42–3, 55
    Hawk-Eye Live, 42, 55

dispute resolution (overview): *see also* CAS
    ADR, role of, 147–8
    ATP dispute resolution, 165–6: *see also* ATP (dispute resolution)
    changes to the ITF Constitution and the ITF internal mechanisms, 148
    contract-based disputes, 7, 147, 167–9: *see also* contract-based disputes
    parties' right to determine dispute resolution mechanics, 147
    doping offences, 147, 148
    Ethics Commission: *see* ethics regulation
    ITF Ethics disputes, 148
    ITF internal mechanisms, 147–8, 149: *see also* dispute resolution (ITF on-site quasi-adjudicatory mechanisms)
        applicability, 6–7
        as the main generator of disputes, 147
        preference over domestic courts, reasons, 5–6
        relationship with CAS, 147
        responsibility for doping and integrity violations, 147
    regulatory and contract-based disputes distinguished, 16–17, 147, 168
    regulatory disputes
        examples of parties involved, 147
        as infractions of ITF, WTA, ATP and tournament rules, 147
        obligatory nature of the rules, 147
    transnational character, 5–9
    WTA dispute resolution, 166–7: *see also* WTA (dispute resolution)
dispute resolution (ITF on-site quasi-adjudicatory mechanisms): *see also* anti-doping rules (TADC/CAS/ITF jurisprudence)
    AHO's first-instance jurisdiction, 149
    procedure, 149
    sanctions, 149

ITF Board's power to prosecute a claim against a national tennis federation, 150-1
  referral of matter to the IAP/ Independent Tribunal, 150-1
ITF Executive Director's authority to suspend a player, 150
ITF Supervisor's role, 150
  right of appeal to the IAP, 150
ITF's investigatory powers, 150
  appointment of independent experts to review the evidence, 150
  challenge to the expert's independence, 150
  referral of finding to the ITF Review Board, 150
  scope (corruption and doping offences as main focus), 149
Djokovic, Novak, 9 n.25, 14, 58, 122, 123-4, 128, 129-30, 131-2, 136, 138, 140, 183-4, 250
Dokic, Jelena, 125, 135
domain name complaints, 66-7: *see also* IP rights (enforcement action)
domestic law and professional tennis, applicability, 1, 9-14
  exceptions to the general rule, benefits, 5-6
  governance laws, 9
  human rights issues: *see* human rights
  issues related to tournaments (criminal and administrative), 2-3, 4-5, 9
  labour laws, 9: *see also* labour status
  NSFs, 5, 9
  relationships between players, academies, coaches and agents, 9, 13
  state's relationship with ITF/IOC, 9, 14

Edberg, Stefan, 120
Elections and Eligibility Panel, 302
  functions, 302
  vetting bodies, 302

endorsement agreements: *see* moral clauses; sponsorship/endorsement agreements
entertainment business, 42-4, 69-72
  competing in the digital age, 43
  digital aids, examples of, 43
  financial statistics 2021-2028, 42
  IP rights, role: *see* IP rights (overview)
  'OneVision' (2022) (ATP), 43
  as part of the global sports industry, 42, 69, 70
  participation statistics
    clubs/courts, 69
    coaches, 69
    fans, 69-70
    gender distribution, 69
    tennis heroes, 71-2
Ethics Code (overview), 285-6
  applicability to all persons serving the ITF, 182
  purpose, 182
Ethics Code by article
  1.3 (covered persons), 189-90
  1.6 (as contractual obligation), 289-90
  2 (overview), 290
  2.1.1 (highest standards of honesty integrity), 290
  2.1.2 (human rights), 290: *see also* human rights and professional tennis (standard-setting role)
  2.1.3 (autonomy from government interference and political neutrality), 290
  2.1.4 (refraint from fraudulent or corrupt act bringing sport into disrepute), 290
  2.2 (undivided loyalty), 291
  2.2.1 (action in the best interests of the ITF, members and tennis as a whole), 291
  2.2.2. (disclosure of a potential disclosure of interest), 291
  2.2.2.1-2.2.3.3 (recusal), 291
  2.3 (bribery and corruption), 291-2
  2.4 (strict confidentiality), 292
    in accordance with local law, 292

Ethics Code by article (cont.)
  2.5.1 (undermining the integrity of a competition), 292
  2.5.2 (avoidance of facilitation of breach of the rules), 292
  2.6 (applicability of ethical rules to Board of Directors elections), 292–3
  2.7 (integrity of the bidding process), 292
  2.8 (cooperation and reporting obligation), 294
Ethics Commission
  establishment (2019), 182
  responsibilities
    compliance with Code principles of integrity and ethics, 182
    investigation of ITF ethical infractions, 6
    monitoring ITF Board elections, 6–7
Ethics Commission (ITF Code of Ethics (Appendix 1)) by article
  1.1 (establishment as independent body to carry out functions under the Code of Ethics), 295
    'independent', 295–6
  1.2 (appointment of Chair and members/legal qualifications), 296
  1.4 (removal for just cause), 296
  1.7 (Legal Secretary's role), 296
  1.9 (oversight of elections and/or appointments to the Board of Directors), 296
  2.1 (eligibility to file a claim), 296
  2.3 (Chair's right to seek further information), 296
  2.5 (appointment of an independent ITF investigator), 296
  2.6/2.7 (Chair's right to raise *ex proprio*/without giving grounds), 296
  2.8 (Chair's options to the challenged official), 296–7
  2.9 (Chair's choices in case of potential breach of local law), 297
  4.2 (finality of the Commission's decision in the absence of a decision to appeal), 298
  4.3 (Chair's right to refer the case to the Independent Tribunal), 295, 297
  4.3.1–4.3.4 (notification of right of appeal), 298
  4.3.5 (notification of hearing by ITC Independent Tribunal: implications), 298–9
  4.4 (provisional suspension), 299
    admissible grounds for challenge (Tribunal's ROP 3.5), 299
  4.4.3 (applicability of Tribunal's Rules), 299
  5.1.1 (official's admission of charges), 300
  5.1.2 (official's dispute of charges: referral to Independent Tribunal), 300
  5.2 (waiver of right to a hearing/acceptance of charges), 300
  5.3 (direct referral to the CAS), 300
  5.3 (proceedings in the name of the Commission), 300
  5.4 (appeal to the CAS), 300
  6.1 (sanctions), 300–2
    Evgenyi Zukin/Iva Majoli cases, 301
    relevant factors, 301
  6.4 (costs to successful official), 299
  7.1 (exclusion of notice of breach more than twelve years after the alleged offence), 298
Ethics Commission (ITF Code of Ethics) by article
  3.1 (investigation initiated by Chair: notification of alleged violations), 297
  4.1 (Chair's alternatives following conclusion of the investigation), 298
ethics regulation, 285–303
  alternative models
    competitive regulation, 287
    outcomes-based, 287
    rules-based, 287

self-enforcement, 287
ethical theories
  consequentialism, 288
  deontology, 288
examples of professions covered
    by, 286
  justification for regulation of the
    legal services (Clement,
    2004), 286
from ethical standard to hard rule
    (international arbitration
    proceedings), 287–8
  core requirements/varying
    standards of impartiality, 288
  courts of the seat as ultimate
    arbiters/reliance on
    institutional standards, 288
international instruments
  UN Convention against
    Corruption (2003), 292
  Whistleblower Directive
    (2019), 292
'liberal professions' (EU Directive on
    Recognition of Professional
    Qualifications (2005)), 286 n.6
  inclusion of non-recognized
    professions, 286–7
as regulatory rules, 286
EU economic law and tennis (overview)
  failure to test compliance of
    regulatory rules of tennis with
    EU rules, reasons, 263
  judicially constructed justifications,
    263–4
    Meca-Medina/Gebhard, 263–4
  SGB conflicts of regulatory and
    commercial functions, 263
  testing compliance (restriction of
    market access/wild cards), 264
EU economic law and tennis (good
    governance standards)
  summary of recommendations,
    283–4
  composition of decision-making
    boards ('red flags'), 265–6
    absence of publicly available ATP
      rules, 265

ATP Chair's conflicting interests,
  265–6
a central aspect, 265
composition of the PAC/casting
  vote, 265
players' consultative role, 265
a 'privilege' to vote (ATP Rule
  1.21), 265
unbalanced board structures,
  266
EU competition law scrutiny, 266
EU recognition of SGB
    independence
  dependence on good governance
    standards, 11–12
  Nice Declaration (2000), 264
  the standards, 264
SGBs' domination of decision-
    making process, 283–4
tennis governance as a network, 264
EU economic law and tennis (market
    access) (summary of the
    challenged ADP Rules), 272–4
OneVision (2021)
  ATP website confirmation of
    market dominance, 275
  exacerbation of existing problems,
    273–4
  failure to consult players, 273 n.37
  Gaudenzi's role, 273 n.37
  manipulating the future, 276–7
  the new commitment, 273–4
  purpose (prevention of an alternative
    tour), 272
Rule 1.07C ('commitment players')
  commitments, 272–3
  definition, 272
  failure to comply/sanctions (Rule
    10.7F), 273
  weight of the commitment, 273
Rule 1.14(1)(B) (restrictions)
  penalties (Rule 8.05A(2)(e)),
    274
  temporal and geographical
    limitations on commitment
    players participation in non-
    ATP events, 274

EU economic law and tennis (market access) (blocking rivals' access)
  manipulating the exploitation market, 267–8
  'organizational market', 266–7
  requiring prior approval of the governing body, 267
  restrictive regulatory measures, 267
EU economic law and tennis (market access) (legal framework)
  'abuse of dominant position' (TFEU 102)
    ATP as dominant undertaking, 274–5
    ATP, Grand Slams and ITF as collectively dominant position, 275
    conflation of regulatory and commercial powers as risk, 268
    qualification as, 268
  jurisprudence
    Bosman, 282
    ESL, 267, 269, 271, 276
    FIA, 268, 269
    Gebhard, 263–4, 282
    Hoöfner and Elser, 268
    ISU cases, 94, 267, 269, 271, 276, 277, 279, 284
    Meca-Medina, 263–4, 268–9, 270–1, 272, 277, 278, 282
    MOTOE (TFEU 106), 269–70, 271, 276, 277, 279, 284
    Ordem dos Técnicos Oficiais de Contas, 272 n.31
    Wouters, 268
  legitimacy requirements
    examples of legitimate objective, 269
    inherence to the objective, 269
    'legitimate objective in the public interest', 269
    proportionality, 269
    summary of requirements (ESL), 283
  prohibition of cartels (TFEU 101 (1)), 268
    'prevention, restriction or distortion of competition' test, 94, 268
  qualification of ATP as, 275
  'undertaking', sports associations as, 268
  unilateral decisions and practices, inclusion, 268
EU economic law and tennis (market access) (legality of ADP Rules/reinforcing practices), 274–9
  ATP as dominant undertaking, 274–5
  ATP, Grand Slams and ITF as a collective dominant position, 275
  legitimate objectives/proportionality
    the arguments and counterarguments, 279
    MOTOE, 277–8
  restrictions (Rule 8.05A(2)(e)/practices)
    cumulative foreclosure effect, 277
    as effective monopolization of opportunities, 275–6
    examples, 276
    failure to comply with *MOTOE* 'restrictions, obligations and review' requirement, 276
Evans, Dan, 83
Evert, Chrissie, 115

fair trial obligations (ECHR 6(1))
  Mutu and Pechstein, 17 n.49
  Riva, Akal, 17 n.50
  waiver of rights, scope for, 157
Federer, Roger, 27, 45, 47, 121, 123–4, 137–8

gambling
  illegal gambling, 101
  ITF's deals with gambling companies, effect, 170, 204–5
  morality clauses, 86
Gaudenzi, Andrea (ATP Chairman)
  as an ATP Media Director, 264–5
  as architect of OneVision, 273 n.37
  conflicts of interest, 266
  PTPA, hostility towards, 138
Gimelstob, Justin, 83

good governance: *see* EU economic law and tennis (good governance standards); ITF (governance); PTPA (governance)
Goolagong, Evonne, 115
Graf, Steffi, 72 n.10
Grand Slam tournaments
   ATP's approach to, 113, 121
      ATP as a dominant undertaking (EU competition law), 274–9
      avoidance of clashes, 187
      players' obligation to play four Grand Slam tournaments, 273
      use of ATP ranking system, 11, 186–7
      wild cards (TFEU 56), 279–82
   commercial value, 28
      merchandising agreements, 60
   controlling on-court behaviour, 245
      grunting, 257
      on-court coaching, 258–9
      Osaka's mental health issues, 262
      variable enforcement, 255
   domain name complaint (*Grand Slam Tennis Properties*), 67
   Grand Slam Board (responsibilities), 8, 210–11
   ITF responsibility for, 7, 10, 11, 16, 174
   morality clauses, 71
   opening to professional players (1968), 25, 194
   prize money arguments 121=124
      IGM's involvement, 128
   Rules
      Grand Slam Code of Conduct, 8, 245
      Grand Slam Tournament Regulations, 8
      objective, 8
   UK ban on Russian/Belarussian athletes post-Ukraine war, 20, 189
   WTA and, 130, 175–6

Halep, Simona, 72 n.10, 83, 133–4
Hawk-Eye Live, 42, 55
Henman, Tim, 72 n.10, 249
Hewitt, Lleyton, 52, 121
human rights and professional tennis (compliance obligations) (international materials)
   CESCR General Comment 24 (2017), 3
   CRC General Comment 19 (2010), 3
   ECSCR General Comment 24 on state obligation in the context of business activities (2017), 3
   EU Commission Working Paper Operational Guidance on taking account of fundamental rights in Commission impact assessments (2011), 3
   EU Directives on Public Procurement and on Non-Financial Information Disclosure, 3 n.11
   HRIAs/due diligence obligations, 3–4, 17, 20, 108–9
   ICCPR (1966), 108
   ICESCR (1966), 108
   ILO principles and standards, 106–10, 138–9
   International Bill of Human Rights, 108
   UDHR (1948), 108
   UDPR (WPA Universal Declaration of Player Rights) (2017), 109
   UNGPs on Business and Investment Rights (2011), 107
   UNGPs on Extreme Poverty and Human Rights (HRC) (2012), 3
   UNGPs on HRIAs for Trade and Investment Agreements (2011), 3
human rights and professional tennis (compliance obligations): *see also* unionization (professional tennis players)
   applicability of rules, principles and fundamental guarantees attaching to other sporting activities, 16
   contractual obligations (domestic law/UNIDROIT), 4, 16–17

human rights and professional (cont.)
  criminal sanctions, 16–17
  domestic law, 17
    Modern Slavery Act 2015 (UK), 3
    Modern Slavery Act 2018 (Australia), 3
  IOC Codes, 20
    ITF emulations, desirability, 20
  ITF's Modern Slavery and Human Trafficking Statement, 17
    ineffectiveness, 20
  ITF's obligations to comply/enforce, 17
  MNCs, 3, 18
  private dispute resolution mechanisms (fair trial obligations), 17
  trade union rights of professional tennis players, 105–10
human rights and professional tennis (standard-setting role), 16–20
  allocation of tournaments as tool, 18
  corporate capture, 18
  criticism of ITF role in Peng Shai case, 18
    WTA approach distinguished, 18
  ITF Code of Ethics, 2.1, 19
    limited value, 19
    text, 19
    Zukin, 19
  ITF Constitution (compliance with Olympic Charter principles), 19
    limited value, 19
  ITF initiatives
    lack of influence on decisions about tournaments, 19–20
    soft approach on Russian/Belarussian athletes post-Ukraine war, 20, 189
    WeThe15, 19–20
  sports diplomacy as a driving force, 17–18

IAP
  overview, 151
  concurrent IAP/Independent Tribunal jurisdiction, 151
  Procedural Rules/ITF Constitution, relationship, 151
  appointment
    ITF Board, 151
    presumption of some legal qualifications, 153
    Sport Resolution's role, 151–2
  Chair
    right to consolidate proceedings/act as emergency arbitrator, 160
    tasks, 159–60
    terms of appointment, 150
  decisions
    appeal to the Independent Tribunal, 152
    enforcement powers, 153–4
    Independent Tribunal Rules/ICC Arbitration Rules distinguished, 153–4
  functions/powers
    composition of the Olympic event, 16
    conduct of investigations, 153
    to invite submissions, 153
    judicial function, evidence of, 153
    kompetenz-kompetenz power, 152
    non-arbitral role, 152
    to require ITF personnel and entities to provide information/attend hearings, 153
    selection of Independent Tribunal, 216
    similarity to expert determination, 152–3
    as a standing committee, 151
  jurisdiction (as an appellate entity), 153, 155–6
    a hotch-potch of conflicting provisions, 155–6
    proceedings requiring a re-hearing vs those not, 156
  jurisdiction (as a first-instance entity), 153, 154–5
    change of nationality requests, 154
    matters covered, 154
    'reciprocity (ITF Code of Conduct, Art. IX), 154–5

INDEX 315

jurisdiction (supervisory
    powers), 153
  arbitral set-aside proceedings
    compared, 156
  scope (complaints not susceptible
    to a judicial hearing), 156
  Sport Resolution's responsibility
    for, 159
ILO principles and standards, 106–10,
    138–9: *see also* unionization
    (professional tennis players)
image rights/rights of publicity
  international diversity, 55
  protection by other IP rights, 55
  revenues from commercial
    exploitation, 55
  a rough definition, 55
IMG, 25–6
  business model, 127–8
  portfolio
    current, 128
    original preference for individual
      players (golf/tennis)/reasons, 25
    vs ProServ, 25–6
IMG Academy, 128
  protégés, 128
injunctions (IP infringements), 68
integrity in tennis (overview), 210–11
international law, relevance to
    professional tennis, 14–16: *see
    also* human rights; Olympic
    movement and professional
    tennis
  limitation of discussion to human
    rights/investment capacity,
    14–15
IOC
  authority over all international
    sports federations, 5
  applicability of IOC-related
    commitments, 5
IP rights (overview), 44–5: *see also*
    broadcasting rights agreements;
    copyright; image rights/rights
    of publicity; merchandising
    agreements; patent rights;
    sponsorship/endorsement
    agreements; trade secrets/
    confidential information;
    trademarks
  ownership of
    complexity of the possibilities,
      44–5
    factors to consider in negotiating
      an IP protection strategy, 45
    territoriality, 44–5
  role, 42–4
IP rights infringements, remedies, 67–8
  overview
    IIP registry proceedings,
      limitations, 67
    judicial litigation, time and cost
      of, 67
  judicial remedies, 68
    award of costs, 68
    damages or account of profits, 68
    delivery up/destruction of infringing
      items, 68
    tracing orders, 68
  injunctions
    definition, 68
    interim injunctions, 68
    perpetual injunctions, 68
IP rights (enforcement action)
  overview
    dependence on local laws, 63
    domain/company name
      complaints, 63
    extra-judicial proceedings
      (registered IP rights), 63
    litigation, 63, 62–8: *see also* ITIA
  cease and desist letters, 63
    mandatory requirement for (UK
      Civil Procedure Rules), 63
    purpose/desirability, 63
  company name complaints
    Company Names Tribunal's list of
      decision, 67
    required elements, 67
    submission to Company Names
      Tribunal option, 67
  domain name complaints
    applicable law (UDRP), 66
    choice of forum, 66
    expedited administrative
      proceedings, 66

IP rights (cont.)
  Grand Slam Tennis Properties, 67
  required elements, 67
  invalidity action
    bad faith, 65–6
    IP rights owners' need to make a strong case, 66
    registration of a later identical or similar trademark, 66
  monitoring infringements, 62–3
    comprehensive brand protection schemes, benefits, 62–3
    manual approach, limitations, 62
    monitoring services, 62
    responsibilities of brand owners, 62
    social media, role, 62
  revocation actions
    action in respect of an entire or partial registration, 64
    genuine use obligation, 65
    grounds for action, 64–5
  trade validity and revocation actions
    grounds for challenge, 64
    importance of maintaining the validity and enforceability of their trademarks, 64
    as part of a wider infringement dispute, 64
    right to initiate action, alternatives, 66
  trademark infringement proceedings
    prevention of the use of an identical or similar trademark as objective, 66
    trademark opposition proceedings distinguished, 66
  trademark oppositions
    absolute vs relative grounds, 64
    prevention of registration as objective, 66
    procedure, 64
    publication of trademark applications, 64
    right to initiate action, 64
    territorial basis, 64
IPIN/ATP/WTA player zone registration, 231

Isner, John, 128, 140, 141
ITF (governance): *see also* Ethics Code; ethics regulation
  Board
    'Athlete Representative Board members'/accountability, 126
    membership, 125–6
  dominant role, 16, 275
  powers (Constitution 3.1), 174–5
  registration (Bahamas)/headquarters (London), 2, 11, 180, 299
    benefits, 2
  responsibilities
    Fed and Hopman Cups, 174
    Grand Slams, Davis Cup and Olympic tennis tournament, 7, 10, 11, 16, 174
    ITF junior circuit tournaments, 7, 174
    as key protagonist, 1, 10–11, 16, 174
  structure
    limited liability company, 125, 180
    membership (NTFs), 11–12
    voting rights, 11–12
  transnational status, 1
ITF Independent Tribunal, 157–65: *see also* anti-doping rules (TADC/CAS/ITF jurisprudence)
  appeals to CAS: *see also* CAS
    appeal against a decision of the Panel or ITF panel, 165
    applicable law, 165
    basis for, 164–5
    CAS procedure, 164–5
    ITF Rules as basis for, 164
    limitation of challenge to set-aside proceedings, 165
    limitation to first-instance awards, 164
  applicable law
    Coleman, 158 n.39
    conflicting provisions, 158
    English law/Arbitration Act 1996, 89, 158
    Houdet, 158
    jurisdiction, 157

INDEX

acceptance of the Tribunal's jurisdiction/waiver of right to another forum, 157
applicability of CAS jurisdiction in absence of ITF jurisdiction, 157
fair trial considerations, 157
ITF Constitution/Tribunal's Rules as agreement to arbitrate (UNCITRAL Model Law), 157
seat of proceedings, 157
waiver of right to litigation/ setting-aside proceedings, 157
legal status
  2005 changes, 148
  as an arbitral tribunal, 89, 158
  exclusive jurisdiction of English courts over appeals from, 89
transitional justice and *Nastase*, 158-9
Tribunal's perception of its extra-dispute resolution role, 158-9
ITF Independent Tribunal (jurisdiction), 162-4
as appellate body, 162
first-instance jurisdiction, 162-4
  major offences (ITF Code of Conduct), 163-4
  Men's/Women's World Tennis Tour Regulations, 162-3
  TADP Rules, 163
as supervisory body, 162
ITF Independent Tribunal (procedures), 159-62
binding effect of a final court award/ competent arbitral decision, 162
constitution, 159-60, 216
  appointment by Panel Chair, 159
  challenge to arbitrator, grounds, 159-60
  parties' lack of control of, 159-60
fairness obligation
  implied contractual duty, 162
  Wilander v. Tobin, 162
powers
  kompetenz-kompetenz/inherent powers, 160
  Tribunal Chairman's right of unilateral action, 160-1
  unusual features, reasons for/ validity, 160
Sport Resolutions, role, 151-2, 159: *see also* Sport Resolutions
Tribunal's Procedural Rules
  as definitive instrument, 159
  as tailor-made, 159
ITF International Adjudication Panel, 181-2
ITIA (introduction)
historical background, 210
  assumption of TIU (corruption)/ ITF (doping) duties, 210
  establishment (2021), 124, 181, 210
status
  funding, 211
  a private company limited by guarantee, 210
  registered office (UK), 210
structure and organization
  employment numbers, 210
  working methods, 210
TISB, 210-11
  funding, 211
  independence of ITIA, 210
  membership, 210
ITIA Sanctioning Guidelines (2021), 241-3
(overview)
  drafting history, 241
  examples of category A1 offenders, 243
  as guidance/a framework, 241
  key principles/scheme for calculating an appropriate remedy, 242
  purpose (proportionate punishment/ deterrence), 240-1
  examples, 240-1
stage 1 (determining the offense category)
  A. high culpability, 241
  B. medium culpability, 241
  C. lesser culpability, 241
  Categories 2 and 3 impact, 242
  Category 1 impact, 241-2
stage 2 (starting point and category range)

ITIA Sanctioning Guidelines (cont.)
    aggravating/mitigating factors, 242
    AHO's discretion to cross the
        boundaries, 242
    itemised outcomes for A1 to C3 on
        the category range, 242
    stage 3 (covered persons'
        cooperation), 242
    stage 4 ('substantial assistance'), 242
    stage 5 (decision on a fine), 242-3

Keothavong, Anne, 247
Kermode, Chris, 128-9
King, Billie Jean, 7, 16, 80, 81, 111, 112, 130, 175
Kramer, Jack, 113, 114, 118, 137
Kroon, Niclas, 52
Kyrgios, Nick, 75, 81, 250, 255

labour status, 2-14: *see also* players and the ATP/WTA
    collective bargaining arrangements/
        institutional protection of
        rights, absence, 13
    excluded benefits, 13
    steps towards/limited scope and
        number, 13-14
    growing unionization/PTPA, 13
    as independent contractors under
        ATW/WTA control, 12-13
    limitation of membership to men,
        131-2
    NTF selections, exclusion from
        challenge in national courts,
        13
    Washington, 13
Lendl, Ivan, 49
lex sportiva (transnational law), 2-9
    applicability
        ethical issues, 287
        organization and allocation of
            tournaments, 2-3
    benefits, 2
    implementation, 4-5
licensing arrangements, 58-9: *see also*
    sponsorship agreements (IP
    rights) (key provisions),
    licensing arrangements

McEnroe, John, 47, 80, 244, 252, 254, 257
McNamee, Paul, 129-30
media rights: *see* broadcasting rights
    agreements
Medvedev, Daniil, 58, 122, 136
merchandising agreements
    description of, 60
    importance of quality control
        provisions, 60
    inclusion of standard licensing IPR
        provisions, 60
moral clauses: *see also* sponsorship/
        endorsement agreements
    alternatives to, 80
    confidentiality of clauses, 83-4
    criticism of, 86-7
    definition issues, 76
        'morality', 79
        'reverse' moral clauses, 79
        terminology, 76
    examples, 83-6, 253-4
        Yonex, 76, 250, 253
    factors impacting on endorsement
        agreements
        activism, 80
        'bringing the game into
            disrepute', 81
        doping offences, 82-3
        sexual orientation, 80-1
        unsportsmanlike behavior on-court,
            80, 82
    frequency/coverage, 76, 77
    geographical spread, 77-8
    history, 77, 86-7
    justification for, 76
    negotiations, 76-7
        achieving a fair protection of both
            parties, 78-9
        a broad vs a narrow clause, 78
        importance of precise language, 78
        inclusion of private behaviour,
            78, 79
        personality of player, relevance,
            79
    sanctions/termination, 79-80, 83
        recommendation for a cautious
            approach, 79-80, 83

INDEX

social media as a danger zone, 78–9, 83, 87
   as a standard-setting tool, 76–7
   termination of tennis contracts on ethical grounds, 80–3
   use of, 79–80

Na, Li, 121
Năstase, Ilie, 6, 75, 80, 83, 101 n.51, 102 n.57, 115, 158–9, 244, 247, 252, 254, 255
nationality
   request to change, 154
Navratilova, Martina, 26, 81–2, 256–7
Netflix, 43
Newcombe, John, 112
Nice Classification system, 52–3
Nice Declaration on the Specific Characteristics of Sport and Its Social Function in Europe, 264
Noah, Yannick/*Noah Clothing*, 65
Nouza, Petr, 123
NSFs and ITC membership (ITC Constitution 3), 179–80
   criteria, 179–80
   membership numbers, 179
   procedure, 180
   sanctions for damage to the image of the ITF/tennis or breach of ITF rules, 180
   voting rights, 179

Olympic movement and professional tennis, 15–16
   history (in date order)
      inclusion in the first Olympic Games (1896), 15
      admission of women players (1900), 15
      clash between the 1912 Olympic Games and Wimbledon, 172
      IOC/ITF frictions leading to the removal of tennis from the 1924 Olympics, 15, 172–3
      failure to resolve the issues/continued exclusion (1924–1968), 15, 173
      rejection of request for readmission (1956), 15, 173
      reinstatement as a demonstration sport (1968), 15, 173
      changes in IOC approaches/re-entry of tennis to the games (1973–1988), 15–16
   current arrangements
      applicability of ITF Regulations, 16
      events, 16
      ITF Independent Tribunal's discretionary powers, 16
      management by ITF, 16, 19
   factors complicating the relationship
      failure of NSFs to safeguard players effectively, 173
      ILTF/national federations insistence on more involvement in decision-making, 15
      IOC conservatism particularly its insistence on amateur status, 15, 172–3
      poor organization of the 1920 and 1924 events, 15
   factors contributing to reinstatement
      ALTC's decision to admit professionals to Wimbledon, 173
      evolution of the amateurism rule, 15, 173–4
      geopolitical dynamics, 173–4
      growing commercialization of professional sport, 15–16
      IOC's financial difficulties, 15
      Los Angeles Games (1988) as a blueprint, 16
      Samaranch doctrine, 15–16
      USLTA's support, 173
   impact of accepting professional tennis on the development of the Olympic Movement, 16, 172
'OneVision' (2022) (ATP), 43: *see also* EU economic law and tennis (market access) (summary of the challenged ADP Rules)
Osaka, Mari, 134–5

Osaka, Naomi, 102, 124, 134–5, 258–9, 262

patent rights
athletes' indirect dependence on, 55
difficulty and expense of maintenance, 55
exclusion from protection, 55
protection offered/requirements for (UK Patents Act 1997), 55
shape marks as alternative, 49
personal branding: *see also* brand investment
brand protection, 43–4
building rapport with a global audience, 43
private lives, growing interest in, 43
ranking required to break even, 134–5
play-agent relations: *see* agency (player-agent relations)
player rights, pay and conditions (the ATP/WTA Rulebooks)
ATP Baseline pilot project (2023), 133
human rights issues
Dokic, 135
Osaka, 134–5
'special ranking rule'
purpose, 133–4
unintended consequences (Halep), 133–4
WTA's proposed alternative, 134
the system
lucrative earnings for the top players/hardly making ends meet for others, 133
outline of the principles, 133
pro-tennis's 1970s' first labour settlement, 132
players and the ATP/WTA, 13–14, 177–9: *see also* labour status
ATP/WTA governance
balancing conflicting interests, 13
Board representation (players), 13
ATP/WTA membership arrangements, 177–8
eligibility, 177
fees, 177
ATP/WTA membership benefits
Baseline (financial safety net), 178
medical insurance, 177–8
pension scheme, 178
code of conduct
dress code, 178–9
media obligations, 178
participation in ATP STARS activities, 178
penalties for breach, 178
professional conduct, 178
registration/membership
dependence of participation in professional tennis on, 177
obligations on players resulting from, 177
Pospisil, Vasek, 123–4, 128–9, 131, 135, 138, 140
prize money
ATP agreement to forgo individual salaries, 113, 132–3
comparison with other sports, 122–4, 140–1
Covid-related unfairness, 128
disparity between men and women, 112, 113–14, 131–2, 136–7 (Tables 6.4 and 6.5)
examples, 114
a Pyrrhic victory (King), 120
US Open awards equal prize money (1973), 115
disparity between prize money and costs (Independent Review of Integrity in Tennis (2018)), 205–6
players' dissatisfaction with prize money pools, 118, 119–24
players' rejection of the collective bargaining model, 118–20
players' varying perspectives on the inequalities in tennis, 123
WCT plans to exclude independent professionals from their tournaments/reversal of decision (1970/1972), 112–13

'professional tennis
  a broad choice, xxxiii–xxxiv
  difficulties of definition, xxxiii–xxxiv
ProServ
  dominance with IMG, 26
  Lendl, 39
  vs IMG, 25–6
PTPA (establishment/reactions to)
  establishment (2020) (Pospisil/
    Djokovic), 123–4, 135–9
  exclusive action
    exclusion of members from the
      ATP Board, 129
    WTA's refusal of players'
      demands to be represented by
      PTPA, 130
  objective
    'a union' (Pospisil), 138
    an independent self-governance
      structure, 138
    'an independent voice from the
      traditional men's tour, 123–4
    scope of envisaged activities, 138
  opposition
    'an existential threat', 138–9
    Federer and Nadal, 137–8
    'Seven Kingdoms', 137
  tension between players happy with
    the existing situation and those
    not as key issue, 138–9
PTPA (governance)
  inaugural Board
    gender equality/cultural
      diversity, 140
    membership, 140
  principles/core tenets, 139–40
    securing players' share of the
      sport's wealth, 140–1
    trade union principles as key, 140
  status (Canadian not-for-profit
    company), 139
public policy/interest
  EU competition law, 263–4, 267–71,
    277–9, 282–3, 284
  jurisprudence
    Patel v. Mirza, 91–2
    Rooney, 91

Zverev, 6, 40–1, 55, 96–9, 127, 136,
  168–9
restraint of trade, 46, 89, 91–4, 98–9,
  100–1
waivers of access to justice, 155, 168–9

Querrey, Sam, 129

regional associations, 44–5, 70, 199,
  292–3
regulating on-court tennis indiscipline,
  overview: *see also* Rules of
  Tennis
  the Code as the principal basis for
    disciplinary action in
    tennis, 245
    ATP/WTA/Grand Slam
      variants, 245
  impact of the social origins of tennis,
    245–6, 250–1
  ITF Rules of Tennis as the definition
    of playing tennis, 245
  the role of rules, 244
regulating on-court tennis indiscipline,
  (changing the rules)
  coaching during a match
    a common practice?, 258
    reasons for resistance to, 258
    trialling change, 259
  a relative rarity in tennis, 258
  subtle shifts (mental health) (Osaka)
    refusal to attend post-match press
      conference (2021), 262
    Roland-Garros's implementation
      of a tool to protect against
      online abuse, 262
    strong support leading to change
      of approach, 262
  subtle shifts (race), 260–2
    experiences of Venus and Serena
      Williams, 260–1
    normalizing a black aesthetic,
      261
    race-based misperceptions/
      misapplication of the rules, 261
    still a white space, 260
    the Wimbledon dress code, 259–60

322   INDEX

regulating on-court tennis indiscipline (commodification of 'bad boy' tennis)
  (introduction), 252
  adjudication and enforcement
    grunting, 256–7
    risk of a 'home advantage/inconsistent decision-making, 255
    'temporal variance, 255
  sponsors' influence
    marked increase in sponsorship/media deals, 253
    negative impact of bad behaviour on players/sports organizations, 253–4
    reluctance to forgo a bad-behaved crowd draw, 252, 254
regulating on-court tennis indiscipline (the Code)
  audible obscenity, visible obscenity and verbal abuse
    examples (Tarango), 251–2
  examples of common code violence, 248
  in-game violations, penalties
    decisions as 'final and irrevocable' (Code IC(R)), 248
    'immediate default' (Code IV (S)), 248
    'point penalty schedule' (Code IV (R)), 248
  physical violence, 248–51
    'abuse of balls', 249–50
    'abuse of racquet or equipment, 250
    rarity of interpersonal physical violence in tennis, reasons, 249
  purpose (Code I(A)), 246
    protection of the sport's aesthetics as key purpose, 250–1
  responsibility for administration of integrity rules, 246: *see also* TACP; TADP
  appeals mechanisms, 247: *see also* CAS, procedure (appeals); ITF Independent Tribunal

sanctions
  criminal liability, 247
  scope (*Nastase*), 247
restraint of trade (English common law) (introduction)
  as a contractual remedy, 89
    effective imposition of restraint, need for, 89
    right to invoke in the absence of a contract, 89
    types of agreements giving rise to, 90
  description of, 88
  domination of English law, reasons for, 88–9
  fluidity of the boundaries, 90
  protection of the weaker party, 90
  guiding principles
    non-violation of competition rules, 90, 92, 94
    protection of the weaker party, 90
  justification/rationale, 89–90
    public policy, 89, 91–4, 96, 99, 103–4
    unenforceability/voidness of an unjustified restriction on trade, 89–90
  unreasonableness as ground for non-enforcement
    balancing the factors, 90–1, 92–3
    interests of the parties, 40–1, 90–1
    interests of the public, 40–1, 91–2
  Zverev, 6, 40–1, 55, 96–9, 127, 136, 168–9
restraint of trade (English common law) (disciplinary bans), 99–102
  heavy sentences
    restraint of trade offences, 99
  jurisprudence
    Luis Suarez, 99
  proportionality and fairness requirement, 99, 101–2
restraint of trade (English common law) (disciplinary bans)
  heavy sentences
    doping/illegal gambling, 99
    tennis offences (ITF Rules), 99–102

breach of rules of conduct, 101–2
  doping and corruption, 99–100
restraint of trade (English common law) (national federation and state regulation), 92–4
  balancing justification and improper restraint, 92–3
  professional/public interest, need for, 93–4
  proportionality, 93
  examples of domestic law constraints, 93
  jurisprudence
    Eastham, 93
    Greig, 93
    ISC attempts to restrict members' rights (EU rules), 94
    Nagle v. Feilden (Jockey Club's refusal of training licences to women), 93
restraint of trade (English common law) (players' contracts with agents), 94–6
  negative consequences for the athlete, 95–6
  non-enforceability
    absence of justification, 96
    proscription by the governing body, 96
  royalties from direct sports earnings, 94–5
  royalties from image rights, 95–6
    Rooney, 95
    Watson v. Praeger, 95–6
restraint of trade (English common law) (professional tennis): *see also* agency (player-agent relations)
  introduction, 96
  agency agreements restraints
    confidential/redacted proceedings, 97–8
    Instone, 97 n.36
    non-financial factors/'trading society' test, 97, 98
    Peninsula Securities, 98–9
    relevant factors, 97–8
    Zverev, 96–9

restraint of trade (English common law) (qualification for national tennis teams), 103–4
  benefits from national team selection, 103
  ITF Constitution (IOC provisions), 103
  Oksana Kalashnikova and Ekaterine Gorgodze, 103–4
  possibility of an amendment to ITF Rules, 194
revocation actions, 64–5: *see also* IP rights (enforcement)
Rules of Tennis: *see also* regulating on-court tennis indiscipline
  ITF International Adjudication Panel, 181–2
  ITF responsibility for, 180
    annual updating/objectives, 181
    objectives (balancing tradition and the development of the sport (Appendix XII)), 246
  Rules of Tennis Committee
    composition, 181
    election to, 181
    removal of a member, 181
    responsibilities, 181
    term of office, 181
  Ruling Board's role, 181
Russian Tennis Federation, 26
Russian/Belarussian players post-invasion of Ukraine, 20, 151, 170, 186, 189, 301

safeguarding in tennis (introduction)
  a catalyst for action, 190
  definition/scope, 191, 192
  examples of action in date order
    2001 (addition of a Child Protection in Sport Unit to NSPCC's portfolio), 190
    2008 (AusAID's implementation of a Child Protection Policy), 190
    2012 (UNICEF's International Safeguards for Children in Sport), 190

safeguarding in tennis (cont.)
  relevant legal materials
    CRC (Art. 19), 190–1
    CRDP (Art. 30), 190–1
    national sport-specific legislation, 191–2
    specific criminal laws, 190
  relevant rules and codes
    ATP draft Code (in progress), 191
    ATP Independent Safeguarding Report (2021), 191
    ATP Tour Director of Safeguarding (2021), 191
    ITF Safeguarding Adults Policy (2023), 191
    ITF Safeguarding Children Policy (2023), 191
    US Center for Safesport's Code for the US Olympic and Paralympic Movement (2023), 191
    USTA Safe Play Handbook (2021), 191, 192
    WTA Safeguarding Code of Conduct (2023), 191
safeguarding in tennis (a duty of care), 192–4
  reasonableness test, 193
  relationship of trust doctrine
    ITF's Safeguarding Policy for Children (relationship of trust doctrine), 193–4
    WTA's Safeguarding Code of Conduct, 194
  relationships giving rise to
    Donoghue v. Stevenson, 192–3
    Shone v. BBSA, 193
safeguarding in tennis (abuse in sport)
  inequality of the relationship across a range of situations as the main factor, 194
  main concerns (sexual, physical and emotional abuse and violence), 194
  main perpetrators, 194
  statistics, 194
    elite athletes as main targets, 194
    IOC, UNICEF and EU documents, focus on, 195

safeguarding in tennis (adult athletes) (notable differences from policy for children), 204–6
  applicability to vulnerability to risk or harm, 204
  dependence on personal circumstances, 204
  failure to address gambling issues, 204–5
  negligible/inappropriate reference to issues affecting adults, 204–5
  social media abuse, ATP/WTA duty to address, 206
  introduction of the Matrix monitoring service, 206
safeguarding in tennis (child-adult relationships) (ITF's safeguarding policy), 196–8
  absence of a published policy, 198 n.32
  accommodation concerns/ITF's attempts to address, 199–200
  absence of an implementing mechanism, 199–200
  appointment of a Safeguarding Manager and Designated Safeguarding Officer, 199
  Safeguarding Manager's responsibilities/necessary skills, 199
  detecting abuse
    key indicators (Art. 18), 202
    a listening culture (Art. 19), 202
    a responsibility of all covered persons and the organization as a whole, 202
  disallowed conduct (Art. 15), an extensive list including
    abuse, harassment, violence and sexual exploitation, 200
    inclusion of 'poor practice', 'neglect' and 'emotional abuse', 200
    social media rules, 200
  examples of
    parents' and caregivers abuse'/ITF's obligation to monitor and report, 201–2

poor practice, 200–1
psychological and emotional neglect, 201–2
unacceptable conduct (Art. 16), 201–2
focus on a safer recruitment policy, 198–9
ITF reports to national authorities/ follow-up action, 201–2
safeguarding in tennis (child-adult relationships) (safeguarding against future harm), 202–4
conditions leading to, 202
doping concerns (WADA Report, January 2024), 204
ITIA responsibility
difficulty of identifying appropriate action/obligations of stakeholders, 204
need for expansion of successful programmes to national federations, 203–4
a responsibility of the ITF, ATP and WTA to address?, 202–3
WTA's initiatives
AERs, 203
high achievements/career longevity, 203
obligation to comply with minimum educational requirements, 203
safeguarding in tennis (child-adult relationships) (WTA)
1994 (review of young women's needs in elite tennis), 195
AER/PDP initiatives, 195–6
2004/2014 reviews, 196
2006 Safety and Security Task Force review, 196
measures introduced following, 196
a holistic approach, 196
safeguarding in tennis (conduct of tennis athletes against non-athletes)
absence of a relationship of trust in the sporting context, 208–9

fiduciary duties of agents to clients (contractual, statutory and common law), 209
stakeholders' safeguarding duties as potential base, 209
Zverev case (reversal of ATP's intention to treat as a 'safeguarding investigation'), 209
safeguarding in tennis (consequences of failure to meet obligations)
ITF options
criminal proceedings in the territorial state, 107
non-criminal activity, 207
liability of the club, NFU or governing body
contractual/absence of evidence of, 207–8
ITF contractual responsibility under the Safeguarding Responsibility for Children, 208
tort-based, 207
safeguarding in tennis (health and safety)
Health and Safety Act at Work 1974 (UK), 206–7
limited ITF reference to/national responsibility for, 206
LTA Coach Qualification Health and Safety Policy, 207
Safin, Marit, 121
Seles, Monica, 256–7
'Seven Kingdoms'
membership of the group (ITF, ATP, WTA and Grand Slams), 124
modes of player and athlete engagement
diversity, 124–5
as internal and subordinate bodies avoiding player unions, 125
responsibility for regulation of player engagement, representation and input into decision-making, 125
roles of
CAS, 124

326   INDEX

'Seven Kingdoms' (cont.)
   IOC/WADC, 124
   TACP, 124
   TADP, 124
Sharapova, María, 74, 81–2, 121, 226, 253
Shuai, Peng, 18
social media
   agents' role, 27
   competition from, 43
   IP infringements, 62–3
   morality clauses and, 78–9, 83
sponsorship agreements (IP rights) (overview): *see also* broadcasting rights agreements; merchandising agreements; sponsorship/endorsement agreements
   commercial factors for consideration, 57
   definition, 56
   endorsement contracts distinguished, 60
   key provisions, 57
   potential benefits, 56
   risks, 56–7
sponsorship agreements (IP rights) (key provisions)
   ambush marketing
      definition, 59
      example (Heineken/Stella Artois (2011)), 59
      legal, statutory and regulatory framework, territorial basis, 59
      legality/illegality/in-between, 59
      mitigating the effects, 59–60
      sponsorship agreements, importance of protective provisions, 59
      trademarks, copyright and designs, role, 59
   details of key rights exploited
      arrangements post-termination of the sponsorship agreement, 58
      details and ownership of rights, 57–8
      potential problems, 58
      protection against ambush marketing, 59
      registration options, 58
   licensing arrangements
      clarity about jurisdiction, 59
      clear list of licences granted/required, 58
      duration, territorial scope and termination provisions, 59
      examples of licence terms, 58–9
      financial terms, 59
sponsorship/endorsement agreements: *see also* brand investment; moral clauses; regulating on-court tennis indiscipline (commodification of 'bad boy' tennis)
   overview
      attractiveness of tennis players, 73
      distinction between, 60, 73
      mutual benefits, 72–3
      risks, 73–4: *see also* scandals *below*
   agents' role, 26, 27–8
   digital aids to finding, 42
   scandals, cancellation of contracts consequent on/examples, 74, 253–4
   scandals, classification as
      by characteristics, 73–4
      by inappropriate behaviour of one of the parties, 74
      by salient feature, 74
      controversial behaviour by member of a player's entourage/endorsement company, 75
      difficulty of definition, 73–4
Sport Resolutions
   as the Independent Tribunal's secretariat, 151–2, 159
   legal status, 159 n.42

TACP overview (vulnerabilities)
   as an individual sport, 229
   appetite/opportunities for online betting, 230, 233–4
   difficulties of funding a professional career, 229–30

triggering an investigation
  covered person alerts, 234
  match alerts, 234
TACP (jurisprudence)
  Affi, Gharsallah and Snene, 238–9
  Crepatte, 232 n.92
  Fayziev, 236
  Feitt, 238
  Grigaitis, 238
  Khabibulin, 236
  Köellerer, 236 n.109
  Lescure, 236
  Okala, 236 n.109
  Oriekhov, 235–6
TACP Procedural Rules in numerical order
  A (introduction) (purpose of the TACP), 230
  B.10 (definitions: 'covered person'), 230–1
  B.22 (definitions: 'major offence'), 232
  B.24 (definitions: 'notice of major offence'), 232
  B.28 (definitions: 'player'), 231 n.89
  B.31 (definitions: 'related person'), 231 n.89
  B.34 (definitions: 'substantial assistance), 242
  B.39 (definitions: 'tournament support personnel'), 231 n.89
  D.1.a (betting by a covered person), 235
  D.1.a–D.1.r (corruption offences), 233–4, 240
  D.1.b (facilitation, encouragement or promotion of betting by a covered person), 235
  D.1.d (contriving the outcome of an event), 216, 236, 239
    financial return, relevance, 237–8
    most common Art. D.1.d offence, 236
    a typical methodology, 236–7
  D.1.e to D.1.g and D.1.o (facilitating others to fix a match), 238
  D.1.m (umpires fixing a match), 238–9
  D.1.q (prohibition on engagement by a tennis betting operator), 235–6
  D.2.a.i and D.2.b.i (reporting an approach to a covered person), 230
  D.2.a.ii and D.2.b.ii (reporting a suspicion of an offence), 230
  F.2.b (obligation to cooperate fully), 239–40
  G.1 (commencement of proceedings), 232
  G.1.a (notice of a major offence: scope), 232–3
  G.1.f.ii (briefing on issues to be raised), 233
  G.2 (conduct of proceedings), 232
  G.3.a (burden of proof (ITIA): preponderance of the evidence), 232
  G.3.b (burden of proof (alleged offender): preponderance of the evidence), 232
  G.3.d (admissibility of evidence: AHO's right to determine facts by any reliable means), 231–2
    use of inference (*Crepatte*), 232
  G.4.a and G.4.b (decision), 233
  H (sanctions), 240–3: *see also* ITIA Sanctioning Guidelines (2021)
    purposes (proportionate punishment/deterrence), 240–3
  H.1.a(i) and (iii)/H.1.b(i) and (iii), 241
  I.1/S.I.1 (right of appeal/scope), 233
  I.4 (time limits), 233
  K.2 (governing law (Florida)), 231–2
    exceptions, 231–2
    reasons for choice, 231
TADP
  conflict with the rankings system (Halep), 133–4, 158
  Independent Tribunal jurisdiction in case of a disputed charge, 163
  WADA implementation/compliance obligation, 6 n.16, 124, 211–12
TADP Procedural Rules in numerical order: *see also* anti-doping rules

(TADC/CAS/ITF jurisprudence); ITF Independent Tribunal
1.1.7 (ITF's delegation of responsibility to ITIA), 212
1.2.6 ('player'), 212
'player support person', 212
1.3 (English courts' exclusive jurisdiction), 89
2.1 (ADRV: presence of a prohibited substance), 212
    establishing a presence, 213
    exceptions, 213
    Prohibited List (WADA), 213
2.1.1 (strict liability), 212, 223–5
    out-of-competition exemption, 213
    player's personal responsibility to ensure compliance, 223–5
    TEU exemption, 213
2.1.1.3 (other ADRVs), 214
2.2 (ADRV: use of a prohibited method), 212
    presumption of use, 213
2.2 (proceedings) (overview), 214–15
2.2.1 (notice), 215
2.2.2 (Charge Letter), 215–16
    player's options, 216
2.2.3 (hearing), 216–17
2.3-2.11 (list of ADRVs), 214
3.1.1 (burden of proof (ADRV) (ITIA)), 100, 161, 218
    'a comfortable satisfaction' between a balance of probability and beyond a reasonable doubt', 101, 218
7.14.2 (ITIA's reasoned decision), 216
8.1 (referral to an Independent Panel), 163, 216–17
8.2-8.3 (establishment of panel/pre-hearing issues), 216
8.4.3/8.4.5 (player's fair hearing rights), 217
8.5.2 (Tribunal's decision), 217
8.5.3/8.5.4 (costs), 217
10 (ineligibility sanctions), 217–21

10.2.1 (ineligibility sanctions: 4-year baseline), 217
10.2.1.1 (intent: non-specified substance (burden of proof on the player)), 219–21
    presumption of intent (CAS jurisprudence), 218–19
10.2.1.2 (intent: specified substance (burden of proof on ITIA)), 218
10.2.2 (ineligibility sanctions: extenuating circumstances), 217–18, 221–2
    finding of no intention, 218, 221–2
    level of fault requirements, 218
10.2.3 ('intentional' (knowledge an ADRV/risk of)), 100, 161, 219
    burden of proof (player), 100, 161, 219
    establishing the source as evidence of lack of intent, 219–21
    'facts established by any reliable means' (ITF Tribunal Procedural Rules), 161
    'other good reason' (a high CAS threshold), 221
10.5 (no fault or negligence (elimination of period of ineligibility)), 222–8
    contaminated substance (Code comment), 225
    definition (TADP Appendix One), 222
    'every conceivable effort' test, 224–5
    examples of successful/unsuccessful defences, 224
    requirements, 222–3
    'utmost caution' test, 223
10.6.1 (no significant fault or negligence (reduction of period of ineligibility)), 222, 225–8
    definition (TADP Appendix One), 225
    examples of successful/unsuccessful defences, 225, 226–8
    a high but not impossible standard (CAS), 226

INDEX

objective assessment/relevant
    factors, 226–7
requirements, 225
subjective assessment (arbitral
    body)/relevant factors, 227
'utmost caution' rest, 225–6
10.6.1.2 (contaminated
    products), 225
definition (TADP Appendix
    One), 225
10.6.2 (no significant fault beyond
    Art. 6.1), 222 n. 47
13.2 (appealable decisions), 228
13.2.1 (appeals involving
    international-level players), 228
13.2.2 (appeals involving other
    players or other persons), 228
13.8.1.1 (time limits: appealing
    player), 228
13.8.1.2 (time-limits: ITIA), 228
13.8.1.3 (time-limits: WADA), 228
tennis governance (ITF/APT/WTA)
    (introduction): *see also* EU
    economic law; unionization
    (professional tennis players)
complicating factors, 9–11: *see also*
    Olympic movement and
    professional tennis
  existence of player-based
    organizations (ATP/WTA)/
    Grand Slams, 71
  fundamental divergence of
    approach between players and
    governing bodies, 105–43
  impact of international
    disarray, 170
  importance of the players/
    pressure for greater
    involvement, 170
  jurisdictional overlap, 170
  ranges of actors involved, 71
  rigid amateurism vs uncontrolled
    professionalism, 174
  sanction-related power of
    governing bodies, 170 n.2
  straddling between not-for-profit
    and intense
    commercialization, 170

structure (overview)
  a classic structure, 70
  evolving role of athletes, coaches
    and competition
    organizations, 171
  fitting the NSFs/regional
    associations in, 79, 171–2
  hybrid regulatory frameworks,
    171–2
  ITF's unusual status as a limited
    liability company, 125, 180
  stability of institutional
    relationships between key
    stakeholders, 171, 180
  a vertical semi-pyramidal
    organizational ladder, 171
tennis governance (ITF/APT/WTA)
    (structure): *see also*
    unionization (professional
    tennis players)
  allocation of tasks, 70–1
  fighting it out/factors influencing,
    174–6
  governing bodies in date order of
    establishment
    USLTA (1881), 175–6
    ILTF (1932) (renamed ITF
      (1977)), 174
    NTL (1967–70), 174
    WCT (1968–89), 174
    Virginia Slims Tour (1971), 175–6
    ATP (1972), 7, 10, 174–5
    WTA (1973), 7, 175
    MIPTC (1974–89), 10, 119, 126,
      174–5
    ITF (1977) (formerly ILTF), 174
  players' councils, 176–7
  WTA Council, 177
  regional associations, 70
  relationship between NSFs and the
    ITF, 70, 179–80: *see also* NSFs
    and the ITC
  relationship between players and the
    ATP/WTA, 13–14, 177–9: *see
    also* labour status; players and
    the ATP/WTA
tennis governance (ITF/ATP/WTA)
    (common features), 9–11

tennis governance (cont.)
  background: *see also* unionization (professional tennis players), key events in date order
    historical changes (1972–1989), 7–8, 10
    impact of commercialization and professionalization, 7
    as key protagonists/domination, 1, 2–3, 174
    rivalries and disputes, 9–10
  applicability of transnational processes, 1, 2–4
  applicable law: *see also* applicable law
    domestic and transnational anti-trust laws, 2–3
    human rights law, 3
    public international law, 1–2
  incorporation
    headquarters distinguished, 2
    limitation to a single state, 4, 9
    preference for liberal arbitration-friendly states, 1
  list of, 70
  responsibilities, 10–11: *see also* human rights
    as non-state actors, 2, 18, 171–2
  status: *see also lex sportiva* (transnational law)
    comparability with NGOs/MNCs, 1–2, 3, 18
    as 'foreign investors' (BTIs), 2, 14
    as transnational corporate actors, 1, 2–9
tennis player unions: *see* unionization (professional tennis players)
Thiem, Dominic, 123, 127
Tilden, Bill, 80 n.45
TISB (Tennis Integrity Supervisory Board), 210–11
TIU (Tennis Integrity Unit) (2009–21), 210, 240: *see also* ITIA
trade secrets/confidential information
  implementation by national IP laws (TRIPS 39), 56
  importance in the tennis world, 56
  requirements for protection, 56

trademarks (general), 42–57: *see also* copyright; design rights; image rights/rights of publicity; IP rights (enforcement action); patent rights; trademarks (general)
  advantages
    indefinite protection, 47
    passing-off action (UK), 47
    strength of protection against third-party infringements, 47
  genuine use obligation
    importance of vigilance, 65
    Noah Clothing, 65
  registration requirements
    definition/purpose of 'trademark' (TRIPS 1(1)/EUTMR 4/national legislation), 46
    grounds for refusal, 46–7
    importance to sporting goods manufacturers, 45
    non-registrable signs (TRIPS 1(1)/EUTMR 7(1)/national legislation), 46–7
    territoriality, 46
  scope of protection
    Nice Classes of particular interest to the tennis sector, 52–3
    Nice Classification system, 52–3
    Nice Declaration on the Specific Characteristics of Sport and Its Social Function in Europe, 264
trademarks (types) (non-traditional)
  general features
    definition, 48
    difficulty of registration, 48
    increase in EU applications, reasons, 48
  colour marks
    AELTC struggles/2016 registration of Wimbledon colours, 49
    balancing factors, 49
    CJEU case law, 48–9
    colour combinations (systematic arrangement requirement), 48–9

INDEX 331

limited number of internationally accepted colours, 49
protection by registered designs and/or copyright as preferred alternative, 49, 50-1
single colour, 48
motion, gesture marks and holograms
    increasing popularity, 31
    likely requirements, 51
    Usain Bolt's 'lightning bolt' gesture, 51
    'Vicht' salute (Kroon/Wilander vs Hewitt), 51-2
shape marks
    AELTC decision to opt for logo protection, 50
    CJEU case law, 50
    non-registrable signs (EUTMR 7 (1)(C) and (e)), 49-50
    other disqualifying factors, 50
    successful applications, 50
smell and taste marks
    'The Smell of Fresh Cut Grass' registration (2009), 51
sound marks
    successful application (BARCA), 51
    tennis possibilities, 51
sound or video files, 48
trademarks (types) (traditional), 47-8
definition/examples, 47
slogans/CJEU jurisprudence, 47-8
transnational law: *see lex sportiva* (transnational law)

unionization (professional tennis players): *see also* player rights, pay and conditions
    introduction (coming in waves), 105, 141-3: *see also* key events *below*
    1960s-70s, 141
    1990s-2010s, 141
    2020 (the third age), 123-4
    collective action vs shared governance, 105-6, 116-24
    ATP/WTA efforts to become governing bodies/transnational businesses/success, 106, 120-1, 174-5
    MLBPA's ground-breaking collective agreement, 117, 119
    PGA/APG choice of the commercial route, 117
    US and European football distinguished/reasons for, 116-17, 118-19
collective action vs shared governance (criticisms of the outcome)
    Ashe on, 119-20
    King on, 120
    a stifling of rewarding and secure contracts in favour of lucrative individualist pay structures, 119
collective action vs shared governance (factors affecting the tennis players' choice)
    absence of a stable managerial counterpart, 228
    a rich man's sport/elite players' domination, 118
defining a professional tennis players' union, 106-8
    ATP/WTA loss of status as player unions/risks to players' rights, 107, 110
    ILO Global Dialogue Forum on Decent Work in the World of Sport (2020), 109-10
    ILO principles and standards, applicability, 106-10
    importance of trade union rights (Shift Project), 109
    recognition of role of human rights, impact, 107-8
    right to organized, independence from an employment relationship (ILO jurisprudence), 109-10
    summary of UNGO obligations, 108-9
    WPA findings on the risks to players' trade union rights (2017), 109

332   INDEX

unionization (cont.)
  initial attempts at unionisation
    (1967–75) (introduction)
    matters requiring resolution, 111
    the old guard resistance, 111
    the Open Tennis vision, 111
    a slow start/breathtaking progress,
      110–11, 116
  key events in date order
    1968 (WCT established), 111–12
    1968 (Wimbledon declared by the
      ITA as open), 112
    1969 (ITFA established), 112
    1970 (establishment of the
      Association of Independent
      Tennis Professionals/ITPA and
      ILTF threats to the WCT),
      112–13
    1970 (The "Original Nine" begin
      the campaign for equality in
      women's tennis), 112
    1972(1) USLTA peace deal, 113
    1972(2) (ATP established with
      Kramer as Executive
      Director), 113
    1972(3) (ATP's refusal to admit
      women players), 113, 132–3
    1973(1) (establishment of the
      WTA/key issues), 113–14
    1973(2) (ATP boycott of
      Wimbledon following the Pilic
      showdowns), 115
    1973(3) (King's intelligence and
      entrepreneurial flare break the
      prize money lock), 115
    1973(4) (settlement of USLTA's to
      ban women players/launch of
      the Virginia Slims tour), 115
    1974 (establishment of the
      MITPC/changes to meet ATP's
      demands), 115–16
    1975 (establishment of the
      WIPTC), 116
    1988 (ATP leaves the MIPTC), 120
    1994 (WTA merger with WIPRC),
      120–1
    2003 (establishment of the IMTA:
      the issues and the failure), 121
    2012 (proposed boycott of the
      Australian Open on prize
      money grounds), 121
    2020 (establishment of PTPA),
      123–4, 135–9

WADA Prohibited List, 213
wild cards
  free movement of services (TFEU 5),
    jurisprudence
    Deliège (proportionality/non-
      discrimination), 281
    Meca-Medina/Gebhard/Bosman
      (rejection of nationality-based
      discrimination), 282–3
    Walrave/Donà (permissible
      nationality-based
      discrimination), 282
  free movement of services (TFEU 56)
    legitimate aim in the public
      interest as sole justification, 281
    unfair distribution of returns from
      tournaments/inequality of
      opportunity, 283
  the system
    definition (ATP Rule 7.12), 279
    discrimination, 281
    disproportionate awards of, 280–1
    French, US and Australian Grand
      Slam deals, 280
    issue 'at the sole discretion of tthe
      tournament', 280
    ITF Rule V(I)/Grand Slam
      tournaments Rule Z(2)(b)
      compared, 280
    typical criteria, 280
Williams, Serena, 72 n.10, 121, 128,
  255–6, 258–9, 260, 261–2
Williams, Venus, 128, 260–1
Wozniacki, Caroline, 121
WTA
  overview, 130
  arrangements for the men's game
    distinguished, 11
  from player association to
    governing body and businesses,
    190–2
  origin, 130

INDEX 333

Board of Directors (membership), 130, 131
development of the safeguarding role: *see* safeguarding in tennis (child-adult relationships) (WTA)
Peng Shuai case, 18
prize money, 131–2
responsibilities (Grand Slams, Davis Cup and Olympic Tennis Event (women's events)), 8, 11, 130
WTA PC
   composition, 130, 131, 177
   election (2023)/demands following, 130–1

WTA (dispute resolution), 166–7
arbitration
   AAA's Expedited Procedures Commercial Arbitration Rules, 167
   limitation to WTA Rulebook-related disputes, 167
   CEO/Board of Directors, 167
   Code of Conduct Committee, 166–7
   Standards Committee, 167

Zverev, 6, 40–1, 55, 96–9, 127, 136, 168–9
Zverev, Alexander, 127, 136, 209

For EU product safety concerns, contact us at Calle de José Abascal, 56–1°,
28003 Madrid, Spain or eugpsr@cambridge.org.

www.ingramcontent.com/pod-product-compliance
Ingram Content Group UK Ltd.
Pitfield, Milton Keynes, MK11 3LW, UK
UKHW020330040925
462578UK00021B/525